THE POLITICS
OF THE PRUSSIAN NOBILITY

THE POLITICS
OF THE PRUSSIAN NOBILITY

THE DEVELOPMENT OF A CONSERVATIVE IDEOLOGY

1770–1848

ROBERT M. BERDAHL

PRINCETON UNIVERSITY PRESS
PRINCETON, NEW JERSEY

Copyright © 1988 by Princeton University Press
Published by Princeton University Press,
41 William Street, Princeton, New Jersey 08540
In the United Kingdom: Princeton University Press,
Guildford, Surrey

All Rights Reserved

Library of Congress Cataloging-in-Publication Data
Berdahl, Robert M.
The politics of the Prussian nobility: the development of a
conservative ideology, 1770–1848
Robert M. Berdahl
p.   cm.
Includes index.
ISBN 0-691-05536-X (alk. paper)
1. Prussia (Germany)—Politics and government—1740–1815.
2. Prussia (Germany)—Politics and government—1806–1848.
3. Conservatism—Prussia (Germany)
4. Prussia (Germany)—Nobility.
I. Title. DD419.B47 1988 943—dc19 88-17616 CIP

This book has been composed in Linotron Baskerville

Clothbound editions of Princeton University Press books
are printed on acid-free paper, and binding materials
are chosen for strength and durability. Paperbacks,
although satisfactory for personal collections,
are not usually suitable for library rebinding

Printed in the United States of America
by Princeton University Press
Princeton, New Jersey

for
PEG
DAPHNE, JENNIFER, AND BARBARA

CONTENTS

LIST OF TABLES	ix
ACKNOWLEDGMENTS	xi
ABBREVIATIONS	xiii
INTRODUCTION	3

1. **NOBLE AND PEASANT: THE CONTOURS OF SOCIAL CLASS** — 14
   - *The Nobility* — 14
   - *The Peasantry* — 28

2. **HABITUS AND HERRSCHAFT: THE SYSTEM OF DOMINATION** — 44
   - *The Framework of Paternalism* — 44
   - *The Institutions of Herrschaft* — 54
   - *The System of Symbolic Herrschaft* — 65

3. **CROSS-CURRENTS OF ECONOMIC AND SOCIAL CHANGE** — 77
   - *Opportunities for a New Agriculture* — 77
   - *The Nobility and the Absolutistic State* — 90
   - *The Allgemeines Landrecht: Between Change and Continuity* — 97

4. **THE REFORM ERA AND THE POLITICS OF THE NOBILITY** — 107
   - *The Collapse of Prussia, the Reformers, and the Stände* — 107
   - *The Emancipation Edict* — 115
   - *The Hardenberg Reforms: Organized Opposition by the Nobility* — 123
   - *The Success of Noble Opposition: Agrarian Legislation, 1810–1816* — 144
   - *The Impact of the Reforms on the Nobility* — 154

CONTENTS

5. ADAM MÜLLER AND THE GENESIS OF A CONSERVATIVE IDEOLOGY — 158
   The Emergence of Formal Ideology — 158
   Müller and His Milieu — 163
   Müller's Conservative Ideology and the Critique of Capitalism — 169
   Some Final Thoughts on Müller and the Nobility — 179

6. THE POLITICS OF RESTORATION — 182
   Between Administration and Constitution, 1815–1822 — 182
   The Reconquest of Local Affairs — 198
   The Changing Concept of Stand — 220

7. THE IDEOLOGY OF RESTORATION — 231
   Haller's Theory of the Patrimonial State — 232
   The Gerlach Circle and Das Berliner Politische Wochenblatt — 246

8. NOBLE AND PEASANT BETWEEN REFORM AND REVOLUTION — 264
   The Depression of the 1820s: Crisis for the Nobility — 264
   Lords and Peasants in the Emergence of Capitalist Agriculture — 286
   Lord and Peasant Confrontations in the "Hungry Forties" — 300

9. POLITICS ON THE EVE OF REVOLUTION — 311
   Constitutional Conflict Renewed. 1840–1847 — 311
   Plans for a New Nobility — 326
   The United Diet — 333

10. IDEOLOGY ON THE EVE OF REVOLUTION: FRIEDRICH JULIUS STAHL — 348
   Friedrich Julius Stahl — 349
   Stahl's Philosophy of Law — 354
   Stahl's Role in Developing Conservative Ideology — 370

EPILOGUE — 374

INDEX — 381

LIST OF TABLES

1. Inflation Index for Estate Costs in Silesia and Brandenburg — 81
2. Changes of Ownership of Estates Mortgaged through East Prussian Landschaft, 1806–1829 — 276
3. Transfer of East Prussian Estates to Commoners, 1806–1829 — 276

ACKNOWLEDGMENTS

The publication of this book at long last gives me an opportunity to thank many of the people who have contributed to it at various stages of its evolution. My oldest and most enduring debt is to Otto Pflanze, who first introduced me to the study of German history more than two decades ago. His friendship and encouragement have sustained me through many critical moments in my career, and his careful criticism of an earlier draft of the book improved it immeasurably. I am also grateful to Felix Gilbert, who enabled me to spend the 1972-1973 academic year at the Institute for Advanced Study in Princeton, during which I formed the initial concept of this project. Felix Gilbert is a rare and wonderful example of a humanist scholar who has contributed much to the profession not only through his work but also through the assistance he has provided to others. The year in Princeton also yielded a friendship with Pierre Bourdieu, whose late-night conversations opened new vistas for me in understanding the manner in which a social environment shapes political thought and action.

From 1975 to 1977, research grants from the Fulbright Commission and the National Endowment for the Humanities enabled me to spend eighteen months in Germany gathering much of the material for this book. In those labors, I was assisted by many people on the staffs of the Niedersächsische Staatsbibliothek in Göttingen, the Deutsches Zentralarchiv II in Merseburg, the Staatsarchiv in Potsdam, and the Staatliches Archivlager in Göttingen, whose material from the East Prussian archives from Königsberg is now located in the Geheimes Staatsarchiv in Dahlem.

By far the most fortunate and important association that began for me with that 1975-1977 stay in Göttingen, however, was my friendship with the people at the Max-Planck-Institut für Geschichte. To Rudolf Vierhaus, its director, goes the credit for having created an environment for historical research that is ideal. I will forever be grateful for the intellectual and material support he has provided through my many visits to Göttingen. To my friends and colleagues at the Institut, especially Hans Medick, Alf Lüdtke, and David Sabean (now at

ACKNOWLEDGMENTS

UCLA), I owe a debt of gratitude I can never repay; their company has always been a remarkable source of intellectual energy.

Although I am no longer at the University of Oregon, this book is a product of my years there. Whatever value it may possess is due to the support and stimulation of my colleagues in the history department at Oregon. They even tolerated my involvement in academic administration with good humor and charity. I want to thank above all Tom Brady, Richard M. Brown, Roger Chickering, Alan Kimball, and Stanley Pierson for all that I have learned from them. My secretary, Hazel Jones, not only typed the entire manuscript but also recognized how important it was that I find the time to work on it, so she organized my administrative duties in a way that made that possible. Her help was vital in every way.

Finally, I am happy to be able to thank the members of my family for their patience, sense of humor, and support during the years I have been at work on this book. My daughters, Daphne, Jennifer, and Barbara, have grown up with this book; they always had the grace to make a virtue out of the necessity of living away from home or tolerating my absence. My wife, Peg, has given me the love and support without which this would have been a much poorer book and I a much poorer person.

ABBREVIATIONS

AHR	*American Historical Review*
ALR	*Allgemeines Landrecht für die Preussischen Staaten.* Hans Hattenhauer, ed., *Allgemeines Landrecht für die Preussichen Staaten von 1794* (Frankfurt a.M. and Berlin, 1970)
FBPG	*Forschungen zur brandenburgischen und preussischen Geschichte*
HZ	*Historiche Zeitschrift*
DZA II	Deutsches Zentralarchiv, Abteilung Merseburg
PSK/B-D	Preussische Staatsarchiv zu Königsberg, now located in Dahlem
STAP	Staatsarchiv Potsdam

THE POLITICS
OF THE PRUSSIAN NOBILITY

INTRODUCTION

Measured by its capacity to endure, the Prussian nobility was the most successful nobility in the modern history of continental Europe. Throughout the long vicissitudes of its history, it displayed a remarkable ability to adapt to new circumstances in ways that ensured the continuation of its political force. In the seventeenth century, the Electors of Brandenburg-Prussia sought to increase their control over the far-flung territories of the state by limiting the power of the nobility; they disbanded noble assemblies and created a new bureaucracy to carry out their policies. The landowning nobility responded by consolidating its control over the rural population living on its estates. By the middle of the eighteenth century, the new bureaucratic elite and the old landowning nobility had reconciled their differences; the bureaucracy had absorbed many of the values and the ethos of the old nobility, while the sons of the old nobility found careers for themselves within the bureaucracy. The two elites, old and new, merged so that by the end of the eighteenth century the nobility again exercised inordinate power within the Prussian state.[1]

Despite the transformation of German society wrought by the growth of cities and industry in the nineteenth century, the nobility continued to dominate political life in Prussia. Even after the creation of the German Empire in 1871, nobles exercised influence in government out of all proportion to their numbers in the society as a whole. Most of the top posts in the government, the diplomatic service, and the army were held by nobles until the collapse of the empire in 1918.[2] Only in 1945 was the influence of the nobility completely eliminated.

[1] This is the theme of Hans Rosenberg, *Bureaucracy, Aristocracy, and Autocracy: The Prussian Experience, 1660–1815* (Cambridge, Mass., 1958).

[2] In 1910, of 11 members of the Prussian State Ministry, 9 were noble, as were 11 out of 12 provincial governors (*Oberpräsidenten*), 25 out of 36 chief officials of the govern-

INTRODUCTION

As a history of the politics of the landowning nobility in Prussia from late eighteenth century until the revolution of 1848, this book is, therefore, the study of a dominant social class. It is the study of how the landowning nobility coped with changes in rural social relations after the emancipation of the serfs in 1807, how it survived the agrarian depression of the 1820s by the development of capitalist agriculture, and how it constructed and refined a formal ideology justifying its continued domination despite these social, economic, and political changes. Throughout the writing of this book, I have tried to bear in mind E. P. Thompson's emphasis that class is "not a thing" but a "historical relationship." In this view, a social class cannot be dissected, measured, and analyzed in and of itself. Rather, class is a relationship or set of relationships that evolves historically; it happens in the social encounter of people engaged in producing the goods they require to live. "Class happens," Thompson writes, "when some men, as a result of common experiences (inherited or shared), feel and articulate the identity of their interests as between themselves and as against other men whose interests are different from (and usually opposed to) theirs. The class experience is largely determined by the productive relations into which men are born—or enter involuntarily."[3]

Because a dominant social class evolves only in relation to those whom it dominates, it is necessary to examine the various dimensions of that domination in order to explain class behavior. This book, therefore, proceeds from the assumption that the crucial fact in the experience of the Prussian nobility was its ownership of land and its direct involvement in the management of its landed estates. The noble estate and village provided the context for the encounter between the nobleman and the peasant. The nobleman's experience of domination was immediate and direct, personal and complete. This relationship with the peasantry over several centuries shaped the class consciousness of the nobility, providing the essential experience that defined,

---

mental districts (*Regierungspräsidenten*), and 271 out of 467 administrators of county government (*Landräte*). In the top ranks of the foreign service in 1914 were 8 princes, 29 counts, 20 barons, 54 ordinary nobles, and only 11 commoners. In the last decades of the empire, the percentage of nobles on the first rungs of the civil service ladder actually increased. See Hans-Ulrich Wehler, *Das deutsche Kaiserreich, 1871–1918*, 5th ed. (Göttingen, 1983), 76. See also Nikolaus von Preradovich, *Die Führungsschichten in Oesterreich und Preussen, 1804–1918* (Wiesbaden, 1955); Lysbeth W. Muncy, *The Junker in Prussian Administration under William II, 1899–1914* (Providence, R.I., 1944); Lamar Cecil, "The Creation of Nobles in Prussia, 1871–1918," *AHR* 75 (1970): 757–95; Arno J. Mayer, *The Persistence of the Old Regime* (New York, 1981), 181.

[3] E. P. Thompson, *The Making of the English Working Class*, Vintage ed. (New York, 1966), 9.

for the nobility, the meaning of authority and thereby the nature of the state. Because the experience of domination was personal and immediate, it had to be justified in terms that were personal and private, in this case through an ideology that can best be described as paternalistic. Patrimonial rule, sanctified by the images of paternalistic concern, became the hallmark of the nobility's accepted mode of domination of the peasantry down to the end of the eighteenth century.

Pierre Bourdieu, who analyzed the form of domination characteristic of precapitalist societies, maintains that they require both "overt violence" (direct physical and economic violence) and "symbolic violence" ("euphemized," unrecognized violence) in order to maintain and reproduce their social relations. He writes the following:

There is an intelligible relation—not a contradiction—between these two forms of violence, which coexist in the same social formation and sometimes in the same relationship: when domination can only be exercised in its elementary form, i.e., directly, between one person and another, it cannot take place overtly and must be disguised under the veil of enchanted relationships, the official model of which is presented by relations between kinsmen; in order to be socially recognized it must get itself misrecognized. The reason for the pre-capitalist economy's great need for symbolic violence is that the only way in which relations of domination can be set up, maintained, or restored, is through strategies which, being expressly oriented towards the establishment of relations of personal dependence, must be disguised and transfigured lest they destroy themselves by revealing their true nature; in a word, they must be *euphemized*. . . . Because the pre-capitalist economy cannot count on the implacable, hidden violence of objective mechanisms, it resorts *simultaneously* to forms of domination which may strike the modern observer as more brutal, more primitive, more barbarous, or at the same time, as gentler, more humane, more respectful of persons.[4]

The central thesis of this book is that the Prussian nobility traditionally justified, or "euphemized," its domination of the peasantry by means of an ideology of paternalism, that this paternalistic model of social relations began to dissolve under the capitalistic transformation of agriculture at the end of the eighteenth century, and that the conservative politics of the nobility during the first half of the nineteenth century were determined by an effort to reestablish the lineaments of patrimonial rule and a paternalist ideology. The ideology of paternal-

[4] Pierre Bourdieu, *Outline of a Theory of Practice*, trans. R. Nice (Cambridge, 1977), 191.

ism contained the core assumption shared by the nobility about the nature of authority: that the family was the essential model of society, with all authority patterned after the stern but caring father. This meant that the essential relationships of superordination and subordination in society were private relationships, that is, relationships that were, like those of the family, personal and individual.

Put another way, it can be said that what Bourdieu calls the "symbolic violence" masking the nature of domination in precapitalist society became less necessary as capitalist relationships developed, for in a capitalist society social relationships were determined, reinforced, and reproduced by the force of the market. The "self-regulating market," to use Polanyi's phrase, created the objective mechanism for social domination; by depersonalizing the system of social relations, it rendered a euphemism based on notions of personal dependency, such as paternalism, both less necessary and less workable. The need for serfdom, both as a means of material production and as a means of social domination, began to disappear with the conditions that made possible and necessary the paternalist ideology justifying it. Reliance on the discipline of the market alone, however, threatened the traditional authority exercised by the nobility; as a result, the conservatism espoused by the nobility attempted to recreate the basis for personal authority at the same time that it initially criticized the emergent market society. The nobility was caught in the contradiction of participating in the advance of capitalist agriculture while trying to maintain a formal ideology that would retain precapitalist forms of domination. This contradiction was overcome only as conservatism gradually accommodated itself to the changed political and economic climate in the 1840s.

The argument here differs from other discussions of the origins of conservatism in Germany. In his fine essay on conservative thought, Karl Mannheim distinguished between "traditionalism" and "conservatism."[5] Traditionalism, he maintained, is subjective; it is the natural, instinctive inclination to do things as they have always been done or to view things as they have always been viewed. Conservatism, on the other hand, is "conscious and reflective"; it is the decision to retain the old when given a choice of the new. "Conservative action," Mannheim wrote, "is always dependent on a *concrete set of circumstances.*" My argument resembles Mannheim's in one important respect: it insists that conservatism is the elevation of traditional patterns of authority to a

[5] Karl Mannheim, "Conservative Thought," in Kurt Wolff, ed., *From Karl Mannheim* (New York, 1971), 153, 157.

conscious and formal level of articulation. Conservatism is the conscious effort to "naturalize," that is, to render traditional once again, existing or previous structures of authority. This is one of the reasons the metaphors used by conservatives are frequently organic, drawn from nature. My argument differs from Mannheim's in that I maintain that the "concrete set of circumstances" generating conscious conservative thought is specific to the experience of domination practiced and rationalized by the actions of the dominant class, in this case, by the nobles on their estates. Conservative political action in Prussia was an effort to retain a specific system of authoritative relations I have summarized with the term *paternalism*. In Mannheim's view, the "concrete set of circumstances" giving rise to conservative thought were broad "styles of thought" and "historical movements" such as the Romantic reaction to the rationalism of the eighteenth century. I have tried throughout this book to avoid the use of broad categories such as Romanticism, for I believe conservatism must be understood, in its fundamentals, as a political ideology defending the specific authority and class interest of the nobility.

Klaus Epstein's imposing study, *The Genesis of German Conservatism*, offers the most comprehensive examination of the eighteenth-century roots of conservative thought; had Epstein lived to complete the second volume of his study, there might not have been a place for my book.[6] Nevertheless, my approach differs substantially from that taken by Epstein. His study is largely an intellectual history; it views conservative thought fundamentally as a response to the German Enlightenment. Even his treatment of political and social controversies in the 1790s operates largely at the level of intellectual discussion. Moreover, Epstein delineated three types of conservatives: "*Status Quo* Conservatives, Reform Conservatives, and Reactionaries." He then placed particular conservative thinkers somewhere along this spectrum. This is a common method for dealing with conservatism. Ernst R. Huber distinguished four types of conservatives in nineteenth-century Germany: *ständisch* conservatives, social conservatives, national conservatives, and state conservatives. He stressed that the boundaries between these groups were fluid and that they frequently overlapped.[7] Sigmund Neumann found three other types—romantic conservatives, liberal conservatives, and realistic conservatives—each of which corresponded roughly to a period of Prussian history in the nineteenth century.[8]

[6] Klaus Epstein, *The Genesis of German Conservatism* (Princeton, 1966).
[7] Ernst R. Huber, *Deutsche Verfassungsgeschichte seit 1789* (Stuttgart, 1960), 2: 331ff.
[8] Sigmund Neumann, *Die Stufen des preussischen Konservatismus: Ein Beitrag zum Staats-*

I have not found the use of such categories very helpful. The typologies employed frequently seem to be the product of heterogeneous criteria; little is delineated because the types usually overlap. One could construct an endless number of categories. In addition, because these definitions are "ideal types" constructed by the historian, to be measured by their deviation from some concept of the "real," the historian tends to impart substantive reality to the types themselves. Rather like a police portrait artist, the historian draws a composite portrait of a particular type, then searches for examples of the portrait in reality, assuming that the type itself explains the essence of the real object of study. It seems more useful to me to try to understand ideology as the result of the constant dialectical process between specific economic and social changes in which the nobility found itself enmeshed, on the one side, and the political situation in Prussia, on the other. I have tried to tie the development of conservatism closely to the social and political history of Prussia between 1815 and 1848. From that perspective, I hope this book contributes not only to our understanding of the history of Prussia but also to the analysis of the genesis of ideology.[9]

The reader should bear in mind several additional points. First, the analysis does not try to deal with all aspects of the nobility in the period prior to 1848. It does not, for example, deal with the army, and it discusses only incidentally the role of the nobility in the bureaucracy, in part because good studies of the army and the bureaucracy already exist. But more important, I maintain that the formative experience of the nobility was ownership of land.[10] We shall be concerned with the people who exercised traditional domination, *Herrschaft*, and whose exercise of that Herrschaft shaped the predominant attitude of their class about the nature of authority. This is not to suggest that the

---

und Gesellschaftsbild Deutschland im 19. Jahrhundert (Berlin, 1930). For a recent treatment of conservatism in Germany and a good survey of the literature, see Martin Greiffenhagen, *Das Dilemma des Konservatismus in Deutschland* (Munich, 1971).

[9] My approach owes much to Hans Rosenberg, "Die Pseudodemokratisierung der Rittergutsbesitzerklasse," in his *Machteliten und Wirtschaftskonjunkturen*, Kritische Studien zur Geschichtswissenschaft, 31 (Göttingen, 1978), 83–101.

[10] Reinhart Koselleck's magisterial work, *Preussen zwischen Reform und Revolution* (Stuttgart, 1967), deals with much more than the bureaucracy, but it offers the best analysis of the Prussian bureaucracy in the period between 1815 and 1848. Koselleck's study is important to any work dealing with Prussian history during this period. John R. Gillis, *The Prussian Bureaucracy in Crisis, 1840–1860* (Stanford, 1971), begins with 1840, but he includes background material on the bureaucracy in the earlier period. On the army, see Gordon Craig, *The Politics of the Prussian Army* (New York, 1955), and Karl Demeter, *The German Officer Corps in Society and State, 1650–1945* (New York, 1965).

Prussian nobility was, more than any other dominant class, completely homogeneous. Differences of view existed within it, and there were nobles who did not own or live on their estates. But those differences of view revolved not around whether the superior position of the nobility should be maintained, but around which strategies would best preserve its superiority. Some recognized earlier than others that patrimonial rule, with its euphemism *paternalism*, could not be sustained in the changing economic and political environment of the 1820s, 1830s, and 1840s.

Second, it should be remembered that the history of the nobility and its experience of domination differed in the various eastern provinces of Prussia. Resistance to change was strongest among the nobility in the older provinces of Brandenburg and Pomerania. Agricultural modernization progressed more slowly in these provinces, and the nobility made a persistent effort to retain paternalistic images of its authority. In the seventeenth century the nobility of East Prussia had engaged in the most protracted fight against the centralized power of the prince; during the reform era after 1807, it guarded jealously its privileges and autonomy. But the social and economic development in East Prussia also differed from that in the other provinces. East Prussia had traditionally the largest class of freeholding peasants (*Kölmer*) in the monarchy; it was the most closely tied to the export of grain, especially to England, so the nobility developed early a strong orientation toward the market; because it was more dependent than the other provinces on the English market, East Prussia suffered most in the depression of the 1820s, when England enacted the Corn Laws, and the East Prussian nobility correspondingly became the strongest advocates of freedom of trade. Silesia had yet a different background and social complexion. Detached from Austria by Prussia in 1740, Silesia was Catholic; it possessed some of the richest and highest-ranking nobles in the entire Prussian state. The peasantry in Silesia, especially in the Polish-speaking regions of the province, was probably the most impoverished and brutalized in the state; peasant unrest occurred more frequently in Silesia than elsewhere in Prussia. In some regions of Silesia, cottage industry, especially linen weaving, provided the basis for the meager livelihood of the rural poor; the poverty of these weavers deepened in the nineteenth century as English cotton began to displace the demand for linen. All of these variations in development contributed to the political differences among the Prussian nobility. After 1815, the Prussian acquisition of the Rhineland introduced an entirely new dimension to the politics of Prussia, for the nobility of the Rhineland had never exercised the kind of control over the peasantry enjoyed by the eastern nobility, and the Rhineland became, in the nineteenth century, a center for Prussian commercial and industrial development.

Third, as the book proceeds, I concentrate increasingly on the political arena. The first three chapters deal with the social conditions surrounding noble domination on estates and the changes in social relations that began to develop in the late eighteenth century. Chapter 4 deals with the politics of the reform era, but primarily as the reforms changed, or threatened to change, the social position of the nobility on the land. With the reconquest of the government in the 1820s, both at the central and at the local level, described in chapter 6, the struggle for the preservation of noble authority moved into the political sphere. Chapter 8 returns to a discussion of the economic and social developments from the 1820s to the 1840s: then chapter 9 offers a detailed study of Prussian political conflicts and the efforts to preserve the nobility between the ascension of Frederick William IV to the throne in 1840 and the outbreak of the revolution of 1848. Chapters 5, 7, and 10 endeavor to illustrate the changing texture of conservative ideology as the nobility encountered economic, social, and political changes throughout the period. This shift of emphasis from the social to the political domain is also a reflection of the growing political consciousness and contestation in Prussia in the era before 1848. This study ends on the eve of the revolution of 1848. The revolution did not by any means end the dominant social and political role of the nobility; but, by introducing a constitution, a parliament, and political parties, it transformed the entire framework for the nobility's defense of its interests.

Finally, throughout the book, two German terms recur, *Herrschaft* and *Stand*. Although I hope that their meanings will become clear to the reader as the terms are elaborated in the text, some definition and clarification at the beginning may be helpful. *Herrschaft* is usually translated into English as "domination," and it has been used in this way here.[11] But the word *domination* does not convey the full range of meaning that is attached to the term. *Herrschaft* is more accurately translated as "dominium," although we also need to remind ourselves of the full meaning of that word. *Dominium* derives from the same Latin root as *dominare* (to rule), but it also shares a common origin with *domus* (house) and *dominus* (lord). *Herrschaft* means lordship, and al-

---

[11] See the article "Herrschaft" in Otto Brunner et al., *Geschichtliche Grundbegriffe. Historisches Lexikon zur politisch-sozialen Sprache in Deutschland* (Stuttgart, 1972), 3: 1–102. My own understanding of *Herrschaft* was enhanced by conversations with David Sabean and by his book *Power in the Blood* (Cambridge, 1984), 20–27.

though, unlike its Latin equivalent, it is not related to the German word for house, the exercise of Herrschaft was always dependent on the ownership of a house on the land and the rule of a household. Otto Brunner stressed this aspect of Herrschaft: "Whoever had no house, but merely possessed individual pieces of land settled by persons paying rent, possessed no Herrschaft, no noble estate, but only 'estate revenues' " (*Gülten*).[12] Herrschaft was not an abstract authority but was always associated with a specific person who exercised lordship in a particular domain—a village lord (*Dorfherr*), the lord of an estate (*Gutsherr*), or the lord of the land (*Landesherr*). Herrschaft also contained the connotation of mutual obligations between lord and subjects. Those subject to Herrschaft were obliged to serve their lord obediently, while those exercising Herrschaft were obliged to provide their subjects with "protection and shelter" (*Schutz und Schirm*) and "advice and help" (*Rat und Hilfe*). Brunner cites the thirteenth-century southern German law book, the *Schwabenspiegel*, as reflecting the reciprocal responsibilities between the lord and his subjects: "We shall serve under the lord who protects us. If he does not protect us, we are no longer legally obligated to serve him."[13] In its close association with the household headed by a *Hausvater* who ruled over his wife, children, and servants, and in its assumption of the mutuality of obligations, the concept of Herrschaft was closely linked with the ideology of paternalism.

From the late eighteenth century, the concept of Herrschaft was gradually emptied of its personal component, so that one spoke of the Herrschaft of the law or used the term for authority with fewer feudal overtones, *Obrigkeit*. The nobility strenuously resisted efforts to depersonalize the nature of authority or to render it more abstract, for the power of the nobility was based on the tradition of individualized, private, and personal control. Noble critics attacked the Prussian General Law Code of 1794 for referring to the king with the impersonal phrase "chief of state" (*Oberhaupt des Staats*). Throughout the first half of the nineteenth century conservative ideologists in Prussia struggled to retain the personal dimension of Herrschaft.

Stand, Stände, and *ständisch* institutions and society are terms with no English equivalents, so I will use them in this study without translation.[14] The term *Stand* was the primary means of social differentiation

[12] Otto Brunner, *Land und Herrschaft*, 5th ed. (Vienna, 1965), 255.
[13] Ibid., 263.
[14] For an extended version of this discussion of *Stand*, see Robert M. Berdahl, "Anthropologie und Geschichte: Einige theoretische Perspektiven und ein Beispiel aus der preus-

in early modern Germany. The traditional triad of Stände—the nobles, peasants, and townspeople—remained the legal distinctions well into the modern period, repeated in the Prussian General Law Code of 1794. The term *Stand*, derived from the verb *stehen* (to stand), is used to describe a person's condition, as in *Zustand*, or marital status, as in *Familienstand*. The English phrase "status group" is not a good translation, for *Stand* lacks the notion of accessibility and relative social mobility usually associated with status groups; on the other hand, it implies more flexibility than caste. *Stand* suggests a kind of stasis, a relatively fixed and durable social order that was reinforced with such aphorisms as, "When each remains in his own Stand, all is well throughout the land." Or, "When each remains in his own Stand, all is ordered by God's own hand."[15]

Although sometimes it has been used to mean class, as when *Mittelstand* has been used to refer to the middle class, the concept of Stand is not the same as class.[16] Max Weber distinguished between the two by suggesting that class is based on a cohesion of economic interests, whereas Stand is based on social privilege, a distinct style of life, and a certain notion of honor. Although Weber sometimes seems to suggest that "class society" supplanted "ständisch society" in the nineteenth century, the two concepts are not mutually exclusive categories; both can coexist in the same society.[17] The fact that class seemed to become the predominant category for social differentiation in the nineteenth century does not mean that classes did not exist before; rather, the cultural veil provided by the notion of Stand could not be stretched to cover the economic interests of classes in a society in which social relationships were increasingly determined by the market. Although *class* and *Stand* are not synonymous, social classes were the soil in which the Stände originally took root. The Stände, which appeared all over Europe from the Middle Ages onward and which everywhere shared in the structure of domination, emerged from elements that

---

sisch-deutschen Geschichte," in Berdahl et al., *Klassen und Kultur: Sozialanthropologische Perspektiven in der Geschichtsschreibung* (Frankfurt a.M., 1982), 263–87.

[15] For some of the aphorisms related to Stand, see K. F. Wander, ed., *Deutsches Sprichtwörter-Lexikon* (Leipzig, 1876). A number of these kinds of expressions were contained in the primers used for schoolchildren. See Friedrich Eberhard von Rochow, *Der Kinderfreund: Ein Lesebuch zum Gebrauch in Landschulen* (Brandenburg and Leipzig, 1776), in F. Jonas and F. Wierecke, eds., *Friedrich Eberhard von Rochows sämtliche pädagogische Schriften* (Berlin, 1907), 1: 186.

[16] On the discussion of the relationship between *class* and *Stand*, see Thomas A. Brady, Jr., *Ruling Class, Regime, and Reformation in Strassbourg, 1520–1525* (Leiden, 1978).

[17] Max Weber, *Wirtschaft und Gesellschaft*, ed. J. Winckelmann, 4th ed. (Tübingen, 1956), 1: 177–80, 285–314, 2: 531–40.

controlled the productive forces of society—the church, the nobility, and the urban patriciate. The concept of Stand, from the outset, was tied closely to the system of Herrschaft.

The Stände emerged in a period when the institutions of Herrschaft were relatively undifferentiated. The distinction between state and society, characteristic of the modern era, did not exist. The Stände were not arrayed against the prince, "representing" the people before the institutions of the state. They were organized institutionally insofar as they shared in the rule; they represented, in real and symbolic terms, the structure of authority before the people. As Otto Brunner put it, "The Stände do not 'represent' the land, rather, they 'are' the land."[18] Thus, a ständisch assembly offered a public presentation of a Herrschaft that was in fact based on private relationships. In this situation, the "public" exercise of authority was fused with the "private." This more or less complete fusion of course did not last beyond the seventeenth century, when the institutions of the modern state began to emerge. But the Herrschaft of the nobility continued to be a mixture of public and private authority, justified by the metaphor of paternalism, until the nineteenth century. During this period, the concept of Stand became an essential element in the cultural system; it provided a meaningful structure, elaborated in a network of symbols, through which one perceived and ordered one's social world. It projected a hierarchical structure of society that was shaped by the social interest of the dominant classes and thus served to mediate and legitimize social and political domination.

These were the objectives of the politics of the Prussian nobility: to preserve the private and personal dimensions of Herrschaft, to preserve the hierarchical structure of society articulated in the symbols of the Stände, and to adapt to the changing economic circumstances and opportunities without at the same time losing the basis for cultural and political hegemony.

[18] Brunner, *Land und Herrschaft*, 423.

1

NOBLE AND PEASANT:
THE CONTOURS OF SOCIAL CLASS

The Nobility

The Prussian nobility, which played so prominent a role in modern German history, was a landowning class. More than for any other aristocracy in Europe, the ownership and management of landed estates formed the core of its ethos. Its power as a class rested, to be sure, not only on its control of the land, but also on its domination of the important institutions of the Prussian state, especially the army and the bureaucracy. Nevertheless, throughout its long history, the Prussian aristocracy remained a landowning class, taking its identity, self-perceptions, habits of authority, and style of domination from its experiences as owner of noble estates. The sons of nobles went off to careers in the army and the civil service, but it was always assumed that, after the interlude of a few successful years, most would return to the family estates to live the remainder of their lives as squires. Even those nobles who attained the highest pinnacle of power within the state frequently continued to concern themselves with the minute details of the operation of their estates.[1] Until the beginning of the nineteenth century, the preservation of the nobility's monopoly of landed estates was a cardinal principle of Hohenzollern policy in Prussia; for decades after that monopoly had been broken, the government worked to maintain a "gentry" class of large landowners considered to be the social foundation of the monarchy.[2] Indeed, it is no exaggeration to suggest that the attitudes and patterns of social relations that matured historically within the framework of the noble estate became the most important ingredient in what came to be called the Prussian spirit.

The Prussian aristocracy was, on the whole, neither splendid nor rich. It did not routinely send its sons on a grand tour of Europe to

[1] Otto von Bismarck, for example, who possessed a voracious appetite for land, was never too busy with official business to pay careful attention to the affairs of his estates; he often retreated for long periods from Berlin to his Pomeranian estate and referred to himself as "the country squire of Varzin." See Fritz Stern, *Gold and Iron: Bismarck, Bleichröder, and the Building of the German Empire* (New York, 1977), 97, 101–3, 290–91.

[2] See chapter 9.

broaden their education and gain a veneer of European culture; in fact, the Hohenzollerns discouraged young Prussian nobles from traveling abroad.[3] It was better to send young noblemen to the cadet schools, where they were taught the habits of command that would serve them in the army and on their estates. Each province boasted a few noble families that were wealthy and controlled vast complexes of estates. Upper Silesia had perhaps the largest concentration of magnates—dukes, princes, and counts who owned more than 882,000 acres of land. The Prince of Pless, for example, owned more than 94,500 acres, whereas one branch of the Henckel-Donnersmarck family had almost one-third that amount.[4] In Brandenburg, the estates of the Arnim-Boitzenburg complex totaled 81,900 acres; the Bredows owned 50,400.[5] In East Prussia, the Dohnas, Finckensteins, and Schliebens held huge networks of estates. Many of these families lived in a grand style, built large and elegant manor houses, had ready access to the king, and occupied positions of influence and honor in the state generation after generation. But they were the exception. Amidst their lands were 420 noble estates whose total area was only 280,350 acres, an average of 667.5 acres.[6] Throughout the monarchy, estates of 945 acres to 1,575 acres were most common; few exceeded 5,000. Some regions were overpopulated with nobles whose estates were little more than peasant homesteads. In South and New East Prussia—territories taken from Poland in the eighteenth century—the nobility impoverished itself through a policy of partible inheritance; in the nineteenth century, it became necessary to forbid the partitioning of any noble estate to less than 94.5 acres.[7] A similar situation prevailed in Hither Pomerania, where a traveler reported late in the eighteenth century that "there are villages which are almost entirely composed of noble persons. Their noble estates [*Rittergüter*] are really peasant and

---

[3] In his *Political Testament* of 1722, Frederick William I wrote the following: "My successor must also grant only to very few of them permits to travel abroad, for first they must stand in your service." G. F. Schmoller, *Das Politische Testament Friedrich Wilhelm des Erstens, 1722* (Berlin, 1896). A translated excerpt is found in C. A. Macartney, *The Habsburg and Hohenzollern Dynasties* (New York, 1970), 310–22.

[4] Georg F. Knapp, *Die Bauernbefreiung und der Ursprung der Landarbeiter in ältern Teilen Preussens*, 2 vols. (Leipzig, 1887), 1: 3; Helmut Bleiber, *Zwischen Reform und Revolution: Lage und Kämpfe der schlesischen Bauern und Landarbeiter im Vormärz, 1840–1847* (Berlin, 1966), 84.

[5] For the holdings of the nobility in the Mark Brandenburg, see Heinrich Berghaus, *Landbuch der Mark Brandenburg und des Markgrafthums Nieder-Lausitz* (Berlin, 1854–1856), 3 vols. The holdings of the Arnims and the Bredows are detailed in vol. 2, 327ff.

[6] Bleiber, *Zwischen Reform und Revolution*, 84.

[7] Freiherrn L. von Zedlitz-Neukirch, *Neues Preussisches Andels-Lexikon* (Leipzig, 1836), 1: 14–18.

CHAPTER 1

half-peasant farms [*Kossätengüter*]. Their customs and style of life are not very different from those of the lower orders."[8]

The older families among this Junker aristocracy descended from a socially and ethnically heterogeneous group that settled the colonized lands east of the Elbe River during the twelfth and thirteenth centuries.[9] As the term *Junker* indicates, some were descended from the "young noblemen" (*junk-herre, junc-herre*), the younger sons of nobles from western Germany who had migrated to the new lands of the east, and others from the native Baltic and Slavic landholders who had inhabited the area and had married among the German settlers; in the areas that became Brandenburg, they had been largely Germanized by the fourteenth century. The forebears of other Junkers were the *locatores*, the land developers, usually of peasant or burgher stock, who had engineered the migration of peasants to the colonized areas, acquired large estates, and gradually blended with the other landowning nobility. Still others were the heirs of military adventurers, the soldiers of fortune who had acquired their estates in exchange for military service. This motley assortment of landholders and petty tyrants originally displayed none of the class cohesion for which their modern descendants became famous; in the turmoil and disorder characteristic of a frontier region, they robbed and feuded with one another, some becoming powerful magnates by crushing the less fortunate squires around them one day only to fall victim to acts of treachery the next.

The emergence of Junker domination in northeastern Germany resulted from a complex process extending from the mid-fifteenth through the sixteenth centuries.[10] During this period, the internal strife and the frequent feuds that characterized their earlier history

[8] [Johann Heinrich Ulrich?] *Bemerkungen eines Reisenden durch die königlichen preussischen Staaten in Briefen* (Altenburg, 1779), 5: 289.

[9] On this general theme, see F. L. Carsten, *The Origins of Prussia* (Oxford, 1954), 89ff.; idem, "The Origins of the Junkers," *English Historical Review* 62 (1947): 145–78; Otto Hintze, *Die Hohenzollern und ihr Werk* (Berlin, 1915); Hans Rosenberg, "The Rise of the Junkers in Brandenburg-Prussia, 1410–1653," *AHR* 49, nos. 1, 2 (1943–1944): 1–22, 228–42. Rosenberg has completely reworked this earlier essay, not only introducing the findings of recent literature, but posing new questions that reveal his remarkable capacity for growth as a social historian over the thirty-five years that separate the two articles. See "Die Ausprägung der Junkerherrschaft in Brandenburg-Preussen, 1410–1618," in his *Machteliten und Wirtschaftskonjukturen*, 24–82. Gustav Aubin, *Zur Geschichte des gutsherrlich-bäuerlichen Verhältnisses in Ostpreussen* (Leipzig, 1910). Walter Görlitz's *Die Junker* (Limburg, 1964) contains some interesting material but is primarily a popular account and too partial to the Junkers.

[10] For the basis of Junker hegemony in Brandenburg and Prussia during the late fifteenth and sixteenth centuries, see Rosenberg, "Die Ausprägung der Junkerherrschaft," 52–59.

declined and the hostility and fear that existed between the powerful "castle-residing" high nobility and the lesser squires abated. In the course of the sixteenth century, a sense of collective interest developed among the nobility, especially against the prince and against the towns.

The disintegration of princely authority in the fourteenth and fifteenth centuries gave the nobility the opportunity to assert its power. The nobles of Brandenburg and Pomerania carved out for themselves broader legal jurisdictions over the local populations; they purchased from impecunious princes the control of castles, domains, and villages. In Brandenburg, the alienation of crown estates in order to obtain revenues began in the thirteenth century and lasted through the sixteenth century, reaching its high point during the reign of Joachim II between 1535 and 1571. Farther east, in Prussia, which had been settled and ruled by the Knights of the Teutonic Order, central authority disintegrated after the knights were defeated by the Poles in 1410. In 1453, the Prussian nobility was bold enough to defy the Order and support the king of Poland. The subsequent defeat of the Teutonic Order in the Thirteen Years' War ended its power; West Prussia was lost to Poland and Prussia itself was henceforth held by the Order in fief to the king of Poland. The extended period of warfare left the Order financially exhausted, forcing it to alienate much of its land to creditors and opening the way for the nobility to assert its independence.

The Reformation provided the nobility with new leverage over the local populations. The Lutheran teaching of authority and obedience may have aided the princes' power, but it also directly enhanced the position of the local nobles who dominated village life and who now obtained the *Patronatsrecht*, the right to appoint the village pastor. The nobility, and not just the princes, gained as well from the disposition of the church lands after the Protestant conversion of the territories. The dukes of Pomerania had to overcome the opposition of some Protestant Junkers who did not wish to share the acquisition of church property with them. Elsewhere, many of the church lands found their way into the hands of the nobility. In Brandenburg, Joachim II's chronic need for money gave the nobility the opportunity to acquire church estates; of the 654 church estates taken with the introduction of Lutheranism in 1540, 286 were owned by the nobility a decade later.

Finally, the emergent nobility was aided by the decline of the towns. Originally, the east Elbian towns were powerful, prosperous, and relatively independent. Many were allied with the Hanseatic League and able to extract broad concessions from the hapless princes: tax exemptions, toll collections, and the important *advocatia*, the right to try criminals, in some cases even nobles, in their own courts.¹¹ With the defeat of the Teutonic Order, the towns began to decline; a diminished population, the debasement of coinage, and the general insecurity of the times plagued these Baltic towns. Thorn and Elbing suffered severely during the Thirteen Years' War, and by 1467 Danzig had lost one-third of its population. In Brandenburg, the more aggressive Hohenzollern Electors began to abrogate urban liberties in the fifteenth century. In 1448, Frederick II forced the twin towns of Berlin and Cölln to vow obedience to him; he deprived them of their self-government, and they were subsequently forced out of the Hanse. Similar concessions were wrung out of Salzwedel, Stendal, Frankfurt-on-the-Oder, and Neustadt; all were declared non-Hanseatic cities by 1525, a symptom of their decline. Similarly, the dukes of Pomerania restricted the urban liberties of Stralsund and Stettin, the two most important trading centers on the Pomeranian coast.¹²

The nobles were the prime beneficiaries of the decline of the towns. They had long chafed at the trade monopoly exercised by the town merchants over the export of agricultural produce; their demands for free trade consistently headed the list of grievances they drew against the towns. The Junkers lent their support to the Hohenzollern efforts against the towns. Eventually, they found it possible to sell their products directly to foreign merchants, bypassing the mediation of the local town merchants. The emergence of the Junkers at the expense of the towns and the subsequent isolation, decline, and exclusion of the towns from the political process became one of the major factors determining the nature of east Elbian society.¹³

The growing independence of the Junkers and the decline of the towns coincided with changing patterns of production on the noble estates. During the twelfth and thirteenth centuries, landlords and developers (locatores) had attracted peasants to the lands they were colonizing east of the Elbe by offering them greater independence than they enjoyed in western Germany. Most landlords granted the peasants hereditary tenure to their holdings, fixed their rental obligations, and demanded only a few days' labor service per year. Then, in the fourteenth and fifteenth centuries, the landowning nobility began to reverse this pattern and to impose heavier servile obligations on their peasants.¹⁴

¹¹ Carsten, *Origins of Prussia*, 92–100.
¹² Ibid., 136–48.
¹³ Rosenberg, "Rise of the Junkers," 6, 234–35.
¹⁴ There is an enormous literature devoted to the problem of the development of serf-

The economic slump that struck western Europe in the fourteenth century relieved the population pressure that had pushed people toward the more thinly populated east. The flow of peasant settlers stopped. Wars, feuds, plagues, and crop failures also contributed to a population decline in the east until, by the end of the fifteenth century, hundreds of peasant holdings and villages stood deserted. Hans Rosenberg summarized the situation succinctly: "In the fifteenth century, the central economic fact facing the rent-receiving landlord and the managing estate proprietor [*Gutsherr*] was the abundance of land and the scarcity of labor."[15] The Junkers responded to this problem by increasing the labor services of the peasants, binding them to the soil, and turning their own energies toward the management of their estates. Their growing political power facilitated this response. In exchange for the assistance rendered the princes in their struggle against the towns, the nobles gained broader jurisdiction over their estates (*Gerichtsherrschaft*), combining in themselves the authority of police, tax collector, magistrate, and judge.[16]

This response of the nobility to its labor shortage was also facilitated by the decline of the towns. In their prime, the towns had provided refuge for peasants who found life on the land too harsh. By the end

---

dom. The best overall guide, in a comparative context, is by Jerome Blum, "The Rise of Serfdom in Eastern Europe," *AHR* 62, no. 4 (1957): 807–36. The earlier interpretation, which tied the rise of demesne farming to the declining military role of the eastern aristocracy, offered by Knapp, in *Bauernbefreiung*, has been largely rejected. F. L. Carsten, in "Origins of the Junkers," also disputes the view made by Rosenberg, in "Rise of the Junkers," 229, that large demesne farming, under a system that later came to be known as *Gutsherrschaft*, "was always there." Carsten's contention is supported by the evidence that there was a steady growth of demesne farming through the fifteenth century; see Siegfried Korth, "Die Entstehung und Entwicklung des Ostdeutschen Grossgrundbesitzes," *Jahrbuch der Albertus-Universität zu Königsberg/Pr.* 3 (1953): 166–67. In his later article, Rosenberg draws a sharper distinction between *Gutsherrschaft*, by which he means the social and legal control of the estate and its villages by the noble lord, and *Gutswirtschaft*, with which he refers to the development of estate agriculture directed by the lord through the use of servile labor. The former developed much earlier, in some regions at the time of German settlement, whereas the latter was a result of the Junkers' response to the economic opportunities presented in the sixteenth century. See "Die Ausprägung der Junkerherrschaft," 59ff. Against the argument that Gutsherrschaft had Slavic origins, advanced by Heinz Maybaum, in "Die Entstehung der Gutsherrschaft im nordwestlichen Mecklenburg," *Vierteljahrschrift für Sozial- und Wirtschaftsgeschichte*, Beiheft 6 (1926), see F. L. Carsten, "Slavs in North-Eastern Germany," *The Economic History Review* 11 (1941): 67ff. See also Friedrich Lütge, *Geschichte der deutschen Agrarverfassung vom frühen Mittelalter bis zum 19. Jahrhundert* (Stuttgart, 1963), 118–45; Carsten, *Origins of Prussia*, 149–64; Hintze, *Die Hohenzollern und ihr Werk*, 108–111.

[15] Rosenberg, "Rise of the Junkers," 230.
[16] Ibid., 232.

of the fifteenth century, the power of the nobles had grown to the point that they could usually compel the towns to return runaway peasants. Where their independence had been broken, as in Brandenburg and Pomerania, the towns could offer no help to the peasants sinking into serfdom. In Prussia, where the emasculated Knights of the Teutonic Order had allowed the towns greater latitude, the unhappy peasants were able to find sympathizers and supporters among the town guilds and commons; as a result, Prussia was the only eastern region that experienced a substantial rebellion during the general uprising of German peasants in 1525. However, the new grand master of the Teutonic Order, Albert von Hohenzollern, who was also the Elector of Brandenburg, quickly dissolved the Order and cooperated with the nobles in crushing the peasants. The new Prussian ordinances of 1526 confirmed the rise of the nobility over the towns and the peasantry; no longer could peasants leave their estates without the permission of the lord and find refuge in the towns.[17]

Economic hegemony went hand in hand with the administrative and political dominion of the Junkers. To the traditional Gerichtsherrschaft, the monopoly of legal jurisdiction over the peasants on his estates and villages, the noble landowner added *Gutswirtschaft*, the absolute control over the production of the estate through the domination of servile labor. With greater control over the peasantry, the landed nobility was able to exploit the favorable market for agricultural products that came with the economic upswing in western Europe during the sixteenth century. Previously, as the limited labor obligations demanded of the peasants indicated, estate productions were relatively restricted. Now, by increasing the labor obligations from as few as three, four, or six days per year to as many as two or three days per week, the lords expanded their estates and became major producers for the market. New lands were brought under cultivation, vacant peasant holdings were resettled, and occasionally peasant farms were seized and incorporated in the lord's estate. As one Pomeranian chronicler reported, "In previous years the noblemen have not been industrious and interested in agriculture; but recently this has changed, and the nobility has never been as rich as now."[18] This social and economic system known simply as Gutsherrschaft—the cultivation of the estate land by the noble owner for his own profit, using the labor of serfs over whom he had complete legal jurisdiction—was securely established by the end of the sixteenth century.

[17] Hintze, *Die Hohenzollern und ihr Werk*, 121; Carsten, *Origins of Prussia*, 151.
[18] Cited in Carsten, *Origins of Prussia*, 54.

The system of Gutsherrschaft became the backbone of Junker power in Prussia for the next two centuries; it provided the noble estate owners with an interlocking control over the social, economic, and political matters immediate to the estate itself. Gutsherrschaft was the central experience of the Prussian aristocracy; it provided the framework and the institutions within which the aristocracy became the dominant class in Prussia and determined both the means by which agricultural commodities were produced and the context for the encounter between the classes involved in that production. Gutsherrschaft granted the aristocracy its primary experience of power, and that experience shaped the aristocracy's attitude toward politics long after the system of Gutsherrschaft had been modified or had disappeared. Not even the emergence of royal absolutism or the development of a state bureaucracy diminished the power of the noble landowner on his estate. In fact, beginning with the compromise contained in the Brandenburg Recess of 1653, the Hohenzollern rulers granted the nobility complete power over their serfs in exchange for the nobility's relinquishing its claims for checks on the central administration of the Elector. Gutsherrschaft molded the Prussian aristocracy in ways substantially different from most of the other aristocracies in Europe; binding them more closely to their estate, it caused noble landowners to see possession and control of land as essential to their preservation as a class.

It is in some respects an anomaly that control of the land should have assumed such real and symbolic importance in the perception of the Prussian aristocracy, for there were, in fact, numerous poor or landless nobles. Despite the efforts of the Hohenzollerns, especially Frederick II in the eighteenth century, to forbid non-nobles from buying noble estates and to ensure that all who were awarded titles of nobility were either granted an estate or had the means to obtain one, many nobles in Prussia by the eighteenth century were without land, largely because of the system of inheritance. By law, all the sons of a nobleman inherited their father's title, virtually assuring that the number of noblemen would always exceed the number of estates available. By 1800, for example, there were roughly 20,000 noble families in the eastern provinces (exclusive of the newly acquired Polish territories in which the nobility was so numerous).[19] The most accurate count of the number of estates in these provinces yields slightly more than

---

[19] Zedlitz-Neukirch, *Neues Preussisches Adels-Lexikon*, 1: 14–15; Reinhard Koselleck, *Preussen zwischen Reform und Revolution* (Stuttgart, 1967), 80, also cites this figure.

11,500—far fewer than the number of noble families.[20] Furthermore, when one considers that many noblemen owned more than one estate, the problem of landless noblemen becomes even more apparent. Statistics compiled by Fritz Martiny reveal that there were 658 adult noblemen living in the Kurmark of Brandenburg in 1800. Of these, 409 were classified as landowning vassals; 133 were vassals' brothers—blood relatives of the vassal: brothers, uncles, cousins, nephews; 116 were vassals' sons—sons or grandsons of the vassal. Twenty-seven percent (177 out of 658) were without land; more significant, however, is the fact that of those classified as vassals' brothers or vassals' sons 71 percent (177 out of 249) were landless. Most of these had sought positions in the military. Sixty-one percent of the vassals' brothers and 83 percent of the vassals' sons had military careers.[21]

That a substantial portion of the nobility was effectively severed from its connection with the land was also apparent in the fact that more than one-fourth of the nobles who owned estates did not live on them. Statistics from Silesia indicate that 26 percent of the noble landowners did not live on their estates.[22] A study of the Kurmark reveals the same pattern. In 1800, of the 409 nobles listed as vassals, 29 percent (119) did not live on their estates. Of the 290 who did, only 31 percent (112) had always lived there; the rest had also pursued careers, usually in the military, that took them away from their estates.[23] Figures for all the eastern provinces, except for the new Polish lands, yield 3,829 noble families living on the land.[24] It is obvious that the dominion over their estates (*Herrschaft*), the cornerstone of noble priv-

---

[20] It is not possible to calculate precisely the number of noble estates. A list of the larger estates about 1800 shows that in the eastern provinces (exclusive of the new Polish territories) there were 5,424 noble estates with a tax value in excess of 5,000 talers. Actually, the total number was considerably larger; because assessments were frequently lower than the market value, the number of estates worth more than 5,000 talers was higher. Moreover, some large estates were subdivided for administrative or inheritance purposes, although they still remained a "unified possession" (*Besitzeinheit*), with unified jurisdiction over the peasantry. Taking these factors into account, the total number of estates, based on the survey of Leopold Krug, was 11,566, still far fewer than the noble families in Prussia. See Leopold Krug, *Betrachtungen über den Nationalreichthum des preussischen Staates*, reprint of 1805 edition by Scientia Verlag (Aalen, 1970), 1: 410; Koselleck's total is not entirely accurate, but the error is insignificant, *Preussen zwischen Reform und Revolution*, 672.

[21] Fritz Martiny, *Die Adelsfrage in Preussen vor 1806*, Beiheft 35 to *Vierteljahrschrift für Sozial- und Wirtschaftsgeschichte* (Berlin, 1938), table AI, insert in the back of the book.

[22] Johannes Ziekursch, *Hundert Jahre schlesischer Agrargeschichte* (Breslau, 1927), 45–47.

[23] Martiny, *Die Adelsfrage*, 110–11.

[24] Krug, *Betrachtungen*, 1: 455.

ilege, actually touched only a portion of those who possessed noble titles.

The relationship between the nobility and the land changed in important ways in the course of the eighteenth century. In 1717, Frederick William I granted allodial title over their estates to the nobles in Brandenburg and Pomerania; the estates in East Prussia were made allodial in 1732.[25] This action dissolved the antiquated notion of the "feudal bond" (*Lehnsverband*) linking the nobility to the monarch. The military service owed by the vassal, a useless anachronism by the eighteenth century, was transformed into an annual tax paid by the nobles (*Lehnpferdgeld*). Because it eroded their privilege of tax exemption, nobles in the old Mark opposed the action. At the same time, however, the monarch renounced his traditional rights over the estates of his vassals (*Heimfallsrecht*), and noble families were given the freedom to dispose of their estates or draft their own inheritance contracts. The effects of this allodialization of the land were neither dramatic nor immediate, but they were significant. Under the feudal bond, the estate had been considered the possession of the noble family, those who were living and those who would possess it in the future. The individual who occupied the estate did not possess it; he could not arbitrarily sell it or encumber it with debt without the approval of the other members of the family. The estate was the property of the entire family, giving the family its name and, presumably, the basis of its noble distinction. It was not merely real property, but a trust; it was not merely the source of income, but the foundation of the aristocratic social order. Allodialization of estates made easier their sale and thus the breaking of the family link to the land that extended over generations.

After the allodialization of the estates, the nobility made an effort to preserve the ideal of family ownership. Various forms of entail (*Fideikommiss, Majorat*, and so on) were followed to prevent the alienation of the family estate, but their usage was uncommon before the middle of the nineteenth century. Inheritance contracts varied from family to family and inheritance custom and law varied from region to region, but the rule customarily acknowledged the claim of the eldest son to the estate and the rights of other children to a portion of the inheritance. In general, this was done by separating real property from movable property (*Absonderung des Lehns und Erbes*). Real property went to

[25] Victor Loewe, "Die Allodifikation der Lehen unter Friedrich Wilhelm I," *FBPG* 11 (1899): 341–74; Hintze, *Die Hohenzollern und ihr Werk*, 295–96; Zedlitz-Neukirch, *Neues Preussisches Adels-Lexikon* 1: 6.

the eldest son; movable property was divided, according to a predetermined formula, among the heirs. Depending on the region, movable property could include farm equipment, livestock, and seed—items whose removal clearly reduced the value of the real property. By the eighteenth century, it was common for daughters to inherit their father's estate if there were no surviving sons. Otherwise, a daughter's inheritance was usually restricted to her dowry, marriage costs, and, in Pomerania, her mourning dress. A widow was generally entitled to a cash settlement equal to the amount she had brought into the marriage if her husband died before an heir was born; otherwise, she was assured an annual income and usually the right to live on the estate for the remainder of her life.[26]

This system of inheritance endeavored to assure that all members of the family had the means to maintain themselves in a manner befitting persons of noble birth. Nevertheless, the system did not succeed in doing that and brought several unfortunate consequences. It provided the elements for frequent disputes and litigations over inheritances, not merely between siblings, but in some cases between widows and their sons. In addition, the financial burden imposed on estate owners by other heirs could often be met by dividing the estate or by mortgaging it in order to pay the cash settlements. Despite the obvious dangers the system posed, up to 10 percent of the estates in the Kurmark had been divided for inheritances by 1800. Usually the estate itself remained intact, whereas the services and rents of peasants were divided among the heirs. More common was the practice of paying the claimants with money borrowed against the estate. The high level of indebtedness of noble landowners during the last decades of the eighteenth century was probably not due primarily to inheritance claims, but nevertheless complaints were common. In 1775, Eberhard von Rochow lamented that it would be difficult to find an estate "that was not troubled with the inheritance debts of widows' payments and daughters' settlements, etc. . . . There are estates that scarcely yield 7,000 talers' income but have inheritance debts of 100,000 talers."[27]

With the allodialization of the noble estates, daughters could inherit the family estates, and to prevent land from falling into the hands of

---

[26] For a discussion of inheritance practices and restrictions see Karl Friedrich Beneckendorff, *Oeconomia Forensis; oder, Kurzer Inbegriff derjenigen Landwirtschaftlichen Wahrheiten*, 8 vols. (Berlin, 1775–1784), vol. 4; see also Martiny, *Die Adelsfrage*, 21–22. Many of the histories of noble families, compiled in the late nineteenth century, contain testaments and wills, which describe inheritances. See, for example, Ernst Devrient, *Das Geschlechte Arnim* (Leipzig, 1914), part 1, "Urkunden"; or Georg Adalbert von Mülverstedt, *Geschichtliche Nachrichten von dem altpreussischen Adelsgeschlecht von Ostau* (Magdeburg, 1886).

[27] Cited in Martiny, *Die Adelsfrage*, 19.

commoners, restrictions against noblewomen's marrying "beneath their Stand" were strict and generally enforced. Noblewomen could marry non-noble army officers, civil servants, and "respected, wealthy burghers and businessmen" without forfeiting their inheritance; however, if they married persons from lower categories of the common citizens, they lost all claims to the family estate and most of the rest of their inheritance.[28] Therefore, wealthier families created family foundations (*Stiftungen*), the proceeds of which were intended to provide a reasonable income for widows and unmarried daughters. Poorer families could send their daughters to the "noble cloisters" (*Adelige Fraülein Kloster* or *Fraüleinstift*) established in each province to ensure that daughters of noblemen could maintain the standard of living and culture appropriate to their Stand. Many of these were medieval cloisters or convents that had been secularized during the Reformation; others were founded in the sixteenth and seventeenth centuries to provide refuge and respectability for unmarried women.[29]

The sons of noblemen were also forbidden to marry beneath their rank.[30] Nevertheless, these injunctions were always dealt with realistically; an ordinance of 1739, for example, permitted "an impoverished nobleman to assist his family through an unequal marriage with a person of low, but respectable, birth and exceptional wealth."[31] How often noblemen married women of lower status for their money is difficult to say; it seems doubtful that many noblemen employed this strategy prior to the nineteenth century.

Marital alliances were a primary means by which the Prussian nobility, like all nobilities, sought to preserve and enlarge its landed property. Bitter conflicts, frequently resulting in the disinheritance of a disobedient son, developed when sons failed to marry in accordance with their fathers' wishes. Family feuds requiring the intervention of the prince sometimes resulted from broken marriage contracts. Although it is seldom possible to discern what property considerations, if any, impelled a particular marriage without a systematic examination of marriage contracts and inheritance settlements, an examination of

[28] On the marriage restrictions for noblewomen, see Beneckendorff, *Oeconomia Forensis* 4: 363–77; Wolf-Gunther Bennecke's *Stand und Stände in Preussen vor den Reformen* (phil. diss., Berlin, 1935), 18–23, also contains a discussion of marriage restrictions in relation to inheritance.

[29] For examples of family foundations, see that of the von Ostau family, Mülverstedt, *Adelsgeschlecht von Ostau*, 73; or Siegmar Graf Dohna, *Aufzeichnungen über die Vergangenheit der Familie Dohna*, part 4, *Die Jungere Dohnas*, Heft A (Berlin, 1885), 50.

[30] *Allgemeines Landrecht für die Preussischen Staaten*, I/7:1/#30. Found in the edition of the text, Hans Hattenhauer, ed., *Allgemeines Landrecht für die Preussischen Staaten von 1794* (Frankfurt a.M. and Berlin, 1970), 346.

[31] Cited in Bennecke, *Stand und Stände in Preussen*, 22.

more than four hundred marriages in several noble families from about 1700 until about 1850 reveals significant aspects of the marriage strategies of the Prussian nobility.[32] In some cases, it is clear that marriage alliances were formed exclusively by property interests. In 1727, for example, Friedrich Ludwig von Dohna-Lauck, excluded from the inheritance of his father's estates by primogeniture, could, because he was the oldest son of his father's second marriage, lay claim to the inheritance of the estates of Reichertswalde through his mother. His claim, however, was contested by Countess Isenburg, who had equally valid rights to the inheritance. To settle the dispute, Dohna married the countess, although, at forty-seven, she was seventeen years his senior. Georg Abraham von Arnim, heir of the vast Boitzenburg domain early in the eighteenth century and without sons, insisted that his daughter marry her cousin, also a von Arnim, in order that the Boitzenburg complex would pass to their son and remain in the family.[33] The relative frequency with which young girls, in their mid-teens, married men well over forty or the cases of men marrying their nieces and very young men marrying considerably older women suggest that inheritance considerations were the basis for many marriages.

In most noble families, especially in the very wealthy and high-ranking ones, the rate of intrafamily marriage was high. An examination of the Dohnas, one of the richest families of East Prussia, which bore the title count, reveals that of 177 marriages that can be identified within the family from about 1700 until about 1860, 22 were marriages in which both partners were Dohnas; an additional 12 were between Dohnas and identifiable relatives with other family names. Thus, 19 percent of the marriages were within the family. Moreover, a large number of marriages within the Dohna family during this period were made with a network of eighteen other families. During this

---

[32] For examples of intra- and interfamilial conflicts over marriage contracts, see Peter-Michael Hahn, *Struktur und Funktion des brandenburgischen Adels im 16. Jahrhundert*, Historische und Pädagogische Studien, 9 (Berlin, 1979), 120–32. My statistics on noble marriages are drawn from a number of family histories, compiled in the late nineteenth or in the early twentieth century, which contained reasonably complete genealogical information on these noble families as well as important documents on their histories. The sample is, admittedly, limited, and it contains a certain bias, of course, in favor of those families who survived the pressures of the nineteenth century and were wealthy enough to hire someone to write their history. This means that the incidence of endogamy was probably higher among the sample than among the Prussian nobility as a whole. Nevertheless, I think the marital patterns suggested by this sample generally hold true for the entire Prussian nobility.

[33] Numerous similar examples can be cited. These are taken from Devrient, *Das Geschlecht von Arnim* 1: 519–26, and Dohna, *Familie Dohna*, vol. 4.

century and a half, 60 out of the 177 marriages (34 percent) were between Dohnas and other families in the network. When added to those 22 marriages within the Dohna family itself, we find that 82 marriages (46 percent) were within the family or a small network of East Prussian noble families.[34]

In each successive generation from the beginning of the eighteenth century until the mid-nineteenth century, the practice of endogamy within the Prussian nobility declined. For example, at the beginning of the eighteenth century the number of marriages within the Dohna family or the network of eighteen families comprised 86 percent of the total; in the next generation, 66 percent were within the family and the network; by the early nineteenth century, this percentage had fallen to 37; and by mid-century, it was only 15.[35] The same pattern of increasing exogamy can be seen in all the noble families surveyed. From 1700 to 1750, 93 percent of all noble marriages were within the ranks of the nobility; during the next fifty years, the percentage of nobles marrying other nobles fell to 75; and during the first half of the nineteenth century, only 64 percent chose their partners from within the nobility.[36] These figures are undoubtedly higher than would be the case if the entire nobility were surveyed, for they are taken from the records of some of the more prominent and wealthy families, who still controlled large estates in Prussia in the late nineteenth century. Nevertheless, the pattern they reveal probably reflects the nobility as a whole—from the mid-eighteenth century until the mid-nineteenth century, the nobility reached increasingly beyond its own ranks in the selection of marriage partners.

From this, we ought not to conclude that members of the nobility were marrying commoners in ever-larger numbers merely because their fortunes needed replenishing with bourgeois wealth. Undoubtedly some marriages were inspired by such needs. But the figures reflect many other factors: greater geographic mobility, broadening the pool of eligible marriage partners; the large number of commoners who purchased estates and intermingled with the nobility after the early decades of the nineteenth century; and the loosening of the

[34] Dohna, *Familie Dohna*, vol. 4.
[35] Ibid.
[36] In addition to the Arnims, Dohnas, and Ostaus already cited, I have consulted the following family histories: Carl August Ludwig von Eickstedt, *Familien Buch des dynastischen Geschlechts von Eickstedt* (Ratibor, 1860); Wichart von Holtzendorff, *Die Holtzendorff in der Mark Brandenburg und Chur-Sachsen: Eine genealogische Studie* (1876); Georg Schmidt, *Die Familie v. Manteuffel* (Berlin, 1905).

castelike ständisch structure of the society that divided nobles from commoners.

No social class, however, is determined solely by its contours, by the relations of its members, and by the strategies it devises to survive and reproduce itself; it is not even determined solely by its role in the economic structure of society. The contours of a dominant social class are shaped by its relationship to the class or classes it dominates. The structure of domination forms the basis of class habitus—that system of dispositions and practices, of habits of mind and perceptions that grows out of the relationship of domination and informs behavior.[37] To understand the habitus of the Prussian nobility, it is necessary to examine the situation of the peasantry it dominated.

The Peasantry

To delineate the structure of the Prussian peasantry in the late eighteenth century requires the use of highly technical, untranslatable language. The term *Bauer*, peasant, was used (and will be used throughout this book) in two different ways. In its broadest meaning, a Bauer was anyone who lived on the land, made his living through agriculture, and had no other rights that could include him in any other class. This is the way in which the Prussian General Law Code of 1794 defined the peasantry.[38] In its narrowest usage, however, *Bauer* was used to refer only to those persons within the rural population who had property rights, inheritance rights, or at least some form of extended contractual rights over their land. As we shall see, there were numerous kinds of such rights and even differences within them; depending on the size of their holdings, some peasants were referred to as full Bauern, half-Bauern, or quarter-Bauern. In general, it may be said that to be considered a Bauer in the narrowest sense one had to hold rights to a *Hufe*, a specified portion (varying in size according to region) of the *Flur*, the large, open fields of the estate in which the strips

[37] The term *habitus* has been coined by Pierre Bourdieu. He writes the following: "Habitus could be considered as a subjective but not individual system of internalized structures, schemes of perception, conception, and action common to all members of the same group or class." It is, he says, "an immanent law, *lex insita*," formed by the objective condition of class, to be "understood as a system of lasting, transposable dispositions which, integrating past experiences, functions at every moment as a matrix of perceptions, apperceptions, and actions and makes possible the achievement of infinitely diversified tasks." *Outline of a Theory of Practice*, trans. R. Nice (Cambridge, 1977), 82–86.

[38] *ALR*, II/7:1/#1: "Under the peasantry [*Bauernstände*] are included all residents who occupy themselves directly with agriculture, insofar as they are not excluded from this Stand by noble birth, office, or other special rights."

of the noble lord were farmed in unison with those belonging to the Bauern.[39]

A small group of peasants in the Prussian provinces was completely free of obligations or subservience to the noble estates and formed a middle stratum of free farmers between the larger estate owners on the one side and the servile peasantry on the other.[40] In some instances their independence was recognized by the fact that they swore an oath of homage directly to the king. In East Prussia, this group was more numerous than elsewhere in the monarchy; referred to as *Kölmer*, these free peasant farmers rejected the term *Bauer* and insisted on being called "owners of *kölmischen* estates."[41] Elsewhere, these free peasant farmers were called *Lehnschulzen*, *Freischulzen*, or *Erbschulzen*. In the Mark Brandenburg, the Lehnschulzen often worked closely with the landowning nobility, serving as *Schulzen*, the chief administrative and police officers of the village. They often directed the labor force of the village, saw to it that the village obligations to the state were fulfilled, and virtually ran the village. One eighteenth-century agronomist referred to them as little Junkers.[42] This group of small peasant farmers comprised a very small percentage of the rural population.

---

[39] The Hufe was of various sizes but was commonly taken to mean 30 morgen; the full Bauer frequently had 2 or 2½ Hufe. See Knapp, *Die Bauernbefreiung* 1: 9. On the requirement that to be considered a Bauer in this narrow sense of the word, that is, having a portion of the Flur, see Hans-Heinrich Müller, *Märkische Landwirtschaft vor den Agrarreformen von 1807*, Veröffentlichung der Bezirksheimatsmuseum Potsdam, Heft 13 (Potsdam, 1967), 18. In the Mark Brandenburg, peasants with such rights were referred to as Bauer or Hufner. See also A. Krenzlin, *Dorf, Feld und Wirtschaft im Gebiet der grossen Täler und Platten Östlich der Elbe*, Forschungen zur deutschen Landeskunde, 70 (Remagen/Rhein, 1952), 26. For a general discussion of the status of peasants, see Heinz Paul, *Zur Frage der Uebereinstimmung der Produktionsverhältnisse mit dem Charakter der Produktivkräfte beim Uebergang vom Feudalismus zum Kapitalismus in der Landwirtschaft Preussens* (Wirtschaft. diss., Leipzig, 1957), 38–51; Gerhard Czybulka, *Die Lage der Ländlichen Klassen Ostdeutschlands im 18. Jahrhundert* (Braunschweig, 1949); Friedrich-Wilhelm Henning, *Dienste und Abgaben der Bauern im 18. Jahrhundert*, Quellen und Forschungen zur Agrargeschichte, 21 (Stuttgart, 1969). Hanna Schissler's *Preussische Agrargesellschaft im Wandel*, Kritische Studien zur Geschichtswissenschaft, 33 (Göttingen, 1978), 66ff., is very general.

[40] See Theodor Freiherr von der Goltz, *Die ländliche Arbeiterklasse und der preussische Staat* (Jena, 1893), 24–25; Müller, *Märkische Landwirtschaft*, 28.

[41] On the homage paid by *Lehnsbauern* (a peasant holding land on feudal tenure), see Werner Lippert, *Geschichte der 110 Bauerndörfer in der nördlichen Uckermark*, Mitteldeutsche Forschungen, vol. 57 (Cologne and Vienna, 1968), 115; W. von Brünneck, *Zur Geschichte des Grundeigenthums in Ost- und Westpreussen*, vol. 1, *Die kölmischen Güter* (Berlin, 1891). See also Knapp, *Bauernbefreiung*, 1: 14–15. On the Kölmer, see also Jerome Blum, *The End of the Old Order in Rural Europe* (Princeton, 1978), 30.

[42] Cited in Müller, *Märkische Landwirtschaft*, 28.

While these free peasant farmers formed a group at one end of the social spectrum free of the authority of the noble lord, a group at the other end was likewise personally free. They were variously referred to as *Einlieger, freie Dorfseinwohner*, or, in East Prussia, *Instleute*; the legal phrase for them was *Schutzuntertanen* (protected subjects).[43] Except in East Prussia, where the Instleute obtained reasonably favorable work contracts that extended for a number of years, these peasants were frequently near the bottom of the village social order. Some of them were former unfree peasants or the sons of unfree peasants who had bought their freedom from their former lord or had successfully run away from him and taken up residence on another estate; others were probably children of small handworkers in the towns who could find no positions and settled on an estate in the country; others may have been vagrants or roamers who settled down. When they presented themselves to the lord and requested his permission to settle on his estate, they subjected themselves to his authority, accepted specified work obligations from him, and worked as day-wage laborers (*Tagelöhner*). Because such employment usually did not provide a subsistence, they also worked as wage laborers for the peasants in the villages. These Einlieger had no cottages and usually rented quarters from peasants. Occasionally, the noble estate owner would offer them fixed rights to a plot of land; if the Einlieger accepted, they forfeited their free status and became the permanent subjects (*Untertanen*) of the estate. In most respects, their existence differed little from the other, unfree Einlieger or Tagelöhner in a village, with one exception: unless they agreed to become permanent subjects, they retained their freedom to leave the estate. The General Law Code of 1794 underscored that freedom: "Such Einlieger are free to move away from the village with their children and to settle elsewhere without having to obtain the permission to leave of the lord."[44]

The remainder of the peasantry, in the broader meaning of that word, lived in the rural villages in lifelong bondage (*Untertänigkeit*), subject to the authority of their lords. *Untertänigkeit* is difficult to define; in the eighteenth century, it was differentiated from *Leibeigenschaft*, whose literal meaning, "bodily property," was associated with slavery. Leibeigenschaft was subsequently outlawed; nevertheless, the qualitative differences between the two forms of bondage were minimal. Untertänigkeit was both a juridical and an economic concept.[45]

[43] Von der Goltz, *Die ländliche Arbeiterklasse*, 30–31.
[44] *ALR*, II/7:3/#121, Hattenhauer, 437.
[45] These general observations on Untertänigkeit are taken from its legal definition in the Prussian General Law Code. Some differences undoubtedly were manifested in ac-

Peasants identified as untertänig were personally bound to the estate, but the character of that bondage often differed according to their status as it was defined by economic obligations to the lord and their tenure rights to land. In general, such peasants were bound to the estates in a number of ways. All their children were born into bondage and were obligated to become *Gesinde*, servants, of their lords for a specified period of time—one year if their fathers had favorable status, three years if not.[46] Bound peasants could not leave the estate without the permission of their lords and could be returned forcibly if they ran away. To obtain their freedom, they had to pay the lord a fixed sum. Bound peasants required the permission of their lords to marry; marriage alliances made against the lord's will were legally valid, but the offending peasant could be punished with imprisonment from three days to four weeks. Bound peasants were liable to the police and judicial authority of the lords, as well as to their arbitrary punishment if their lord considered them to be "lazy, disorderly, or disobedient."[47] The lords, on the other hand, were obligated to see that their bound peasants were adequately fed, that their children received a "Christian education," that orphaned children were cared for, and that they were protected against the effects of natural misfortunes, as when the harvest failed.[48]

There were several categories of bound peasants who were Bauern in the narrow sense of the word, that is, whose strips of farm land were part of the large open fields, the Flur, of the estate. Those with

---

cordance with the traditional customs of the various provinces, but the code probably defined *Untertänigkeit* as it was practiced most commonly. For the general provisions of the code, see *ALR*, II/7:3 and 4; Hattenhauer, 436–41. On the issue of Untertänigkeit versus Leibeigenschaft, much was written in the last half of the eighteenth century. For example, in 1792, the *Lausitzische Monatsschrift* contained the following: "The *Leibeigene* is a slave, who is dependent on the arbitrary actions of his master; the hereditary Untertan is a free man, whose freedom is merely limited in other ways than that of the other citizens of the state." The duties performed by him were merely the repayment for the paternal obligations he undertook for him; they were "similar to the payment of interest on borrowed capital." Cited in Rudolf Lehmann, *Quellen zur Lage der Privatbauern in der Niederlausitz im Zeitalter des Absolutismus* (Berlin, 1957), 211–13. On Leibeigenschaft, see Blum, *Old Order*, 39.

[46] There were exceptions to the general rule that the children of bound peasants were forced into the service of the lord. Most peasants could win an exception to the rule if they could demonstrate their son was needed in their service; if a peasant had only one son, he was generally excused from this compulsory service. See *ALR*, II/7:4/#196–200. Also the children of Erbpächter or Erbsinzbauer, who held the most favorable tenure status, were not obliged to service. Müller, *Märkische Landwirtschaft*, 29.

[47] *ALR*, II/7:4/#228; Hattenhauer, 440.

[48] *ALR*, II/7:3/#122–32; Hattenhauer, 437.

the most favorable rights were the *Erbzinsbauern* or *Erbpachtbauern*. Although they did not "own" their lands in the sense that they had the free dispositon of them, they could sell their holdings with the permission of the estate owner. Moreover, their hereditary rights to their lands extended beyond their direct descendants, although the lords retained the right to deny the inheritance to anyone they deemed "unfit."[49] Erbzinsbauern were subject to the lord's authority, that is untertänig, only with respect to their property rights; if they sold their land, their Untertänigkeit was ended and they could leave the estate without having to purchase their freedom. In addition, their children were generally not untertänig and therefore did not owe personal service to the lord.[50] A second, much more numerous category of such genuine Bauern was that of the *Lassbauern*, or the *Lassiten*, who held a somewhat less favorable status.[51] Within this group, there was a considerable range in the size of the landholdings and the nature of the tenure rights. Some Lassbauern had hereditary rights to their lands similar to those of the Erbzinsbauern, but with notable differences. Their personal bondage was greater. In the event they were to sell their holdings, which required the lord's approval, they still remained bound to the estate and could not leave it without paying for their emancipation. Their lands could be inherited only by their wives or sons, but the noble estate owner had the right to select the son who would inherit the holdings. Their children were born into bondage and owed one year of personal service to the lord. Those Lassbauern who did not hold hereditary rights were more common and formed the classic model of Untertänigkeit, especially in the older regions of the Mark Brandenburg. As in the case of Lassbauern with hereditary tenure, they were bound to the estate, although they held their lands only for their lifetime; the lord had the right, nevertheless, to break their lifetime contract if he deemed their service inadequate. Most often, a son would be selected by the lord to assume the holding upon his father's death. The children of nonhereditary Lassbauern were bound to the estate and liable for three years of personal service to the lord. A category of peasants with similar rights, but with less than lifetime tenure, were the *Zeitpächter*, who held a lease to their lands for a fixed period of time.[52] Because the lord could exercise greater control over Zeitpächter, there was constant pressure by the lord to transform

[49] *ALR*, II/7:5/#272; Hattenhauer, 442.
[50] Müller, *Märkische Landwirtschaft*, 29; Knapp, *Bauernbefreiung*, 16.
[51] Ibid., 17ff; Müller, *Märkische Landwirtschaft*, 30–31; Lippert, *Geschichte der 110 Bauerndörfer*, 115–16.
[52] Lippert, *Geschichte der 110 Bauerndörfer*, 116; Müller, *Märkische Landwirtschaft*, 31.

hereditary or lifetime tenure rights into fixed-term leaseholds. This pressure became especially pronounced in the last half of the eighteenth century.

Within each of these categories, there were further differentiations according to the size of the holdings and the number of draft animals the peasants could support; these differentiations, in turn, determined the nature of labor service performed for the estate owner. A full Bauer generally had at least four teams (*Spannen*) of two horses or oxen each, a half-Bauer (*Halbbauer*) generally had at least two teams, and so on.[53] Peasants with enough land to support a team of draft animals were usually liable to perform *Spanndienst*, labor service with a team of draft animals, for the lord. Those without such teams, usually only some of the nonhereditary Lassiten, were liable for *Handdienst*, manual labor.

The majority of the rural population in Prussia, however, did not enjoy property rights as favorable as these; with rare exceptions, they possessed no strips of land in the Flur, and if they had any land at all, it consisted of smaller plots adjacent to the large open fields or small gardens in which they raised vegetables for their own consumption. The size of their holdings, the security of their tenures, and the level of their subsistences varied widely. Of equal importance is the fact that those who were not true Bauern stood on a lower rung of the social structure, commanded less respect, and had virtually no voice in village affairs.

In the Mark Brandenburg the class of the peasantry immediately below the Bauern were the *Kossäten*, who were almost always excluded from the Flur and leased smaller holdings from the estate owner for a fixed period of time.[54] They were seldom capable of supporting a team, so they were usually bound to perform substantial hand labor for the lord. Peasants with somewhat similar rights and obligations in Silesia were called *Häusler* (cottagers) or *Gärtner* (gardeners).[55] Even within these categories there were further differentiations—for example, *Freihäusler* and *Freigärtner*. These were by no means free persons, as their titles might indicate; rather, they were relatively free of labor service and paid substantially higher rents for their cottages and gardens. In addition to the subsistence they squeezed out of their small plots, they often worked as wage laborers for peasants with larger holdings or supplemented their meager earnings with cottage

---

[53] Ziekursch, *Hundert Jahre*, 75.
[54] Müller, *Märkische Landwirtschaft*, 18; Knapp, *Die Bauernbefreiung*, 12.
[55] Ziekursch, *Hundert Jahre*, 73–74, 89–94.

industry, especially weaving. *Dreschgärtner*, for example, were obligated to supply the lord with the daily service of two persons, a man and a woman.

Well below these groups on the social scale were the multitude of peasants who possessed no land whatsoever.[56] In rare cases, they were given cottages in which to live; most commonly, they rented quarters from peasants in the village. Variously referred to as *Inleute, Büdner, Kätner, Instleute, Kammerleute, Hausleute,* or *Mietshäusler,* they worked as day-wage earners (Tagelöhner) on the lord's estate or on the lands of the peasants. Usually they were hired by the peasants to perform services they owed to the estate owner. Because much of their work was seasonal, they supplemented their agricultural wages, wherever possible, with spinning and weaving. Below these, at the very bottom of society, were the *Knechte* or *Mägde,* the servants of the peasants in the village, who frequently had no place to sleep but in stalls and barns. All of these landless peasants lived in severe misery; as one official reported from Silesia in 1792, "I know of villages in which 70 and 80 families live as landless renters and lead, for the most part, a miserable existence."[57] John Quincy Adams, touring Silesia in 1800, was appalled at the conditions of the peasantry but was inclined to blame the peasants for their misery. "Of their persons they appear to take no concern at all, and are, of course, as dirty as any other peasant in the most wretched hovels of Europe. The houses are generally full of children, clad in no other garb than a coarse shirt; often times stark naked, and loaded with vermin like the land of Egypt at the last of its plagues."[58]

To obtain anything approaching a precise statistical profile of the Prussian peasantry for the late eighteenth century is difficult, but it seems clear that those without land or with very small plots outnumbered those with secure tenure. Moreover, during the last half of the century, the number of landless peasants appears to have been growing at a much faster rate than that of landowning peasants. This increase is related to some of the fundamental changes in agricultural production, which I will describe in chapter 3; it suffices here to note the nature of that increase. The most reliable estimates do not include all Prussian provinces, but we may assume that they reflect a general

---

[56] Ibid., 69–72; Lippert, *Geschichte der 110 Bauerndörfer,* 115; Müller, *Märkische Landwirtschaft,* 28.

[57] Cited in Ziekursch, *Hundert Jahre,* 72.

[58] Cited in Blum, *Old Order,* 183.

tendency.⁵⁹ Hartmut Harnisch calculates that peasants with land (Bauern, Halbbauern, Kossäten) comprised 52.6 percent, whereas those without land (Einlieger, Hirten, Handwerker) made up 47.4 percent of the population of the villages in the Kurmark of Brandenburg in 1748; a half-century later, the balance tipped the other way— only 44.2 percent of the peasants had land, whereas 55.8 percent were landless. His figures for Pomerania also indicate a substantial growth of the landless peasantry: between 1795 and 1805, the number of free peasants (Schulzen, Kölmer) actually declined; those with larger holdings (Bauern, Halbbauern) increased by 1.5 percent; those with small plots (Kossäten, Gärtner, Häusler) increased by 12.8 percent; and the number of landless peasants grew by 14.3 percent.⁶⁰ Figures from Silesia yield similar conclusions: the numbers of poor, landless peasants increased at a rate far faster than the rest of the population during the last half of the century.⁶¹

It is also difficult to characterize the various rents, dues, and services owed by peasants to their lords, for they varied according to the status of the peasant and according to region. In general, the service obligations of the peasantry were probably greatest in Silesia and smallest in parts of East Prussia and Brandenburg. Peasants with substantial rent obligations as a rule owed only one or two days of service per week, whereas those who paid less worked more. Service obligations were tied to the land held by the peasant; thus, full peasants frequently were required to provide daily service to the estate owner.⁶² This they rarely performed themselves but gave instead to the Einlieger or Tagelöhner in their employ. Peasants lower on the social scale often fulfilled their obligations themselves.⁶³ By the eighteenth century, labor contracts, *Urbaren*, were common in most regions of Prussia; they defined precisely the services owed. A summary of such an Urbar from Silesia in 1790 offers a glimpse of the nature of peasant service on one estate.⁶⁴ The full peasants were each obligated to pro-

---

⁵⁹ The statistics of Leopold Krug, *Betrachtungen über den Nationalreichthum des preussischen Staates* 1: 472–79, are informative but not very reliable. Some conclusions can be gleaned from Otto Behre's statistics in *Geschichte der Statistik in Brandenburg–Preussen bis zur Gründung des königlichen Statistischen Bureaus* (Berlin, 1905), 159, 179.

⁶⁰ Hartmut Harnisch, "Bevölkerung und Wirtschaft: Ueber die Zusammenhänge zwischen sozialökonomischer und demographischer Entwicklung im Spätfeudalismus," *Jahrbuch für Wirtschaftsgeschichte* 2 (1975): 79–83.

⁶¹ Ziekursch, *Hundert Jahre*, 71–77.

⁶² See the tables in Willi Boelcke, *Bauer und Gutsherr in der Oberlausitz* (Bautzen, 1957), 89–91.

⁶³ Knapp, *Die Bauernbefreiung*, 21.

⁶⁴ This Urbar is from A. Meitzen, *Urkunden schlesischer Dörfer* (Berlin, n.d.), 332–40;

vide, without compensation, the daily service of four draft teams with their equipment throughout the year. When the peasant was called upon to do hand service, he was not obligated to provide the draft teams. Each workday was divided according to the season. From spring until fall, it was divided into three parts: from sunrise until nine A.M., from ten A.M. until two P.M., and from three P.M. until sunset. The peasants did not have to work during the second period. In the shorter winter days, the workday extended from sunrise until eleven A.M. and from two P.M. until sunset. The peasant had to haul the harvested grain to the market. Dreschgärtner were required to supply the daily hand service of two persons, a man and a woman, except during the harvest season, when they were required to supply three. The work periods during the harvest season were also clearly specified, including the times when the women worked in the fields and when they were released to prepare meals. The children of all Untertanen were obligated to serve the lord personally, "as long as he desires it and has need of them, until the girls marry or the young men have the opportunity to take over a peasant plot."

In many regions, the drafting of Urbaren came only at the end of the eighteenth century and then only under some duress from the government. In 1784, as a result of numerous conflicts between lords and serfs concerning work obligations, Frederick II attempted to require noble estate owners to agree to such contracts with their peasants; in the face of opposition from the nobility, this order was changed after Frederick's death two years later to read as follows: "The acceptance of Urbaren shall take place only in those places where conflicts over services or debts of the Untertanen are present."[65]

The increasing usage of Urbaren to regulate the services and dues of peasants represents an important change in lord-peasant relations. Urbaren protected the peasants by restricting the arbitrary authority of the lord to enlarge his demands for services and by giving peasants a contract that could form the basis of legal action. Urbaren also provided an opportunity for the lord to acknowledge officially, both for the benefit of his own conscience and the education of his peasants, his beneficent paternalism. The Urbar excerpted earlier, for example, contained the following declaration: "With the establishment of this Urbar, the lord [*Grundherrschaft*] has indicated a special proof of his

---

other examples of Urbaren are found in estate archives. See, for example, STAP, Pr. Br. 37, Herrschaft Buchow, 294, Bl. 30. The service obligations in other areas, such as the Mark Brandenburg, were perhaps less than in Silesia. See Joachim Sack, *Die Herrschaft Stavenow*, Mitteldeutsche Forschungen, vol. 18 (Cologne-Graz, 1959), 99–107.

[65] Cited in Sack, *Herrschaft Stavenow*, 100.

love and grace, both now and for all time, by granting the full exemption from service during the week in which Christmas falls." In addition, it specified what each servant would be given to eat and what special meals would be granted at Christmas, Easter, and Pentecost.[66]

In the absence of a contract, the peasant was frequently liable for "unspecified service" to the lord, especially in Silesia.[67] The lord could virtually demand service of the peasant whenever he wished; "unspecified service" was most often used to press peasants into labor during a hunt or for the reconstruction of buildings on the estate. Another obligation Silesian peasants owed was the *Laudemien*—a tax in the amount of 10 percent of the purchase price of a peasant holding at the time of its sale or transfer. This tax was also levied against a peasant farm when ownership changed through inheritance. It was one of the burdens about which Silesian peasants complained most bitterly. The tax provided noble estate owners with considerable income. When, for example, during the revolution of 1848 demands were made for the termination of the Laudemien, Graf Schaffgotsch ordered his administrator to calculate the income he received from the Laudemien on his estates; he was told the average annual income was 10,900 taler.[68]

The division of labor on an estate grew out of the different service obligations and reflected the differentiation of peasant status. Peasants owing the service of draft animals were responsible for plowing, harrowing, hauling grain to market, and all other jobs requiring horsepower. Most of the sowing, weeding of root crops, fertilizing, harvesting, and threshing was done by those performing hand services. Women prepared flax for spinning, men chopped wood, and children helped to herd livestock.

These objective conditions of their existence—hereditary servitude, incessant and overwhelming work obligations, meager subsistences, miserable living conditions, and little knowledge of the world beyond their village—gave peasants few opportunities to improve their circumstances or to break out of their bondage. Some were able to buy their freedom; it was not uncommon for peasants to buy the freedom of their sons and daughters, who, excluded from an inheritance, faced a hopeless future.[69] Some fled or tried to flee. Runaway peasants, however, appear to have been few; unless they lived near the border, they had nowhere to go, since the law prohibited anyone from giving ref-

[66] Meitzen, *Urkunden schlesischer Dörfer*, 333, 336–37.
[67] Ziekursch, *Hundert Jahre*, 85–86.
[68] Helmut Bleiber, *Zwischen Reform und Revolution*, 34.
[69] Ziekursch, *Hundert Jahre*, 73.

uge.[70] Their whereabouts were not difficult to ascertain and the machinery of the state cooperated in their return.[71] Occasionally, as a result of brutal mistreatment, the extension of work obligations beyond those permitted in the Urbar, or the appropriation of peasant holdings, peasants submitted protests to authorities. These became more frequent after 1779, when, in the miller Arnold case, Frederick II intervened on behalf of a common miller against the judgment of noblemen.[72]

The complaint of four peasants from Lower Lusatia reveals both the misery of the peasantry and the cruel and arbitrary exercise of power by some lords.[73] It also demonstrates that peasants had a clear understanding of their rights, however minimal those may have been, and that at least some peasants were capable of resisting violations of their rights. The complaint of these peasants is worth some attention, for it is typical of hundreds of others. Friedrich Krüger, George Kerck, Hans Suppera, and Martin Noack lived on the estate Briesen, which had been bought in 1766 by a Herr von Röbel. Von Röbel proceeded to treat his peasants "in an unspeakable and barbarous manner" and to demand far greater services than had ever been the case in the past. In their appeal to the king, they described their situation as follows:

As we made a moving presentation to him [Herr von Röbel], and explained that we had never performed such extended service in the past, and also because of a shortage of draft teams owing to the well-known losses we suffered by disease, that therefore we were not in a position to fulfill such services without leaving our own fields, from which we had to pay the land tax, to deteriorate, we received his answer: He cared about none of these things; we could plant our own fields or not, pay the taxes or not, stay on the land or go to the devil, he would not chase after us. Neither pleas nor supplications affected his mercilessness and his cruelty. In the September court session, since we were to accommodate ourselves to the newly demanded services, we were not allowed to speak a word, but were threatened with beatings and given a short time to reconsider, with the implication that, if we came to an understanding and performed the services that were

---

[70] *ALR*, II/7:3/#155–58; Hattenhauer, 438.

[71] The documents from Lower Lusatia contain a number of cases of runaway peasants. In some cases, the estate owner gives the authorities the exact location of the peasant. See Rudolf Lehmann, *Quellen zur Lage der Privatbauern in Niederlausitz*, 89–90, 125, 131–33.

[72] Ziekursch, *Hundert Jahre*, 203.

[73] Lehmann, *Quellen zur Lage der Privatbauern in Niederlausitz*, 171–75.

demanded, we would be treated differently. In the October court session, it was required that each of us, one after the other, should come forward and make our declaration. Immediately, the first three were thrown into the jail in which, for four entire days and nights, they were compelled to lie like animals, until finally they were released after many pleas. The rest of us had our necessary clothes and beds seized and confiscated; indeed, the judge levied a fine of 3 taler against each of us, and since not one of us could pay a groschen, much less 3 taler, our livestock, furniture, clothes, and necessary equipment were taken away.

When the court met again in November, most of the people in the village did not appear out of fear of beatings and arrests. Of those who appeared, however, the four of us, Friedrich Krüger, George Kerck, Hans Suppera, and Martin Noack, were locked up in the courtroom, . . . and the next day taken to Cotbus and locked up in a dark hole in the city tower, where, because no one looked after us or listened to us, we would most certainly have died of cold and hunger and vermin had we not, after twenty-three days, escaped from this most dangerous prison and fled over the Saxon border into safety. We are presently there. . . . The day after our flight, Herr von Röbel confiscated from George Kerck 4 horses, an ox, a wagon, a plow and farrow, and declared that when we returned it would and should be more terrible for us.

All of this has happened only because we refused to submit blindly to the pitiless demands of Herr von Röbel for more service and because we would not do that which so transgressed our rights.

The cruelty of Herr von Röbel is indescribable, for during our work on his estate, not only did he beat us and our animals—as he recently beat an old peasant more than forty times, with the result that the old man soon died; not only did he punish us with the "Spanish Coat" because of any little thing; but he also took away much of the land that was rightfully ours and told us, under the threat of severe punishment, to plant in the fields where the soil is thin, with the result that we have forfeited 16 *Scheffel* and more of our yield.

We can get no one to work for us anymore, because everyone fears the cruelty of Herr von Röbel; we are expected to pay taxes and fees, but the means are withheld from us.

Your Gracious Majesty and Lord, certainly our demise is unavoidable unless Herr von Röbel's cruelty is halted, for in the last war we suffered more than any other regions and in the last few years, we have lost our livestock to the plague. Through borrowing, we had

CHAPTER 1

scarcely begun to recover when this Herr von Röbel seeks to ruin us anew, and all because of his impermissible self-interest.

In short, our misery is unimaginable. We have done all that we have been obliged to do, and in many cases, more. Our lord is not satisfied with that, but believes that we have been created solely and alone for his advantage and that he can do with us whatever he wishes.

In this case, the state intervened on behalf of the peasants and enjoined von Röbel from further punitive action. Whether or not the injunction was effective is unknown.

Cruel treatment, increased work obligations, and the appropriation of their lands sometimes led peasants to open rebellion. As a result of brutal treatment, causing a number of peasants to flee from their estate over the Polish border, a peasant revolt spread in 1765 and 1766 to a number of estates in Polish Silesia.[74] It ultimately spread to forty villages and the peasantry, armed with axes, scythes, and pitchforks, were easily put down by the military. Some of the estate owners, emboldened by the presence of troops, took brutal revenge on their serfs. Again the state intervened; at least one estate owner known to have tortured his peasants was forced by the authorities to sell his estate. After the emancipation of the serfs in Austria and the outbreak of the French Revolution, there were further incidents of peasant uprisings in Silesia. Anonymous letters circulated throughout the province. One contained the following: "The nobles and the authorities are carrion. We want a king. . . . God did not create noblemen or authorities. . . . We will promise quiet only when we get relief from the nobles, otherwise the world will come apart. . . . When the lords cease beating us, it will be better. . . . We want kings, but they must help us."[75] The rebellion was again forcibly put down. To punish the ringleaders, Silesian governor von Hoym recommended the gauntlet, which had been introduced for civilian punishment in 1787. In his instructions, Hoym made the nature and the purpose of the punishment clear: the guilty should be brought to their own villages on market days and forced to run the gauntlet between two hundred soldiers six times; they should not be murderously beaten, for "if they are released in their hometowns, not severely injured or beaten to death, but with right bloody welts, the goal of frightening the other disturbers of the peace will be completely achieved."[76]

It is important to note several factors about the peasant social struc-

[74] Ziekursch, *Hundert Jahre*, 193–94.
[75] Ibid., 229–30.
[76] Ibid., 235–36.

ture in Prussia I have described here. It was clearly a highly differentiated society. Because the peasantry was divided into many different classifications of title, property rights, and work obligations, it was not a society in which the lords were aligned on one side and the peasants on the other. Rather, the power of the lord was mediated; it radiated throughout the estate, touching all, but with differing degrees of immediacy. The poor, landless Einlieger or Tagelöhner may occasionally have felt the lord's whip, but he probably felt more often that of the Gärtner or Bauer for whom he worked. The Gärtner was excluded from holding land in the open fields, but he did have his plot somewhere on the estate and the right to graze his cow on the common; his conditions were not as favorable as those of the full Bauer, but neither were they as poor as the Tagelöhner. The Bauer had to pay high rents or provide substantial labor for the lord, but he rarely performed that work himself; it was done by one of the laborers in his employ. Thus the peasantry both was exploited and, except for those at the very bottom of the scale, participated in the process of exploitation. In a society in which each was subservient to the lord, though with different personal obligations, and in which most were also subservient to other peasants, it was difficult, if not impossible, for class solidarity to develop. The lord's power was mediated by the fact that a great many of his subjects participated in the process of domination and exploitation. In fact, in this eighteenth-century German society, in which social differentiation was expressed in the language of the Stände, or estates, peasants commonly viewed other peasants with different rights as members of a different Stand.[77] This social differentiation was recognized in the Prussian General Law Code of 1794, which defined members of the *Gemeinde*, the village community, as those holding property rights to land; landless peasants were excluded.[78]

The social differentiation also functioned to enhance the lord's means of social control over the peasants at the same time that it offered opportunity for upward mobility for peasants locked within the framework of servile bondage. Noble estate owners could, legally, replace inefficient or disobedient peasants who had no hereditary rights; moreover, in the eighteenth century, as more land was brought under cultivation, the peasants could improve their status by settling on new lands. Thus the lords had the opportunity to ventilate the suffocating structure of serfdom with select drafts of paternal grace. They were

[77] C. Büchsel, *Erinnerungen aus dem Leben eines Landgeistlichen*, 10th ed. (Berlin, 1925), 37–38.
[78] *ALR*, II/7:2/#18; Hattenhauer, 433.

not ignorant of the advantages this system offered and manipulated it quite consciously. The eighteenth-century agronomist Karl Friedrich Beneckendorff, commenting on the mechanisms of social control available to the lord, wrote the following:

The difference between the peasant with property rights and the Tagelöhner does not consist of the fact that one has more or less work than the other, but in the fact that the former has the hope of accumulating something and leaving it to his family upon his death, while the latter must be contented merely to give his family their daily sustenance as long as he lives.

If, however, the poor peasant can take no more pleasure in this hope than can a Tagelöhner, it follows that because there is no reason for him to fear the deprivation or hope for improvement of that which is entrusted to him for his support, there is nothing at hand with which to require him to remain obedient and orderly except for the application of corporal punishment.[79]

This system of mediated social relations broke down when the noble estate owners exercised their power too directly by demanding services that violated the sense of justice the peasants had developed over time or by brutalizing them with extreme physical punishment and torture. At such times, a degree of class solidarity developed as peasants fled or rebelled. When that occurred, the state intervened to reestablish the paternal image of society. Offenders were punished, often severely, but just as often in a measured way, such as the punishment prescribed by von Hoym during the uprising of 1793: public beatings, severe but not fatal, that would serve as an example. When necessary, the state assumed the role of the strict father, punishing with a purpose. But it also gave exemplary punishment to those noble estate owners whose brutality was excessive enough to break the delicate balance of oppression and paternalism. In 1750, when Countess von Gessler was sentenced to six years of personal arrest for beating a servant to death, Frederick II refused the request of her husband, one of his generals, that the sentence be commuted because, as he wrote to his minister of justice, he hoped the lesson would prevent other nobles from committing "cruel and inhumane acts against their subjects." To Count Gessler, he wrote the following: "As a reasonable man, you will yourself be drawn to the conclusion that justice is the same for everyone and all people without exception and that, there-

[79] Beneckendorff, *Oeconomia Forensis* 5: 33.

fore, when persons of higher status or noble persons commit wrong, they must also atone and be punished according to the law."[80]

The contours of each social class, lords and peasants, shaped their habits of mind and behavior. The encounter of each with the other, however mediated, took place largely within the confines of the estate and village. It was there that authority was articulated, and it was there that it was met with obedience or resistance—or both. It was on the local estate that the strengths and limitations of the paternalist ideology found their expression.

[80] R. Stadelmann, *Preussens Könige in Ihrer Thätigkeit für die Landeskultur*, Publicationen aus den K. Preussischen Staatsarchiven (1882), 2: 296–97. See also Reinhold Koser, *Geschichte Friedrichs des Grossen*, 4th ed. (Stuttgart and Berlin, 1912), 2: 94–95.

2

HABITUS AND HERRSCHAFT: THE SYSTEM OF DOMINATION

The Framework of Paternalism

The east Elbian noble estates, together with their attendant villages, formed relatively self-contained communities; at the same time they had important economic ties with distant European markets. Indeed, it can be shown how extensively the economic welfare of remote estates was dependent on the flow of trade from the Baltic seaports to western Europe and England.[1] During the nineteenth century, the greater mechanization of agriculture increased that dependency. Nevertheless, for most daily requirements, the estates and villages were largely self-sufficient. The needs that the peasants could not themselves satisfy could be met in their village or in a town a few miles away. Except for Silesia, where a large industry of cottage linen weaving flourished until the early nineteenth century, there was very little cottage industry in the eastern provinces of Brandenburg-Prussia, except for those products the peasants produced for home consumption or the local market.

A good indication of this self-sufficiency is provided by the estate records. For example, Herrschaft Buckow, in Lebus County (*Kreis*) in Brandenburg, was a large demesne owned by the von Flemming family. It was composed of several estates and five villages, the largest of which was Buckow, with a population of 937 in 1805. Buckow served as the major market and service center for the smaller neighboring villages of the demesne. Among its population in 1805 were 6 saddlemakers, 6 wheelwrights, 3 coopers, 2 potters, 2 ropemakers, 9 cabinetmakers, 22 shoemakers, 11 weavers, 2 dyers, 20 tailors, 1 smith, and 1 glassblower. The grain mill and brewery were also located in

---

[1] On the importance of Baltic trade for the eastern estates, see Gunther Franz, Wilhelm Abel, and Gisbert Cascorbi, *Der Deutsche Landwarenhandel* (Hannover, 1960), 41–53, 77–92. For the question of the wider market dependency of the estates, see Immintraut Richarz, *Herrschaftliche Haushalte in vorindustriellen Zeit im Wesserraum*, Beiträge zur Oekonomie und Verbrauch, Heft 6 (Berlin, 1971). For what promises to be a splendid examination of lord-peasant relations on a single estate in Brandenburg, see the forthcoming work by William W. Hagen.

Buckow. Smaller estates with only one village were composed predominantly of peasants whose needs could usually be met by local, or at most, regional markets.[2]

It was this enclosed, self-contained quality of the estate and village to which Otto Brunner has called our attention with the concept of *das ganze Haus*. Noting that the Greek root for economy, *oikos*, is the word for house, Brunner has shown that the notions of economy were, until the nineteenth century, primarily associated with household management. The household formed the primary unit of production and consumption in early modern Europe; das ganze Haus, was a social microcosm, comprising not only the lord and his family, but his servants and subjects as well.[3] Thus, the essential unit of production in society, das ganze Haus, also framed the fundamental structure of social relations. It was in relation to the household that domination and authority were experienced. As Brunner has written, "The house is the nucleus of all Herrschaft. . . . For in order to be a lord [*Herr*] in a legal sense . . . one had to 'belong to the land and reside in the land,' one had to own a house in the land. Whoever had no house, but merely possessed individual pieces of land settled by persons paying rent, possessed no Herrschaft, no noble estate, but only the right to 'estate revenues' [*Gülten*]."[4]

The role of the lord in das ganze Haus was articulated in what came to be known as *Hausväterliteratur* (literature for house-fathers), which became extremely popular from the end of the sixteenth century until the middle of the eighteenth century.[5] The first such book, by Johann

---

[2] For population lists of estate villages, see STAP, Pr. Br. 37, Buckow, Herrschaft Buckow, 288, Bl. 16–17; STAP, Pr. Br. 37, Marwitz-Friedersdorf, 163, Bl. 1–4.

[3] Otto Brunner, "Das 'ganze Haus' und die alteuropäische Oekonomik," in *Neue Wege der Verfassungs- und Sozialgeschichte*, 2d ed. (Göttingen, 1968), 103–27. Brunner's phrase, *das ganze Haus* was first coined by the nineteenth-century folklorist Wilhelm Riehl in his book *Die Naturgeschichte des deutschen Volkes*, ed. Gunther Ipsen (Leipzig, 1935). Riehl's use of the concept is loaded with romantic assumptions, and he laments the decline of the structure of family and household in the advent of industrialization. It is against Brunner's and Riehl's formulation that Richarz, *Herrschaftliche Haushalte in vorindustriellen Zeit im Weserraum*, argues, by insisting that the estate was always dependent on distant markets and that the kind of autonomy Brunner posits never existed. The two positions do not seem to me to be mutually exclusive. Although the estate depended on foreign markets both for its own needs and the sale of its produce, the essential relations of production and consumption shaped the system of social relations on the land and were locally determined.

[4] Otto Brunner, *Land und Herrschaft*, Veröffentlichungen des Instituts für Geschichtsforschung und Archivwissenschaft in Wien, 1 (Vienna, Brünn, and Munich, 1947), 293.

[5] On the Hausväterliteratur in general, see Julius Hoffmann, *Die "Hausväterliteratur"*

CHAPTER 2

Colerus, appeared between 1593 and 1603; during the next century, it went through numerous editions and revisions and many anonymous authors plagiarized it.[6] The popularity of Hausväterliteratur grew from the fact that it offered practical information on agronomy; the books were textbooks on the agricultural methods of the period. They contain chapters on how to select an estate, assess its value, and purchase it; every conceivable topic related to the management of an estate was covered: how to raise every kind of crop and livestock; how to utilize the woodlands, lakes, and streams; how to build sawmills and brew beer; how to organize the work calendar and divide the labor tasks; how to keep books and records; how to settle disputes between peasants; and how to treat animal and human illnesses.

The popularity of Hausväterliteratur reached a peak precisely during the period in which the eastern nobility turned increasingly toward the management of its estates and forced the peasantry deeper into serfdom. Because the organization of labor on the estates structured the social relations, these textbooks also may be seen as offering an ideology for the emerging agricultural nobility. The very term *Hausvater* conveyed the domesticity of the estate and village as well as the paternal concern the lord claimed to have for all of its inhabitants.

Hausväterliteratur offered a description of rural society that was based on existing social relationships; at the same time, it sanctioned that system of domination and, with its widespread circulation and influence, helped reinforce that system. The rule of the Hausvater was natural, taken for granted. Coler wrote the following: "The manager of the house must be the lord of the house; everything in the house must be ordered according to his rule."[7] Von Hohberg also wrote: "A Hausvater should fear God, work with his wife, educate his children,

---

und die *"Predigten über den christlichen Hausstand": Ein Beitrag zur Geschichte der Lehre vom Haus und der Bilding für das Häusliche Leben* (phil. diss., Göttingen, 1954).

[6] The title of Colerus's first book was *Calendarium perpetuum et sex libri oeconomici* or, in German, *Ein stetswerender Calender dazu sehr nützlich und nötige Hausbücher für die Hauswirth, Ackerleut, Apotheker, Kaufleute, Wandersleute, Weinherrn, Gärtner, den gemeinen Handswerksleuten, und all denen so mit Wirtschafften oder Gastungen umgehen* (Wittenberg, 1604). Colerus's other books had the titles *Oeconomia ruralis et domestica* (1645) and *Oeconomia oder Hausbuch* (1604). For a brief biographical treatment of Colerus, see *Allgemeine Deutsche Biographie* (Leipzig, 1876), 4: 402–3. In addition to Colerus, see the works of Franz Florinus, *Oeconomus Prudens et Legalis* (Basel, 1748), and *Der Hausvater* (Hanover, 1764–1773); Christian Friedrich Germershausen, *Die Hausmutter in alle ihren Geschäften* (Leipzig, 1778) and *Der Hausvater* (Leipzig, 1783–1786). The work of the south Austrian nobleman Wolf Helmhard von Hohberg, *Georgica Curiosa*, 2 vols. (Nuremberg, 1682), has been analyzed carefully by Otto Brunner in *Adeliges Landleben und Europäischer Geist: Leben und Werk Wolf Helmhards von Hohberg, 1612–1688* (Salzburg, 1949).

[7] Cited in Hoffmann, *"Die Hausväterliteratur,"* 92.

rule his servants and subjects, and manage his estates from month to month."[8] The subservience and compulsory labor of the serfs were likewise thought to be ordained by God. According to von Hohberg:

> The robot and compulsory labor services [*Robathen- und Frohn-Dienste*] appeared soon after the first sinful "Fall" of Adam, as a result of which God ordained that man should earn his bread by the sweat of his brow, that he should cultivate the fields and labor; thereafter, because of the increase of the human race, with which arrogance and disorder grew, the stronger forced the weak, the slow, and the helpless to do their bidding, giving rise to conflict and murder. Finally, necessity advised that men would improve themselves if they submitted, under certain conditions, to a strong and famous hero. . . . Thus originated kings, princes, and lords, as well as certain laws out of which emerged privilege, respect for authority, and the obedience of subjects. Out of this source also sprang the compulsory servitude and robot labor common in the world.[9]

While advising noble estate owners on how to deal with the peasantry, the Hausväterliteratur also transmitted popular perceptions of the peasantry. The peasant was considered to be a creature of the senses, his entire being shaped by his physical labor. One eighteenth-century author, Karl Friedrich Beneckendorff, wrote thus: "The peasant has a heart nearly devoid of feelings, one that cannot be moved by suggestions of reason. . . . His conduct is governed only by his physical senses, and it is only through these that he can be brought to order and that he can be held to the fulfillment of his obligations."[10] Similarly, a rural pastor reported that descriptions of Christ's spiritual suffering made no impression on the peasantry, for it corresponded so little to their experiences. Describing hell as a separation from goodness and God was ineffective; rather, to impress the peasant, it had to be expressed in terms of physical suffering. Only when the physical suffering of Christ was described was "the peasant all ears and sympathy."[11] Christian Garve, the popular philosopher, also attributed the

[8] Cited in Brunner, "Das 'ganze Haus,' " 111.
[9] Hohberg, *Georgica Curiosa* 1: 63.
[10] Karl Friedrich Beneckendorff, *Oeconomia Forensis; oder, Kurzer Inbegriff derjenigen Landwirtschaftlichen Wahrheiten* (Berlin, 1775–1784), 5: 51. Beneckendorff's eight volumes represent the very last form of Hausväterliteratur; thereafter, literature on "scientific agriculture" began to emerge.
[11] Karl Aner, "Zwei märkische Landesgeistliche aus der Aufklärungszeit," *Jahrbuch für Brandenburgische Kirchengeschichte* (Berlin, 1919), 17.

CHAPTER 2

character of the peasant to his "physical, heavy, and monotonous work."[12]

Garve represented the attitude of an enlightened *philosoph*, yet it is useful to note his description of the servile peasantry in eastern Germany for he, too, shared many values of the Hausväterliteratur. For Garve, the character of the peasant was formed not only by his heavy physical labor, but also by the fact that, within the context of the estate, peasants were isolated from the rest of society and therefore entirely subject to the lord. "They are simultaneously servants of the former [the noble lord], for whom they must work, and vassals, who are judged and punished by him. This two-fold authority naturally carries an arbitrary quality and, though it is proper [*gerecht*], it is also oppressive."[13] In this sense, Garve suggested, the peasant was similar to the Jew: both were severed from the rest of civil society and concerned only with their immediate business—commerce for the Jew and agriculture for the peasant. Both developed cleverness and guile, both were suspicious and mistrustful of others, especially superiors, and this mistrust frequently was translated into hatred.[14] Confined to the estate, having daily contact largely with one another, the peasants developed a degree of solidarity and shared experiences that gave to each village characteristics that carried over from one generation to another—"indolence and dishonesty, stubbornness and crudity or thievery in one and diligence and thrift in another."[15]

Garve repeated the common aphorism "If he is not made to, the peasant will move neither hand nor foot" (*Wenn der Bauer nicht muss, so rüht er weder Hand noch Fuss*).[16] The slow, plodding character of the peasant was clearly visible, Garve declared, and it had several causes. First, it came from the heavy physical labor that peasants performed, which could be done only with measured slowness over the course of a day. Second, "indolence was the result of emptiness of spirit.... The peasant, devoid of thought, is lazy because he does not wish for an

---

[12] See Christian Garve, *Ueber den Charakter der Bauern und ihr Verhältnisse gegen die Gutsherr und gegen die Regierung*, reprinted in Garve, *Popularphilosophische Schriften*, ed. Kurt Wölfel (Stuttgart, 1974), 7–8. For a translation of parts of Garve's essay, see Robert M. Berdahl, "Christian Garve on the German Peasantry," *Peasant Studies* 8, no. 2 (1979): 86–102.

[13] Ibid., 10.

[14] Ibid., 14.

[15] Ibid., 22.

[16] Ibid., 24. Similar aphorisms are also found in the Hausväterliteratur. See Beneckendorff, *Oeconomia Forensis* 5: 46ff. The slow, plodding character of the peasant was brilliantly described as a result of work processes by E. P. Thompson at a meeting in Göttingen in the summer of 1978 which was devoted to the nature of work processes.

improvement of his situation and sees no means by which to accomplish it."[17] Contact with a wider world was essential for ambition, Garve argued, and the most industrious peasants were always on estates located close to towns or rivers. Moreover, the incapacity of the peasantry also resulted from poor nourishment and inadequate clothing.

Garve found the moral life of the peasants on the land inferior to handworkers in the towns. Their "inclination to drink" was a factor in their indolence. Sexual morality was also very poor: "When I have been in the countryside, often in very small villages, I have heard so much of young maids who have been seduced, so many cases of broken marriages, even of unnatural vices, that I can scarcely believe that more examples can be found in a similar number of lower bourgeois families."[18] The chief characteristic he found in the peasant was "malicious guile" (*Tück*). In describing this characteristic, he painted a memorable picture of a *tückisch* peasant youth.

Aside from the peasants, it is principally the children of whom it is said that they have a guileful [tückisch] look. It is without doubt a mixture of childishness, of simplicity, of languor—shown with some malice and guile. I will use physiognomy in order to clarify the mentality that expression represents. Everyone undoubtedly remembers having seen such faces among peasant youths, whose one eye, or perhaps both, squint furtively beneath half-closed eyelids, whose mouth is twisted open in a scornful, somewhat dumb smile, whose head hangs on his chest or even sinks toward the ground as if trying to conceal itself: in a word, faces in which fear, stupidity, and simplicity are mixed with ridicule and antipathy. When one says something to them or asks something of them, such youths stand as motionless and silent as a post; they answer no questions put to them by passersby. Their muscles are as if benumbed and without movement. As soon as the stranger moves away, they run to their comrades and break out into loud laughter.[19]

Here we can observe the two essential sides of the peasant character as seen by his superiors. There was, on the one hand, his childlike simplicity, his uncomplicated naiveté and innocence—those qualities which later romantic folklorists found so attractive. On the other hand, he was cunning, untrustworthy, dishonest, and insolent—those

---

[17] Ibid., 25, 28.
[18] Ibid., 51.
[19] Ibid., 57.

qualities which the authors of the Hausväterliteratur warned the lords against. Beneckendorff referred to the peasants' "intentional malice." "The peasant is, on the whole," he warned, ". . . a very dangerous creature. As the saying goes, one dare not give him an inch or he will take a mile."[20] Coler warned, "However many subjects [Knechte] one has in his house, he has exactly so many thieves."[21] Garve had a greater understanding of the peasantry than did these authors of Hausväterliteratur, but he nevertheless expressed some of the same apprehensions. There was a difference, he suggested, between complete slaves and half-bound serfs. The slave was so oppressed that he could imagine no other existence; if circumstances once awakened him from his "slumber," however, the slave became "like a tiger and lost, at once, both the submissiveness of the slave and all feelings of humanity." The half-bound serf, by contrast, "did not bear his grievances without sensitivity."

One need not fear that he will seek to break it [the yoke] on his neck by open acts of violence, as rebellion; however he carries on a constant, secret war with his lord. To reduce the advantages of his lord, to improve his own is a desire that he carries constantly at the base of his heart and it is an objective which he seeks to achieve, in secret, as often as possible. Dishonesty and small thievery, carried out against the property of his lord, he does not consider nearly so bad as if it were practiced against one of his equals. He is not the completely submissive slave of his lord, nor is he a fearful enemy. However, he is also not an obedient subject who voluntarily obeys out of good intentions.[22]

This hidden conflict at the core of rural society frequently revealed itself most vividly in crises. Friedrich August Ludwig von der Marwitz, who considered himself to be, and probably was, a model Hausvater, provided an example, reporting the reactions of his peasants when fire destroyed much of his manor, Friedersdorf, in May 1806.[23] When the fire broke out in the middle of the night, no one sounded the alarm immediately; Marwitz, awakened by the fire, had to order the alarm

---

[20] Beneckendorff, *Oeconomia Forensis* 5: 53, 46.
[21] Hoffmann, *Hausväterliteratur*, 185.
[22] Garve, *Charakter der Bauern*, 59–60.
[23] Friedrich August Ludwig von der Marwitz, *Friedrich August Ludwig von der Marwitz: Ein märkischer Edelmann im Zeitalter der Befreiungskriege*, ed. Freidrich Meusel, 3 vols. (Berlin, 1908–1913), 1: 266–74. For examples of conflicts between lords and peasants in Brandenburg that show how strained the relationships often were, see William W. Hagen, "The Junkers' Faithless Servants," in Richard J. Evans and R. R. Lee, eds., *The German Peasantry* (London and Sidney, 1986), 71–101.

and drag the water wagons from the barn himself, as it apparently had not occurred to anyone to do so; while waiting for the draft horses to be brought, he ran to harness his riding and carriage horses to the wagons only to find that they had been harnessed to the plows instead, though the implement building was not yet imperiled. His peasants simply considered the plows more important than the manor house. When he returned to the courtyard, he found his peasants sitting on the "barrels and boards" (furniture) they had saved from their own dwellings; they had not yet bothered to get out the fire hose. He whipped them into action. When he glanced up at the manor house, he saw his domestic servants heaving the furniture from the upstairs windows; what was not smashed by the fall was being carried off by others. He reported other men standing around "laughing themselves dead" over the antics of a two-year-old. When others arrived from the village, he had to promise them brandy in order to entice them into manning the fire hoses. Some wanted brandy immediately and only the threat of severe punishment forced them to help. As onlookers gathered from the neighboring village, Marwitz had to organize a watch to keep them from looting. In the end, the manor house and numerous outbuildings burned to the ground, and although there was clear evidence of arson, no charge could be brought.

Descriptions such as these serve to remind us of the limitations of paternalism as a category of social relations. The idea of das ganze Haus describes a reality: the enclosed, self-sufficient estate and village, whose head was the Hausvater. But it is only a partial reality. Too often the idea of das ganze Haus has been infused with romantic qualities, as it was by Riehl, to suggest a harmonious community, a Gemeinschaft whose bonds were severed in the commercial and urban Gesellschaft of the nineteenth century.[24] In fact, at the very center of the social relations in das ganze Haus, there was both deference and conflict—outward deference toward authority and an inward, "secret war" of peasants against masters.[25] Deference was frequently coupled with the mocking laugh behind the master's back, the smirk that undermined the bow. Obedience to commands was joined with exagger-

[24] Later in the nineteenth century, the sociologist Ferdinand Tönnies's famous work, *Gemeinschaft und Gesellschaft*, associated the former with family economy. Otto Brunner sees the two as combined in das ganze Haus, "Das 'ganze Haus,'" 111. As Brunner notes, Tönnies was influenced by the early-nineteenth-century conservative ideologist Adam Müller. See chapter 5.

[25] I am indebted to E. P. Thompson for much of what I have to say here, both to his essay "Patrician Society, Plebeian Culture," *Journal of Social History* 7, no. 4: 382–405, and to the comments he made during the meeting at Göttingen I mentioned in footnote 16.

CHAPTER 2

atedly slow action; new work orders were greeted with motionless stupidity; and outward respect for superiors was negated by secret theft from them. To their superiors, as well as to middle-class observers, peasants appeared to be both incorrigibly ignorant and wickedly cunning; in fact, the very appearance of ignorance was often an act of cunning, one that confused and confounded superiors. It was a subtle defense, one that frequently drove the masters to resort to physical force and was, therefore, in its way, an assertion of dignity and control. The close relationships on an estate did not permit much open defiance, and punishment for such acts was swift and severe; yet the secret war Garve describes was a daily defiance, an expression of class conflict within a framework of an ostensibly paternalist society. It posed the ever-present threat of open rebellion, which occasionally broke out, and it reveals the basis for the fear of the "dangerous creature," the peasant, that lurked beneath the harmonious surface of das ganze Haus.

The strategies with which peasants dealt with the oppressive reality of serfdom formed an essential part of the peasant's habitus. Developed over centuries, these strategies were learned and manipulated by each generation. In many ways, their behavior represented a kind of self-mockery, or what E. P. Thompson has referred to as countertheater, to be contrasted with the theatrical style of self-presentation developed, as we shall see, within the habitus of the nobility.[26] Indeed, it became a part of the ideology of the nobility to contrast itself with the peasantry. One of the principal qualities claimed by the nobility was virtue (*Tugend*). "Since the time of Homer," writes Brunner, "the world of the nobility lived with the conviction that a man of noble extraction is born with virtue."[27] The archetypal opposite of the nobleman was the fool, who could not control his appetites and impulses. This was most often translated as the peasant, a creature of uncontrolled impulses. Beneckendorff considered virtue to be a quality quite foreign to the peasantry: "Virtue and its effects are generally unknown to peasants because of their ignorance and poor education."[28] Much of the courtesy literature written for young noble persons in the eighteenth century stressed the self-control expressed by noble behavior to contrast it with that of commoners; one writer stressed that the dance of nobles exhibited self-control, restraint, grace, and order, not

[26] Ibid., 400–405.

[27] Otto Brunner, *Adeliges Landleben und Europäischer Geist*, 77.

[28] Beneckendorff, *Oeconomia Forensis*, 5: 50; Garve speaks of the peasants' lack of "refined sensibilities," as indicated by the filth in which they were content to live.

to be confused with the "crazy spinning, twisting, and strange leaping that characterize the dance of the rabble [*Pöbel*]."[29]

The habitus of the peasantry was thus closely tied to the nobility's definition of itself. To the perceived ignorance, malice, indolence, immorality, stubbornness, slowness, insolence, and cunning of the peasantry, the landowning nobility offered guidance and control. Over the childlike peasant stood the paternal nobleman. Paternalism was prescribed in all the literature touching on lord-peasant relations. It was intended to soften the harsh reality of serfdom as well as to render the peasants more docile. Beneckendorff advised, "The enduring bonds that tie the lord to his serfs and subjects do not permit him to be indifferent to their condition, to whether they are happy or unhappy. An unhappy subject is not only far less useful to the entire state, but also to the noble lord himself."[30] An essayist wrote the following in 1798: "Actually, the relationship of the subject to his lord should be that of a child to his father. Superiors should be the first advisers and protectors of their subjects." Garve, too, expressed similar sentiments.[31]

In numerous cases lords undoubtedly did provide paternal care for their peasants.[32] Many peasants referred to their master and mistress as Father and Mother.[33] Friedrich Eberhard von Rochow described the assistance, "in word and deed," that he provided his peasants during 1771 and 1772 when poor weather ruined the harvests. Marwitz,

---

[29] Julius Bernhard v. Rohr, *Einleitung zur Ceremonial Wissenschaft der Privat-Person* (Berlin, 1730), 484.

[30] Beneckendorff, *Oeconomia Forensis* 5: 305.

[31] "Ein Wort über Dienstprozesse wider ihre Gutsherrschaften," *Jahrbuch der Preussischen Monarchie* 2 (1798): 389. Cited in Klaus Spies, *Gutherr und Untertan in der Mittelmark Brandenburg zu Beginn der Bauernbefreiung* (Berlin, 1972), 2. For comments from Garve, see *Ueber den Charakter der Bauern*, 114–20. "There are those lords who really see themselves as fathers of their subjects, and who, on many occasions, have a direct influence on the economy of the peasants, keep them orderly and diligent, and improve their well-being."

[32] The extent to which the nobles' paternal concern for peasants was a reality, as against the reality of exploitation, is disputed among historians. It seems clear that historians have frequently exaggerated the beneficence of paternalism; others deny that it had any reality. Recently an excellent work by a historian from the German Democratic Republic, Hartmut Harnisch's *Die Herrschaft Boitzenburg* (Weimar, 1968), denies the existence of any paternal relationships. A careful examination by Karl Spies, *Gutsherr und Untertan*, concludes the following: "This investigation demonstrates the impossibility of describing the peasant-lord relationship in the Mittelmark Brandenburg and Prignitz, during the period from 1780 until the beginning of emancipation in 1811, as patriarchal or considerate" (390).

[33] C. Büchsel, *Erinnerung aus dem Leben eines Landgeistlichen*, 10th ed. (Berlin, 1925), 38.

CHAPTER 2

too, offers examples of concern for his peasants.[34] Yet, the prescription of paternal concern offered by the Hausväterliteratur ought not be taken as a description of the reality. The instances of extraordinary paternalism by lords were so rare that the Prussian king Frederick William III was moved to write in 1800, when such an instance was brought to his attention: "This is so fine an example of the reciprocal affection and trust between noble lords and subjects that I am heartily cheered by it, the more so since it is so rare."[35]

The concept of paternalism, however, was central to the ideology that justified noble domination of the peasantry. The word was a practical metaphor, for it suggested a hierarchy of authority that extended from the lord of the estate (Hausvater), to the king (*Landesvater*), to God, the Father of all.[36] But to understand how the noble landowners governed their estates, we must examine more closely the institutions of control through which the paternalist ideology was articulated.

The Institutions of Herrschaft

In a speech addressed to fellow noble estate owners, Adolph von Thadden declared, "The king is a large estate owner and landowner; the noble estate owner is a small king."[37] Although uttered in 1842, von Thadden's description of the noble estate owner as a small king was even more accurate in earlier centuries. With few exceptions, the residents of his estate and village were subject to his legal authority; they were referred to as his subjects (Untertanen), just as everyone was a subject of the king. It was said that the authority of the state stopped at the boundary of the noble estate. As we shall see in the next chapter, efforts of even the "absolute" state in the eighteenth century to intrude upon the traditional prerogatives of the estate owners, especially efforts to protect the peasantry, were frustrated by the enormous power that the landowning nobility retained at the local level. The

---

[34] *Friedrich Eberhard von Rochows sämtliche pädagogische Schriften*, ed. Jonas Weinecke (Berlin, 1909), 3: 9–11. See Marwitz, 1: 713ff., for his charge to his son, in his last testament, to be a Hausvater and not an "isolated farmer."

[35] R. Stadelmann, *Preussens Könige und ihrer Thätigkeit für die Landeskultur*, Publicationen aus den K. Preussischen Staatsarchiven (1882), 4: 254.

[36] See Wilhelm Roessler, *Die Entstehung des modernen Erziehungswesens in Deutschland* (Stuttgart, 1961), 39–43.

[37] Eleonor Fürstin Reuss, *Adolf von Thadden-Trieglaff: Ein Lebensbild* (Berlin, 1894), 222. The historian Johannes Ziekursch wrote, "The estate lord and possessor of the police and judicial power was a small king, the absolute lord in the house and manor and in the peasant huts, in the church and school as in the entire village: the exact image of the Prussian King in miniature." *Hundert Jahre schlesischer Agrargeschichte* (Breslau, 1927), 131.

serfs were bound to the state in such a way that obligations to the state—payment of taxes and military service—were even mediated by the noble lord. He collected their taxes, and their military obligation was so tied to servile bondage that runaway peasants were regarded in the same way as military deserters.[38] In the paternalist idiom of the aristocracy, this mediation was an important function of the noble estate lord. Marwitz wrote, "The state itself is a nonentity for the peasant, because he can neither see it nor comprehend it, except for the taxes that he pays to it. ... The intermediate authority (the noble lord), however, he knows completely because he lives with him and through him he comes to know the state."[39]

The authority of the noble lord over his subjects extended far beyond his control of their labor; he held complete police power over those in his estate and village. He possessed patrimonial judicial authority (*Patrimonialgerichtsbarkeit*) over all; he was granted the right to appoint the village pastor (Patronatsrecht). With the responsibility for the education of his subjects came the power to name the village schoolmaster. In addition, his authority penetrated deeply into the private lives of his subjects; it included, as we have already noted, control over their marriage alliances, their inheritance rights, and the labor of their children.

Although many of the powers of the lord to intrude into the lives of peasants legally ended with peasant emancipation in 1807, noble estate owners continued to exercise police and judicial powers over the residents of their estates and villages well into the nineteenth century. These powers were extensive. Because their authority was recognized and sanctioned by public law, noble estate owners carried out their responsibilities with quasi-official status. Indeed, throughout the *Vormärz* period, there was considerable confusion about the status of noble estate owners; on some occasions, the government explicitly denied that they were public officials (*Beamte*), whereas at other times, it recognized them as such.[40]

---

[38] See Otto Büsch, *Militärsystem und Sozialleben im alten Preussen*, Veröffentlichungen der Berliner Historischen Kommission, 7 (Berlin, 1962), 27. See also Beneckendorff, *Oeconomia Forensis* 5: 170ff.

[39] Marwitz, II/1:242.

[40] For a brief description of some aspects of this confusion, see Dorothee Mussgnug-Stürmer, *Landgemeinde und Untertänigkeit: Zur preussischen Verfassungsentwicklung vom Erlass des Allgemeinen Landrechts 1794 bis zum Jahre 1842* (phil. diss., Heidelberg, 1971), 136–37, 152–53. In the General Law Code of 1794 (*ALR*, II/17:1/#31, #32, #33), the judicial authority was vested in the king and granted by him to noble estate owners. They were not named Beamte. In 1825, this was reiterated. However, the question of police powers was treated differently. The question of whether the Schulze, who was named by the lord

CHAPTER 2

This confusion over the official character of the noble estate owner is significant, for it indicates how closely intertwined the categories "public" and "private" remained in German society. This is why nobles such as Marwitz insisted that estate ownership was an office (*Amt*).[41] The fusion of public and private, the investing of the person with the office, meant that the instruments of coercion were closely united with those of cultural hegemony and that the structure of official control was joined with personal dependency in such a way as to make authority seem natural, as inevitable and irreversible as the seasons of the year or the relationship of father to child. In the ideology of the aristocracy, therefore, privileges, rights, and authority were not to be seen as expressions of private interest, as we know it, but as public functions associated with Herrschaft.

Moreover, the paternalist ideology of the landed nobility justified the use of its public authority to control the private lives of the peasantry. Not only was an unruly and debauched peasantry of little value to the noble lord, but he had also a positive social obligation, as Hausvater, to ensure the moral behavior of the peasantry. Christian Garve considered the estate owner's police power to be an important means for the moral control and education of the peasant, who remained, "to a certain degree, always a child." This kind of moral education could not be provided for any other class of citizens, Garve suggested, in so positive a fashion. The estate owner can, he wrote, "because of the relationship he presently has with his vassals, be the censor of their morals. . . . He can punish drunkenness, he can punish gross indecency, he can punish deceit or physical violence. He can intervene in the internal affairs of the family, in the economic and marital affairs of the peasants, in the relationships between parents and children, relatives and neighbors."[42]

The ordinances enforced in noble villages reflected this combination of public authority and private interest.[43] They were a mixture of

---

and carried out the police powers in the village in his name, was a Beamte arose in 1843 when a Jew was named Schulze in a village. The Ministry of Interior declared that such a communal office was an office of the state and therefore could not be held by a Jew. The issue arose in other contexts as well, as the legal controls of the state were extended to cover more fully the police powers on the estate. See STAP, Pr. Br. Oberpräsidium, Bd. 993 (Tit. 26: Polizeisachen), Bl. 1–4, 22–35.

[41] STAP, Pr. Br. 37, Marwitz/Friedersdorff, 584, Bl. 56.

[42] Garve, *Ueber den Charakter der Bauern*, 108–9, 112–13.

[43] Almost all the estate archives contain copies of the village ordinances. See for example, that of the village Garzin, in Herrschaft Buckow, from 1796; STAP, Pr. Br. 37, Herrschaft Buckow, 294, Bl. 54–62. Some have also been published. See several examples in August Freiherrn von Haxthausen, "Die patrimoniale Gesetzgebung in der Altmark,"

56

legal restraints, labor regulations, explications of the legal rights of the lords, and ethical constraints imposed on the residents of the village. They contained, for example, ordinary provisions for public order and safety—regulations concerning fire safety, curfew regulations, controls on vagrants and gypsies, prohibitions against disturbances of the peace and against theft, and so on. They also reinforced the labor controls the lord exercised over his peasants by indicating the punishments awaiting peasants who failed to fulfill their service obligations, such as not appearing to work at the appointed time; seeking to shirk their duties by supplying the lord with "delinquent field hands, unfit or worn-out wagons or horses";[44] or treating carelessly the property of the lord. The village ordinances also underscored the rights and privileges reserved for the lord and prescribed the punishments for peasants who violated them. In some instances, for example, peasants could be fined for going into the lord's woods with an axe. Finally, consistent with the lord's role as the Hausvater of the estate and village, the ordinances regulated much of the moral behavior of the peasants. Some ordinances called upon the peasants to attend church services; all regulated the hours of taverns, forbidding them to have, in some instances, dance music or gambling or to sell beer to peasants on credit; many prescribed the fines levied on unmarried persons found guilty of having sexual relations.

The police power in the village was carried out by the village Schulze, who was chosen by the noble estate owner from among the residents of the village who could read and write.[45] As the police official of the village, the Schulze was responsible for enforcing all village ordinances. He saw to it that the night watch protected the village from theft and arson; he organized the peasants in the search for deserters; he did the fire inspections and led the fire brigade; and he carried out some of the punishments ordered by the patrimonial court. As an agent of the lord, his duties went well beyond those of law enforcement, and he cooperated closely with the overseers, or "field police," as they were sometimes called, who supervised the work of the peasants in the lord's fields. Either the Schulze or the overseer could lodge complaints or charges against peasants in the patrimonial courts.[46]

Patrimonial courts were the lowest rung of the judicial ladder in Prussia. They were, for the peasantry, the courts of the first instance,

---

Jahrbücher für die preussische Gesetzgebung, Rechtswissenschaft, und Rechtsverwaltung (Berlin, 1832), 39: 3–70.

[44] Ibid., 51.

[45] *ALR*, II/7:2/#47, 51; Hattenhauer, 434–35.

[46] See *ALR*, II/7:2/#37–72; Hattenhauer, 434–35.

and, because few peasants or rural laborers could afford litigation at any higher level, they usually served also as courts of the last instance. The awesome legal power of the lord could be exercised against the peasant through the patrimonial court. The lord could force, under penalty of a fine, the peasant to appear in court at his will; either the lord or his estate overseer could bring charges against a peasant that would be decided by a judge appointed by the lord and dependent on his grace for continued employment. The peasant, on the other hand, had no such right to call the lord to court; he was compelled by law to prefer charges in a higher court, which was usually beyond his means.[47]

Most of the cases appearing in patrimonial courts involved disputes between peasants.[48] One peasant would complain that another had permitted his livestock to wander into his fields, that he had failed to repay a debt, or that he had moved the field markers to his own advantage. A large number of cases involved physical violence, usually a husband beating his wife or children, but sometimes fights between peasants. Occasionally, patrimonial courts also served as "divorce courts" in which peasants could dissolve marriages.[49]

Patrimonial courts provided the best example of the fusion of the private and public authority of the noble estate owner. They could be used, with the full force of the law, for quite private purposes—the punishment of peasants who were derelict in fulfilling their duties or who showed insolence to their superiors. The courts functioned to sanction the arbitrary treatment or punishment of peasants by their masters. Indeed, most of the physical brutality that occurred on an estate was the result of the explicit right of a lord to punish his servants; the patrimonial courts stood as a reinforcement of that right. This was the case, for example, when an overseer in Brandenburg brought charges of insolent behavior against three peasant boys who, when he set about to beat them for not doing their work properly, told

---

[47] *ALR*, II/17:1/#41–45; Hattenhauer, 621.

[48] Examples of cases are drawn from estate archives. See STAP, Pr. Br. 37, Branitz, Bd. 20, Bl. 7–8, 44–45, 53, 71; STAP, Pr. Br. 37, Wiesenburg, Bd. 194, Bl. 19–21, 21–24, 27–28, 38, 74. The records of some cases have been published by Haxthausen, "Die patrimoniale Gesetzgebung," 71ff.

[49] I have found only one such case in the estate archives: STAP, Pr. Br. 37, Wiesenburg, Bd. 223. In this instance a peasant's wife left him after three months of marriage. He went to court, submitted the request that she return "immediately"—within three days. This was delivered to her, she acknowledged her receipt of it, and failed to return. Thereupon, she lost all property claims and forfeited her dowry; the marriage was then dissolved.

him to "stick his whip up his ass."[50] Likewise, the court sanctioned the action of a lord who punished one of his peasants caught stealing fruit from the manor orchard by descending upon the peasant's own orchard and taking all the fruit in it. The East Prussian judge, who told the story as an illustration of the frequent injustices committed in the patrimonial court system, said, "The lord was unmoved by the tears of the peasant's wife and children and he took perhaps three times more fruit than he had lost—and his actions were approved by the other noblemen."[51]

Because of the alleged childlike qualities of the peasant and the primacy of his physical sensibilities, corporal punishment was generally considered the most efficacious manner of keeping him in line. To be most effective, instructed the primers on disciplinary control, corporal punishment should be immediate and performed publicly as an example to others. The primary function of corporal punishment was to induce fear, and therefore discipline, in the peasants; if it was administered too often, it lost its effect.[52] Punishment was required, Beneckendorff advised the Hausvater at length, because of the peasants' "laziness, indolence, and carelessness"; except in extreme cases, however, it ought not to interfere with the productive operation of the estate, either by breaking into the work process or by reducing the peasants' capacity to work. "Most cases can be dealt with and finished conveniently with a punishment that lasts only a few minutes or, in any case, a few hours."[53] To this end, of course, the whip was the most convenient and therefore the most constantly available tool of punishment for the use of the overseer or the noble estate owner himself. "A pair of painful blows with a staff or lashes with a whip, as everyone knows, have the best effect—more than most other means of punishment . . . which make less of an impression on the other peasants."[54] More serious offenses were punished in other ways. Women who committed petty theft were often punished with the use of "neck irons" or a similar device known as the "gent." Because it was not terribly painful, Beneckendorff commented, women who had once been punished with it lost their fear of it, so that it lost its effectiveness. Male offenders were commonly put in stocks in the village square; a more

---

[50] STAP, Pr. Br. 37, Branitz, Bd. 19, Bl. 38–39.

[51] Cited in Dirk Blasius, *Bürgerliche Gesellschaft und Kriminalität*, Kritische Studien zur Geschichtswissenschaft, 22 (Göttingen, 1976), 26.

[52] The same justification was given for corporal punishment in the case of slavery in the American South. See Eugene Genovese, *Roll, Jordan, Roll* (New York, 1974), 64–67.

[53] Beneckendorff, *Oeconomia Forensis* 5: 59.

[54] Ibid., 70–73.

painful version of stocks forced them to sit on a plank whose sharp edge pressed into their flesh. Serious offenses by both men and women were sometimes punished by confinement in a *Klause* or a *Kamurke*, a small hut in which it was impossible to sit upright; this, too, had its torturous version, for it was sometimes constructed with a floor composed of slats with narrow or sharp edges.[55] Other methods of punishment included forced labor and confinement in jail; noble estate owners could, according to the General Law Code of 1794, confine their subjects to jail for up to forty-eight hours without court action.[56]

The discussion surrounding corporal punishment in Prussia at the end of the eighteenth century illuminates another feature of paternalism as the idiom of social relations.[57] Although the chief author of the General Law Code of 1794, Carl Gottlieb Svarez, considered corporal punishment to be incompatible with the concept of free citizenship toward which the code aspired, he nevertheless tolerated it as a "fatherly method of improvement." Social control by means of corporal punishment was thus implicit in the very essence of paternalist notions of society; it was closely tied to the idea that social relations were essentially personal ones of superordination and subordination. The General Law Code explicitly approved corporal punishment by superiors of those in their charge—parents could so punish their children, heads of households their servants, lords their peasants, masters their apprentices, and teachers their pupils. In each instance, the fear of pain was seen as a means of education, of ensuring good behavior. The exercise of corporal punishment was limited only by the stricture that it ought not cause permanent bodily injury or damage one's honor. Again, the latter restriction is compatible only with a hierarchical society in which honor is based on birth and social station; persons of honor—that is, of authority and respect—were not subject to corporal punishment.

Frederick II attempted to limit the arbitrary nature of patrimonial justice by denying noble estate owners the right to act as judges unless they had the proper legal training and had passed an examination.[58] If they lacked such training, they were required to appoint a judge

---

[55] Ibid., 72–73; see also the summary of corporal punishment in Lower Lusatia in *Lausitzische Monatsschrift* of 1792, cited in Rudolf Lehmann, *Quellen zur Lage der Privatbauern in Niederlausitz im Zeitalter des Absolutismus* (Berlin, 1957), 203–4.

[56] *ALR*, II/7:4/#233; Hattenhauer, 441.

[57] See the discussion of corporal punishment in Reinhart Koselleck, *Preussen zwischen Reform und Revolution* (Stuttgart, 1967), 641–59.

[58] This was repeated in *ALR*, II/7:1/#73; Hattenhauer, 435.

with such an education to conduct patrimonial court proceedings. This was another example of the effort of the state to impose some of the structure of public law on the private authority possessed by noble lords. It had, however, little effect. The judges were largely dependent on the good will of the lord; they ate at his table and shared his views of the peasantry.[59] In 1798, Frederick William III wrote to his minister of justice, Goldbeck: "I have noticed that most of the complaints about patrimonial jurisdictions originate from the fact that patrimonial lords select, at will, the judges for their courts, that they pay them and dismiss them at their pleasure, that they also use them simultaneously as their counsel in legal affairs. With such a dependency of the judges on the patrimonial lords, the residents can scarcely have confidence in them and it cannot be denied that from this source a variety of injustices develops."[60] A decade later, one of the reform bureaucrats, von Merckel, summarized the problem even more pointedly: "In brief, despotism and illegality on the one side, dissatisfaction, disobedience, perversity, malice, and the inclination to mobs and tumult on the other, [are] conditions that hardly serve the holy name of justice."[61] These criticisms of patrimonial justice, which continued throughout the entire period prior to the revolution of 1848, were opposed by most noble estate owners on the grounds that patrimonial justice was an essential aspect of their roles as Hausvater.[62]

The patrimonial courts had other important weaknesses for which they were also criticized. Because noble estate owners bore the direct costs of criminal investigations, the transport of criminals to prison, and even the costs of their executions, they were frequently less than diligent in their prosecution of cases in which they themselves had not been injured. A Silesian nobleman claimed that it was "truly no exaggeration" when he reported cases of murderers being charged with lesser offenses by lords so they could save money or of thieves being

---

[59] One East Prussian Kölmer complained: "The poor Untertan is often merely the victim of the hospitality, which the judge enjoys at the house of his patrimonial lord. The selfish mistreatment of the bound residents of the estate is made possible under these circumstances." Robert Stein, *Die Umwandlung der Agrarverfassung Ostpreussens durch die Reformen des neunzehnten Jahrhunderts* (Jena, 1918), 1: 142ff. See also Stein (1933), 2: 116 n. 119. Eduard Pelz, the former Silesian peasant who became an outspoken critic of patrimonial justice, likewise wrote, "They eat often at the table of their patron, their horses are fed in his stable, their coachmen and servants are served in the manor kitchen." Treumund Welp [Eduard Pelz], *Die Patrimonial-Gerichtsbarkeit: Bruchstück aus den Memoiren eines schlesischen Bauern* (Leipzig, 1843), 19.

[60] Cited in Pelz, *Die Patrimonial-Gerichtsbarkeit*, 11–12.

[61] Cited in Ziekursch, *Hundert Jahre*, 123.

[62] See Pelz, *Die Patrimonial-Gerichtsbarkeit*.

CHAPTER 2

released "to locate witnesses of their prior good conduct," in the full knowledge that they would escape, in order to save the costs of incarceration.[63] These costs were ultimately borne by the peasants through such assessments as the *Sporteln* (court fees), with which the judges were paid, and *Schutzgeld* (literally, protection money), paid by Einlieger who fell into the category of *Schutzuntertanen*. In the end, a number of noble estate owners themselves doubted whether the expenses related to the patrimonial courts were worth the advantages they gained from them.[64]

The village school was another institution over which the noble estate owner exercised direct control. He appointed the schoolmaster and wrote the instructions under which the school was to operate; he sometimes even prescribed what was to be taught and how.[65] Nevertheless, it took a long time and a great deal of government pressure before noblemen, themselves often poorly educated, realized that schooling could be used as an effective instrument of social control. Frederick William I called for the establishment of elementary schools in the countryside in an ordinance of 1736; it remained, however, largely unenforced, so that Frederick II also ordered the creation of schools in each noble village shortly after he ascended the throne.[66] This too remained a dead letter in most villages, for it met with the indifference or opposition of many nobles. They considered education to be, at best, unnecessary, and at worst, dangerous. As one village pastor wrote in 1764, "Many [noble estate owners] consider a reasonable and Christian education of their Untertanen to be superfluous and unnecessary. If the peasant is only able to plow, reap, and thresh, he is already a good peasant. . . . It is thought . . . that if the peasant cannot write and cannot move without the knowledge of the noble-

---

[63] See the criticisms of Carl Freiherrn von Vincke, *Die Patrimonial- und Polizeigerichtsbarkeit auf dem Lande in den östlichen Provinzen des preussischen Staates* (Breslau, 1847), 12.

[64] Helmut Bleiber, *Zwischen Reform und Revolution: Lage und Kämpfe der schlesischen Bauern und Landarbeiter im Vormärz, 1840–1847* (Berlin, 1966), 99–111.

[65] Marwitz gave detailed instructions to his schoolmaster, describing what was to be taught and calling for an annual exam of all the pupils "in order to persuade me who has been diligent and who has been lazy." STAP, Pr. Br. 37, Marwitz/Friedersdorf, III, Bl. 2–6.

[66] The best discussion of elementary education in Prussia is in Anthony J. LaVopa, *Prussian Schoolmasters* (Chapel Hill, N.C., 1980). On the general development of rural education in Prussia, see Stadelmann, *Preussens Könige und ihrer Thätigkeit für die Landeskultur*, 3: 45–55; Wilhelm Roessler, *Die Entstehung des modernen Erziehungswesens in Deutschland*; H. Heppe, *Geschichte des deutschen Volksschulwesens* (Gotha, 1858; reprint, Olms, 1971), 1, 3: 1–154.

man, the barbarism of our land will be most severely hidden."[67] Even where village schools were created, they accomplished little. The schoolmaster was very poorly paid; in fact, in some parts of the Mark Brandenburg, schoolmasters were paid nothing except what they received from the peasants. In Silesia, the schoolmaster was generally also a peasant or herder who held school only when his other duties were not pressing. Schoolmasters had to contend not only with the indifference of the lord, but frequently also with the hostility of the peasantry. One report in 1799 declared: "The parents permit or command their children to stay out of school, not just for days, but for weeks at a time. In addition, in many regions, the parents let their children stop attending school at all just as soon as they are eleven or twelve years of age and can do work as Mägde or Knechte."[68]

By the end of the eighteenth century, village schools had become more widespread. This was partially due to the efforts of the government to develop practical schools on the crown estates that would teach some of the skills needed for rural life—animal husbandry for boys, spinning and weaving for girls, for example. Some enlightened noble estate owners, the most noteworthy of whom was Eberhard von Rochow, built model peasant schools. Rochow also wrote primers for use in village schools; they were filled with brief homilies about virtuous peasants and were meant to teach obedience to authority as well as literacy.[69]

Historians of the eighteenth century frequently see efforts to improve literacy and expand education as expressions of the liberal humanism of the Enlightenment. Klaus Epstein, for example, believed that early expressions of conservatism arose in opposition to efforts at popular education.[70] While the close association between the Enlightenment and education cannot be denied, demands for more village schools for the peasantry also represented efforts to introduce more social control, to "domesticate" the wild and ignorant peasant. Popular education, even in the eyes of the *Aufklärer*, also served as an instrument of social control. Garve saw this very clearly. "Those who defend

---

[67] Cited in Heppe, *Geschichte des deutschen Volksschulwesens*, 3: 37 n.

[68] Cited in ibid., 77.

[69] Rochow's books were filled with aphorisms for the peasantry, intended to reinforce the rectitude of existing social relations. "In the world there are various Stände; that is, there are some men who must give orders and some men who must obey." Friedrich Eberhard von Rochow, *Versuch eines Schulbuchs für Kinder der Landleute; oder, Unterricht für Lehrer in niederen Landschulen*, 3d ed. (Berlin, 1790), 88; and again, "It is good when each loves his own Stand," the wise peasant counsels in the primer. *Rochows sämtliche pädagogische Schriften* (Berlin, 1907), 1: 186.

[70] Klaus Epstein, *The Genesis of German Conservatism* (Princeton, 1966), 76–79.

the *Aufklärung*," he wrote, "say, with justice, that the dissipations of the common man and, from time to time, the most fearful rebellions, are always to be seen in those lands and periods where the peasants are most dumb and raw. . . . They say that it is not possible for men, and therefore even less for peasants, to be able to be more evil and bad when they obtain more proper notions of God, of their duty, and of happiness than they had before; that it is not possible for them to become poorer workers when they are able to think, and above all to have better understanding related to their work."[71] Similarly, a series of articles in the "enlightened" journal *Neues Wittenbergsches Wochenblatt* in 1797 showed how humanism and education could serve the ends of social control.

Nothing lies closer to the hearts of those friends of humanity, especially those forthright preachers on the land, than the improvement of the education for the large masses on the land. . . . It is a principle of general validity: That also the peasant, in our age, must receive a better instruction and education than has heretofore generally been the case in the village schools if he is to be held true and obedient to his duty.

Here and there, wrong-thinking enemies of humanity consider it extremely dangerous if their Untertanen obtain more understanding and insight than they previously had; they always consider them only as human beasts of burden that are allowed to grow up in all ignorance and must not be made more intelligent because their reason can only be guided by coercion and tyranny. . . . It seems clear that this bad and malicious principle be cast aside, so that the lower classes of the people are given a better foundation and more incentive, if they are, as rational human beings to fulfill their obligations as Untertanen with zeal and fidelity, and it cannot happen in any other way than to give them better instruction in the schools.[72]

Although the level of physical brutality against the peasants may have abated somewhat in the aftermath of emancipation and the level of education improved slowly over the course of the nineteenth century, many noble estate owners continued to think a little education was dangerous for peasants. They should be able to read and write a bit, to know their Bible and hymnal, and perhaps to do some simple figuring; but more than that usually, as one county administrator

---

[71] Garve, *Ueber den Charakter der Bauern*, 201–2. Epstein quotes Garve's rendering of the other side of the argument, 78.

[72] "Ein leicht ausführbares Mittel, die Dorfschulen, in Ansehung des Unterrichts und guter Ordnung zu verbessern," *Neues Wittenbergsches Wochenblatt* 5 (1797): 185–86.

(*Landrat*) wrote in 1831, "causes a certain decline in their level of productivity." "The contemporary theoreticians," he continued, "believe it a great service to the human race when they are able to elevate the common man to a higher level of knowledge and so-called culture. They might well be asked whether, after the elevation to such a level, the common man will still be willing to walk behind a plow for ten hours a day. And yet, the overwhelming majority of human beings must spend their days in physical labor to earn their daily bread."[73]

The final institution through which the noble estate owner exercised authority was the Patronatsrecht, the power, with minor limitations, to appoint the village pastor.[74] As with the control of the schools, and in contrast to the police and the judges, this authority was indirect; it represented, instead of coercion, the power of persuasion and, on occasion, of paternalist compassion. If the role of the schoolmaster was to educate the peasant to appreciate the importance of his duties, that of the pastor was to preach passivity and obedience as the will of God. Even those pastors who sympathized deeply with the plight of the peasants dared not openly criticize their patron. As one former village preacher cautioned others, "Even when the estate lord and patron misunderstands his God-given position and abuses it, the pastor must not intervene. A bad king remains still the king of the land, and a godless patron remains still the patron of the village and must be respected and honored as such. One gains nothing by disagreeing with such lords and one can easily provoke dissatisfaction."[75] The impact of such pastors on their peasant parishioners, though difficult to assess, ought not be underestimated.

The System of Symbolic Herrschaft

Thus far, we have considered the relationship between the Prussian nobility and the peasantry in two of its dimensions: First, the description of a noble estate as a self-contained community, *das ganze Haus*, in which the ideology of paternalism, despite its limitations, provided the justification for the nobility's domination of the peasantry; second, the description of the noble estate as a system in which the institutions of direct control served both the public functions of the state and, simultaneously, the private interests of the lords. In this connection, we

---

[73] DZA II, Merseburg, Rep. 92, v. Rochow, A III, no. 22, no pagination.

[74] The *Patronatsrecht*, with its limitations, is found in *ALR*, II/9:43; and II/11:8/#568–617. Jewish estate owners were excluded from exercising the Patronatsrecht, #582; Hattenhauer, 532, 562–63.

[75] C. Büchsel, *Erinnerungen aus dem Leben eines Landesgeistlichen*, 80.

have stressed the domination by the nobility as a fusion of public and private functions. There is a third dimension, closely related to this, that must be considered. It can be defined somewhat imprecisely as a system of symbolic domination, that is, a system in which the superiority of the dominant class was expressed in numerous symbolic forms and in language and behavior that legitimized its rule. The concept of paternalism legitimized domination by stressing the interdependency, the mutuality of rights and obligations, within the lord-peasant relationship. It brought both classes together into a familial relationship, naturalizing the role of the lord as Hausvater. The broader structures of symbolic domination, without contradicting the ideology of paternalism, worked the other way. They separated the ruled from their rulers, legitimizing the structure of subordination and superordination by underscoring the innate differences between the groups. The structures of symbolic domination worked to show that those who governed were a different order of persons altogether from those whom they governed.

The system of symbolic domination can be described in various ways. Antonio Gramsci used the phrase "cultural hegemony" to refer to the entire system of institutions, laws, symbols, rituals, and norms by which a dominated class exercised its control. This cultural hegemony was the means by which, in rural Prussia, social relations were mediated to the advantage of the nobility. Although Gramsci's concept was broader than what might be referred to as symbolic domination, it had the similar effect of setting the nobility apart from the rest of society and making its superiority seem natural.[76] Jürgen Habermas, for example, has used the phrase "representative publicness" in connection with the symbolic representation of authority "before the people" in feudal society.[77] Also calling attention to the fact that feudal society did not distinguish between the private person and the public office—the king's person was invested with his public office—Habermas pointed to the array of symbolic manifestations developed to separate the public person from those who were merely private, that is, common. Insignias, coats-of-arms, dress, hair styles, gesture, forms of address, dialects, all of these were used as status symbols, giving the

---

[76] Gramsci's notion of hegemony is contained in scattered references through selections from the *Prison Notebooks* (New York, 1971); see especially 12–13, 55–60, 207, 245–46, 258, 263, 275–76. See also Raymond Williams, *Marxism and Literature* (Oxford, 1977), esp. 108–9; John Cammet, *Antonio Gramsci and the Origins of Italian Communism* (Stanford, 1967), 204–12; Stuart Hall, Bob Lumley, and Gregor McLennan, "Politics and Ideology: Gramsci," *Working Papers in Cultural Studies* 10 (1977): 45–76.

[77] Jürgen Habermas, *Strukturwandel der Oeffentlichkeit* (Neuwied, 1962), 13–24.

public person an "aura" of authority. The baroque style and the court life of the seventeenth century especially reflected this "representative publicness" which, Habermas suggests, "reached a highly refined point" in the elaborate etiquette of the court of Louis XIV, where even the most private aspects of the king's life were given public display. In a similar fashion, Edward P. Thompson has used the notion of theater in describing the manner in which the dominant class exercised its cultural hegemony; it provoked, from plebeian society, the response of a countertheater.[78] Of the ceremonials and pomp of the ruling class in England in the eighteenth century, Thompson has written the following:

We have here a studied and elaborate hegemonic style, a theatrical role in which the great were schooled in infancy and which they maintained until death. And if we speak of it as theatre, it is not to diminish its importance. A great part of politics and law is always theatre; once a social system has become "set," it does not need to be endorsed daily by exhibitions of power (although occasional punctuations of force will be made to define the limits of the system's tolerance); what matters more is a continuing theatrical style. What one remarks of the eighteenth century is elaboration of this style and the self-consciousness with which it was deployed.[79]

Such ceremonials and baroque behavior have different meanings in different social settings. For the French nobility of the seventeenth and eighteenth centuries, they provided a justification for the contest with the king and, later, compensations for the loss of power. But they were always intended to set the nobility above the rest of the society so as to justify the privileges it continued to enjoy. In eighteenth-century England, the use of theater was most often associated with the law; it was meant to overawe the plebs with the sense of majesty and justice and certitude of the law, as well as to terrify them with such spectacles as public hangings.[80]

In Prussia, the social context was different so that the nature of the nobility's symbolic domination had quite other functions and took different forms. Because the nobility retained the direct, physical control of the peasantry throughout the eighteenth century, it had less need for ostentatious symbols to express its power. Moreover, Prussian nobles were not wealthy enough to afford the majestic trappings associ-

[78] E. P. Thompson, "Patrician Society, Plebian Culture," 382–405.
[79] Ibid., 389.
[80] See especially Douglas Hay, "Property, Authority, and Criminal Law," in Douglas Hay et al., *Albion's Fatal Tree* (New York, 1975), 17–63.

ated with the grand nobility of western Europe; they were often only slightly less crude than the peasantry whom they ruled. A few wealthy families with large estate complexes built handsome châteaus, but most manor houses were simple and functional, often resembling large peasant houses.[81] To those noble persons accustomed to life in Berlin, with its culture and court, the rural nobles appeared boorish and ignorant.[82]

Precisely because of the nobility's proximity to the peasantry and because its control of the peasantry was relatively direct and unmediated (a whip is not a subtle instrument), it had need of a symbolic system that would establish distance between itself and the peasantry. Indeed, the very credibility of the paternalist ideology required the establishment of both intimacy and distance between the ruled and their rulers. This is why, for example, peasants often hated their overseers but considered their lords to be genuinely concerned with their welfare. In 1790, when the peasants on the estate Leuthen, in Lower Lusatia, rebelled against the additional demands made on them by the leaseholder of the estate, they sent a delegation to Berlin to request the intervention of the owner of the estate, Countess von Hordt, on their behalf.[83]

This symbolic domination, manifested in many small ways, was expressed in the fact that the lord always addressed his peasants with the informal "*Du*," as with children, while they could address him only with the formal "*Sie*."[84] It was obvious in the village church, where the lord sat in a separate pew and where all the symbols of religious worship, representing God the Father, were intermingled with statues, busts, and sarcophagi of the noble forebears, representing the peasants' earthly "father."[85] Symbolic domination was reinforced in such ceremonies as those in which the peasant, upon acquiring a plot, swore an oath of allegiance and loyalty to his lord, not unlike that which a vassal had traditionally sworn to his lord in the feudal structure.[86] Similarly, when a new estate owner assumed possession of an estate, a

---

[81] See Carl von Lorck, *Ostpreussische Gutshäuser: Bauform und Kulturgehalt* (Kitzingen, 1953); H. J. Helmigk, *Oberschlesische Landbaukunst um 1800* (Berlin, 1937).

[82] Caroline von Rochow, *Vom Leben am Preussischen Hofe, 1815–1852* (Berlin, 1908), 111–12.

[83] Lehmann, *Quellen zur Lage der Privatbauern*, 195–203.

[84] Werne Pöls, ed., *Deutsche Sozialgeschichte* (Munich, 1976), 1: 36–38.

[85] For examples of village churches see the volumes edited by Paul Eichholz, Friedrich Solger, and Willy Spatz, *Die Kunstdenkmäler der Provinz Brandenburg* (Berlin, 1907–).

[86] STAP, Pr. Br. 37, Marwitz/Friedersdorf, 137, Bl. 5–8; see also his comment in his memoirs, Marwitz, 1: 133.

transfer ceremony took place at which all Untertanen were present and required to swear their loyalty to the new owner.[87]

The intimacy of paternalism and the distance of symbolic domination were both manifested in the special occasions in the life of an estate and village—baptisms, marriages, and funerals in the family of the noble lord. Marwitz offers an excellent example of such an occasion in his account of the baptism of his son, when he gathered the residents of his village, Friedersdorf, in front of the manor house and addressed them thus:

> Here I present my newborn son. Since my older sons are buried there, and since my brother has fallen on the field of battle, I have been the last of my family. If heaven had denied me a son, you would have fallen into the hands of strangers.
>
> How detrimental to the common good is the change of lords and subjects; how detrimental when the possession of land constantly passes from the hands of one to another, like the wares of businessmen. That is visible to you by so many of your neighbors. . . . The poor and the weak lack a father who cares for them in a time of need, as we have experienced it; the whole is deprived of a true spokesman and provider.
>
> God be praised that it has not been this way with us for the past 150 years. After the Thirty Years' War, my forefathers who settled here rebuilt the destroyed village; they built the church that still stands, they established the school that remains free, they fed the poor. I myself . . . have defended you against injustice in the land; I have led your youth against foreign foes. I have tried to follow in the footsteps of my ancestors.
>
> If this bond which has existed between us for so long is to endure longer and pass on to your children, pray that my son lives. In the hope that you will do so, in the hope that you will transfer to him the obedience and loyalty that you have always shown me, I have invited you all to his baptism. I will take care to raise him in the fear of God and the love of his neighbors. I will take care to infuse in him such convictions that he will never shy from that which is best for you and for the country, that he will not fear the powerful nor the face of the enemy, that he will fear neither imprisonment, nor injury, nor death. That is my intention. What is yours?
>
> Is it your will, as upright and true subjects, to live and die with him in the future, to hold firm to him and not to abandon him in fortune or misfortune? If you wish always to be mindful of this day, where-

---

[87] Beneckendorff, *Oeconomia Forensis* 2: 284.

upon you have sealed a baptismal bond with him, answer me with a loud and clear "Yes!"

(Here the entire community said a loud "yes" and gave me their hands, and so on.)

Now I ask God the All Powerful to bless and protect him. We shall enter the church together.

(Then the baptism took place in the church. Thereafter, the Schulze, in the name of 13 Kossäten—six had not participated—presented me with a silver bowl with an incription for my son. In the church, the Schulze held the child and, in addition to the Schulze, the two oldest Kossäten, the two servants who had been longest in my household service, and the two oldest women who were born in Friedersdorf were presented to the community and stepped to the altar. On the following Sunday, the 13 who had given the gift were invited for a meal at the manor house.)[88]

In this simple ceremony, Marwitz succeeded in reminding his peasants of their mutual bond with the past and the future. He stressed the continuity of their relationship over generations, rendering it natural and a part of the order of things. He reminded them of his paternal concern for their well-being, that his ownership of the estate was not merely a commercial undertaking, but a personal commitment. He called upon them to voice their loyalty to his son, who though a child, was thus set above them and at a distance from them from the outset. The figures of authority within the peasant community—the Schulze and the elders—were also recognized and set apart from the rest. Both peasants and lord renewed their relationship with an exchange of gifts. In short, the entire ceremony reconfirmed the structure of relationships on the estate, enforcing the habitus of Herrschaft and obedience.

Some rural festivals and celebrations also contained the kind of ritual that allowed the noble estate owner to display a degree of paternalist intimacy within the context of a clearly defined hierarchy. For example, it was the custom in most east Elbian provinces for the lord to give a festival for his peasants after the fall harvest had been gathered. This began, typically, with the peasants' gathering to present the lord with a crown made of harvest grain, accompanied in some cases by the ritualized recitation of a poem by one of the peasants. One from Silesia is representative of a number of such presentations:

> *Ich bringe dem Herrn einen Kranz von Korn,*
> *Er ist gewachsen unter Distel und Dorn*

[88] Marwitz, II/1:258–59.

HABITUS AND HERRSCHAFT

Hat ausgestanden Schnee, Hagel und Regen.
Ich wünsche dem Herrn viel Segen,
Soviel Hocken, soviel Dukaten
In des Herrn Kasten!
Soviel Ähren,
Soviel gute Jahre!
Ich bringe dem Herrn einen Kranz
und Wünsche für uns einen Tanz![89]

The lord then responded, sometimes in a similar ritual, thanking the peasants for their work, assuring them of his concern for their welfare, and inviting them to enjoy the festival. In some cases, he then withdrew, allowing the peasants to celebrate alone; in others, he and his wife had the first dance, bedecked with the crown of grain, which was then passed next to the overseer, and then downward through the ranks of the peasantry.

The importance of such festivals in the reproduction of social relations should not be underestimated.[90] They were important ingredients in the "representative publicness" or the theater of the landowning nobility, underscoring the essential connections of paternalist social relations. With the growth of capitalist agriculture in the nineteenth century and the concomitant decline of paternalism, such festivals changed their form or disappeared. One nineteenth-century observer reported about harvest festivals, "These festivities were earlier more general; these days they disappear more and more, and the landowners endeavor to get their grain into their barns as cheaply as possible."[91]

---

[89] Ingeborg Weber-Kellermann, *Erntebrauch in der ländlichen Arbeitswelt des 19. Jahrhunderts* (Marburg, 1965), 48–171, contains a description of harvest festivals. The poem is on page 170. An unpoetic translation is the following:

> I bring the lord a crown of grain,
> It has grown amid thorns and thistles
> And has withstood snow, hail, and rain.
> I wish the lord much blessing,
> Many sheaves, many ducats
> for the lord's treasury!
> So many honors,
> So many good years!
> I bring the lord a crown
> And the wish that we may have a dance!

[90] On the relationship of festival to social reproduction, see Gerald Sider, "Christmas Mumming and the New Year in Outport Newfoundland," *Past and Present*, no. 71, 102–25.

[91] Cited in Weber-Kellermann, *Erntebrauch in der ländlichen Arbeitswelt*, 162.

CHAPTER 2

Systems of symbolic domination are directed at both the ruled and the rulers. To the ruled, they are intended to impart the sense that the social order is natural and immutable. To the rulers, they are intended to impart essential aspects of the habitus, to equip them to wear the mantle of authority as if it were natural to them. There are instances, however, when these two objectives come into conflict and the authority of the dominant class is unmasked and shown to be arbitrary, raw privilege. An example is noble hunting rights. The exclusive privilege of hunting formed an important aspect of the self-definition of the nobility; as the military significance of the nobility declined in the late Middle Ages, the hunt came to be seen as an activity in which virtues acquired in war could be symbolically reenacted. Hohberg, author of the classic Hausväterliteratur, stressed the importance of the hunt for nobles.

The hunt is the training for the brave and knightly and, at the same time, it is for the nobility a praeludium belli in which the noble learns to attack, combat, and kill a wild animal with cunning and speed. He learns to use his weapons on foot or on horseback, patiently to bear and to endure cold, heat, rain, and storm . . . , to suffer hunger, thirst, and exhaustion, and to clear the neighborhood of destructive and dangerous animals.[92]

Another writer in the eighteenth century relished the dangers of the hunt.

I have seen two men killed and others injured, but those are the hazards of the hunt, turns of fate, and often the injured are themselves responsible because they quest after the honor of killing the deer. I want the danger to be great, the threat of death frequent; I want to see falls and broken limbs; the hunt retains its brilliance and purity. If it is not accompanied by danger, even chambermaids will develop a passion for it and not kings, princes, strong men who bear a masculine character.[93]

By the eighteenth century, the hunt could no longer be justified, if it ever could be, as a praeludium belli. It had only a symbolic function as the means by which noblemen could display those virtues over which they claimed an exclusive monopoly—strength, bravery, self-denial, self-control, immunity to discomfort, skill as a horseman and

---

[92] Hohberg, *Georgica Curiosa* 2: 684; cited also by Brunner, *Adeliges Landleben und europäischer Geist*, 292–93.

[93] Cited in Ulrich Wendt, *Kultur und Jagd* (Berlin, 1907–1908), 2: 164. See also, "Jagd," in Johann Heinrich Zedler, ed., *Grosses Vollständiges Universal-Lexikon* (Leipzig and Halle, 1735), 14: 151–52.

combatant, love of danger, masculinity. Having no practical function, it was an expensive luxury that took peasants away from productive labor, for they were obligated to serve their lord during the hunt; it often left the peasant fields in waste after a herd of noble horsemen in pursuit of game trampled them; and it cost the peasants the grain they were not allowed to protect from foraging wild animals. Yet, despite the bitterness that it provoked among the peasants and their demands that it be set aside, the nobility fought strenuously throughout the entire Vormärz period to retain its exclusive hunting privilege. The most recent study of noble hunting privileges stresses its significance as a status symbol and self-confirmation of the nobility: "The right to hunt was especially well suited as a symbol, because it was reserved exclusively for one Stand; as a monopolized symbol, it helped to maintain the belief in the inaccessibility of those qualities that it represented and, thereby, to stabilize the hierarchical order that rested on the claim and acknowledgment of the special position of the nobility."[94]

It is important to appreciate how completely the cultural system of Prussia served to set the nobility apart from the rest of society and thus to justify its hegemonic position. This was possible because the concept of the Stände, the estates of which the society was composed, was deeply embossed on the Prussian social and cultural structure.[95] The *Ständestaat* of the late Middle Ages, in which the nobility reached the peak of its political power and thus restricted and shared the power of the prince, had been set aside during the seventeenth and eighteenth centuries with the triumph of princely absolutism. But as Hans Rosenberg has shown, this was accomplished in such a way that the influence of the nobility was carried out through the new bureaucracy and therefore served to revalidate the nobility as a separate Stand.[96] Moreover, as we shall note in the next chapter, the political power of the nobility continued in the ständisch institutions of local government.

Ständisch distinctions were symbolized and cultivated in many ways. The vacant chair between nobles and commoners at dinner, the ceremonial sword, sumptuary ordinances, courtesy books teaching noble

[94] Hans Wilhelm Eckhardt, *Herrschaftliche Jagd, Bäuerliche Not, und bürgerliche Kritik*, Veröffentlichungen des Max-Planck-Instituts für Geschichte, 48 (Göttingen, 1976), 272. Eckhardt's analysis concentrates on Württemburg, but his conclusions on the symbolic nature of the hunt apply elsewhere as well. His focus on both the lords and the peasants is especially good.

[95] Robert M. Berdahl, "Anthropologie und Geschichte," in Berdahl et al., *Klassen und Kultur*.

[96] Hans Rosenberg, *Bureaucracy, Aristocracy, and Autocracy: The Prussian Experience, 1660–1815* (Cambridge, Mass., 1958).

etiquette, titles, genealogies and the portraits of ancestors hanging in the manor house, all of these served to set the nobles apart and to give them a sense of their special position in society.[97] Nobles frequently avoided contact with commoners. As one eighteenth-century observer noted, "I know noblemen who refuse to send their children to any public school because they are convinced they will acquire too little honor there.... Others keep their children at home because they fear their good morals will be injured by contact with the children of commoners."[98]

Ständisch distinctions permeated the Prussian legal system throughout the eighteenth century. This can be seen in the laws regulating the marriage of nobles to commoners, in the fact that commoners were ostensibly prohibited from owning noble estates, and in the fact that noblemen were not permitted to enter a profession deemed unsuitable for their Stand, especially one involving the most "common" place of all, the marketplace. Perhaps most significant was the fact that notions of honor, a cultural symbol over which the nobility claimed to hold a monopoly, remained a legal category.[99] From the Middle Ages onward, the notion of honor had been closely associated with Stand; different recognitions of honor were accorded to the different Stände. But the nobleman's honor was of a different order from that of the other Stände. As late as 1836, the conservative weekly, the *Berliner Politische Wochenblatt*, declared that the nobleman's "sole profession is the striving for honor and as soon as the Stand loses sight of this goal, it will cease to exist."[100] The Prussian General Law Code of 1794 contained 152 paragraphs dealing with offenses against the honor of a person; it proceeded from the principle that persons of a higher Stand had more to lose if their honor were injured than did persons of a

---

[97] See Alexandra Schlingsiepen-Pogge, *Das Sozialethos der lutherischen Aufklärungstheologie am Vorabend der Industriellen Revolution*, Göttinger Baustein zu Geschichtswissenschaft, 39 (Göttingen, 1967), 46; for an example of courtesy literature, see Bernard von Rohr, *Einleitung zur Ceremonial Wissenschaft der Privat-Person*; on the role of ständisch thought on sumptuary ordinances in general, see L. C. Eisenbart, *Kleiderordnung der deutschen Städte zwischen 1350 und 1700*, Göttinger Baustein zu Geschichtswissenschaft, 32 (Göttingen, 1962), 52–65.

[98] Cited in Gert Zang, *Sozialstruktur und Sozialization des Adels im 18. Jahrhundert: Exemplarisch Dargestellt an Kurbayern* (phil. diss., Constance, 1972), 160.

[99] A good treatment of "honor," as it evolved historically and was claimed by various social groups, is in the article "Ehre," in Otto Brunner et al., eds., *Geschichtliche Grundbegriffe: Historisches Lexikon zur politisch-sozialen Sprache im Deutschland* (Stuttgart, 1972–), 2: 1–63.

[100] *Berliner Politische Wochenblatt*, 1836, 126.

lower Stand.[101] If persons of higher station injured the honor of a person of lower station, they could be punished with a fine of from ten to thirteen taler; if, however, persons of lower station injured the honor of someone higher, they could receive from fourteen to twenty-eight days in jail. This differentiation remained an article of Prussian law until 1850.[102]

The concept of honor was important to the paternalist ideology espoused by the nobility. Not only did it set the nobility in a different category from the rest of the society, but it suggested that, because the nobility was invested with honor, it was above self-interest. The bourgeois, by contrast, was mired in self-interest and lacked true honor. Possessed of honor, devoid of self-interest, the nobility saw itself as a *Mittelstand*, an intermediary authority, transmitting the authority of the monarchy downward to the peasantry. Without a Mittelstand between the crown and the people, a monarchy could not exist, argued Marwitz. "A Mittelstand is therefore necessary in order to separate the masses of the people and to observe them. If there should be a Mittelstand between the king and the people, it must also have certain privileges, for without these it belongs to the people and is unable to exert influence on them."[103]

The concept of Stand was more than a political organization or a premodern form of representation. It was a system of symbolic domination that permeated the entire culture, from the highest to the lowest group of society. It provided the framework for deference and authority. Shaped in the interest of the dominant groups of society, it projected a system of social differentiation based on the assumption that men and women were innately endowed with the qualities in the collective personality of their Stand. The concept of Stand provided an essential category through which people perceived their society and their place in that society, giving shape to the contours of their behavior. This is not to suggest that the concept of Stand functioned so perfectly as to eliminate conflict; far from it. As we have noted, conflict was constantly present, floating just beneath the surface and occasionally breaking into the open. But the symbolic domination represented

---

[101] *ALR*, II/20:10/#538–690; Hattenhauer, 689–94.

[102] "Ehre," *Geschichtliche Grundbegriffe*, 34.

[103] Marwitz, II/1:196–98. The view of the nobility as a Mittelstand was a common one in the eighteenth century. Montesquieu considered the nobility as *pouvoirs intermédiaires*, and Johann Georg Schlosser described the nobility in 1787 as a Mittelstand between regent and people. Kant also used the concept of the Mittelstand to describe the nobility as a stratum between sovereign and people. See "Adel," in *Geschichtliche Grundbegriffe* 1: 20–21.

by ständisch differentiation functioned well enough to suppress conflict and, in many instances, to achieve its objective of bringing about the internalization of the structures of authority. Its success as a symbolic system can be seen in the commentary of a village pastor.

As the children were gathered in the church, it struck me that each had seated himself in another row, as in the school. At the front sat the son of the Schulze and the church warden, then followed the sons of the Bauern, then the sons of the Büdner, and so on, the last being the son of the renderer. The young girls ordered themselves in a similar fashion. The sexton strongly advised me to allow the children to remain seated in this manner because otherwise it would cause too much turmoil and because it was quite doubtful whether such things could be altered. The difference between Bauern, Büdnern, and Tagelöhner was constantly made valid by the one side and respected by the other side. This was especially evident in all festive occasions and likewise the pews in the church were divided accordingly. The Knecht and the Magd called the lord and his wife mother and father, and das ganze Haus ate at one table, but each had and retained a consciousness of his own position. It seldom happened that the boundaries of the Stand were crossed in a marriage. The Bauer wife would say, "My daughter is still too young to marry beneath her Stand," even when the girl was already thirty years of age.[104]

[104] Büchsel, *Erinnerungen aus dem Leben eines Landgeistlichen*, 37–38.

3

CROSS-CURRENTS OF ECONOMIC AND SOCIAL CHANGE

Opportunities for a New Agriculture

There is a danger that these descriptions of the status and conditions of the servitude of the east Elbian peasantry may convey an image of a static social system, one that continued for several centuries without any apparent change. It is true that change came slowly, that many of the conditions that existed at the end of the seventeenth century continued into the nineteenth century, even after the agrarian reforms. The habits of authority and deference, deeply ingrained in this rural culture, did not disappear readily, even with later changes in the legal relationships between lords and peasants. But the situation was not static. During the last three decades of the eighteenth century, the profound upswing of economic life that overtook western Europe, ending a long period of stagnation reaching back to the 1620s, also effected changes in the rural society of Prussia.

The most striking change in European society was the rapid increase in population. Between 1750 and 1800, the European population increased by 34 percent, from 139.6 million to 186.8 million, bringing a greater demand for grain.[1] England, with its urban growth and new industrial population, became a major market for the grain produced in central and eastern Europe. Indeed, England passed from being an exporter of grain in the middle of the eighteenth century to a net importer by 1800. By 1800, the Polish and German grain shipped to the west, primarily to England, from the three Baltic ports of Danzig, Elbing, and Königsberg, accounted for nearly one-third of the volume of the entire international grain trade. In 1769, between 200 and 300 ships with Prussian grain passed through the Danish sound; in 1798, the number had grown to 1,671 ships.[2] Increased demand drove grain prices up, gradually at first, then sharply in the 1780s. Between the 1730s and the first decade of the nineteenth cen-

---

[1] Jerome Blum, *The End of the Old Order in Rural Europe* (Princeton, 1978) 241.
[2] Ibid., 243; Hajo Holborn, *A History of Modern Germany* (New York, 1966), 2: 267.

tury, cereal grain prices shot up by 283 percent in Denmark, 259 percent in Austria, 210 percent in Germany, and 163 percent in France.[3]

Increasing grain prices gave the noble landowners a new affluence; according to one estimate, their income doubled during the last thirty years of the eighteenth century.[4] At the same time that these rising prices and an expanding European market provided new opportunities for profit, Frederick the Great endeavored to strengthen the economic basis of the nobility, which he deemed essential to the preservation of the state. He sponsored programs for clearing and draining new lands for cultivation; in the region that became Prussian Silesia, for example, arable land increased by about 15 percent between 1721 and 1798. In Further Pomerania, the equivalent of 10 percent of the land of the entire region was added to the arable land in the 1760s and 1770s. Frederick encouraged the publication of journals about techniques for improving agricultural yields. He elevated few persons to the ranks of the nobility who were unable to purchase a noble estate, thus preserving the link between nobility and land ownership.[5]

By far the most important innovation of Frederick the Great, however, was the creation of *Landschaften*, rural credit institutes that made funds available to nobles for the improvement of their estates.[6] Frederick established the first Landschaft in Silesia in 1769; that in the Mark Brandenburg was established in 1777, in Pomerania in 1781. The Landschaft in East Prussia was founded in 1788, two years after Frederick the Great's death. Membership in the Landschaft was limited to noble estate owners. The entire membership of the Landschaft stood behind the notes issued, and the state also provided guarantees,

---

[3] Wilhelm Abel, *Agrarkrisen und Agrarkonjunktur* (Hamburg and Berlin, 1966), 182–83.

[4] Fritz Martiny, *Die Adelsfrage in Preussen vor 1806*, Beiheft 35 to *Vierteljahrschrift für Sozial- und Wirtschaftsgeschichte* (Berlin, 1938), 13; Walter Görlitz, *Die Junker* (Limburg, 1964), 113–14.

[5] Otto Hintze, "Die Hohenzollern und der Adel," in *Geschichtliche Abhandlungen*, vol. 3, *Regierung und Verwaltung* (Göttingen, 1967), 30–55; idem, *Die Hohenzollern und ihr Werk*, 383–87; idem, "Zur Agrarpolitik Friedrichs des Grossen," *FBPG* 10 (1898): 275–309; Elsbeth Schwenke, *Friedrich der Grosse und der Adel* (diss., Berlin, 1911), 50–56; August Skalweit, "Wie Viel Kolonisten hat Friedrich des Grossen angesiedelt?" *FBPG* 24 (1924): 243–48. A.M.F. Gritzner, *Chronologische Matrikel der brandenburgischen-preussischen Standeserhebungen 1600 bis 1873* (Berlin, 1874).

[6] Wilhelm von Brünneck, *Die Pfandbriefsystem der preussischen Landschaften* (Berlin, 1910), 1–35; for a discussion of the legal regulations governing the Landschaften, see 82–181. Johannes Ziekursch, *Hundert Jahre schlesischer Agrargeschichte* (Breslau, 1927), 6–12, has a discussion of the Silesian Landschaft. An excellent study of the East Prussian Landschaft is forthcoming by Bernd Ristau, whose Master's thesis, *Die Anfänge der Landschaftlichen Kreditanstalt in Ostpreussen im späten 18. Jahrhundert* (Göttingen, 1976), is already one of the best works on the subject.

so the notes (*Pfandbriefe*) circulated publicly like bank notes. Estate owners could mortgage their estates to half or, in some provinces, two-thirds of their assessed value, while the Landschaft had the powers of sequestration and foreclosure if the borrower was unable to repay the loan.

The Landschaften had one overwhelming advantage: they secured capital from the middle class without endangering the exclusive ownership of the estates by noblemen. Middle-class purchasers of the notes had a reasonably secure investment since the entire Landschaft stood behind the value of the notes; because only the Landschaft could foreclose on a bad debt, there was no danger that default on the loan could result in the estate's passing into the hands of a non-noble. Because the loans were secured by the Landschaft, the interest rates available to the estate owners were low, usually 4 to 6 percent—considerably less than estate owners had in the past been compelled to pay to moneylenders.[7]

The creation of the Landschaften had dramatic and far-reaching effects. As the rapidly rising prices of grain made land more valuable, estate owners found that they could mortgage their estates for ever-larger amounts. The availability of cheap credit through the Landschaft also provided the means for expanding the family holdings by purchasing additional estates. Originally, most of the Landschaften required the estate owner to obtain the approval of several agnates before encumbering the estate with debt, except that incurred to pay the claims of other heirs or for "useful improvements on the estate." "Useful improvements" provided ample latitude, however, and by the end of the eighteenth century, most estate owners regarded their lands as fully allodial and mortgaged them without consulting the agnates.[8] They also stopped consulting agnates before selling the estate. By the last decades of the century, the easy and cheap credit offered by the Landschaften, as well as the rising land values fostered by grain prices, fueled a heated market of land speculation. Although some nobles borrowed money to improve their estates, others used the borrowed money to purchase another estate, which in turn they mortgaged to the limit. Frequently, the level of the mortgage exceeded the legal limit, but, as the value of land appreciated through the inflation fired by speculation and grain prices, additional money could be borrowed on it. One contemporary described how many estate owners used the system: "Through the introduction of the credit system, it has come

[7] Ziekursch, *Hundert Jahre*, 7–9, 27–32.
[8] Martiny, *Die Adelsfrage*, 21–22.

CHAPTER 3

to be that families with little wealth have accumulated many large estates. For they first buy an estate, or perhaps they already own one, which they have assessed, borrow as much money on it as they can get from the Landschaft, buy a second, which they again have assessed, borrow money on it, and again are in the position to purchase a third estate."[9]

Until the middle of the eighteenth century, most of the estates that changed hands through sale were purchased for cash or exchanged as settlements for debts. Few were bought and sold, for land was still considered a family possession, to be sold outside the family only under dire conditions. The availability of cheap credit, however, led to land speculation and prices shot upward. The following examples indicate the scale of this speculation and the subsequent inflation: One estate in the Kurmark of Brandenburg sold for almost 20,000 talers in 1744; in 1787, its market value had increased to 25,000 talers; ten years later, the same estate sold for 60,000. Another estate in the Kurmark changed hands five times in as many years. In 1800 it sold for 12,000 talers; in 1801 for 13,225; in 1802 and again in 1803 for 15,000; and in 1804, it went for 22,000 talers. Reports from the other provinces show the same pattern. An estate in Silesia sold for 20,000 in 1771, for 100,000 in 1799; one in West Prussia brought 11,300 in 1771 and 41,000 in 1804.[10] Table 1, an index of estate prices in Silesia and Brandenburg, shows the steep inflation during the closing decades of the century.[11]

The social implications of this speculation are obvious. With the constant transfer of estates from one noble to another, the longstanding link between lord and peasant, the entire context for the ideology of paternalism, and with it, the justification for the system of social relations in rural Prussia became difficult to maintain. Paternalist arguments in defense of serfdom became obviously absurd. Many were

---

[9] U. J. Seetzen, "Ueber dem Handel mit Landgüter," *Annalen der niedersächsischen Landwirtschaft* 3 (1801): 89–90. See August Meitzen, *Der Boden und die landwirtschaftlichen Verhältnisse des Preussischen Staates*, 8 vols. (Berlin, 1868–1908), 3: 200–202. Ziekursch, *Hundert Jahre*, 54–55, offers statistics that indicate that the level of indebtedness of estates in Silesia was increasing at a much faster rate than were their price levels during the second half of the eighteenth century.

[10] It is possible to find many more examples. For Silesia, see Ziekursch, *Hundert Jahre*, 23–26; for the Kurmark, see Martiny, *Die Adelsfrage*, 32–33; for a sample of prices from all the provinces, see Leopold Krug, *Betrachtungen über den Nationalreichtum des preussischen Staates*, reprint of 1805 edition by Scientia Verlag (Aalen, 1970), 1: 404–9.

[11] Wilhelm Abel, *Geschichte der deutschen Landwirtschaft vom frühen Mittelalter bis zum 19. Jahrhundert* (Stuttgart, 1967), 331. See also Schissler, *Preussische Agrargesellschaft im Wandel*, 217.

TABLE 1
Inflation Index for Estate Costs in Silesia and Brandenburg

	Silesia	Brandenburg
1740–1760	100	100
1761–1770	117	158
1771–1780	121	183
1781–1790	158	205
1791–1800	203	326
1801–1805	325	494

concerned about the effect of estate transfers on the rural social structure. Frederick William III wrote to "condemn . . . the trading in estates according to which the estates with their subjects [Untertanen] pass from one hand to another and their lords change one after the other."[12] Another contemporary wrote, "The uninterrupted progress in the buying and selling of estates naturally tears the moral connection, built over years of inheritance, between the subject and his lord; both view each other as strangers."[13] Those closer to the situation were even more explicit in describing the effects of estate transfers. One Silesian Landrat commented, "One cannot deny that the accumulation of so many estates in one hand must contribute to the destruction of the lord-peasant relationship. The estate owner learns neither his subjects nor their needs; everything is left to a bribable justiciary and a hard-hearted administrator."[14] Another Silesian Landrat feared the process would destroy the social fabric. He wrote:

After the nobleman for the most part has exchanged the time-honored principle of his forebears, to be a father to his subjects, for the role of a usurer and an estate broker, the condition of the peasantry has grown worse each year. A single individual now owns the property of ten noble families and, in what to him is a trivial business speculation, he trades an estate as quickly as a suit in his wardrobe and, with the estate, unfortunately also the poor peasants, who in the course of a year often have many lords, each of whom demands more of them than the previous master. In this way it is unavoidable that the bond that once intimately united the lord with his peasants is completely dissolved. The peasant loses the sources of his livelihood, for the con-

[12] See the documentation in R. Stadelmann, *Preussens Könige und ihrer Thätigkeit für Landeskultur* (1882; reprint, Osnbrück, 1965), 3: 265.

[13] K. A. Menzel, *Geschichte Schlesiens* (Breslau, 1810), 3: 614–15.

[14] Cited in Ziekursch, *Hundert Jahre*, 60.

tinually changing estate owners think only of how to extract the greatest possible revenue from the estate they have purchased at an exaggerated price; thus, it is natural that all the mainsprings of commercial production are strained in every conceivable way and the peasant, who can find no possible help from such short-term masters, is handled harshly. When the estate has been sucked dry like a lemon, the owner casts it aside and begins this pattern anew on another acquisition. For some years, this spreading brokerage of estates . . . has had the most injurious effects not only on the common man, but on the entire monarchy.[15]

For those nobles who engaged in land speculation, it was difficult and impractical to try to preserve the concept of the estate as a possession of the family to be nurtured for future generations of Hausväter or that it was an "office" bestowing on its owners certain privileges and obligations. Land speculation introduced a new economic variable with which estate owners now had to contend; the market for land drew them more tightly into a society dominated by market relations as land became merely another commodity in which they dealt. One agricultural reporter articulated this new attitude toward land when he wrote the following in 1801: "The noble estates are viewed as a ware in which one deals, for many buy estates, not in order to keep them, but in order to sell them again for a profit."[16]

Because of the emergence of this attitude toward land, noble estate owners who engaged in land speculation frequently found it advantageous to seek permission to sell their estates to non-nobles. Bourgeois buyers usually paid higher prices. After the death of Frederick the Great, restrictions against commoners' buying noble estates were relaxed; if permission was not granted to commoners, they frequently purchased estates through noble straw men.[17] By 1800 approximately 10 percent of all the noble estates in the Prussian provinces were in the hands of commoners.[18] To that number should be added the commoners who were "general leaseholders" (*Generalpächter*) of the crown estates. These royal estates in Prussia amounted to 11 percent of the total usable land; since 1732 only commoners were permitted to lease

---

[15] Ibid., 60. For further discussion of the effects of the market in estates on lord-peasant relationships, see Max Lehmann, *Freiherr vom Stein* (Leipzig, 1903), 2: 55ff.

[16] Seetzen, "Ueber dem Handel mit Landgüter," 90–91.

[17] Martiny, *Die Adelsfrage*, 34–35.

[18] Ibid., 35–36, 114–15; Ziekursch, *Hundert Jahre*, 47–49; Reinhart Koselleck, *Preussen zwischen Reform und Revolution* (Stuttgart, 1967), 83.

them.[19] By 1800 there were about 2,000 commoners leasing or administering royal demesne.[20] Non-noble estate owners and leaseholders were primarily concerned with making a profit on their investments. Leopold Krug observed the following in 1805: "The prosperity of bourgeois and non-noble estate owners and above all the leaseholders of crown lands and other large estates is almost universally recognized in the Prussian provinces, and it has become proverbial in many regions, above all in those in which the land is fertile."[21]

The passage of noble estates into the hands of commoners raised a significant question about the future of the nobility: could the nobility be preserved if severed from its foundation on the land?[22] By the end of the century, this question had become pressing. In 1802, Karl Ernst von Saldern, a nobleman from the Kurmark, requested permission to dismember his estates, distributing them among his peasants on hereditary leasehold. Frederick William III instructed his ministers Eberhard Friedrich Freiherr von der Reck and Otto Karl Friedrich von Voss to examine the implications of such dismemberment and hereditary leasing of noble estates. Nearly all the evidence presented in their reports warned against the dangers that such a process posed for the nobility. Even the moderately liberal finance counselor, August Heinrich von Borgstede, cautioned against terminating the restrictions on the purchase of noble estates by commoners.

If now the nobles are permitted to sell their estates, or are given the right of unrestricted hereditary leasing of them, which would have the same effect, to a large extent the result would be that only the rich and powerful families, whose wealth puts them in such a position, would be able to accumulate many estates . . . while the less wealthy noble, enticed by momentary advantage, would frequently sell or lease his estates and gradually lose his present existence. The noble with money instead of estates, or largely without money if the estates are expended, will be forced to the occupations of the other classes. . . . We cannot recommend such a significant alteration in the structure of the state [*Verfassung*] without a compelling reason.[23]

---

[19] Krug, *Betrachtungen* 1: 341; the cabinet order prohibiting nobles from leasing crown lands was issued on March 23, 1732; it is found in *Acta Borussica, Die Behördenorganisation und die Allgemeine Staatsverwaltung*, ed. Gustav Schmoller, W. Stolze, and Otto Hintze (Berlin, 1894–1910), v/1:386. Hereafter cited as *A.B.B.*

[20] Koselleck, *Preussen zwischen Reform und Re olution*, 84.

[21] Cited in ibid., 84.

[22] See Martiny, *Die Adelsfrage*, 39–40.

[23] Ibid., 41–46.

Reck concluded in a similar vein, "The name of the nobleman without sufficient estates is only a nominal title, a nobleman who lacks the power and the vital interest to fulfill the purpose of the state." Dismemberment of estates and their transformation into hereditary leaseholds parcelled out to peasants would transform the system of Gutsherrschaft into one of *Grundherrschaft*, whereby the estate owners lease their estates rather than administer them directly. It would make the nobility into a *rentier* class and undermine the system of paternalist Herrschaft that shaped its style and rule and its social and political role in the state. Count Finck von Finckenstein, one of the leaders of the aristocracy in the Mark Brandenburg who subsequently became a vigorous opponent of the reforms of Hardenberg, argued that if the sale of an estate to a burgher were unavoidable, the commoner who purchased it should be ennobled in order to preserve the nobility's monopoly of the land. He also suggested that to prevent impoverishment of the nobility nobles be permitted to lease crown lands.[24]

In addition to the manner in which the buying and selling of noble estates undermined the principles of a paternalist ideology of lords and peasants, a second major change in the social relations of Prussia was prompted by the introduction of new agricultural methods during the closing decades of the eighteenth century. The expanding demand for agricultural produce, increasing food prices, and higher land values led to an intensive interest in the improvement of agriculture everywhere in Europe at this time. François Quesnay and the French physiocrats emphasized the primacy of agriculture within a national economy; Johann Heinrich Gottlob von Justi, the leading German cameralist of the period, also devoted much attention to it; Johann Christian Schubart was an early exponent of new agricultural techniques.[25] New treatises on agriculture, the latter-day successors to the Hausväterliteratur of the seventeenth and early eighteenth centuries, offered information on new methods of farming, reorganization of the fields, elimination of the commons, and the improvement of the organization of agricultural labor.[26] Local agricultural societies sprang up in Prussia and began circulating journals devoted to increasing the productivity of the land.[27] Frederick the Great was keenly interested

---

[24] Ibid.

[25] Abel, *Geschichte der deutschen Landwirtschaft*, 282ff.

[26] Theodor Freiherr von der Goltz, *Geschichte der deutschen Landwirtschaft*, 2 vols. (Stuttgart and Berlin, 1902), 1: 358–69; August Skalweit, "Beneckendorff's Oeconomia Forensis," *Zeitschrift für Agrargeschichte und Agrarsoziologie* 1 (1953): 40–55; Blum, *The End of the Old Order*, 247–49.

[27] Von der Goltz, *Geschichte der deutschen Landwirtschaft* 1: 376–77; Johannes Schultze,

in these projects. In order to introduce modern English methods in Prussia, he installed English experts on several royal estates. Both he and Frederick William III endeavored to lease the crown lands only to those who would employ such new methods to improve their yield, and they hoped these prosperous examples would lead private estate owners to introduce similar changes.[28]

However, it was not an easy task to modernize Prussian agriculture. At mid-century, estates were still organized in much the same pattern as they had been since the Middle Ages.[29] Estates were composed of "undivided" and "divided" lands. The undivided lands, or commons (*Gemeinheit*), were composed of pastures or woodlands that were, with certain restrictions, available to all the peasants on the estate. The divided lands fell into two categories. First, there were the small plots allocated to the individual peasants, according to their status; these plots, as we have seen when examining the various categories of peasants in chapter 1, served as vegetable gardens. The second form of divided land, comprising the bulk of the land under cultivation on the estate, consisted of the large open fields (Flur), divided into narrow strips. Some strips were the lord's, others were parcelled out to individual peasants according to their rights and status. Neither the lord's nor the peasants' holdings were consolidated; their strips were scat-

---

"Die märkische Ökonomische Gesellschaft," in *Forschungen zur brandenburgischen und preussischen Geschichte: Ausgewählte Aufsätze* (Berlin, 1964), 231–39. The journals frequently extolled the virtues of the ständisch social structure, preserving morality in the countryside. Schultze cites the following poem from the pages of the journal published in the Mark Brandenburg:

> Ich bin ein Bauernmädchen
> Und liebe meine Stand
> Und bin von meinem Rädchen
> Nie nach Berlin gerannt.
>
> Sein Glanz soll mich nicht rühren
> So viel er Reiz auch hat,
> Die Unschuld nur verlieren
> Kann man in dieser Stadt.

I am a peasant maiden / And am fond of my station / I'll never leave my little spinning wheel / And run off to Berlin. / Its brilliance shall not tempt me / Despite its many charms / One can only lose one's innocence / In a city such as this.

[28] Von der Goltz, *Geschichte der deutschen Landwirtschaft* 1: 453–54; Stadelmann, *Preussens Könige und ihrer Thätigkeit für Landeskultur* 3: 80–90. Friedrich's cabinet order of June 21, 1774, sought to introduce English agriculture into Prussia.

[29] Georg Friedrich Knapp, *Die Bauernbefreiung und der Ursprung der Landarbeiter in ältern Teilen Preussens*, 2 vols. (Leipzig, 1887), 1: 4ff.; Ziekursch, *Hundert Jahre*, 33–39; von der Goltz, *Geschichte der deutschen Landwirtschaft* 1: 447–85.

tered throughout the fields, minimizing the dangers to each if the harvest was poor in certain portions of the estate. One estate owner described the appearance of his estate when he inherited it as follows: "Looking at the map of Stargordt, which was surveyed in 1732, one would think that my ancestors had carefully divided the whole land into narrow strips and dispersed them by casting lots. Thus the fields of lords, clergymen, and peasants were interspersed."[30]

This pattern of scattered holdings made any change from the three-field system of agriculture difficult. Because each open field contained strips belonging to the lord and to individual peasants, no individual, whether lord or peasant, could introduce a new pattern of crop rotation on his strips alone; each was compelled to farm his strips in unison with the others (*Flurzwang*). Any attempt to introduce change encountered the hereditary rights of many peasants; any effort to "separate" the lands of the lord from those of the peasants or the lands of the peasants from one another introduced lacerating disputes over equitable redistributions and eliminated some of the safeguards offered by the pattern of scattered fields. It is not surprising, therefore, that the three-field system still prevailed in most parts of Prussia late in the eighteenth century.[31]

In addition to the difficulties that the distribution of the estate lands posed, the enormously complex mosaic of peasants with different kinds of status and different claims to the land offered a substantial obstacle to change.[32] To end the system of servile labor would require the difficult adjudication of these complex claims. Changes in the organization of the estate would work to the disadvantage of those whose tenure rights were least secure. Division of the commons, for example, often made it impossible for poorer peasants to maintain livestock. Moreover, such changes threatening the well-being of the peasantry ran counter to the government's ostensible aim of protecting the peasantry from expropriation. As we have seen, at the end of the century, the impoverished and landless segments of the population seemed to be growing the most rapidly.

Despite these difficulties, important changes in agricultural produc-

---

[30] Cited in O. Eggert, *Die Massnahmen der preussischen Regierung zur Bauernbefreiung in Pommern* (Cologne and Graz, 1965), 8–9.

[31] Hans-Heinrich Müller, "Die Bodennutzungssysteme und die Separation in Brandenburg vor der Agrarreformen von 1807," *Jahrbuch für Wirtschaftsgeschichte* 3 (1965): 82–96; Ziekursch, *Hundert Jahre*, 33–35; Abel, *Geschichte der deutschen Landwirtschaft*, 306–7.

[32] Knapp, *Bauernbefreiung* 1: 12ff.; Karl Böhme, *Gutsherrlich-Bauerliche Verhältnisse in Ostpreussen während der Reformzeit von 1770 bis 1830* (Leipzig, 1902), 12–47; Ziekursch, *Hundert Jahre*, 77–95; Eggert, *Die Massnahmen*, 22–28.

tion were introduced during the last decades of the century, especially on the royal estates. And changes in one aspect of production often required changes in another. The first innovations, which did not necessitate a redistribution of the land or a reorganization of labor, were usually merely improved versions of the three-field system.[33] New crops were planted in the fallow fields—above all, clover and other fodder crops, the so-called green fallow. By 1800, the fallow land had disappeared in many parts of Prussia. The increased quantity of fodder produced by these new crops made possible the stall-feeding of cattle; the result was an increase in cattle production and, equally important, greater quantities of manure.[34] As the practice of stall-feeding spread, the need for pasture land declined, opening the possibility of the division of the commons. Division of the commons, however, proceeded slowly; by 1775, only about 18 percent of the villages in the Kurmark of Brandenburg had divided their commons.[35]

More common than the division of the commons was the "separation" of those portions of the estate that belonged to the lord from those belonging to the peasants.[36] Some acts of separation had taken place already before mid-century; in 1766, Frederick established the Commission for Separations, charged with overseeing the practice. Separation freed the lord from the necessity of farming his land according to the same pattern as the peasant strips, thus enabling him to introduce new methods. But the process of separating the lands was difficult and proceeded slowly.

Other innovations included different systems of crop rotation; in some areas, a four-field system was used, with greater cultivation of legumes and potatoes. Potatoes became one of the most important new crops during the last decades of the century; in the Kurmark, for example, the potato harvest jumped from 5,862 Scheffel in 1765 to 129,598 Scheffel in 1801.[37] In regions of the Mark Brandenburg, a more complex system of crop rotation, borrowed from Mecklenburg (the Mecklenburg *Koppelwirtschaft*) was used by some. Its cycle involved

[33] Müller, "Die Bodennutzungssysteme und Separation in Brandenburg," 96–99; Abel, *Geschichte der deutschen Landwirtschaft*, 306–10.

[34] Stall-feeding was one of the things that agricultural reformers stressed because they understood that it was essential to other changes. See, for example, Albrecht Thaer, *Annalen der niedersächsischen Landwirtschaft*, vol. 1 (1799), 233ff.; von der Goltz, *Geschichte der deutschen Landwirtschaft* 1: 450.

[35] Abel, *Geschichte der deutschen Landwirtschaft*, 300. See also von der Goltz, *Geschichte der deutschen Landwirtshaft* 1: 406–14.

[36] See Müller, "Die Bodennutzungssysteme und Separation in Brandenburg," 113–21.

[37] F.W.A. Bratring, *Statistisch-Topographische Beschreibung der Gesamten Mark Brandenburg*, ed. Otto Busch und Gerd Heinrich (1804; reprint, Berlin, 1968), 93.

eight to fifteen phases. Although these new systems were common on royal estates and some of the noble estates that had undergone separation, they were by no means universal at the end of the eighteenth century. They were especially uncommon on peasant holdings; in many cases even after separation, through habit and lack of capital necessary to innovate, peasants went back to their old methods.[38] In some cases, however, the peasants were also involved in the introduction of new methods.[39]

New crops and new patterns of cultivation naturally raised problems with the organization of labor. Peasants whose work obligations to their lords had frequently remained unchanged for decades now found new demands which, if they did not require more work, at least often required a different kind of work, which many considered more onerous. Centuries of conflict had made the peasants suspicious of changes introduced by the lords, and they frequently considered new work patterns to increase their compulsory service. As a result, many agricultural innovators considered serfdom a major obstacle to the improvement of agricultural productivity. Serfdom came to be seen by many as too inefficient. Albrecht Thaer, the most important proponent of new agricultural methods in Prussia, advocated the emancipation of the serfs; he claimed to be able to distinguish fields farmed by servile labor from those of free peasants simply by their appearance.[40] A few estate owners liberated their serfs and adopted a system of wage labor; others reduced the work obligations in exchange for increased rents.[41] But most retained serfdom. Between 1798 and 1805, however, peasants on the crown lands were freed from their compulsory labor obligations, were emancipated from their bondage to the land, and gained proprietary rights to the plots of land they held.[42]

The quest for higher yields through new techniques, crops, and in

---

[38] Müller, "Bodennutzungssysteme und Separation in Brandenburg," 116.

[39] Hartmut Harnisch, in *Kapitalistische Agrarreform und Industrielle Revolution* (Weimar, 1984), 48–51, argues persuasively that a number of peasants were interested in improving their lands but were blocked by the lack of capital.

[40] Albrecht Thaer, *Grundsätze der rationellen Landwirtschaft* (Berlin, 1831), vol. 1; Eggert, *Die Massnahmen*, 30.

[41] Hans Haussherr, *Wirtschaftsgeschichte der Neuzeit* (Weimar, 1954), 380, 464; Böhme, *Gutsherrlich-Bäuerliche Verhältnisse*, 14–15; Albrecht Thaer, *Annalen der niedersächsischen Landwirtschaft*, vol. 3 (1801), 204–5.

[42] Otto Hintze, "Preussische Reformbestrebungen vor 1806," in *Geist und Epochen der preussischen Geschichte*, ed. Fritz Hartung (Berlin, 1943), 537 ff.; Knapp, *Die Bauernbefreiung* 1: 108; Friedrich Lüdtke, *Geschichte der deutschen Agrarverfassung* (Stuttgart, 1967), 225–29; Eggert, *Die Massnahmen*, 69–71.

some cases, a new system of labor, brought about changes in the attitude toward land and the whole complex of das ganze Haus. These changes were especially evident in the thought of Thaer.[43] Thaer's interest in agriculture began as an avocation, the result of an experimental garden he developed outside Celle, where he practiced medicine. By the 1790s he was devoting most of his time to agriculture; in 1798, he published a treatise on English agriculture, and the following year he began publishing a small journal advocating new methods of farming. Prior to 1806, however, Thaer's teachings were known primarily among a small circle of enlightened bureaucrats, leaseholders of crown estates, and progressive agriculturists. Frederick William III was sufficiently impressed with Thaer's findings in 1804 to persuade him to move to Prussia, where he was enabled to purchase an estate, Möglin, that would serve both as an experimental farm and an institute for teaching "rational agriculture." Thaer was made a governmental adviser and named to the Prussian Academy of Science.[44] His most important book, *Grundsätze der rationellen Landwirtschaft* (Fundamentals of rational agriculture), appeared between 1809 and 1812.

Thaer considered it imperative that agriculture be viewed from a new perspective. He began his major study of rational agriculture with the words, "Agriculture is a trade [*Gewerbe*] whose purpose is to earn a profit through the production of vegetables and livestock. The greater the profit, the more completely is its purpose fulfilled. The most successful agriculture is that which extracts from this operation the highest, most sustained possible profit according to the relationship of wealth, labor, and circumstance."[45] To achieve this goal, agriculture must be brought under the chastening rationalism of the market economy. Serfdom bound unproductive and unenlightened peasants to the soil and should be abolished. Restrictions on the ownership of noble estates, which prevented those with talent from becoming farmers, should be eliminated. "Those who believe in the duty of the estate owner to manage his estate himself," he wrote, "can base

[43] On Thaer, see the biography by his son-in-law, Wilhelm Korte, *Albrecht Thaer: Sein Leben und Wirken, als Arzt und Landwirth* (Leipzig, 1839); also Walter Simons, *Albrecht Thaer* (Berlin, 1929); Franz Schnabel, *Deutsche Geschichte im neunzehnten Jahrhundert* (Freiburg i. Breisgau, 1929), 1: 464–68, grasps clearly the significance of Thaer's teaching, suggesting it "dealt a death blow to the patriarchal economic ethic." See also Volker Klemm and Günther Meyer, *Albrecht Daniel Thaer: Pionier der Landwirtschaftswissenschaft in Deutschland* (Halle, 1968).

[44] Stadelmann, *Preussens Könige in ihrer Thätigkeit für Landeskultur* 4: 210, 257, 287, 294–96, 324–26, reproduces the correspondence between Thaer and Frederick William III, outlining the conditions offered Thaer upon his immigration to Prussia.

[45] Thaer, *Grundsätze*, 1: 1.

their argument only on a certain strict concept of the feudal system, which currently exists in practically no state in Europe and which has been ousted by the mercantile spirit of the times."[46] Thaer stressed that the successful farmer should expect as much return on his capital invested in land as he would from any other form of investment. To do that, he would have to adopt a more scientific approach; he would have to understand the nature of his soil, the systems and functions of crop rotation, animal husbandry, fertilization, drainage and irrigation, and, not least, bookkeeping.

Thaer's thought thus further undermined the view of a landed estate as familial property and the basis of noble status. His approach owed much to the influence of the French physiocrats and the English economists; his concerns were dictated by the market. Uninterested in the particular tradition of Prussian agriculture or in preserving the structure of rural society, he was willing to impose a foreign model on Prussia because it was more efficient. Fundamentally at odds with the traditional assumptions of the paternalist ideology of the Prussian nobility, his attitudes had much more in common with emergent bourgeois values than they did with the ständisch society of the *ancien régime*.

The Nobility and the Absolutistic State

The Prussian landowning nobility secured its domination of the peasantry, as we have noted in chapter 1, as a result of the political compromise forced on it by the electors of Brandenburg-Prussia during the seventeenth century. Beginning with the Brandenburg Recess of 1653, the electors gradually suppressed the nobility's capacity to obstruct central authority by disbanding or emasculating the provincial diets (*Landtage*) in which the nobility's opposition was commonly expressed. In so doing, the electors gained control of foreign policy, introduced permanent taxes, established a standing army, and began to build up a corps of bureaucratic officials to carry out their policies. The nobility, in turn, obtained official recognition of its absolute power over the peasantry on its estates, secured a monopoly on the ownership of noble estates, and gained control of the institutions of county (*Kreis*) government. This "compromise" between the crown and the nobility had obvious advantages for both parties.[47] The Hohenzollern rulers were granted the opportunity to build a unified state

---

[46] Ibid., 3.

[47] The best description of the "compromise" is in Carsten, *The Origins of Prussia*, 179–228.

out of the far-flung territories that comprised their inheritance; they gradually constructed the state apparatus that established bureaucratic absolutism. The nobility received the freedom to enserf the peasantry further and to exploit the land for its sole advantage.

The compromise was always filled with tension, however, for the interests of the state and those of the nobility did not always coincide. The nobility, for example, did not completely recognize as legitimate the power of the bureaucracy; in the eyes of the nobility, conditioned by its experience in governing its landed estates, political authority rightfully resided only with those who exercised personal authority. Public authority was a reflection of private responsibility; the authoritative structure of the polity should parallel that of the society. The landowning nobles considered the new bureaucratic officials to be interlopers whose political power was divorced from any genuine personal authority.[48]

With its political voice silenced at the provincial level after the decline and disappearance of the provincial diets, the nobility utilized the institutions of the county to assert itself. The chief instrument for the representation of the political views of the nobility became the county assembly (*Kreistag*), which met regularly in all the provinces; the county assemblies became the chief guardians of noble privileges and the means of collective action by the nobility to preserve its control of the land and the peasantry. Through these county assemblies, the nobility continued to exercise some influence at the provincial level as well, frequently frustrating the wishes of the bureaucracy.[49] Although the Brandenburg diet did not meet again after the Recess of 1653, the county assemblies of Brandenburg sent representatives annually to administer the provincial treasury. The importance of this meeting gradually declined, but it continued to meet until the eighteenth century. In the New Mark, the eleven county administrators (Landräte) met annually to discuss provincial affairs. In Further Pomerania, agents of the crown met with representatives of the nobility to discuss tax levies each year.[50] The persistence of these bodies helped the no-

[48] Hans Rosenberg, *Bureaucracy, Aristocracy, and Autocracy: The Prussian Experience, 1660–1815* (Cambridge, Mass., 1958).

[49] A.B.B., VI/1:260–64. Carsten has probably exaggerated the collapse of the corporate influence of the nobility in the face of princely absolutism. There is a great deal of evidence that suggests tht corporate institutions at the local level even gained in vitality through the attacks on the Landtage. See also Kurt von Raumer, "Absoluter Staat, korporativer Libertaet, persönliche Freiheit," *HZ* 183 (1957): 55–96; Fritz Valjavec, *Die Entstehung der politischen Strömungen in Deutschland, 1770–1815* (Munich, 1951), 41–52.

[50] A.B.B., VI/1:347–54, 377–79, 395–98, 415–24, 433–38, 446–52.

bility retain its consciousness as a ruling Stand; although their power was limited, they provided so sufficient a stumbling block to central authority that King Frederick William I felt compelled to warn his successors against them in his last political testament:

> The vassals of the Old Mark are a bad and disobedient group who do nothing good.... My dear successor must keep them under his thumb and not associate with them.... When you command the Landräte to do something of importance or something trifling and they do not obey but argue against it ... you must immediately cashier them and choose new ones from the province whom the nobles do not nominate. This will show that you want to be lord and that they must be vassals and that they must not try to govern together with you.[51]

Despite the obvious tensions between the nobility and the emerging absolutistic state, it was clear that the state was intent on preserving the social structure with the dominant position of the nobility. The power of the absolutistic state was built on the presence of the army, and the army, in turn, reflected perfectly the structure of the society.[52] After the creation of the canton system of recruitment in 1733, the organization of the army and the structure of authority in the countryside were mutually reinforcing. Each regiment drew its recruits from its canton, a district composed of 5,000 hearths for infantry regiments and 1,800 for cavalry regiments. Recruits for the army came largely from the unfree peasantry, noncommissioned officers often from the free peasantry (Kölmer), and the officer corps almost exclusively from the ranks of the landowning nobility. Thus, the structure of domination on the land was perpetuated in the army; the techniques of military command learned by the noble-officer enabled him to militarize his control of the estate, while the traits of subservience and obedience acquired by the peasant-recruit in the army made him a more pliable subject on the land. The military system penetrated deeply into the daily life of the peasant village. Because recruits were furloughed for nine or ten months of the year in peacetime in order to work the fields, attempts to flee the estate to which they were bound were treated as acts of military desertion, so the military authority assisted estate owners in securing the return of runaway peasant-recruits. Some villages were required to provide night watchmen to prevent this "soldier-peasant desertion," as it was called. Peasants had to

---

[51] *A.B.B.*, III:452.

[52] This discussion of the relationship between the military and society is based on the excellent study by Otto Busch, *Militärsystem und Sozialleben im alten Preussen* (Berlin, 1962); on the role of the Landräte in this social-military system, see *A.B.B.*, VI/1:264–67.

be ready at any moment to join in the pursuit of deserters. Villages near garrisons were especially apt to be pressed into service in pursuing deserters and, if it could be shown that peasants had been inattentive in their watch for them, the entire village was subject to a fine of 100 taler. Because recruits could sell their uniforms when they were finished with them, the civilian population was frequently partially clothed with uniforms, giving the villages a military hue. Moreover, the Landräte were largely responsible for collecting the *Kontribution*, the chief tax levied in rural areas and paid by the peasantry, and for quartering troops in the county, if necessary. These powers were in themselves a significant means of social control, and they demonstrate how closely fused the military and social structure had become by the middle of the eighteenth century. This fusion of the military system and the social system meant that a change in one, the emancipation of the serfs, necessitated a change in the other, a reform of the military. This, of course, was to happen after 1806.

Because of the close link between the army and the social system in Prussia, changes in the nature of agricultural production in the eighteenth century were a serious concern to the state. As the expanding markets and higher prices for grain provided the noble landowners with new opportunities for greater profits, many of them responded by appropriating peasant holdings, a practice called *Bauernlegen*. Bauernlegen occurred in a number of ways. In East Prussia, where there were a number of free peasants (Kölmer), the noble estate owners began to buy peasant holdings; of 8,390 peasant farms recorded by the reports of the East Prussian Landräte in 1818, more than 600 had been appropriated by lords before 1806.[53] In other instances, noble owners dislodged a full peasant from his holding and divided it between two or three Büdner or Häusler, who had inferior rights and were compelled to provide more labor service to the lord. Other lords changed hereditary leaseholds (*Erbpachten*) into temporary or lifetime leaseholds (*Zeitpachten*), then proceeded to confiscate the land upon the death of the leaseholder.[54] Because the peasants contributed the bulk of the taxes and supplied the army with its recruits, the crown opposed this practice, which was especially prevalent in Silesia and Pomerania, where the conditions of serfdom were most severe. In 1748–1749, Frederick the Great initiated a policy aimed at preserving the peasantry (*Bauernschutz*). He demanded that all vacant peasant

[53] Hanna Schissler, *Preussische Agrargesellschaft im Wandel*, Kritische Studien zur Geschichtswissenschaft, 33 (Göttingen, 1978), 81.

[54] Peter Schutiakoff, *Die Bauern-Gesetzgebung unter Friedrich dem Grossen* (diss., Strasbourg, 1895), 7–12.

CHAPTER 3

holdings be reported to the government and settled by landless soldiers returning from the war. He ordered a sharp reduction in the number of days per week peasants were compelled to serve their lords and the elimination of the most onerous form of serfdom, Leibeigenschaft. Not only were estate owners who were guilty of Bauernlegen to be fined, but so, too, were the public officials who condoned it.[55] The entire proposal met severe opposition from the nobility; the nobles of Further Pomerania argued that any reduction in peasant services would ruin the nobility.[56] Consequently, the whole project was scuttled.

In 1763, Frederick tried again, this time concentrating on Pomerania. He ordered the elimination of Leibeigenschaft on the crown lands, town estates, and noble estates.[57] Again, he encountered intense opposition. The assembly of nobles in Cammin declared that although the burden of Leibeigenschaft may have been too harsh, they had the right to hold their peasants in this form of bondage. The Stände meeting in Demmin argued that Leibeigenschaft no longer really existed, whereas those gathered in Stettin agreed that Leibeigenschaft should be eliminated but that *Erbuntertänigkeit*, hereditary bondage, should be maintained. This was no concession at all, for there was no qualitative difference between the two.[58] Frederick's program was carried out only in the crown estates; elsewhere in Pomerania, Bauernlegen continued.[59]

The landed nobility of Silesia was even more energetic in blocking royal intervention on behalf of the peasantry. In their endeavor to protect the estate owners in their counties, Landräte consistently lied, falsified reports, and refused to announce royal edicts. In 1753, when several instances of serfs' being sold as chattel came to light, most Lan-

[55] Ibid., 12–15; Knapp, *Die Bauernbefreiung* 2: 37–52; Otto Hintze, "Zur Agrarpolitik Friedrich des Grossen," *FBPG* 10 (1898): 275–309. See especially the documents Hintze published, 294–309.

[56] Oskar Eggert, *Die Massnahmen der preussischen Regierung*, 47.

[57] W. von Brünneck, "Die Aufhebung der Leibeigenschaft durch die Gesetzgebung Friedrich des Grossen und das Allgemeines Landrecht," *Zeitschrift der Savigny-Stiftung für Rechtsgeschichte, Germ. Abt.* 10 (1889): 31.

[58] Leibeigenschaft, literally "ownership of the body," was usually associated with the most severe forms of serfdom; *Erbuntertänigkeit*, hereditary servitude, meant that a man and his children were bound to the service of their master. Thus, the elimination of Leibeigenschaft alone did not constitute a significant step toward the elimination of serfdom. For the objections of the noble estates, see Stadelmann, *Preussens Könige in ihrer Thätigkeit* 2: 104–5; Eggert, *Die Massnahmen*, 53–54.

[59] Hintze, "Zur Agrarpolitik Friedrichs des Grossen," 293. Between 1782 and 1798, 1,346 peasant holdings were absorbed by lords in Pomerania. See Eggert, *Die Massnahmen*, 20–22.

dräte supported the estate owner's right to treat serfs "as with other pieces of property, to sell, trade, or give away."[60] The practice was strictly forbidden, but it continued for years.

Ernst von Schlabrendorff, Frederick's able governor of Silesia, was one of the most vigorous champions of peasant rights. Bauernlegen had become an enormous problem in Silesia, where noble estate owners had seized peasant holdings during the turmoil of the wars or appropriated them if the occupant died during the wars. In June 1764, Schlabrendorff ordered all peasant possessions restored to the status they had in 1723, the first year for which records were available. The Silesian nobles protested so vehemently that the command was reissued as a royal edict the following month. Landlords who failed to comply within one year were to be fined up to 1,000 taler; when that threat failed, Schlabrendorff first doubled the fine, then threatened to quarter troops on the estates of noncompliant nobles.[61] Neither of these actions, however, was completely successful; Schlabrendorff had to rely on Landräte to report offenders and this they rarely did. Attacked by an angry nobility, his authority constantly undermined by recalcitrant Landräte, Schlabrendorff was finally forced from office.[62]

After the death of Frederick the Great, the nobility reasserted its interests more vigorously. A chief target was the Frederician policy of maintaining grain magazines. By purchasing grain in years of plenty and selling it in lean years, the magazines aimed at maintaining a constant supply of grain at a relatively stable price, especially in times of harvest failures. In addition, Frederick carefully controlled the export of grain. Ostensibly intended for the army, the magazines obviously had profound economic consequences for the noble estate owners who produced large amounts of grain. Irritated by the restrictions that held down the price of their products, nobles worked with export dealers and key bureaucrats who advocated free trade to persuade Frederick William II to remove all restrictions. He acceded to their demands. The change was disastrous; the price shot up and Frederick William II later was forced to reimpose restraints on grain exports. But the grain magazine system never again functioned the way it had under Frederick the Great.[63]

---

[60] Cited in Ziekursch, *Hundert Jahre*, 98.

[61] Ibid., 164–69, 170–85, 192–98.

[62] Johann Heinrich von Carmer, who later became chief adviser to Frederick the Great, was largely responsible for Schlabrendorff's dismissal. He criticized Schlabrendorff's methods as "despotic"; Carmer supported reforms that in no way threatened the interests of the landlords. See ibid., 192–98.

[63] For a description of the conflict over the grain magazines after Frederick's death, see

CHAPTER 3

In significant ways, the resistance of the landowning nobility to the effort of the state to protect the peasantry from Bauernlegen was made possible by changes in the nature of the bureaucratic state and by Frederick the Great's own policies in support of the nobility. For example, in the middle of the eighteenth century, the hostility between the nobility and the centralized bureaucracy began to ease. One reason for this was the fact that the bureaucracy, originally established to curtail the independent power of the nobility, began to assume an aristocratic outlook itself. Under Frederick the Great, more officials were drawn from the ranks of the nobility, and commoners were often given patents of nobility for their service in the bureaucracy. The two elites, bureaucratic and aristocratic, began to merge. In his brilliant analysis of this transformation, Hans Rosenberg has concluded the following:

> Thus, the development of the new bureaucracy's sense of social status was largely molded in the image of the aristocratic standards inherited from the *Ständestaat*. Concomitantly, the political mentality of the haughty owners of the supreme courts became more bureaucratic and more Prussian. ... Toward the middle of the eighteenth century, cleavage gave way to a spirit of reasonable, almost amicable cooperation, of live and let live, of give and take. The subtle transmutation had important historic repercussions which greatly aided the resurgence of the nobility as a ruling force in the polity. The appeased and reconciled official elite of the Ständestaat began to amalgamate with the commissioned executives of the absolute monarchy and that recast the structure of the dynastic-aristocratic body politic.[64]

This "resurgence of the nobility as a ruling force in the polity" was also a result of Frederick the Great's endeavor to make the nobles the "foundations and pillars of the state," as he wrote in his political testament. Frederick sanctioned or even encouraged the revival of certain institutions dominated by the nobility at various levels of local government. In 1755 he restored to the county assemblies the privilege, curtailed by his predecessors, of selecting candidates for the post of Landrat.[65] Under Frederick, the noble monopoly over the officer corps in the army grew stronger. The legal reform of his minister, Samuel von Cocceji, assured the noble control of the *Regierungen*, the provincial courts that had played a central role in the political power

---

August Skalweit, *Die Getreidehandelspolitik und Kriegsmagazinverwaltung Preussens 1756–1806. Acta Borussica: Getreidehandelspolitik* (Berlin, 1931), 4: 149–217, 579–99.

[64] Rosenberg, *Bureaucracy, Aristocracy, Autocracy*, 122.

[65] A.B.B., III:267–68.

earlier held by the nobility. After the devastating Seven Years' War, Frederick declared a five-year moratorium on all debts owed by noble estate owners. To provide new capital for agricultural recovery and improvement, he established the Landschaften, the rural credit institutes, in nearly every province.[66] These Landschaften ultimately concerned themselves with far more than agricultural credit; by the end of the eighteenth century, they had assumed the role of representative institutions for provincial nobles. The Landschaften submitted requests, petitions, complaints, and advice to the officers of the central government; they exerted their considerable influence to pressure provincial authorities on numerous matters of economic, social, and political importance.

The powers of these institutions of local government, dominated by the nobility, should not be exaggerated. In most matters, they could never seriously challenge royal authority. Their continued existence, however, served to indicate that royal absolutism in the Prussian ancien régime did not destroy all of the political power of the nobility and that it did not curtail—indeed, it probably even enhanced—the domination of the peasantry by the nobility. Most important, as we shall see, is the fact that they came to the fore once again when, after the defeat of 1806, the central government was in disarray. These institutions, which had preserved the continuity of the noble social position, became the instruments through which the nobility opposed the social reforms initiated by Stein and Hardenberg.

The Allgemeines Landrecht: Between Change and Continuity

By the 1780s, two identifiable currents flowed through Prussian society. One flowed rapidly toward the nineteenth century; it resulted from the changing economic order in Europe, and it opened new markets for the agricultural products of the Prussian provinces east of the Elbe. It brought higher prices for grain and touched off the buying and selling of landed estates in Prussia at an unprecedented scale. This current brought with it demands for a new agriculture and, thereby, for a new system of agrarian labor and social relations. The other current carried more of the past with it; it resulted from the "resurgence of the nobility" in Prussia. The nobility was now able to employ the state more fully to its advantage than at any other time since the middle of the seventeenth century; the nobility could reassert

---

[66] See above, 78–79.

its privileges and control over local affairs, so that it could appropriate peasant farms with relative impunity. At the same time, the nobility chose to view itself in traditional terms, to justify its domination of the peasantry with reference to the idea of paternalism.

The convergence of these two currents is what makes the *Allgemeines Landrecht* (General law code) of the Prussian states, published in 1794, so significant a document. The presence of these two currents in Prussian society has caused some historians to view the *ALR* as the culmination of Frederician Prussia, the last chapter in the social history of the ancien régime.[67] Other historians view it as the beginning of the nineteenth century, a "hint of the future," as one of its authors understood it.[68] In fact, it was both.

Issued during the last decade of the century, the *ALR* summarized and codified the system of social relations that had developed in Prussia since the seventeenth century, and, at the same time, its assumptions opened the doors to the social changes Prussia would undergo during the early nineteenth century. The *ALR* is rather like an archaeological excavation; in it, the historian can discern several different layers, different patterns of thought, some reflecting the traditional structure of society divided by Stände, others revealing the bourgeois society that would emerge. As the landowning nobility opposed its promulgation, it used many of the same weapons and arguments that had been used against centralistic absolutism since the seventeenth century; those arguments, however, no less than the *ALR* itself, contained a "hint of the future," traces of the political conservatism the nobility would espouse in the early nineteenth century.

The *ALR* was the product of Frederick II's desire to reform the legal structure of Prussia. During the early part of his reign, he had commissioned *Grosskanzler* Samuel von Cocceji to reorder the administration of justice by simplifying the cumbersome legal procedures and by drawing up a uniform code of law for the Prussian provinces. Cocceji accomplished the first goal, but his death in 1755 ended plans for the codification of Prussian law.[69] It was not until 1780 that Frederick re-

---

[67] This has been the most common interpretation of the *ALR*. It is the view taken, for example, by Kurt von Raumer, "Absoluter Staat, korporative Libertaet, persönliche Freiheit," 77, when he calls the *ALR* the "late fruit of Frederician absolutism." It is also the general approach taken by Klaus Epstein, *The Genesis of German Conservatism* (Princeton, 1966), 372–87.

[68] This interpretation has been most cogently argued by Koselleck, *Preussen zwischen Reform und Revolution*. For the context of Carl Gottlieb Svarez's phrase "hint of the future," see Koselleck, 44. My analysis owes much to Koselleck.

[69] See Herman Weill, *Frederick the Great and Samuel von Cocceji: A Study in the Reform of*

turned to his project; on April 14, his cabinet order instructed *Grosskanzler* Johann Heinrich von Carmer to prepare a general law code that would eliminate the existing anachronisms and contradictions in the law and synthesize Roman and natural law with the Germanic legal practices in the provinces.[70] The work of preparing the code fell to Carmer's able assistant, Carl Gottlieb Svarez.[71]

Although he was joined by a number of legal experts, most notably Ernst Ferdinand Klein, Svarez himself was primarily responsible for the final shape of the *ALR*. Therefore, it cannot be understood apart from him and his political philosophy. Svarez studied law at Frankfurt on the Oder under Joachim Georg Darjes, a student of the philosopher Christian Wolff. Wolff's ideas appear to have influenced Svarez. Wolff's philosophy was one of the most extreme statements made in Germany both in defense of individual natural rights and on behalf of rigorous monarchical absolutism. Because of his far-reaching view of natural rights, he granted the individual extreme civil liberties, including the right of active resistance against a monarch who violated constitutional and fundamental laws. At the same time, Wolff granted extensive sovereign power to the monarch, including absolute control of the economy and education and the power to assure that his subjects "fulfill their duties toward themselves, toward others, and toward God." Wolff reconciled this peculiar polarity between the individual and the sovereign by insisting that the purpose of the social contract was to provide more than security; it was the duty of the individual to assist others in achieving "whatever is required for life—that is, an abundance of the things which serve the necessities, the comforts, and the pleasures of life and an abundance of the means of felicity." The sovereign was to see that individuals met this obligation; "there would be no right if there were no obligation."[72]

Svarez did not go as far as Wolff; he granted neither the extensive civil liberties to the individual nor the extreme power to the monarch. Like Montesquieu, he believed that natural law was to be found less in abstract formulas than in the reason of humankind, and the positive

---

the *Prussian Judicial System, 1740–1755* (Madison, Wis., 1961); Rosenberg, *Bureaucracy, Aristocracy, Autocracy,* 123–34.

[70] The cabinet order is found in *Novum Corpus Constitutionum Prussico-Brandenburgensium praecipue Monarchicum,* vol. 6 (Berlin, 1781), 1935–44.

[71] The dated but useful biography of Svarez is by Adolf Stölzel, *C. G. Svarez: Ein Zeitbild aus der 2. Hälfte des 18. Jahrhunderts* (Berlin, 1885).

[72] For a splendid brief treatment of Wolff and his place in German political thought, see Leonard Krieger, *The German Idea of Freedom* (Boston, 1957), 66–71. My citations of Wolff are from Krieger. Koselleck also discusses the influence of Wolff in *Preussen zwischen Reform und Revolution,* 54ff.

law must therefore reflect both rationality and the customs, traditions, and culture of each locality.[73] As Svarez wrote to one of the critics of the *ALR*, the Silesian minister of justice Freiherr von Danckelmann, "the legal system of the Wolffians is logical and chiefly influenced by Roman law; the system of the Landrecht is chiefly influenced by German Law."[74]

There are, nevertheless, many similarities between the political thought of Svarez and Wolff. In a state of nature, Svarez believed, every person was born equal and possessed equal rights—one had the right to protect oneself and one's possessions and one was the judge and guarantor of one's own rights.[75] It is instructive, however, to note the heavy emphasis Svarez placed on intellectual and moral freedom as essential to all the other rights. "Man has therefore the natural right to preserve his existence, because it is the only condition according to which he can enjoy all his other properties [*Güter*]; he has the right to enlighten his understanding, to seek truth, and to enlarge the storehouse of his ideas and knowledge; he has the right to maintain his freedom of will and, in his decisions and undertakings, to be deter-

---

[73] Montesquieu influenced the concept of natural law in the late eighteenth century. In *Spirit of the Laws*, book 1, chapter 3, he wrote, "Law in general is human reason, inasmuch as it governs all the inhabitants of the earth: the political and civil laws of each nation ought to be only the particular cases in which human reason is applied. They should be adapted in such a manner to the people for whom they are framed that it should be a great chance if those of one nation suit another." For a discussion of the later, more historical and philosophical view of natural law, in contrast to an older, a more abstract and mathematical view, see two articles by Hans Thieme, "Die Zeit des späten Naturrechts," *Zeitschrift der Savigny-Stiftung für Rechtsgeschichte, Germ. Abt.* 56 (1936); and "Die preussishce Kodifikation," ibid. 57 (1937): 355ff. According to Thieme, Svarez was most concerned that the law code conform to legal traditions in Prussia, not merely to an abstract concept of justice. "Die preussische Kodifikation," 370–72. Svarez once commented, "They [the laws] must not shape things according to theory, but their theory must be shaped according to the nature of things." Cited in Uwe-Jens Heuer, *Allgemeines Landrecht und Klassenkampf* (East Berlin, 1960), 103.

[74] Cited in Thieme, "Die preussische Kodifikation," 366.

[75] Svarez articulated his political philosophy in the lectures on law he presented to the crown prince, *Vorträge über Recht und Staat*, ed. Hermann Conrad und Gerd Kleinheyer (Cologne and Opladen, 1960); see also Gerd Kleinheyer, *Staat und Burger im Recht: Die Vorträge des Carl Gottlieb Svarez vor dem Kronprinzen* (diss., Bonn, 1959); Hermann Conrad, "Die geistigen Grundlagen des Allgemeinen Landrechts für die preussischen Staaten von 1794," *Arbeitsgemeinschaft für Forschung des Landes Nordrhein-Westfalen: Geisteswissenschaft*, Heft 77 (Cologne and Opladen, 1958). Suggestive but tendentious is Heuer, *ALR und Klassenkampf*. Some of the political thought behind the *ALR* was presented by Svarez and Klein for the discussion of the confidential Berlin group, the *Mittwochengesellschaft*. Heuer, 277–82, reproduces Svarez's essay for the Mittwochengesellschaft, "Ueber den Zweck des Staates." In addition, see the discussion in Koselleck, *Preussen zwischen Reform und Revolution*, 25–51.

mined only through the insight of his understanding, not through blind impulses [*Triebe*] or external compulsion."[76]

Because the state of nature was one of confusion and unrest, in which human beings found it difficult to preserve their rights, they joined in a contract with others to form civil society. Then, through a second contract, in which individuals and families agreed to subordinate themselves to a higher authority, they formed the state. The state is thus not of divine creation, nor does it originate in the power of the stronger; it originates in a contract and its authority is limited by that contract. The authority of the state should extend no further than is necessary to fulfill its purpose of maintaining "the security of property and the rights of each individual through the unified strength of all."[77] This means that the individual does not forfeit his or her natural rights upon entry into civil society and the state; the individual submits them to certain restrictions as are necessary for the state to fulfill its purpose of protecting the rights of all. Indeed, the individual even possesses certain "inalienable rights" which the state may not transgress; but as one might gather from Svarez's definition of natural rights, the inalienable rights reside in the realm of spiritual and moral freedom, not in the realm of action. In times of emergency, the state may call upon the individual to sacrifice all rights, even life, but never moral freedom.[78] In his lectures to the crown prince, which elaborated his political thought, Svarez repeated the message of Frederick the Great: "The despot says: 'Do not think [*räsoniere*].' The sovereign says: 'You may think, only obey.'"[79] Thus, Svarez stopped far short of Wolff; he denied the subject any right of resistance to absolute authority; he also denied the ruler the right to intrude into all aspects of the subject's life.

The *ALR* expressed this attempted balance between individual and sovereign. It acknowledged a person's natural rights and the function of the state in protecting them. All individuals, including unborn children, possessed the "general rights of man." "The general rights of man are founded on the natural freedom to be able to seek and promote his general welfare without injuring the rights of others," stated the introduction to the *ALR*.[80] Each inhabitant of the state was justified in securing them "through his own power," that is, by returning to a state of nature, only in cases in which the power of the state was un-

---

[76] Svarez, *Vortäge über Recht und Staat*, 455.
[77] Ibid., 464–65.
[78] Ibid., 585–86; see also Conrad, "Die Geistigen Grundlagen," 23–26.
[79] Svarez, *Vorträge über Recht und Staat*, 587.
[80] *ALR*, Einleitung, #83; see also 1/1/#10; Hattenhauer, 54–55.

available.[81] The power of the monarch was also limited; in an earlier version of the code, Svarez had eliminated the *Machtsprüche*, the right of the king to intervene arbitrarily in judicial proceedings, but he was forced to restore it in the final draft of the *ALR*. Still, moral and spiritual freedom were secure from the intrusion of the king; "each inhabitant of the state must be permitted a complete freedom of belief and of conscience," declared the *ALR*.[82]

In addition to the natural rights individuals retained in civil society, they acquired certain new rights and obligations from civil society, based not on natural law, but on the needs of civil society. These rights and obligations were the result of the positive law of civil society and thus legitimized the inequalities that existed in the social order. "Every difference in rights which originates merely from birth," Svarez instructed the crown prince, "is not founded on the laws [*Rechte*] of nature, . . . but only on the positive legislation [*Gesetze*] of the state."[83]

This was Svarez's most important formulation, for it enabled him to reconcile a natural-rights political philosophy with the manifest social and legal inequities of the Prussian ancien régime. It points up two things. First, it shows how much Svarez's legal theory owed to existing laws in Prussia and how unwilling he was to move beyond the framework of tradition. Second, it demonstrates the continuing vitality of the ständisch ethos embedded in Prussian society. Indeed, the entire outline of civil society offered by the *ALR* is built on the ständisch scheme. It declares the following: "Through nature or legislation, or both together, civil society consists of many small, connected societies [*Gesellschaften*] and Stände. . . . The member of each Stand as such, considered individually, has certain rights and duties."[84]

At this level, the *ALR* was an extremely conservative document, retaining most of the essential elements of a status society. Rights and duties were not accorded to individuals, but to members of the corporate groups, above all, the traditional Stände—nobles, burghers, and peasants. The freedom of the vast majority, the peasantry, was qualified by countless stipulations of the *ALR*, some of which contained astounding contradictions. "Except for the relationship to the estate to which they are bound, subject persons [*Untertanen*] are viewed as free citizens of the state. . . . They may not leave the estate to which they are bound without the permission of their lord."[85] Their

---

[81] *ALR*, Einleitung, #76, 77, 78; Hattenhauer, 53.
[82] *ALR*, II/11/#2; Hattenhauer, 543.
[83] Svarez, *Vortäge über Recht und Staat*, 261–62.
[84] *ALR*, I/1/#2–7; Hattenhauer, 55.
[85] *ALR*, II/7:1/#1, 2; Hattenhauer, 433. *ALR*, II/7:4/#147, 150; Hattenhauer, 438.

labor was unfree; work obligations were reinforced by the strength of the written code. "As a rule, the subjects who are obligated to service are bound to perform all forms of transport and hand labor that are required for the agricultural utility of the lord's estate."[86] Moreover, the market for land was as constrained as the market for labor. "Only the noble is permitted the ownership of noble estates."[87] And finally, the most substantial concession the *ALR* granted to traditional society was the fact that it was not intended to supplant provincial law, but to operate only in a subsidiary capacity, effective only when provincial law was unclear or nonexistent, as in the case of newly acquired territories.[88]

At another level, however, the *ALR* undermined the status society that it appeared to reinforce. It acknowledged that the ständisch structure was not natural; rather, ständisch differentiations were artificial products of civil society. These differentiations existed to facilitate the achievement of the objective of civil society—the maintenance of domestic peace and the preservation of property. The implications of this were clear; if the ständisch structure failed in these objectives, or if it interfered in the achievement of them, it could be altered. The privileges of the nobility were civil rights, not natural rights, and they might be abrogated by the state if necessary. At the same time, the Stände were defined not only in terms of birth, but also in terms of occupation, that is, their role within civil society.[89] The duty of a person, his or her role in civil society, was determined by the needs of the state. As those requirements changed, so might obligations. And there is ample evidence that both Svarez and his collaborator, Klein, had already begun to reexamine the relationship of serfdom to the function of the state. In a group of essays on freedom and property published in 1790, Klein favored the abolition of serfdom and the creation of a free market for labor, so "that a man will choose, when he may, that occupation which pays better." The entire economy would improve. Svarez came to the same conclusions more slowly, but in 1796 he too advocated the abolition of hereditary serfdom. Moreover, Svarez showed his preference for free economic relationships when he told the crown prince that the practice of *Fideikommiss*, a form of entail allowed the nobility that removed land from the market and rendered it virtually unmortgageable, should be discouraged because such entail

---

[86] *ALR*, II/7:6/#308–13; Hattenhauer, 443–44.
[87] *ALR*, II/9#37; Hattenhauer, 535; see also II/7:3/#91, 92; Hattenhauer, 436.
[88] *ALR*, Einleitung, #1, 2; Hattenhauer, 51.
[89] *ALR*, I/1#6; Hattenhauer, 55; on this point see also Koselleck, *Preussen zwischen Reform und Revolution*, 74–75.

forestalled the modernization of agriculture and the development of the economy.[90]

The *ALR* undermined ständisch institutions in other significant ways as well. For example, it made virtually no mention of the political role played by ständisch institutions at the county and provincial level, a glaring omission from so comprehensive a document. The Stände described by the *ALR* bore no connection with local institutions; the broad categories of peasant, burgher, and noble were supraprovincial, defining the subject's relationship with others in the state and with the head (*Oberhaupt*) of state. Furthermore, the traditional division of society into three Stände no longer sufficed to describe Prussia at the end of the eighteenth century; the authors of the *ALR* found it necessary to give special attention to the ständisch privileges and obligations of the "servants of the state"—the military, church authorities (*Geistlichen*), and teachers.[91] It introduced three distinct categories of burghers: those who enjoyed special legal privileges and "dignities" (*Eximirte*), ordinary burghers, and burghers with a dependent status (*Schutzverwandte*).[92] It interlaced the ständisch society with categories that corresponded more to class than to status; indeed, in a surprising number of instances, the *ALR* used the term *class* to describe groups of subjects.[93]

The Stände dominated by the nobility attacked the proposed law code precisely because they thought it would erode the foundation of their existence. In fact, they used the occasion to reassert their role in the legislative process. Already in 1780, shortly after the plans for the new code became known, deputies of the "great committee" of the Landschaft of the Mark Brandenburg, which had assumed many of the functions of a provincial diet, demanded that they be permitted to cooperate in the preparation of the code. Carmer did not object, for Frederick II had intended that the Stände be consulted; he did, however, insist that the Stände be allowed to offer suggestions only after a draft of the code had been prepared, thus ensuring that his justice department would retain command.[94] After coming to the throne in

---

[90] Ernst Ferdinand Klein, *Freyheit und Eigenthum, abgehandelt in acht Gesprächen uber die Beschlüsse der französischen Nationalversammlung* (Berlin and Stetten, 1790), 23; Stölzel, *Svarez*, 155, 421; Svarez, *Vorträge über Recht und Staat*, 338–40.

[91] On this point see Koselleck, *Preussen zwischen Reform und Revolution*, 73–74, 76.

[92] *ALR*, II/8:1/#1–12; Hattenhauer, 452–53.

[93] *ALR*, II/7:2/#23; Hattenhauer, 433; *ALR*, II/8:1/#50; Hattenhauer, 454; *ALR*, II/10/#52; Hattenhauer, 539; *ALR*, II/14/#3, 4, 7, 78; Hattenhauer, 590, 593; *ALR*, II/17:2/#130; Hattenhauer, 624.

[94] Günter Birtsch, "Gesetzgebung und Repräsentation im späten Absolutismus," *HZ* 208 (1969): 270–73.

1786, Frederick William II issued a cabinet order instructing Carmer to convene a conference of deputies from all of the provincial Stände in order to discuss the proposed code. In these deliberations, he declared, "all obstinacy, partisanship, or stubborn persistence in certain preconceived opinions must be set aside" and the code must represent "the wishes and convictions of a majority of the Stände and the nation."[95] The conference was planned for 1789, but after the outbreak of the French Revolution, such a meeting of the Stände was no longer considered opportune; no general conference was held.[96] As believers in enlightened despotism, the authors of the *ALR* felt such a conference was unnecessary; Klein wrote in 1790, "These laws may be given by the prince or by a national assembly; they contain the will of the individual only insofar as they are reasonable and further his own interest."[97]

Through the various ständisch institutions that had survived in the provinces, however, the nobility launched an attack on the proposed code. The arguments varied. Some did not deserve serious consideration. The spokesmen from the Old Mark of Brandenburg, for example, considered as "incitement to sin" the financial support peasant girls would now be able to claim from young noblemen who made them pregnant. Or the representatives from Silesia suggested that the code should not be promulgated publicly, or if it were, only in Latin, because it might cause unrest among the peasantry.[98]

Others attacked the failure of the government to consult the local assemblies formally. Count Friedrich Ludwig von Finckenstein, from the Kurmark, went so far as to question the applicability of the code in the provinces because the provincial diet had not been convened and was not consulted. Indeed, the most persistent complaint of the nobility was the failure of the code to provide a permanent place for provincial diets in the legislative structure. Representatives from Minden-Ravensberg declared that every new law should have not only its advice, but also its consent, "as is in keeping with constitutional practice everywhere in Germany where provincial diets are to be found." Representatives of the Kurmark demanded a restoration of the guarantee of the Recess of 1653, that the provincial diet would have the right to "concur in the legislation." Others demanded the institution-

---

[95] *Novum Corpus Constitutionum Prussico-Brandenburgensium praecipue Monarchicum*, vol. 8 (Berlin, 1790), 147.
[96] Epstein, *Genesis of German Conservatism*, 381.
[97] Klein, *Freyheit und Eigenthum*, 169.
[98] Birtsch, "Gesetzgebung und Repräsentation," 290; Koselleck, *Preussen zwischen Reform und Revolution*, 138.

CHAPTER 3

alization and regularization of consultations between the government and the estates.⁹⁹

In a fundamental way, however, the most penetrating critique of the proposed law code appeared to be the most self-seeking. Landrat von Ostau, from East Prussia, objected to the code's few provisions, which limited, however slightly, the authority of the lords over their serfs. Significantly, he argued that the inequality between a serf and his lord was not merely the artificial creation of civil society, as suggested by the proposed code. This inequality was a product of "nature and necessity." The relationship between lord and peasant was as natural "as that between parents and children." The "mutual well-being" of both lord and peasant, brought about "through love and reciprocal trust," would be destroyed if the authority of the "parents" over the "children" were limited and "the rod for chastising their children were taken from their hands." This argument, insisting that inequality was natural, in the nature of things, was repeated in numerous other comments of noblemen. It was a clear, formal expression of the paternalist ideology that grew out of the social relations that prevailed on the land.¹⁰⁰

Most of the objections of the provincial nobility were ignored by the framers of the *ALR*, but they had their effect on Frederick William II, who canceled its promulgation in 1792. After twelve years of labor, it appeared the code would never become law. In an angry letter to the king, Carmer denounced "all the insinuations that have been made to Your Royal Majesty from some few who proceed with heads filled with an aristocratic form of government, who intend first to postpone the event, then after awhile to bury it, and in such a way bring their own plans and presumptions into being."¹⁰¹ Continued legal confusion, exacerbated by the desire to Germanize the legal practices in the newly acquired Polish territories, caused Frederick William to reverse himself, and a slightly modified version of the code became the law of the Prussian states on June 1, 1794. Although it provided the essential framework for Prussian law until 1918, it underwent essential revisions, the most important of which began only a few years after its promulgation, when the reforms of Stein and Hardenberg were introduced.

⁹⁹ Birtsch, "Gesetzgebung und Repräsentation," 282, 285–88.
¹⁰⁰ Ibid., 288–89.
¹⁰¹ Cited in Heuer, *ALR und Klassenkampf*, 201.

4

THE REFORM ERA
AND THE POLITICS OF THE NOBILITY

The Collapse of Prussia, the Reformers, and the Stände

The defeat of the Prussian army at Jena and Auerstädt on October 14, 1806, brought an end to the ancien régime in Prussia. By the end of October, the main contingents of the army had surrendered, the garrisons had capitulated with astonishing alacrity, the king and his advisers had fled to Königsberg and later to Memel, and Napoleon had occupied Berlin. Through an alliance with Russia, Prussia prolonged the hostilities until the spring of 1807, but the defeat of the Russians at Friedland on June 14 left Prussia no alternative but to accept the harsh stipulations of the Peace of Tilsit. The Prussia of Frederick the Great disappeared. The treaty stripped Prussia of most of its Polish provinces and all of its territories west of the Elbe, reducing the state to its four eastern provinces of Brandenburg, Pomerania, Silesia, and Prussia. It called for the occupation by French troops of the entire region west of the Vistula River pending Prussia's payment of a substantial indemnity, later set at 120 million francs.[1]

The flight of the court from Berlin signaled the disintegration of central bureaucratic authority in Prussia. The officials who remained behind swore oaths of allegiance to Napoleon. The terms of the Treaty of Tilsit left Frederick William III in direct control only of the administration of East Prussia and the county of Glatz in Silesia. In the provinces occupied by the French, Prussian officials were left only in charge of the church, the schools, and the administration of justice; all other matters fell directly under French jurisdiction.[2]

Economic disorder accompanied military defeat and administrative disintegration. Much of the land suffered severe damage from the war; villages were destroyed and livestock was either killed or requisitioned by the armies that traversed the landscape. Economic collapse continued after the end of the war. During the period of official French occupation, from August 1807 to December 1808, the French

---
[1] Hajo Holborn, *A History of Modern Germany* (New York, 1966), 2: 384–85.
[2] Rudolf Ibbeken, *Preussen 1807–1813* (Cologne and Berlin, 1970), 95.

CHAPTER 4

requisitioned 108,802 draft horses and the services of 54,000 farm workers (Knechte) from the Kurmark in Brandenburg.[3] Moreover, by forcing Prussia into the continental system, Napoleon eliminated the English market, destroying the price of grain. The inflated land values of the decades before 1806 collapsed and numerous estates were threatened with bankruptcy. According to one report, "The landowners cannot raise the interest for the capital investment in their devastated estates; therefore, the mortgage notes [Pfandbriefe], heretofore a valued means of exchange, have fallen to as much as one-third their face value."[4] The cities fared no better. Hunger, epidemics, and poverty brought much higher death rates, especially among infants. In Berlin, during 1807 and 1808, 5,846 children were born and 4,300 died. The suicide rate climbed from six to ten cases per week in Berlin and Potsdam. Johann August Sack, the governor of Brandenburg, offered this dismal report: "We are not exaggerating the facts when we maintain that many poor people, such as the subaltern officials and the pensioners, have sold their furniture down to their last beds, and some have perished from hunger and despair."[5] From this economically prostrate state, the administration had to find a way to pay the large French indemnity.

The military disaster and the subsequent collapse of the Prussian state presented an opportunity for reform bureaucrats to initiate a program intended to modernize the administrative structure of the state, introduce legislation to reform the social and political constitution, and emancipate the economy from the remaining fetters of feudalism. All of this was made more imperative by the financial burdens of the French indemnity, which required that the state maximize its productive capacity. At the same time, however, the downfall of the state also gave new impetus to the ständisch institutions of local government dominated by the nobility. These local institutions, driven to the periphery of political influence during the preceding century and a half, became more prominent after 1807. The utter collapse of the central administration during the French occupation gave new importance to the ständisch bodies of the credit institutes (Landschaften). Napoleon saw them as the proper agencies for raising the military contributions he demanded from the occupied provinces; in some

[3] Ibid., 92; M. F. von Bassewitz, *Die Kurmark Brandenburg im Zusammenhang mit den Schicksalen des Gesammtstaats Preussen während der Zeit vom 22. Oktober 1807 bis zu Ende des Jahres 1808. Von einem ehemaligen höhern Staatsbeamten* (Leipzig, 1851–1852), 2: 601ff.

[4] Cited in Ibbeken, *Preussen 1807–1813*, 93.

[5] Hermann Granier, *Berichte aus der Berliner Franzosen Zeit*, Publikationen aus den Preussischen Staatsarchiven, 88 (Leipzig, 1913), 41; Ibbeken, 94.

areas, committees of the provincial Stände took over important financial operations, negotiated loans, and even issued paper money, usually with the approval of the remaining bureaucratic authorities, and occasionally even in opposition to them.[6] The reassertion of these ständisch bodies after 1807 provided the institutional framework for the noble resistance to many reforms.

A collision between the reform bureaucrats and the conservative nobility, entrenched in the revitalized Stände, was almost unavoidable. The two overriding problems confronting the reformers were the disintegration of administrative authority and the economic crisis; these problems were closely connected and their solutions were intertwined. The reformers were convinced that confidence in the administrative authority of the state could be restored only through some system of popular representation. Only by allowing the participation of the population at all levels of government could the state develop the strength and self-assurance necessary to rid itself of the French occupation. Yet such representation was impossible without the principle of free citizenship, which required the elimination of privileges, legal inequalities, and the more obvious instruments of noble superiority in Prussia. Economic recovery was also essential; for the reformers, the economic equivalent and prerequisite of free citizenship was the creation of a free market for labor and land. A free economy would be more productive and efficient. Moreover, it would provide greater revenues for the state. Hardenberg, for example, argued for free peasant ownership of farms, the elimination of the peasants' servile obligations, "the abolition of their drudgery," because it would produce an annual increase of four million taler in state revenue.[7] The reformers considered the participation of citizens in the governmental process to be the most important goal of administrative reform; a precondition of that participation, however, was an economic reform that would change the structure of Prussian society. A difficulty for the reformers was that the traditional Stände, revitalized by the French occupation, now

---

[6] Bassewitz, *Die Kurmark Brandenburg . . . während der Zeit vom 22. Oktober 1807 bis zu Ende des Jahres 1808* 2: 12; Otto Schönbeck, "Der kurmärkische Landtag vom Frühjahr 1809," *FBPG* 20 (1907): 2–3; Klaus Vetter, *Kurmärkischer Adel und preussische Reformen*, Veröffentlichungen des Staatsarchivs Potsdam, 15 (Weimar, 1979), 36–37. For a discussion of the manner in which the ständische institutions of the Landschaften were revitalized by the actions of the French, see Herbert Obenaus, *Anfänge des Parlamentarismus in Preussen bis 1848* (Düsseldorf, 1984), 52ff.

[7] For a discussion of Hardenberg's economic views and the question of peasant emancipation, see Hans Hausherr, *Hardenberg: Eine Politische Biographie* (Cologne and Graz, 1965), 3: 238ff.; Peter G. Thielen, *Karl August von Hardenberg* (Cologne and Berlin, 1967), 309ff.

CHAPTER 4

asserted that they were the proper institutions of representation; because they were dominated by the nobility, these estates naturally opposed many of the reforms aimed at creating free citizens. In sum, to achieve their goal of a constitutional state of free citizens, the reformers had to depend on, or to overcome, representative bodies drawn from those elements of the society that were most resistant to change and that had regained some of their former strength since the collapse of the Frederician state. The task was extraordinarily difficult.

Stein approached the task of reform with pragmatic assumptions. He objected to abstract theories of government and dismissed political philosophers as "metaphysicians"; he once remarked that the science of statecraft was the science of cunning (*Pfiffologie*).[8] He often used the vocabulary of the Enlightenment, as when he described the Emancipation Edict as the "first fundamental law of our state, our *habeas corpus* act," expressive of the "original and inalienable rights of humanity."[9] But his conception of the reforms was always tempered by practicality: emancipation would increase agricultural productivity, local government would save the state money, and full representation would have to wait until the citizenry was "habituated" to self-government. He was most critical of the Prussian bureaucracy. Officials, he charged, governed with a "machinelike mentality," a "spirit of hirelings," remote from the people they governed. The bureaucracy too often possessed an "ignorance of the district it administered," an "indifference, often a ridiculous antipathy" toward its subjects, and a "fear of change and innovation that might increase its work."[10] Stein repeatedly stressed the link between administrative reform and the development of representative institutions. His emphasis throughout was on the phrase "participation in the administration" (*Teilnahme an der Verwaltung*).[11] This would give the citizens a stake in the future of the state and draw the bureaucracy closer to the needs and aspirations of the people. He wrote the following in his famous Nassau Memorandum:

If the property owner is excluded from all participation in the provincial administration, then the bond that binds him to the fatherland remains unutilized, the knowledge which the relationships with his

[8] See the assessment of Stein made by his coworker Theodor von Schön, *Aus den Papieren Theodor von Schön* (Berlin, 1875), 1: 54.
[9] Erich Botzenhart and Walter Hubatsch, eds., *Freiherr vom Stein* (Stuttgart, 1969), II/2:990.
[10] Botzenhart, *Stein*, II/1:389.
[11] Ibid., II/1:390, 393, 395 (in the Nassau Memorandum); II/2:852, 854, 990. Subsequent page numbers referring to volume 2 of *Stein* are given in the text in parentheses.

properties and his fellow citizens provide for him remains unproductive. His desires for improvement, for the redress of the grievances that oppress him, are weakened or overcome, and his leisure time and the talents which, under other circumstances, he would gladly devote to the state, are wasted on other kinds of pleasures or idleness. If the property owner is prevented from participating in the administration, the civic spirit [*Gemeingeist*] and the spirit of the monarchy are killed; exclusion nourishes opposition to the government, complicates the task of the bureaucracy, and increases the cost of administration. (II/1:389–90)

Stein's example for this "participation in the administration" was England. In the Nassau Memorandum, he cited the study by Count Ivernois on public administration in England, which, Ivernois suggested, was inexpensive because the local communities were willing to bear the cost of an administration in which they participated. In his report to the king on November 23, 1807, Stein stated that the "chief point of view from which the plan of reorganization proceeds" was the desire to reduce the high cost of administration that resulted from the intrusion of "ignorant" and "indifferent" paid officials into local affairs (II/2:500–506). The existing bureaucratic hierarchy should be replaced, or at least supplemented, by a system that gave representation to local property owners. Participation, however, should not be limited to noble landowners but should extend to all the propertied classes. "We must not replace the bureaucracy," he wrote in the Nassau Memorandum, "with a miserable and weak structure based on the domination of a few estate owners, but we must involve in provincial affairs an assembly of significant property owners of all types, whereby all are bound to the state with equal obligations and equal rights" (II/1:393). In fact, the monopoly of rights exercised by noble estate owners through their police and judicial authority would have to be broken before any genuine sense of citizenship could develop (II/2:886, 904).

Stein's plans called for the participation of "elected officials" at various levels of government. In the local communities, rural and urban, he hoped for the broadest exercise of authority by elected representatives of the property owners; at the intermediate or provincial level, he intended to draw representatives of the estates into the administration; and at the ministerial level, he wanted technical advice from representatives of the estates as members, for example, of the commission that drafted legislation (*Gesetzkommission*) (II/2:532). His ultimate objective was a system of "national representation." "Every active citizen of the state, whether he possesses a hundred peasant plots [Hufen] or one, whether he is engaged in agriculture or manufacturing or trade, whether he has a bourgeois occupation or is united with the state through spiritual [geistige] bonds, has the right to representation" (II/ 2:990). On the other hand, he also said, paradoxically, that he considered the expression "representatives" to be unsuitable. "The deputies of the provincial estates" were to be regarded "really as officials, not as representatives of the people" (II/2:835). They were to act as counselors, bringing insight and information to the administration, enabling it to govern more intelligently.

This emphasis on participation in the administration blurred the distinction between the executive and the legislative process. The same attitude was carried forward by Hardenberg. He made it clear that the Assembly of Notables that he convened in 1811 was to have only consultative power: "The new institution . . . must emanate directly from the government alone; it must come as a welcome gift from above. . . . It can only be advisory, otherwise . . . the monarchical form of government would be impaired."[12] There was an inherent contradiction between the reformers' desire to create institutions representative of the popular will and their insistence that those institutions should not impinge in any way on the autonomy of administrative authority.

This contradiction was compounded by the fact that, although deputies or officials were to be elected by all property owners of the provinces, they were still to be elected by the Stände. As a liberal, Stein believed it necessary to base the right of representation on property, including the right of an individual to regard his or her own person and labor as property. A precondition of this representation, however, was the success of the social and economic reforms—the emancipation of property and persons. Stein still thought in terms of a society di-

---

[12] Cited in Walter Simon, *The Failure of the Prussian Reform Movement, 1807–1819* (Ithaca, N.Y., 1955), 62–63. Hardenberg was less interested even than Stein in any genuine form of representation; he considered it the responsibility of the "representatives" to bring their insight to the government and to carry the views of the government back to the people. Herbert Obenaus points out that the French experience with the Estates-General of 1789 always worried authorities when discussions of representation were undertaken. He argues that this was typical of the era of transition from absolutism to constitutionalism, so that there was frequently an effort to integrate the Stände into the administration, where they could be limited and controlled. Herbert Obenaus, "Die Immediatkommission für die ständische Angelegenheiten als Instrument der Preussischen Reaktion im Vormärz," in *Festschrift für Heinrich Heimpel*, Veröffentlichungen des Max-Planck-Instituts für Geschichte (Göttingen, 1971), 1: 410. Obenaus has done the most comprehensive study of representative institutions in Prussia. See *Anfänge des Parlamentarismus*; see also his "Verwaltung und ständische Repräsentation in den Reformen des Freiherrn vom Stein," *Jahrbuch für die Geschichte Mittel- und Ostdeutschlands* 18 (1969): 130–79.

vided into Stände, an assumption that enhanced the authority of the preexisting and revived estates of the provinces. Thus, although property was to be the basis, the ständisch system still provided the framework for representation. In fact, few of the preconditions necessary for a system of representation based only on property existed. The status of the "emancipated peasantry" remained ambiguous, as we shall see, after 1807; when subsequent "regulations" pertaining to the peasantry were issued in 1811 and 1816, it became clear that few peasants actually were free property owners. Thus, by preserving the Stände as the basis for representation without creating a free peasantry, genuine citizenship never evolved, and the system actually reinforced the position of the landowning nobility. Indeed, the only administrative reform that introduced a degree of representation and self-government was the municipal ordinance, and that primarily because administrative reform was coordinated with economic reform, freedom for the trades (*Gewerbefreiheit*), and because it embraced only one Stand as defined by the *ALR*, the Bürgerstand.

Stein's comments on Karl von Rehdiger's proposals for a system of national representation for Prussia illustrate the difficulties the reformers encountered in trying to create such a system. Stein recognized that any system of representation would have to displace the domination of the nobility in the ständisch institutions inherited from the past. "The nobleman is a burden for the nation," he wrote, "because he is numerous, for the large part, poor, and demanding of allowances, privileges, and preferences of every sort. A result of his poverty is his lack of education . . . and incapacity for higher positions." Stein's hopes for a system of representation required a reduction in the number of noble families and an official recognition of only a limited number of rich nobles. These nobles could be trained for service and seated in an upper chamber, along with other citizens of great wealth, insight, or service to the state. This was never accomplished, and representation still lay in the hands of the traditional nobility.[13]

The integral relationship of the financial problems of the state, the plans for representative provincial bodies, and the reinvigorated position of the noble estates can be seen in the diet of the East Prussian credit institute (Landschaft) that Stein convened in February 1808.[14]

---

[13] Botzenhart, *Stein*, II/2:852–56. Rehdiger was a Silesian estate owner. For a discussion of Rehdiger's proposals and Stein's reactions, see Obenaus, *Anfänge des Parlamentarismus*, 38–40.

[14] Botzenhart, *Stein*, II/2:562, 579, 580–81, 642. Stein made it clear that the diet would have only advisory powers; see ibid., 629. Gerhard Ritter, *Stein: Eine politische Biographie*, 3d ed. (Stuttgart, 1958), 275–77.

CHAPTER 4

This diet was broadened beyond the nobility to include free peasants (Kölmer); future East Prussian diets were also to include burghers. The assembly had many characteristics of a modern system of representation; the representatives were to vote as individuals and, free from instructions from their counties, to vote their convictions. But the role of the diet was largely consultative. It was called to approve two proposals of the government for raising revenue. One proposal would set aside the prohibition against the alienation of royal estates. According to the plan, the East Prussian Landschaft was to issue mortgage notes (Pfandbriefe) against the value of the royal estates; these notes would be sold or delivered directly to Napoleon. They would then be redeemed through the gradual sale of crown lands. The second proposal called for the enactment of a general income tax for East Prussia. After some hesitation, the diet approved both proposals; it then approved the creation of the standing Committee of the Stände as the representative body of the province when the diet was not in session.[15]

East Prussia was the only province over which the central administration retained control during Stein's tenure of office. Although it was expected that representative assemblies in the other provinces would be built on the East Prussian model, they never were. Governor von Massow, in Silesia, had little desire to include the peasantry, and Sack, the governor of Pomerania and Brandenburg, faced a strong and determined nobility. When the diet of the Kurmark of Brandenburg met, beginning on February 27, 1809, to consider the same proposals that had been submitted to the Estates in East Prussia, the nobility was clearly in charge. After considerable discussion and some opposition, the diet agreed to issue the government 8.5 million taler in mortgage notes against royal estates valued at 12 million. The diet also approved an income tax, but unlike that of East Prussia, the tax in Brandenburg was clearly framed in the interest of the nobility, which paid at a lower rate than the peasantry.[16]

It is evident that the financial requirements of the government had a deleterious impact on the political and social reforms. The need for revenue forced the government to tolerate the perpetuation of assemblies of estates dominated by the nobility, rather than along the lines of representation originally envisaged. Belatedly, Count Alexander von Dohna, who followed Stein as minister of interior, realized that

[15] Max Hein, *Geschichte der ostpreussischen Landschaft von 1788 bis 1888* (Königsberg, 1938), 39–45; Simon, *Failure of the Prussian Reform*, 31.
[16] Otto Schönbeck, "Der kurmärkische Landtag vom Frühjahr 1809," 1–103; Klaus Vetter, *Kurmärkischer Adel und preussische Reformen*, 36–43.

any reorganization of the system of representation would have to be introduced without the estates or against them, otherwise they "would merely advance their corporate interests in the fashion of a party."[17] Indeed, this statement could be applied to all of the proposals for reform.

THE EMANCIPATION EDICT

The Emancipation Edict of October 9, 1807, was the first and most important legislative decree of the reform era in Prussia. Although its enactment was precipitated by the Prussian military defeat and subsequent economic collapse, the emancipation of the peasants on private estates of the nobility had been discussed since the initiation of emancipation on the crown lands in 1799.[18] As early as 1798, impressed by "the unbelievably large number of complaints" he had received from peasants, King Frederick William III began to give consideration to the elimination of serfdom.[19] After the Peace of Tilsit, he ordered Theodor von Schön and Frederick von Schroetter to prepare an emancipation decree for the entire monarchy. "The abolition of serfdom," he wrote, "has consistently been my goal since the beginning of my reign. I desired to attain it gradually; but the disasters that have befallen the country now justify, and indeed require, speedier action."[20] Thus, plans for emancipation were well under way before Stein was called to office early in October 1807.[21]

[17] Cited in Ernst Walter Zeeden, *Hardenberg und der Gedanke einer Volksvertretung in Preussen, 1807–1812*, Historische Studien, Heft 365 (Berlin, 1940), 71.

[18] For the reforms on the crown lands see Hartmut Harnisch, "Die agrarpolitischen Reformmassnahmen der preussischen Staatsführung in dem Jahrzehnt vor 1806–1807," *Jahrbuch für Wirtschaftsgeschichte, 1977*, part 3, 36ff.; Hartmut Harnisch, in *Kapitalistische Agrarreform und Industrielle Revolution* (Weimar, 1984), 62, argues that there was a qualitative difference between the pre–1806 efforts by the state to improve the conditions of the peasants and the subsequent reforms. Crown peasants were not free to sell their holdings to anyone but the crown, so the pre–1806 reforms on crown estates did not create a free market for peasant lands. See also Hanna Schissler, *Preussische Agrargesellschaft im Wandel*, Kritische Studien zur Geschichtswissenschaft, 33 (Göttingen, 1978), 106ff.; Otto Hintze, "Preussische Reformbestrebungen vor 1806," in *Geist und Epochen der preussischen Geschichte*, ed. Fritz Hartung (Berlin, 1943); Georg Friedrich Knapp, *Die Bauernbefreiung und der Ursprung der Landarbeiter in ältern Teilen Preussens*, 2 vols. (Leipzig, 1887), 1: 91–114.

[19] See R. Stadelmann, *Preussens Könige und Ihrer Thätigkeit für die Landeskultur* (1882; reprint, Osnabrück, 1965), 4: 209–10, 213–14.

[20] Ibid., 327–29.

[21] For the background to the Emancipation Edict, see Georg Winter, "Zur Enstehungs-

CHAPTER 4

During discussions preparatory to the drafting of the Emancipation Edict, representatives of the East Prussian nobility indicated their primary concerns about the impending emancipation. On August 29, 1807, they petitioned the king, requesting that each noble estate owner be granted "free disposition over his peasant plots [*Bauernhufen*], without the interference of higher authorities"; that the publication of an edict be delayed until a new servants' ordinance (*Gesindeordnung*) had been issued that would require five years' service for the lord by all peasant children; and, finally, that emancipated peasants be required to stay on the land and be prevented from migrating to the towns in order to maintain a sufficient labor supply for agriculture.[22] The king replied, reassuring the nobles, "The elimination of serfdom, which has become a pressing necessity, nevertheless requires great caution, so that the nobleman obtains compensation through free disposition over his estates and peasant plots, insofar as the latter can take place without injury to the culture and the population."[23]

The framers of the Emancipation Edict, Schroetter and Schön, both realized that "the free disposition over his peasant plots" by the noble landowner constituted an end to the state policy protecting the peasantry (*Bauernschutz*).[24] Accordingly, Schroetter made no allowance for continuing Bauernschutz; his plan simply granted the peasant the freedom over his person and the lord freedom over his land. Schön argued from a strict, economic logic. First, Schön argued that any limitation on the ownership of land restricted its value and therefore the ability to command credit; if it remained difficult or impossible for persons with capital to own estates, the value and productivity of the land were arbitrarily suppressed. "The state authority can never, in my opinion, be interested in whether this or that person has possession of an estate," Schön concluded.[25] Second, Schön argued that the laws offering Bauernschutz preserved marginal peasants and resulted in the division of peasant holdings into small, inefficient plots; Bauernschutz should be gradually abolished. Finally, at the end of his

---

geschichte des Oktoberedikts und der Verordnung vom 14. Februar 1808," *FBPG* 60 (1927): 1–33; Knapp, *Bauernbefreiung* 1: 130ff.; Ritter, *Stein*, 233ff.

[22] The document is printed in Knapp, *Bauernbefreiung* 2: 157–59; see also Vetter, *Kurmärkischer Adel und preussische Reformen*, 123.

[23] Knapp, *Bauernbefreiung* 2: 60.

[24] For a discussion of the two recommendations, see Simon, *The Failure of the Prussian Reform Movement*, 19ff.; Georg Winter, "Zur Entstehungsgeschichte des Oktoberedikts und der Verordnung vom 14. Februar 1808," 15ff.; Knapp, *Bauernbefreiung* 1: 126ff., 2: 147ff.; Lehmann, *Stein* 2: 269–75.

[25] The text of Schön's recommendations is found in *Aus den Papieren des Ministers und Burggrafen von Marienburg Theodor von Schön* 2: 101–29; this statement is from p. 117.

report, Schön acknowledged the injustice of serfdom but argued for its abolition on largely economic grounds. The number of people seeking work was greater than the supply of work; therefore, the elimination of serfdom not only would not create a labor shortage, but contrary to the fears of the nobility would also lead to a healthy competition for work. Peasants who had difficulty keeping places were probably inefficient; landlords who had difficulty keeping peasants probably mistreated them. The state had no interest in preserving either. Schön, however, did suggest the continuation of Bauernschutz for a period of time. To forestall the massive appropriation of small peasant holdings by the lords, he recommended that peasant plots too small to be maintained be combined into larger peasant farms.

Schön's report became the basis for the Emancipation Edict.[26] The edict did essentially three things: it ended the restrictions against commoners' owning noble estates, thereby creating a free market for land; it opened all occupations to all classes, including the nobility, thereby creating a free market for labor; and it ended the hereditary bondage of the servile peasantry, declaring that after Saint Martin's Day (November 11), 1810, there would be only "free persons" in the Prussian monarchy. In addition, the edict contained an important provision, which allowed estate owners to absorb the small, individual holdings of peasants who did not have hereditary claims to their plots. Such action required the approval of the provincial authorities. The edict left several questions open for later interpretation. It neither distinguished between those obligations that peasants owed their lords as a result of their personal status of subjection and those that were owed as a consequence of their land tenures, nor did it enumerate the conditions under which the obligatory connections between the lord and peasant were to be severed. These ambiguities gave the nobility an opportunity to agitate for a favorable interpretation of the edict.

Responses to the edict varied among nobles, both within and among the various regions of the monarchy.[27] Indeed, it was characteristic of

---

[26] For the edict, see Stadelmann, *Preussens Könige und Ihrer Thätigkeit für die Landeskultur* 4: 230–33; Botzenhart, *Stein*, II/2:257–60.

[27] The expression, made by one nobleman, "Better three more lost battles of Auerstädt than one October Edict," cited by Theodor von Schön, *Weitere Beiträge und Nachträge zu den Papieren des Ministers und Burggrafen von Marienburg Theodor von Schön* (Berlin, 1881), 51, is often given as evidence of the general hostility of the nobility to the Emancipation Edict. The subsequent opposition of the nobility to the reform proposals of Hardenberg has frequently colored the analysis of the reaction to the Emancipation Edict itself. Thus, for example, Hanna Schissler, in *Preussische Agrargesellschaft im Wandel*, 123, writes somewhat inaccurately: "The landowning noble received the agrarian reforms just as the proclaimed tax and administrative reforms as a frontal assault on his economic position and

CHAPTER 4

their provincial identity that concerted efforts by opponents of the edict to organize opposition did not extend across provincial boundaries. Local ständisch assemblies remained the vehicles of expression. Typically, the greatest opposition came from those areas in which the modernization of agriculture had progressed the least, in which servile labor was still considered essential to production, or from those areas which had suffered most from the war. Moreover, the French occupation of most of the monarchy outside of East Prussia gave provincial authorities an excuse to try to delay publication of the edict; they claimed not to want the French to receive credit for peasant emancipation. In Pomerania and Silesia, Landräte conspired with estate owners to keep secret the contents of the edict; in Silesia, where peasant disturbances had been common for more than two decades, a peasant rebellion broke out in the summer of 1808 because the peasants believed they were being held illegally in bondage.[28] It required the intervention of French troops to quell the rebellion.

Elsewhere, opposition to the edict was relatively slight. Many estate owners recognized that the edict ended the policy of Bauernschutz and opened the door to the seizure of the holdings of peasants who lacked hereditary rights. Stein had originally intended that peasant farms be absorbed only in those cases "where the estate owner is incapable of rebuilding or maintaining the devastated peasant farm."[29] The war had left many peasant holdings vacant and in shambles; it was estimated, for example, that as many as 1,700 peasant plots were without tenants on the noble estates of East Prussia.[30] Nevertheless, it became obvious that many nobles used the edict as a pretext for seizing peasant lands. There were cases in which lords took the lands of thirty peasants, greatly enlarging their own estates, and reduced the peasants to Gärtner, with only a few acres of land each.[31] As a result of the growing threat of the appropriation of peasant farms by estate owners, the ministry was compelled to issue the Ordinance of February 14, 1808, elaborating limitations on the conditions under which

---

political privileges." It is necessary to differentiate carefully among the various reforms to discern the nobles' general response.

[28] Johannes Ziekursch, *Hundert Jahre schlesischer Agrargeschichte* (Breslau, 1927), 277–90; Vetter, *Kurmärkischer Adel und preussische Reformen*, 132; Botzenhart, *Stein*, II/2:571, 614, 861, 899–900, 936–37; Max Lehmann, *Freiherr vom Stein* (Leipzig, 1903), 2: 349ff.

[29] Botzenhart, *Stein*, II/2:555–56.

[30] Hartmut Harnisch, "Vom Oktoberedikt des Jahres 1807 zur Deklaration von 1816: Problematik und Charakter der preussischen Agrarreformgesetzgebung zwischen 1807 und 1816," *Jahrbuch für Wirtschaftsgeschichte*, Sonderband, 1978, 234.

[31] Knapp, *Bauernbefreiung* 1: 138–39.

peasant farms could be taken by the landlords.[32] As the October Edict had stipulated, the holdings of hereditary peasants (Erbpächter, Erbzinsen, Erbzinsbauern, and so on) could not be absorbed without their agreement. Those of nonhereditary peasants (Zeitpächter) could be seized and incorporated into the lord's estate only with the approval of the authorities. In such a case, however, according to the February Ordinance, only one-half of the peasant land could be attached to the lord's estate; the remaining half was to be combined with other peasant holdings and leased to hereditary peasants. With this ordinance, Schön and Schroetter sought to build a class of peasants with substantial holdings. Similar ordinances were subsequently issued for the other provinces as well.[33]

This February Ordinance, far more than the Emancipation Edict itself, touched off a storm of protest, for the nobles considered the ordinance to be a violation of their right of "free disposition" of their estates, promised them by the king in his letter of September 3, 1807. From 1808 until 1811, first to Stein, then to his successors, the Committee of the East Prussian Estates protested against the ordinance.[34] The committee's arguments were based on the assumption that all the holdings of nonhereditary peasants were, in fact, the property of the lord and that to compel the lord to relinquish half was a violation of his property rights. The committee charged that the integration into his estate of only half "of his peasant holdings, which he had, until then, permitted the peasants to cultivate," and the transformation of the other half into hereditary leasehold "ruin the estate owners and the peasants and injure the property rights of the lord." The nobles "wish merely the restoration of their original rights," claimed the committee.[35] Stein rejected these arguments, based on property rights, as "completely false," for noble estate owners had never had the right arbitrarily to absorb peasant holdings.[36] Even more pointedly, Chris-

[32] Botzenhart, *Stein*, II/2:651–53. For details of the February 14 Ordinance and its implications, see Harnisch, *Kapitalistische Agrarreform und Industrielle Revolution*, 71–72.

[33] Schön's objective of creating a class of substantial peasants, because of their higher productivity, coincided, in this instance, with Stein's objective of a substantial peasantry that could be represented in the provincial estates. See Harnisch, "Vom Oktoberedikt des Jahres 1807 zur Deklaration von 1816," 238; for Stein's intentions, see Botzenhart, *Stein*, II/2:842–44.

[34] For the numerous protests of the East Prussian estates, see Knapp, *Bauernbefreiung* 2: 207–16.

[35] Cited in Harnisch, "Vom Oktoberedikt des Jahres 1807 zur Deklaration von 1816," 237.

[36] Botzenhart, *Stein*, II/2:773–76, 818–20.

CHAPTER 4

tian Friedrich Scharnweber, who later guided agrarian policy during Hardenberg's ministry, responded to the demands of the committee as follows:

The East Prussian–Lithuanian estates appear to have forgotten that in the past no peasant holdings could be absorbed into the estate and they complain that the permission to do this now is limited to half of the peasant farm and also that this permission is only conditional. The intention of this limitation is clear and wise. It is intended to retain for the peasant families, who are able to eke only a miserable existence from their plots of land, the means of their continued subsistence, to prevent the father of the family from becoming a Knecht, who can no longer provide for his family. . . . To the Committee of the Estates, human beings appear to be extraneous issues.[37]

Others defended the appropriation of peasant farms on the grounds that it would make agriculture more efficient. Governor Sack of Brandenburg commented that "the peasant who is unable to maintain his farm without support is far better off as a Büdner." Albrecht Thaer, who began to play an important role in the drafting of agrarian legislation in 1810 and 1811, advocated the absorption of small peasant holdings into larger estates.[38]

The discussions prompted by the February Ordinance were of commanding interest at the time that the estates of Brandenburg were called into session to approve the mortgaging of the royal estates. A large committee, composed of fourteen landowning nobles and five burghers, assumed the task of making recommendations on the question of agrarian reform. As a basis for the committee's discussions, Governor Sack provided the report drafted by one of his advisers from Pomerania, von Balthasar. Balthasar's recommendations were radical and sprang from purely economic assumptions. He advocated drawing together peasant plots, whether hereditary or not, into farms of between one hundred and six hundred morgen; larger farms suffered by the lack of intensive farming, smaller farms from the inapplicablity of new agricultural methods. He called for the complete separation of noble estates from peasant farms, with compensation paid to the lord; the division of the commons, with the legal costs of division and separation paid by the lord; the elimination of servile obli-

[37] Knapp, *Bauernbefreiung* 2: 213.
[38] Ibid. 1: 147–61.

gations; and, implicitly, the equalization of tax burdens on all forms of real property.[39]

Although Balthasar's recommendations would have introduced far more radical changes in the structure of rural society than were envisaged by the reformers who drafted the edict, the Committee of the Brandenburg Estates agreed with most of Balthasar's suggestions. The response, drafted largely by H. J. von Goldbeck, sought only to amend the recommendations to the further advantage of the noble estate owners. Goldbeck called for the elimination of all restraints on the exchange of property, allowing estate owners to absorb peasant holdings. While the committee accepted the abolition of compulsory peasant service with a team of draft animals (*Spanndienst*), it insisted on the retention of compulsory manual service (*Handdienst*). Other actions of the estates were aimed at the preservation of noble privileges and the introduction of the unrestricted export of grain.[40]

It may be said, therefore, that during the period from the promulgation of the Emancipation Edict in 1807 until the appointment of Hardenberg as chancellor in 1810, the Prussian nobility generally sought to exploit the opportunities offered by the edict to improve its financial position by expanding its estates at the expense of the peasantry. This effort was facilitated in large part, as we have noted, by the policies of the reformers themselves, who, endeavoring to increase the productivity of agriculture, favored the consolidation of peasant holdings or their partial appropriation by estate owners. Although the February Ordinance was intended to preserve or enlarge the holdings of hereditary leaseholders, it sacrificed the smaller, nonhereditary peasants to the noble estate owners and to the demand for greater efficiency.

Stein recognized that emancipation alone would not lift the burden of servility from the backs of the peasants; to do that, it would also be necessary to restrict the powers of the lord on his estate, especially the power of the patrimonial courts. As one of Stein's friends, Friedrich Ludwig von Vincke, put it, "What difference does it make in the daily life of the servile peasant if the formula is proclaimed: After today there shall be no more serfdom?"[41] The peasant uprisings in Silesia in the summer of 1808 persuaded Stein that peasant unrest was due

---

[39] Schönbeck, "Der kurmärkische Landtag vom Frühjahr 1809," 43–51; Vetter, *Kurmärkischer Adel und preussische Reformen*, 125–27.

[40] Schönbeck, "Der kurmärkische Landtag vom Frühjahr 1809," 51–62; Vetter, *Kurmärkischer Adel und preussische Reformen*, 127–32.

[41] Cited in Simon, *The Failure of the Prussian Reform Movement*, 22.

CHAPTER 4

largely to the system of patrimonial justice, so he ordered the formulation of a plan to abolish patrimonial courts.[42] Within a few days, the Committee of the East Prussian Estates registered its objection to any plan to eliminate patrimonial courts. The abolition of patrimonial courts, the committee charged, would injure the dignity of the nobility as the most important Stand in the state; it would weaken the confidence that the people placed in the nobility. Although the maintenance of patrimonial courts was an expensive burden to the estate owner, the committee asserted, the owner assumed the responsibility willingly, not because of a desire for power or gain, but because of his paternal concern for the welfare of his peasants. In many villages, it had not been necessary to convene patrimonial courts for years, for the lord had been able to settle disagreements without the need for formal proceedings. Moreover, the committee concluded, the charge that the lord exerted undue influence over his judges was greatly exaggerated, for patrimonial judges were public officials.[43]

A letter to Stein from a Herr von Richthofen repeated many of these arguments in defense of the system of patrimonial courts. Subordination, he asserted, was the foundation of all states; the teaching of obedience, which must begin with youth, would disappear if the noble estate owners, to whom this responsibility was entrusted, lost the right of patrimonial police powers and justice. Other petitions in defense of patrimonial justice stressed the king's promise, at his coronation, to preserve the existing constitution (*Verfassung*) of the land, of which the patrimonial courts were an essential element; they were, it was claimed, "the dearest of our rights," a bond that bound the lord to his subjects through affection and loyalty.[44]

Those to whom Stein entrusted the task of drafting a new system of local justice sympathized with the attitude of the nobility.[45] No action was taken before Stein was forced to leave office in late November 1808.[46] The failure to link emancipation of the peasantry with a new

---

[42] Lehmann, *Stein* 2: 361; Botzenhart, *Stein*, II/2:861, 886–87; H. Scheel, *Das Reformministerium Stein: Akten zur Verfassungs- und Verwaltungs Geschichte aus den Jahren 1807/08* (Berlin, 1966), 3: 1025.

[43] Lehmann, *Stein* 2: 365–66.

[44] Ibid., 595.

[45] Simon, *The Failure of the Prussian Reform Movement*, 27.

[46] The elimination of patrimonial courts was urged by Stein in his *Political Testament*. He wrote: "When a subject is compelled to seek justice where the judge is dependent on the opponent, belief in the impartiality of law is weakened, the confidence in its higher dignity and the sense of its impregnable holiness are destroyed. The abolition of patrimonial jurisdiction has already been initiated."

system of police and justice in rural Prussia left the agrarian reforms compromised from the outset.

The Hardenberg Reforms: Organized Opposition by the Nobility

The second major wave of reform began in 1810, after the appointment of Hardenberg as chancellor. Hardenberg differed from Stein in many ways. As an eighteenth-century bureaucrat, "the last representative of that same enlightened absolutism which he was supposed to overcome," as Ranke so aptly described him,[47] Hardenberg was primarily concerned with the primacy and power of the state. He was less skeptical than Stein of the efficiency of the bureaucracy and more reluctant to give any voice to representative institutions. They should be called into existence only by the authorities and should be used by the government to convey its wishes to the people. Hardenberg was much more of a rationalist and much less a traditionalist than Stein; less sensitive to the historic evolution of localities, he insisted that Prussia be referred to, and thought of, as one state. Nevertheless, he lacked Stein's detachment; as a noble landowner, he was reluctant to relinquish the patrimonial authority he exercised over his peasants. In his Riga Memorandum of 1807, he proposed the abolition of patrimonial justice only in criminal cases; that is, only in those cases in which the landowner had the least interest and which were the most expensive for him. In other cases, he wrote, "the landowner must retain the means of compelling his peasants, laborers, and servants, swiftly and without cost, to fulfill their obligations; and though these people must not be denied a hearing, neither must the landlord be made dependent in these matters on the arbitrary decisions of a judge who may be far away."[48] Later, in 1810, when it was becoming apparent that retention of patrimonial justice was a hindrance to any genuine emancipation of the peasantry, Hardenberg was still reluctant to abolish it.[49]

---

[47] Cited in Schnabel, *Deutsche Geschichte im neunzehnten Jahrhundert*, 2d ed. (Freiburg/Br., 1948–51), 1: 459; on Hardenberg's approach to statecraft generally, see also Simon, *The Failure of the Prussian Reform Movement*, 51–56; Koselleck, *Preussen zwischen Reform und Revolution*, 163ff., Ernst Klein, *Von der Reform zur Restauration*, Veröffentlichungen der Historischen Kommission zu Berlin, 16 (Berlin, 1965).

[48] Cited in Simon, *The Failure of the Prussian Reform Movement*, 54; for the entire text of the Riga Memorandum, see Leopold von Ranke, ed., *Denkwürdigkeiten des Staatskanzlers Fürsten von Hardenberg* (Leipzig, 1877), Appendix. See also Hans Haussherr, "Hardenbergs Reformdenkschrift Riga 1807," *HZ* 157 (1938).

[49] Wilhelm Steffens, *Hardenberg und die ständische Opposition 1810/1811*, Veröffentlichungen des Vereins für Geschichte der Mark Brandenburg (Leipzig, 1907), 142.

CHAPTER 4

Hardenberg was, moreover, confronted with problems different from those of Stein. From the beginning of his ministry, he was compelled to consider domestic reforms within the context of the financial plight of the Prussian state. Prussia had fallen behind schedule in repaying the French indemnity and Napoleon was exerting pressure. "Pay! Pay!—That is the song of the emperor [Napoleon]," complained Hardenberg.[50] The heavy burden of indemnity, in addition to the increasing expenditures of the state, could not be met under the existing tax structure. As was typical of much of Prussian law, even at the end of the eighteenth century, taxes differed from province to province. The two taxes, however, that provided the bulk of the state's revenue were the excise tax levied on most staples, above all food and drink sold in the towns, and the "contribution" tax, a land tax levied on the countryside. In some provinces, as in Brandenburg and Pomerania, only "contributing farms" were subject to this; all noble estates were exempt. In Silesia and West Prussia, noble estates were taxed, but at a much lower rate than peasant farms; only in East Prussia had the principle of equal taxation on land held by nobles and commoners been established.[51]

The reformers intended their programs both to increase the state's revenue and to end the inequities and provincial differences within the tax structure. Again, the financial requirements of the state were inextricably intertwined with social and political reform. Accordingly, Hardenberg's Finance Edict of October 27, 1810, began by acknowledging that "the most pressing concern is the complete fulfillment of our obligations to France." This required sacrifices by all. It required higher taxes on consumer products and luxuries, the elimination of "all exemptions" on land taxes, and the levying of equal land taxes on all property owners. It necessitated an end to the preferential treatment of some segments of the monarchy and the equalization of tax burdens between the towns and the countryside. The edict, together with subsequent legislation, eliminated guild monopolies, established the complete freedom to pursue a trade (*Gewerbefreiheit*), subject only to a trade tax. The legislation eliminated the noble monopoly on mill-

---

[50] Hans Haussherr, *Die Stunde Hardenbergs* (Hamburg, 1943), 109. Ernst Klein, in *Von der Reform zur Restauration*, sees Hardenberg's policies as shaped throughout largely by the financial crisis of the Prussian state. Klein's thesis is strongly rejected by Harnisch, *Kapitalistische Agrarreform und Industrielle Revolution*, 60.

[51] On the system of taxation, see Rolf Grabower, *Preussens Steuern vor und nach den Befreiungskriegen* (Berlin, 1932), and Karl Mamroth, *Geschichte der preussischen Staats-Besteurung, 1806–1816* (Leipzig, 1890), 241ff.

ing, brewing, and distilling in the countryside. The Finance Edict closed with the promise to create a new system of representation, both at the provincial and the national level, "whose advice we will gladly use and through which ... we will continuously impart to our loyal subjects our convictions in order that the condition of the state and the finances may improve, and that the sacrifices brought to that end are not in vain."[52]

Hardenberg anticipated opposition to his finance plans; indeed, three days after their publication, he warned officials to deal generously with opponents and to deal with offenders "not according to the severity of the new penal code, but with measured punishments, in a paternalistic spirit."[53] Even Hardenberg, however, may not have reckoned with the strenuous protests launched against the plans. Within a few weeks, opponents of the edict had organized and begun to flood Berlin with their petitions of protest. In some cases, especially those representing the towns and the peasantry, the appeals reflected legitimate concerns about the burden additional taxes would impose at a time when the economy still suffered from the devastation of war.[54] More numerous and vigorous, because they were better organized, were the objections of the landed nobility. Throughout Prussia, the nobility seized on the county and provincial assemblies that had been revitalized since 1808 to voice their protest. The assembly of Sehesten County, in East Prussia, resolved to suspend the collection of any taxes under the new edict until they received a clarification from the king as to why these unreasonable demands were necessary. Ignoring his own admonition to deal with resistance in a measured way, Hardenberg ordered the two leaders of the recalcitrant group of nobles thrown in prison for more than a month.[55] Tapiau County, also in East Prussia, sent an impassioned petition to Hardenberg; objecting to most of the reforms because they were a violation of the "constitution" of the state, the petition charged that with "the stroke of a pen, the welfare of thousands of families is destroyed."

[52] *Gesetz-Sammlung für die königlich Preussischen Staaten, 1810* (Berlin, 1810), 25–31. For a summary, see Klein, *Von der Reform zur Restauration*, 21ff.; Thielen, *Karl August von Hardenberg*, 256–57; Hans Hausherr, *Hardenberg* (Cologne, 1965), 3: 86–111.

[53] Klein, *Von der Reform zur Restauration*, 39–40.

[54] Schön reported on the hardship the edict would bring to East Prussia. See Steffens, *Hardenberg und die ständische Opposition*, 11–12. On peasant fears, see Conrad Bornhak, "Die preussische Finanzreform von 1810," *FBPG* 3 (1890): 592; Mamroth, *Geschichte der preussischen Staats-Besteuerung, 1806–1816*, 442.

[55] Georg Bujack, *Das Commissorium der Landesdeputirten der Provinz Preussen und Littauen in Berlin im Jahre 1811* (Königsberg, 1889), 1–4.

CHAPTER 4

If such [the Finance Edict] should be carried out, nine out of ten of the present estate owners will become beggars and the other tenth so weakened that he will be unable to offer alms to his impoverished brothers. The Revocation of the Edict of Nantes in France had the unfortunate effect of forcing many thousands to flee with their property, among whom many came to Prussia. But no one will accept us, impoverished by wars and indemnities, when we are driven from our estates and compelled to wander. Every state has too many beggars already.[56]

Similar exaggerated protests came from other provinces. The nobility in Silesia claimed that peasant emancipation would cost fifty million taler, in addition to which they were now expected to pay substantially higher taxes.[57] In the Mark Brandenburg, the Landräte coordinated the protests. Their leader, Landrat Wilhelm von Pannwitz, of County Niederbarnim, after having stirred up opposition to the finance plans, warned Hardenberg that he was "no longer able to quiet the estates," for many "respectable men are sickened and extremely embittered" and, unless Hardenberg agreed to hear their protests, they would go directly to the king.[58] Another leader of the opposition in Brandenburg, Friedrich August Ludwig von der Marwitz, forbade the Schulze in his village to collect the new taxes ordered by the authorities; Marwitz claimed that the Schulze was his subject (Untertan) and could therefore not be commanded to do anything without Marwitz's permission.[59] This single incident reveals the complexity of the impact made by the financial reforms: not only did they threaten the financial status and tax exemptions of the nobility, they also threatened to impose the authority of the state on the relationships of the village, which had previously been under the control of the noble lord.

The organization of this vehement opposition within the local ständisch bodies forced Hardenberg to develop a plan for some form of national representation that would "represent" the government to the people. Since his chief objective was to free the state from the French yoke and restore its power and authority, national representation was useful only as it contributed to that end. Insofar as the existing estates were an obstacle, they needed to be replaced. Hardenberg's advisers

[56] Ibid., 6–8.
[57] Steffens, *Hardenberg und die ständische Opposition*, 36–37.
[58] Vetter, *Kurmärkischer Adel und preussische Reformen*, 45–46; Pannwitz sent his warning to Hardenberg through one of Hardenberg's assistants, Friedrich von Schuckmann. See Steffens, *Hardenberg und die ständische Opposition*, 16–17.
[59] Marwitz's activities are revealed in Marwitz, II/1:172 ff. On Marwitz's refusal to allow his Schulze to cooperate in the collection of new taxes, see ibid., II/1:308–13.

shared this view. Already in August and September 1810, Governor Sack of Brandenburg and Pomerania complained to Stein of the nobility, who would "move heaven and earth in order to preserve themselves in their old self-interest" (*Egoismus*). "The finance plan is the first and most important thing," he wrote. "I am thoroughly convinced that no cure can be achieved without radical means. These must begin with a constitution and another organization of the Stände. This radical cure can be achieved only through the elimination of all traces of the feudal system, the casting aside of all differences between the provinces and the various classes of citizens within them."[60]

Accordingly, in order to bypass the existing ständisch institutions, Hardenberg announced on December 27, 1810, the convocation of an Assembly of Notables, selected by the government. Drawn from a broader spectrum of the populace than the traditional Estates, the Assembly of Notables would give the appearance of being representative. Still, the assembly was dominated by the nobility; thirty of its sixty-four members were noble, and the small landholders and peasants were represented by administrators of royal lands, well-to-do peasants, and village Schulzen.[61] In no sense, however, was the assembly to be a legislative body; its function was merely consultative. Hardenberg declared the following in his speech opening the assembly on February 23, 1811:

> The intention is not, and may not be, to alter this [the character of the Finance Edict]; it is, rather, to assemble here men from all provinces and all Stände who understand and are familiar with local conditions, and thereby to ensure and ease the execution of this system. It is to create an exact understanding of this [tax system], to eliminate misunderstanding, and to enable those who have been convened to return to the provinces to create a healthy general attitude and to build confidence and obedience.[62]

The notables, thus, were to be an extension of the government; they were to mold public opinion according to the wishes of the central administration.

The problem with Hardenberg's view of national representation was that it failed to deal with the fact that, since 1807, the traditional institutions of the Stände in the provinces, dominated by the nobility, had been given new life and considered themselves the only legitimate

[60] Sack to Stein, 31 August and 11 September 1819, in Botzenhart, *Stein* 3: 172ff.
[61] See Zeeden, *Hardenberg und der Gedanke einer Volksvertretung in Preussen*, 100ff.; Obenaus, *Anfänge des Parlamentarismus in Preussen*, 62.
[62] Cited in Klein, *Von der Reform zur Restauration*, 179–80.

CHAPTER 4

representatives in the land. Indeed, Marwitz went so far as to claim that the nobility was "the only constitutionally recognized Stand in the state."[63] Short of suppressing these institutions, the government could do little to prevent them from continuing to serve as focal points for noble opposition to the reforms. The actions of the Stände in East Prussia and the Mark Brandenburg indicate the difficulties Hardenberg had in bypassing them to create a new system of representation.

Since 1808, as we have already noted, a committee of the East Prussian–Lithuanian diet, composed of four nobles and one commoner, had served continuously in the place of the diet, coordinating the activities of the various county assemblies and acting as a clearing house for appeals to the government. In 1810, this committee orchestrated the selection of deputies to go to Berlin to protest the Finance Edict; the committee also helped draft the instructions for these deputies and remained in frequent contact with them while they were in Berlin.[64] When this deputation from East Prussia arrived in Berlin on January 18, 1811, it found delegations from other provinces already there.[65] A group of nobles, selected by the county assemblies of the Mark Brandenburg, had already met with Hardenberg on January 8 to request the convening of a diet. Hardenberg refused but agreed to permit the delegation from the Mark Brandenburg to remain in Berlin to confer with the notables. Prior to their second meeting with Hardenberg, this group of nobles from Brandenburg submitted a petition again requesting convocation of a diet; they argued that because the constitutional structure of Prussia grew out of agreements between the crown and the Estates, no change in that structure, such as the Finance Edict would initiate, could be made without the consent of a diet. Those signing the petition referred to themselves as deputies of the Stände. By the time of their second meeting with the chancellor on January 28, Hardenberg's attitude had stiffened; delegations from the other provinces had also arrived in Berlin, also demanding the convocation of diets. He objected to their referring to themselves as dep-

---

[63] Marwitz, II/1:162.

[64] At least one nobleman from East Prussia, chosen by his fellow noblemen to participate in the delegation to Berlin to protest the Finance Edict, refused to join in the delegation after he learned of the creation of the Assembly of Notables. "I cannot deny," wrote Count Dönhoff, "that the timing of such a deputation appears unfavorable, because at this moment, when the king believes he has done all that has been demanded through the convening of an assembly of notables, he may not be inclined to listen to a special deputation. I also believe that this is a commonly held opinion." Bujack, *Commissorium*, 36. For important documents, including correspondence between the Berlin delegation and the Committee of the Stände in Königsberg, see Bujack, *Commissorium*.

[65] Bujack, *Commissorium*, 63; Vetter, *Kurmärkischer Adel und preussische Reformen*, 47.

uties since no diet had deputized them. Some of those signing the petition, he charged, did not even live in the Kurmark of Brandenburg.[66]

In other respects, however, Hardenberg compromised. Confronted with delegations chosen by the provinces and gathered in Berlin well in advance of the opening of the Assembly of Notables, he tried to silence the opposition by increasing the number of nobles in the assembly.[67] But this merely created new problems. First, it caused a number of proponents of the reform to doubt Hardenberg's willingness to carry through against opposition.[68] More important, in adding new notables to the assembly, Hardenberg selected some who had come to Berlin as deputies from their provinces. This contributed to the fusion of the two groups: deputies, chosen by local assemblies, and notables, called by Hardenberg. Moreover, most of the deputies were bound by their provincial Stände by some form of written instructions. This ran counter to Hardenberg's demand that the notables consider themselves independent consultants—above all, free of any narrow, provincial outlook. "You will consider yourselves citizens of the entire state, and individual welfare and individual interests will be subordinated to the whole."[69] When Notables von Kalkreuth and von Sydow, from East Prussia, told Hardenberg that they considered themselves bound by their instructions as deputies, Hardenberg replied firmly that they were "not bound by these instructions and views, but are obligated only by your own insight."[70]

Hardenberg attempted to distinguish between the deputies and the notables in other ways. Referring to the deputies merely as estate owners, he reserved the title deputies of the Estates only for the notables whom he had appointed, endeavoring to endow the Assembly of Notables with a constitutional authority. Marwitz complained bitterly of

[66] For reports on the meetings of the Kurmark deputies, their petitions to Hardenberg, and his responses, see Marwitz, II/1:211–38.

[67] Simon, *The Failure of the Prussian Reform Movement*, 63; Steffens, *Hardenberg und die ständische Opposition*, 53.

[68] For example, Barthold Georg Niebuhr wrote in January 1811 that Hardenberg was giving in to the nobles on the financial issue; he feared that Hardenberg was "becoming an instrument of the aristocracy." See Dietrich Gerhard and William Norwin, eds., *Briefe Niebuhrs* (Berlin, 1929), 2: 180. Both Sack and Gneisenau complained to Stein of Hardenberg's failure to take a firm stand against the demands of the nobility; see Botzenhart, *Stein* 3: 497, 522–23. Schleiermacher complained that Hardenberg's administration had abandoned completely the direction that Stein had set; ibid., 537.

[69] Excerpts of Hardenberg's address to the notables is in Marwitz, II/2:135–41.

[70] See the exchange of Kalkreuth and Sydow with Hardenberg, Bujack, *Commissorium*, 78–79.

CHAPTER 4

this tactic: "Through such an exchange of names, the concepts are also confused, and the old Brandenburg constitution is carried to its grave."[71] Nevertheless, Hardenberg's attempt to separate the notables from the deputies failed; those notables who were also deputies remained in close contact with their fellow deputies, often acted on their instructions, or explained the discussions in the assembly to their colleagues.[72] The ständisch institutions and outlooks were simply too powerfully entrenched to be bypassed or easily overcome.

The Assembly of Notables was divided into four sections, each of which was led by a president of a governmental district (*Regierungspräsident*) and contained representatives from every province. The discussions were thus segmented and it was not easy for provincial interests to consolidate. The assembly had no power to initiate legislation, and its discussions were limited to the issues that were presented to it by the government. The notables met regularly from late February until late March 1811, and periodically until September 16, 1811. Hardenberg's hope that the notables would become loyal advocates of the government's reform proposals never materialized; the provincial representatives, dominated by the nobility, more often criticized the government.[73]

In their arguments against the Hardenberg reforms, members of the Prussian nobility insisted on the preservation of the *Verfassung des Landes* (the constitution of the land). *Verfassung* means "constitution" in both the narrow and the broad sense of the term. The nobility's use of the phrase "constitution of the land" was intended, on the one hand, as an answer to those who agitated for a written constitution by suggesting that Prussia already had a constitution and, on the other hand, as an indictment of reformers altering and violating the time-honored constitution of the land. The constitution comprised, first of all, the royal guarantees that had been given to the provincial estates during the preceding centuries, both through the settlements between the crown and the diets and through the promises given by the kings on the occasion of their coronation.[74] For the nobles, the constitution

[71] Marwitz, II/2:43; see also Koselleck, *Preussen zwischen Reform und Revolution*, 191.

[72] Steffens, *Hardenberg und die ständische Opposition*, 49; for evidence of the intrusion of the attitudes of deputies into the considerations of the notables, see Bornhak, "Die preussische Finanzreform von 1810," 603.

[73] Obenaus, *Anfänge des Parlamentarismus*, 64–65.

[74] All of the protests of the provincial estates recalled the history of settlements between the crown and the estates. Bujack, *Commissorium*; Marwitz, II/1:342. Marwitz himself cited the Recess of 1653 often as the "constitution" of the Mark Brandenburg; see especially ibid., II/1:170, 172, 229, 232–35, 310, 342–45; II/2:6–8, 55, 68–72.

was contained in provincial law, a fact that had been recognized even by the Allgemeines Landrecht, in many ways the functional equivalent of a national constitution, when it acknowledged the primacy of provincial law over the subsidiary law of the Landrecht. The constitution was thus grounded in provincialism and in the powers of the Stände, dominated by the nobility. But the phrase "constitution of the land" also referred to the entire structure of social relations and the "constituted" authority of the nobility on the land. Also part of the constitution of the land was the fact that the powers of the state stopped at the boundaries of the noble estate, except for taxes, military conscription, and the state's unsuccessful attempts at Bauernschutz. Hereditary serfdom was, to be sure, a part of the constitutional structure, but many had come to realize that hereditary bondage was not an essential element of the constitution. Inefficient, unpopular, and frequently brutal, serfdom had already been abolished by many nobles on their own estates without dire consequences. Hence, the Emancipation Edict had not been strenuously opposed, especially in those regions where the effects of voluntary emancipation were relatively well known. If by 1810 serfdom per se was not considered essential to the constitution, the preservation of noble authority on the estate still was thought essential by many. The entire ethos of paternalism associated with das ganze Haus—patrimonial courts, police powers, and church and school patronage—was still considered to be an essential feature of the Verfassung des Landes. It was in the defense of this constitution, broadly understood, that self-conscious conservatism first developed among the Prussian nobility.

Because of this understanding of the constitution, the nobility was itself, in a fundamental way, a provincial institution. The conflict between Hardenberg and the aristocracy was, at one level, therefore, a conflict between Prussian nationalism and Prussian provincialism. Hardenberg recognized this clearly. In outlining his financial program in 1810, he insisted on the consolidation of all provincial debts; "concentration must take place in one administration," he wrote, "because we do not want to perpetuate provincialism, but to introduce nationalism."[75] In his first speech to the notables, Hardenberg declared that his purpose was to create "one spirit, one national interest," and he believed this was not possible with the provincial Stände as they then existed.[76] Precisely this formulation alarmed those nobles who believed that their preservation as a privileged class depended on the

[75] Botzenhart, *Stein* 3: 385.
[76] Marwitz, II/2:136.

perpetuation of their provincial rights. The conservative political writer Adam Müller warned Marwitz that Hardenberg would create French "departments" in Prussia and that the destruction of the provinces would bring with it the destruction of the nobility. "No nation without the old provinces, no nation without the old nobility," he wrote.[77] Marwitz, too, stressed the need for preservation of the provincial structure of Prussia. In response to Hardenberg's first speech to the notables, he wrote the following:

> Prussia ... is an assemblage of many provinces that varied widely in their laws and customs; it can also never become a nation ... because each province has as its neighbors other provinces to which, though not a part of the same state, it feels basically more closely related than it does to the distant and, to it, unknown other provinces of the Prussian state, as for example, the Mark Brandenburg is to Saxony, Silesia to German Bohemia and Moravia, Prussia to Curland and Lithuania. To endeavor to meld them into one means to rob them of their individuality and to create a dead carcass out of a living body.[78]

The primacy of the provincial outlook among the Prussian nobility was apparent in its reaction to Hardenberg's plan for the election of the so-called provisional National Assembly, first announced on September 7, 1811. More than the Assembly of Notables appointed by the government, the provisional National Assembly was intended to be a forerunner of a system of national representation. It was to be composed of representatives elected by the Stände of the various governmental districts of the monarchy. Although the nobility, with eighteen representatives, was the most heavily represented, it did not control a majority; the cities elected thirteen representatives, and the peasants, the *Rustikalstand*, elected nine. Because the Landräte presided over the election of the peasants, the peasant representatives tended to be conservative; most were Schulzen in their villages and thus well integrated into the traditional hierarchy of authority.[79] As was true of the Assembly of Notables, the National Assembly was to have only consultative powers. Indeed, Hardenberg did not even bother to inform the assembly in advance of the promulgation of the Gendarmerie Edict on July 30, 1812, an edict that altered more radically than any other the constitutional structure of rural Prussia.

Although some nobles counseled cooperation with the National As-

[77] Ibid., II/1:265.
[78] Ibid., II/1:323.
[79] Vetter, *Kurmärkischer Adel und preussische Reformen*, 55–56.

sembly as a means of forestalling the loss of further noble privileges, a majority opposed any form of national representation. Their chief objection lay in their belief that each province had special needs and unique legal traditions, which would be obliterated by a national assembly. Count Dönhoff expressed this view in a letter to Hardenberg. Defending the "wholesome provincialism" as a condition for "true nationality," he insisted that it would be "injurious for one or another of the provinces if the principle would be established that a majority of votes in a general representative assembly is taken to be the expression of the general, national wishes of all the provinces."[80]

Despite these reservations, the National Assembly functioned, from its inception in 1812 until its dissolution in 1815, as a tool of the nobility rather than as an arm of the administration. Like Stein before him, Hardenberg was incapable of considering representation on any other basis than that of the Stände; but the power of the traditional Stände, rooted in local and provincial assemblies, was too strong to surmount. The national representatives never overcame their provincialism and, because they remained in contact with the Stände from whom they were elected, they became agents through whom the nobility worked to overthrow Hardenberg's reforms.

In a number of small skirmishes, some of which assumed comic proportions, the nobility struggled to maintain the symbols of paternalism, which it considered essential to the preservation of the "constitution of the land." For example, an ordinance issued in 1808 removed the administration of poor relief from the Stände of the counties and placed it under the central bureaucracy. Poor relief, which included workhouses for beggars and care for military invalids, was an important, visible symbol of the nobility's paternal concern for the poor. When, in 1811, the government got around to carrying out the ordinance, the nobility in the Mark Brandenburg balked; Marwitz took the key to the poor-relief treasury and left town, compelling the authorities to appropriate the treasury forcibly. Their actions prompted a series of complaints by the nobility.[81] Elsewhere, nobles complained that the behavior of the peasantry had changed since the Emancipation Edict. From Silesia came the lament that the peasants no longer treated their lords with respect: "The lower classes refuse respect to the lords, refuse to take off their hats, address them all with *Du*, as signs of equality and freedom. Such scenes . . . indicate not merely a misinterpretation of the edict, but a psychological truth that freedom,

[80] Cited in Koselleck, *Preussen zwischen Reform und Revolution*, 210.
[81] Marwitz, II/1:277–80; Vetter, *Kurmärkischer Adel und preussische Reformen*, 91–93.

given to the raw classes of the people, produces a lack of restraint and a licentiousness that can shake the state itself."[82]

To separate these broad constitutional concerns of the nobility from its narrower economic interests was difficult—the lord's legal privileges on his estate, many argued, were part of the capital value of the estate. Some nobles argued primarily against reforms that had adverse effects on their finances. Obviously, the most immediate impact of the Finance Edict was economic; by removing noble tax exemptions and abolishing the milling, distilling, and brewing monopoly of the nobility, the edict threatened the nobility with a reduction of income. The petitions directed to Hardenberg and the instructions written to the provincial deputies in Berlin gave high priority to financial questions.[83] To be sure, the deputies argued on constitutional grounds that new taxes could not be imposed without the approval of provincial estates and that these taxes violated their constitutional rights, but their protests were primarily directed against the taxes themselves. For some, the violations of traditional noble privileges were less threatening than the financial repercussions of the reforms.

The question of the priority of economic above constitutional concerns divided the deputies of the Mark Brandenburg. Marwitz recognized the division most clearly. In April 1811, a small group of nobles from the Mark had met with Hardenberg again to request the convocation of a provincial Landtag. Marwitz disagreed with the thrust of their appeal and in a significant and penetrating statement enunciated the differences between his position and theirs:

> The point of view from which the Right Honorable Gentlemen consider our affairs is economic. My point of view, on the contrary, is legal [*rechtlich*]. ... In a word, the Right Honorable Gentlemen want to avert the present pecuniary pressure; I will not suffer that law be replaced by power. ... If the only objectives before us are economic, it would be best to remain completely silent in order not to lose more; if we have a legal objective, then we must do or claim what our rights—the essence of our Stand—and the consequences of our understanding demand from us, unconcerned whether the results are beneficial or injurious.
>
> What is the primary objective? It is for me none other than the preservation of the laws and the constitution of this land—for this end, as

---

[82] Cited in Steffens, *Hardenberg und die ständische Opposition*, 141.
[83] Bujack, *Commissorium*, 11–15.

far as I am concerned, all the new taxes can remain and still three times as much can be demanded from me than now.[84]

Marwitz's most extreme formulation of this theme came with the famous *Final Remonstrance*, which he drafted and which was approved by the county assemblies of Lebus, Beeskow, and Storkow before being submitted to the king in early June 1811. The cornerstone of the Prussian constitution, he argued, was the dualistic *Ständestaat* in which the crown consulted with the Estates. The Estates had met the initial demands of Napoleon and had been consulted over the alienation of crown estates in 1809. "We learned through the edict of October 28," he charged, "that all of this was only a dream and that now foreign laws governed the state, so that really the traditional, old Brandenburg-Prussian state has been dissolved." The problem was not, he declared, a "monetary deficiency," but a "moral deficiency," which came from the imposition of "foreign laws." Venting his anger at Hardenberg and at his associates Friedrich von Raumer and Christian Friedrich von Scharnweber, none of whom was a native Prussian, Marwitz charged: "Instead of consulting with the men who live in the land and are acquainted with its needs before the execution of the laws, the young foreigners who influence Your Majesty's ministers carry out experiments with their new-fangled theories on our country." The new laws would have two results: First, they would bring about the equalization of all classes, thereby eliminating the intermediate class, the nobility, which exercised direct control over the masses. Henceforth, he warned, "only one, large, undivided mass will confront the throne." Second, they would facilitate the mobility of all landed property. The new legislation no longer respected the nobleman but spoke only of "the large landed properties, which are commonly referred to as noble estates"; this would encourage the frequent sale of estates, so that most would eventually pass into the hands of Jews and thus "our venerable old Brandenburg-Prussia will become a new-fangled Jew-state."[85]

But Marwitz and the twenty other nobles who signed this petition did not represent a majority of their class. Indeed, Hardenberg himself recognized that only "one portion—in no way a majority—of noble estate owners" took so extreme a position, and he recommended to the king that the two ringleaders, Marwitz and Finckenstein, be im-

[84] Marwitz, II/1:334–38; see also, ibid., 220–21.
[85] Ibid., II/2:2–23.

CHAPTER 4

prisoned for their insolence and insubordination.[86] Their relative isolation from the rest of the nobility may be seen in the fact that while the two outraged noblemen sat in Spandau Prison for six weeks, few of their fellow nobles made an effort to obtain their release.[87] Although Marwitz's criticism was ineffectual, so that Hardenberg could punish him without fearing a groundswell of indignation, Marwitz's position was significant, for it constituted a penetrating and relatively insightful commentary on the society emerging in Prussia at the beginning of the nineteenth century.

For Marwitz, the true Prussian constitution was based on the existence of the two Stände within the monarchy: the nobles, who represented rural, agricultural society, and the burghers, who represented urban, industrial society. Each Stand had different rights, different obligations, and a different ethos. Each formed a vital Mittelstand between the king and the masses, essential for the maintenance of order. In the towns, this Mittelstand was composed of the guild masters; in the countryside, the noble estate owners. The exclusive rights of the guildsman was to pursue his trade under the protection of a legal monopoly, that of a nobleman was to own a noble estate.[88] These exclusive rights were necessary for the two Stände to occupy their intermediate position of authority in society, for they needed to be separated from the masses whom they controlled by special privileges. If those privileges were set aside, and no distinctions separated the Mittelstände from the masses, chaos would ensue. This, Marwitz insisted, was the lesson of the French Revolution. As soon as the nobility lost its exclusive privileges in France, the revolution could not be halted and the monarchy was lost. "Without a Mittelstand, a pure democracy can exist, but not a monarchy."[89] Each Stand served the state differently, the burghers through payment of taxes, the nobles through military service.

Out of these different rights and obligations, Marwitz continued, grew a different ethos and a different sense of honor in each of the two Stände. The nobleman was born to nobility. His identity, the meaning of his life, his title, his name, all of these were the product of his inheritance. The noble estate, from which he drew his name, provided the natural link with both the past and the future generations

[86] For Hardenberg's response to the king, see the marginal notes he made on the petition, ibid., and his recommendations, ibid., II/2:224–26.

[87] Marwitz complained bitterly about the failure of others, especially his friend von Prittwitz, to protest his imprisonment. See ibid., II/2:114. Bülow-Cummerow won his friendship, despite their political differences, by visiting him in prison.

[88] STAP, Pr. Br. 37, Marwitz-Friedersdorf, 583, Bl. 3–4; Marwitz, II/1:245 ff., II/2:60 ff.

[89] Marwitz, II/1:195–200.

of his family. Generations of military service endowed the young nobleman with a special sense of honor and a tradition to uphold. Noblemen were born, not made, and their titles were an outward and visible sign of their inward qualities. Marwitz wrote, "Kings can grant titles for favors or money, and thus confer the name of noble; they can thereby create lords, but not noblemen. In the children of bankers, businessmen, ideologues, and cosmopolitans, in ninety-nine out of a hundred cases, the speculator or boorish shopkeeper shows through ... that is, they are, and remain, common. The son of a nobleman ... will always shun that which could be called common."[90]

Nobles were more closely tied to nature than were townspeople because they lived on the land and all that they acquired came from the soil. Ownership of landed estates was essential to the ethos of the nobility. It made the nobility the backbone of the state, for the land would always remain the essence of the nation. Military service was natural for the nobility because it defended the nobility's own land. Land was the basis of the nobleman's wealth; it was his "immobile capital." Control of the land was also the basis of the nobleman's role as a Mittelstand over the peasantry.[91] This nexus between landownership and control of the rural population gave the nobleman his office, his duty.[92] "Hereditary serfdom was not a 'residue of slavery,' " as Stein had claimed, Marwitz insisted. "Hereditary serfdom was much more of a patriarchal bond that joined the peasant to the nobleman, a bond that plants the idea of a higher law and a more noble morality, as well as the respect for a more civilized life in the hearts of the lowest classses. Its abolition can only make way for the most extreme licentiousness and the most dangerous political irreligiosity." The patriarchal nature of authority on a landed estate led to the "inner subordination" of the peasantry. Through the relationship with his lord, the peasant came to understand the authority that the state represented, "The state," Marwitz said, "is a nonentity for the peasant because he can neither see it nor comprehend it. . . . The intermediate authority, the noble lord, however, he knows completely because he lives with him, and through him he learns to know the state."[93]

The Bürgerstand was different from the nobility. Its wealth and station were the product not of inheritance, but of achievement. It was not dependent on nature for its acquisitions, but on learning and abil-

[90] Ibid., 1: 510–11.

[91] See Marwitz's essay "Von den Ursachen des Verfalls des Preussischen Staates," ibid., II/2:57–100.

[92] STAP, Br. 37, Marwitz-Friedersdorf, 584, Bl. 56.

[93] See Marwitz's essay "Kritik des Steinschen Testaments," Marwitz, II/1:238–51, esp. 240–42.

ity. The wealth of the Bürgerstand was not fixed and stable, like the land of the nobility, but "mobile capital." Thus, Marwitz declared, it was appropriate that its service to the state should be in the payment of taxes. Townsmen should not play a prominent role in the military, for their capital, being mobile, worked against their developing strong national loyalties. Marwitz stressed the fact that the Rothschilds were a family with no essential national loyalty.[94]

The Bürgerstand, however, was changing. No longer was the Bürgerstand led by men of achievement in the trades and leaders in the guilds; the guilds were being abolished and the leadership of the towns was passing to "parvenus" and "speculators." "It is now possible," Marwitz charged, "without any work, but merely through speculation, to make a profit. . . . There is now a mob of people in Berlin who, without the slightest occupation, without the least work, live merely from the stock exchange." Because of this, the moral fiber of the nation had deteriorated. Usurers ("such a person is now referred to as a *rentier*") had formed a "money oligarchy." This condition was the product of "the revolution," which "has built a European money oligarchy that actually dominates the states. Through the power which money has acquired over all human relationships during the past three centuries—and above all, during the last thirty years—this oligarchy has put itself into the position to compel the states to raise taxes and deliver them to it."[95]

The position of the nobility, Marwitz lamented, had also been destroyed. First, the princes robbed the nobility of many of its powers and cut the bond of vassalage that previously tied the nobles to the state and defined their legal function in society. "Of their former lordliness, nothing remains but shadows and illusions," he wrote. Second, the acquisitive spirit that had infected the towns also had invaded the countryside. At the end of the eighteenth century, the nobles had engaged in land speculation, buying and selling estates, and thereby severing their hereditary and familial ties to the land and the patrimonial bond to their peasants. They ceased to be lords of their estates; "they are farmers, somewhat more competent than peasants," Marwitz admitted.[96] Deprived of their constitutional function as vassals and having relinquished much of their authority as noble landlords, they had become merely nominal nobles. The pride that they had in their Stand had become an empty arrogance, and the privileges they continued to

[94] Ibid., 1:636–37.
[95] Ibid., 595–635.
[96] Ibid., II/1:163–64.

enjoy had become a source of irritation and an object of scorn and ridicule. "The noble has not only been brought down in his status as a citizen of the state, but in his own opinion [*Meinung*]!" The criticism and scorn to which the nobility was subjected by others did not originate in the traditional Bürgerstand, Marwitz insisted, but from the new elite, "the class of men torn loose from the state," who were irritated that they were not also addressed as "Herr von ——."[97]

This gradual dissolution of the ständisch constitution of Prussia, begun in the seventeenth and eighteenth centuries, Marwitz believed, had assumed revolutionary proportions under the reforms of Stein and Hardenberg. The reforms, he thought, endeavored to remove the last barriers between the Stände; in doing so, they had introduced the basis for conflict at all levels of the society. "Stein . . . initiated the revolutionizing of the fatherland, the war of the propertyless against property, industry against agriculture, the mobile against the stabile, crass materialism against the God-given order."[98] Everyone had become dissatisfied with his station in society, Marwitz claimed.

Once, the Stände were separate and to move from one Stand into another was difficult, although not impossible, given capacity and talent. Now, all Stände have been let loose [*losgelassen*], and in each of them, an upward drive from below has been unleashed. . . . Every peasant's son wants to be an artisan, every artisan's son wants to be a clerk, every clerk's son wants to be a high official, every schoolteacher a professor, and every professor or businessman wants to become a great lord. In the end, who will plow the fields and polish the boots of all these great lords?[99]

On other occasions, Marwitz complained that the reforms, instead of inciting ambition among the lower classes, had merely made them lazy and disrespectful. Peasants no longer wanted to work and servants were difficult to find, although the roads were crowded with beggars. But Marwitz was also honest enough to admit that the agrarian reforms had seriously hurt the peasants by depriving them of land.

For Marwitz, preservation of the Prussian constitution depended on the preservation of the nobility. This, he recognized, could not be achieved unless the nobility itself were reformed. Marwitz's proposals for the reform of the nobility, made first in 1812, included recommendations that were to be repeated often by others during the period

[97] Ibid., II/2:73–77.
[98] Ibid., I:492.
[99] STAP, Pr. Br., 37, Marwitz-Friedersdorf, 583, Bl. 3.

before 1848. His suggestions stressed the two functions he considered essential for the nobility: control of the landed estates and service in the army.[100] To survive, the nobility must retain control of land; to ensure, therefore, that the land did not pass into the hands of commoners, it must be made inalienable. It must not be mortgaged or sold and it must be passed on to only the eldest son without being burdened by the inheritance claims of other children. With the exception of the eldest son, whose military service would be terminated when he was called upon to take over his father's estate, all noblemen would be obligated to serve in the army for their entire careers. In the event that a nobleman inherited an estate before service in war, he would be obliged to return to the army during the next outbreak of hostilities and to serve in a specified number of campaigns. Any nobleman judged unfit for the army would have to forfeit his title, as would any nobleman convicted of cowardice. No patents of nobility should be awarded without the simultaneous granting of a noble estate, so that Prussia would cease to have landless noblemen, other than those in the army. Very few should be ennobled and only those who were truly worthy.

Marwitz's proposals were hopelessly reactionary. His insistence on restoration of a bond of vassalage between the king and the nobility was a futile effort to recapture a symbolic nexus that had long since been emptied of meaning. His suggestion that the sons of noblemen be bound to lifelong careers in the army contradicted not only contemporary notions that careers should be opened to talent, but also the military lessons of the French Revolution and the Prussian defeat at Jena and Auerstädt. The belief that the nobility should retain its monopoly of land and that noble estates should never be mortgaged would have denied agriculture the capital necessary for modernization.

Marwitz was a spokesman for the most conservative wing of the Prussian nobility during the reform era; the attitudes he represented were shared by many other nobles, who, for tactical reasons, refused to take such an extreme position. His ideas were the first fairly systematic expression of political conservatism by a Prussian noble, and they indicate how closely that conservatism was related to the social and political experience of the nobility on its landed estates. Marwitz was the spokesman for the paternalist ideology; he defended the social institutions of east Elbian Prussia because he believed they were based on a balanced system of mutual rights and obligations. He recognized

[100] For Marwitz's suggestions for a reform of the nobility, see Marwitz, II/2:156–59.

THE REFORM ERA

that they served the interest of the dominant nobility and that in many cases the nobility abused the trust implicit in this system of paternalism. But he also believed that paternalism served and protected the peasantry. He attacked the reforms, the dissolution of the Stände, and the emergence of the "money oligarchy" because he felt they were tearing people loose from a society based on human relations of mutual concern. He did not object to the modernization of agriculture or the granting to the peasants of proprietary rights to their lands; indeed, he himself did both even before the advent of the reforms. But he did not want to see land lose its traditional meaning for the nobility and become mere property, a commodity bought and sold. Marwitz did not oppose the introduction of important elements of capitalist agriculture; he simply did not want to see traditional social relations and values undermined by the dictates of the market economy and capitalism.

The "constitutional rights" of the nobility, as Marwitz understood them, were severely threatened by the reorganization of county government prescribed by Hardenberg's Gendarmerie Edict of July 30, 1812. The Gendarmerie Edict was the most extreme act of administrative reform and centralization of bureaucratic authority during the Hardenberg era.[101] It divided the monarchy into new administrative districts; within these districts, 164 counties were designated, according to size and population, and without regard to traditional boundaries. Except for the largest cities (Berlin, Königsberg, Elbing, Stettin, Potsdam, Frankfurt-on-the-Oder, and Breslau), which formed special administrative units, the cities were incorporated into the new counties. The chief executive officer in each county, replacing the Landrat, was the county director, who was appointed by the central government without formal consultation or nomination by the estates of the county. The county director supervised the administration of the police, finances, tax collection, military conscription, and the quartering of troops in the county; his supervision of the police extended to the community level, and he was also responsible for overseeing village schools and the appointment of village pastors. The traditional county assembly (Kreistag), dominated by the nobility, was replaced by a system of representation that granted equal voice to the towns, noble es-

---

[101] On the edict in general, see Heinrich von Treitschke, *Deutsche Geschichte im neunzehnten Jahrhundert* (Leipzig, 1927), 1: 370; R. Röpell, *Zur inneren Geschichte Preussens in den Jahren 1811–1812*, Publikationen der Schlesischen Gesellschaft für vaterländische Kultur (1847), 349ff.; Koselleck, *Preussen zwischen Reform und Revolution*, 196ff.; Klein, *Von der Reform zur Restauration*, 183ff.; Ernst von Meier, *Die Reform der Verwaltungsorganisation unter Stein und Hardenberg* (Munich and Leipzig, 1912), 388ff.

CHAPTER 4

tate owners, and peasants. In addition, county courts replaced the patrimonial courts of the noble estate owners.[102] In this single edict, then, the institutions of patrimonial domination—police, justice, church, and schools—were taken from noble estate owners and placed under the control of the central bureaucracy.

Hardenberg originally had not intended to introduce so radical a reform. As we have noted, he did not want to strip noble estate owners of their patrimonial police or judicial authority; in fact, even the Edict of Regulation of September 14, 1811, which initially outlined the conditions for peasant emancipation, explicitly declared the following: "The judicial and police relationships will not be altered by this ordinance." However, just as peasant unrest in Silesia in the summer of 1808 convinced Stein of the necessity of abolishing patrimonial justice, so, too, did peasant uprisings in Silesia in 1811 persuade Hardenberg that the power of the noble landowners and the Landräte had to be restricted. Scharnweber, who drafted the Gendarmerie Edict, estimated that only one-third of the Landräte in the monarchy could be trusted to carry out the reforms initiated by the central administration. So long as the Landräte were incompetent, or insufficiently responsive to the commands of the central government, the reforms would remain ineffective.[103]

The Gendarmerie Edict aroused a storm of protest from the Prussian nobility. Although the provisional National Assembly was in session at the time that the Gendarmerie Edict was being prepared, it was not consulted on the contents of the ordinance. Upset by this lack of consultation, the representative from Breslau, Lange, complained, "Either our advice and judgment are considered to be of value or they are not; if of value, they should be made use of; if of no value, we should be told why not." Another representative charged that the edict "destroyed the last vestige of political freedom" in Prussia.[104] Ignoring Hardenberg's request that the assembly act independently, free of influence from the provincial Stände, the assembly acted, as had the notables before it, as an agent of the conservative nobility in the provinces. It voted overwhelmingly against the government's effort to forestall discussion of the Gendarmerie Edict and, despite the objections of several peasant representatives, voted to recommend the retention of patrimonial courts, control of church and school, and traditional noble domination of the county assemblies.

[102] Meier, *Die Reform der Verwaltungsorganisation*, 396–404.
[103] Koselleck, *Preussen zwischen Reform und Revolution*, 196, 201.
[104] Klein, *Von der Reform zur Restauration*, 183–84.

During the next year and a half, protests against the Gendarmerie Edict poured into Berlin. The Pomeranian nobility claimed: "The edict establishing the gendarmerie ... eliminates the entire relationship of the former Ländstande and all of their rights. The Landrat of the county is no longer the representative of his fellow citizens but a royal official."[105] Similarly, the nobles from the Mark Brandenburg complained, "In the future, the Stand of the noble estate owners will be placed into an assembly with the peasant Stand, robbing it of all its special rights of representation and forcing it into a local commune in which it must adhere to the recommendaitons of this assembly. A majority of votes is sovereign, even though the highest interests of the landowner require him to oppose such communal conclusions as those that work against his preservation."[106] The Brandenburg nobles charged that the intrusion of central, bureaucratic police into the village would upset the relationships that prevailed there. "In our view," they wrote, "the police must not involve themselves in private and family relationships unless those relationships collide with the state or its security."[107] Marwitz also found the separation of the peasantry into its own Stand lamentable: "Noblemen and peasants are not of a different Stand, but of the same, and it cannot be represented by the fist that digs and plows, but by the head, which knows the land and its conditions."[108] By destroying the institutions of patrimonial Herrschaft and imposing the state police onto the "private" relationships of the noble estate, by pitting noble and peasant against each other in their representative assemblies, the law promised to introduce conflict into a situation where, according to the traditional myth, paternalism had produced harmony.

Because of stubborn opposition by provincial nobility, the Gendarmerie Edict was not carried out before the war with France interfered with its enactment. In February 1814, a majority of the National Assembly demanded the right to debate the issue again. By that time, however, the impulse for reform had disappeared and the entire edict was ultimately suspended.[109] The nobility had succeeded in preserving control of its subjects in the villages.

[105] For a discussion of the opposition of the nobility from Brandenburg, see Vetter, *Kurmärkischer Adel und preussische Reformen*, 94–98. This statement is found in DZA II, Rep. 74, H. 9, Stände, no. 15, Bl. 12.

[106] DZA II, Rep. 74, H. 9, Stände, no. 20, no pages.

[107] Ibid.; for other opposition, see DZA II, Rep. 74, H. 9, no. 3, Bl. 85–92; Rep. 74, H. 9, no. 9, Bl. 69ff.

[108] Marwitz, II/2:169ff.

[109] Vetter, *Kurmärkischer Adel und preussische Reformen*, 98.

CHAPTER 4

THE SUCCESS OF NOBLE OPPOSITION: AGRARIAN LEGISLATION,
1810–1816

The suspension of the Gendarmerie Edict was not the only instance of successful noble opposition to Hardenberg's reforms. During 1811, Hardenberg also made major modifications in the tax system that he had introduced the previous year. These modifications did not result, to be sure, solely from the opposition—the new taxes had not produced the revenues anticipated. This was due, in some cases, to noncompliance, or to "the inexcusable negligence and purposeful neglect on the part of local government and the magistrates," as Hardenberg later complained. But it was also true that the new legislation, calling for freedom of occupation (*Gewerbefreiheit*), had not stimulated the economy as had been expected.[110] In announcing his revisions, Hardenberg maintained that the government had not abandoned the principle of equal taxation for all citizens; nevertheless, the changes were almost all to the advantage of the landholding nobility. Numerous grain taxes were eliminated; the brandy tax was reduced to the advantage of small distilleries on noble estates, and, where it had previously existed, the noble monopoly on brewing and distilling was reinstated; uniform taxation between towns and the countryside was abandoned; and, most important, noble land tax exemptions were restored where they had previously existed.[111]

The nobles won significant victories on other issues as well. For example, in 1807 Stein had declared a moratorium on repayment of debts owed by noble estate owners; this was renewed for one year in 1810 and came up for discussion in the Assembly of Notables in 1811. Although the moratorium was class legislation, favoring noble estate owners over "capitalists," as Schön argued, and therefore in violation of the spirit of the free market in land promised by the October Edict, it was extended, with slight modifications, until 1815. One nobleman claimed that this saved "hundreds of estate owners from ruin."[112] The government also acquiesced to many of the nobles' demands in drafting a new servants' ordinance (*Gesindeordung*). Alarmed at the prospect of losing control over their servants after emancipation, nobles agitated for legislation that would hold servants on the estates and limit the wages that might be paid to them. Stein had earlier considered these demands an effort to "undermine" the "spirit of emancipation"

[110] Klein, *Von der Reform zur Restauration*, 41–43.
[111] Steffens, *Hardenberg und die ständische Opposition*, 189–95.
[112] See Stein's comments on the moratorium (*Indult*), Botzenhart, *Stein*, II/2:547–48; see also Ziekursch, *Hundert Jahre*, 286–88; Lehmann, *Stein* 2: 292–95; Schissler, *Preussische Agrargesellschaft im Wandel*, 115, 133.

and to "reconstitute serfdom in some new form."[113] The nobility was not completely satisfied with the ordinance of 1810 because it specified no maximum wage and asserted that the relationship of lord and servant was based on a free contract; nevertheless, under specific circumstances, servants were prohibited from leaving the estate without the approval of the lord, and he was permitted to exercise corporal punishment against insubordinate servants. It was a significant step back from the notion of a completely free market for labor.[114]

By far the most important concessions won by the nobility, however, had to do with the "regulation" (*Regulierung*) of the peasantry, that is, with the conditions under which complete peasant emancipation would actually take place. From Stein's departure until Hardenberg's appointment as chancellor, nothing was done to solve the problems accompanying emancipation. The questions were vexing: What were the property rights of the lord or of the peasant to the lands formerly allotted to peasant cultivation? To what extent were those lands to be considered as having constituted wages for the obligatory labor services owed by peasants to their lords? For which categories of peasants, if not all, should these labor services be dissolved? Were the lords legally bound to offer the kind of paternal care and protection to the free peasants living in their villages that they had formerly owed unfree peasants? To all of these questions the wide variety of peasant rights, differing, as we have seen, from province to province and even within provinces, added confusion. Few reformers had sufficient knowledge of the enormous variety of peasant rights to make distinctions between them, and no general legislation could encompass all of these differences. Moreover, the discussion of the agrarian legislation became pressing in 1810 and 1811, at just the moment when the provincial nobility mustered its strength to oppose Hardenberg's financial plans. All of these factors shaped the strategy pursued by the nobility. The nobility sought constantly to delay the enactment of the "regulation" of the peasantry, to postpone compliance with the legislation after it had been enacted, to manipulate the enactment to serve its own interests, to bypass the reform bureaucracy with appeals directly to the king, and to exclude as many peasants as possible from "regulation" by denying their rights to the land and insisting on a continuation of obligatory labor service.

The nobility constantly charged that the reformers were determined to destroy the basis of its existence. This was untrue, as the extension of the debt moratorium for noble estate owners demon-

---

[113] Botzenhart, *Stein*, II/2:803–4; Lehmann, *Stein*, 338–44.
[114] Schissler, *Preussische Agrargesellschaft im Wandel*, 129.

strated. In fact, even Scharnweber, who was most sympathetic to the peasants and therefore hated by the nobility, insisted that the objective of government policy must be to sustain the noble estate owners. Surveying the disastrous condition of Prussian agriculture brought about by the war, Scharnweber wrote to Hardenberg, "Exactly this sad condition makes it necessary and indispensable that the peasants acquire the means for a self-sufficient existence and the estate owners the means to rebuild their estates and to maintain them."[115] It must be remembered that, even for the most "radical" of the reformers, the preservation of a class of large landholders, whether common or noble, was a primary objective of policy.

Two questions stood at the center of the discussions about the "regulation" of peasant emancipation: (1) What property rights did peasants have to their lands? (2) Could compulsory labor services be continued after emancipation and, if so, for which peasants?

It was generally acknowledged that peasants with hereditary rights to their holdings also possessed strong proprietary claims. Thus, the October Edict did not permit the appropriation of hereditary leaseholds by noble estate owners without the permission of the leaseholder and, presumably, without the payment of compensation to him. The property rights of nonhereditary leaseholders, however, were not so secure; as we have seen, the October Edict allowed estate owners to appropriate such holdings with the approval of the authorities. This was modified only slightly by the Ordinance of February 14, 1808, which permitted the estate owner to attach only half of such a holding to his estate; the other half he was required to lease to a peasant, who combined several such plots, on hereditary leasehold. In this way, Schön and Stein hoped to build a class of landholding peasants.[116] The February Ordinance, and the subsequent ordinances for the other provinces that were based on it, acknowledged the lord's property rights over all of the land of a nonhereditary peasant. If such a holding were dissolved, the estate owner could keep half but must lease the other half; the estate owner thus disposed of all of it. Especially in East Prussia, where nonhereditary, fixed-term leaseholds were relatively common, it was widely held that the estate owner's property rights extended to the entire peasant holding. A group of East Prussian nobles explained their rights in this way: "In lieu of the present abolition of hereditary serfdom, we have leased the peasant plots of

---

[115] Scharnweber's draft response of Hardenberg to criticism of Count von Schlieben of East Prussia. DZA II, Rep. 74, H. 9. Stände, no. 9, Bl. 62. Another draft is cited in Klein, *Von der Reform zur Restauration*, 136.

[116] See footnote 115.

our free estates . . . to free persons. A free contract between both parties, of a specified duration, is now the bond that joins the peasant to his lord. It is completely that of a leaseholder of land, in which both parties draft a contract according to their convenience."[117] The implication was clear: at the expiration of the contract, the entire plot reverted to the estate owner to dispose of as he pleased. Ernst von Bülow-Cummerow, by no means a reactionary nobleman, also held the opinion that all of the land leased in a nonhereditary contract belonged to the lord.[118] The landowning nobility was thus quite willing to interpret emancipation and the introduction of free contracts to its own advantage.

Friedrich von Raumer and Christian Friedrich Scharnweber, given the task by Hardenberg of drafting agrarian policy in 1810 and 1811, took a different view. Critical of the effects of the ordinances based on that of February 1808, Scharnweber wrote Hardenberg: "Two results follow: (a) that the area of peasant land will be reduced by half and the number of peasant plots reduced to one-eighth, . . . (b) that the larger portion of the peasant Stand will disappear, since there will be nothing left for it but to become day laborers" (Tagelöhner). "The estate owners solely and exclusively have gained all the advantages of the abolition of the peasant relationships." The countryside, he predicted, would be populated by a few substantial peasants of 300 to 400 morgen, a few large estate owners, and a mass of day laborers who had no land.[119]

Raumer's draft of a decree "regulating" the conditions of peasant emancipation went further than any other in attempting to secure firm property rights for the peasants.[120] He set aside, for the moment, the Erbpächter and the Erbzinsbauern, peasants who had the best

[117] Cited in Hartmut Harnisch, "Vom Oktoberedikt des Jahres 1807 zur Deklaration von 1816," 237–38. Harnisch stresses that the sacrifice of peasant property rights began with the February Ordinance of Stein, not later under Hardenberg's leadership. This article, based on a great deal of new archival material, is very persuasive. It offers an especially thorough and sympathetic treatment of Scharnweber. Much of my argument in these pages relies heavily on Harnisch.

[118] Ernst von Bülow-Cummerow, *Ueber die Verwaltung des Staatskanzlers Fürsten von Hardenberg* (Zerbst, 1821), 53.

[119] Cited in Harnisch, "Vom Oktoberedikt des Jahre 1807 zur Deklaration von 1816," 241–42. Scharnweber's logic that the number of peasant holdings would be reduced to one-eighth of their present number was based on the following logic: the average peasant holding consisted of 3 Hufen; since half of that went to the lord, only 1½ Hufen remained. The ordinances required that the minimum size of the newly gathered peasant farm should be at least 12 Hufen, so it would take the sacrifice, on an average, of eight peasant holdings to bring together one substantial new farm.

[120] Knapp, *Bauernbefreiung* 2: 243–49.

CHAPTER 4

hereditary rights to their land and whose property rights were uncontested; instead, Raumer's draft dealt with those peasants whose rights were less clear. These he divided into two groups. The first group was composed of the Lassbauern or Lassiten, some of whom had hereditary rights to their land, though of a lesser order than the Erbpächter, and some of whom had lifelong tenure but no hereditary rights to their lands. These Lassbauern, whether hereditary or nonhereditary, were to obtain full property rights to their land immediately, without having to pay compensation to their lord; thereafter, any compensation that might be allowed would be calculated by weighing the losses suffered by the lord because of the abolition of compulsory labor services against the losses suffered by the peasant because of the abolition of the paternal obligations of the lord. Raumer believed the latter to be significant: "the gain for the peasant by obtaining property may frequently not be as large as the loss through the elimination of the so-called *Beneficien*."[121] The second group of peasants were composed of the fixed-term leaseholders (Zeitpächter). The "regulation" of these peasants was left up to the lord. He could either retain the existing lease contract, with the obligation to keep the peasant plot as such, or he could dissolve the contract, in which case half of the land went to the lord as compensation for the loss of labor services and half went to the peasant.

Members of the Assembly of Notables were invited to comment on Raumer's draft in early 1811.[122] One major criticism focused on Raumer's categorization of the peasants. Hereditary and nonhereditary Lassbauern should not be accorded the same rights; also, Kossäten and Büdner should be excluded from the category of fixed-term leaseholders, Zeitpächter, and thus excluded from regulation altogether. Another objection reflected the estate owners' fear of the loss of labor on their estates; they questioned the elimination of all compulsory labor services. Although it might be possible for an estate to function without the services of those peasants bound to provide draft animals (Spanndienst), it would be difficult to get along without the manual labor (Handdienst) of the peasants, they argued. Indeed, one of their major reasons for wanting to exclude Kossäten and Büdner from regulation was that these lowly peasants usually provided only

---

[121] Friedrich von Raumer, *Lebenserinnerungen und Briefwechsel* (Leipzig, 1861), 1: 105.

[122] For comments from various nobles, see Knapp, *Bauernbefreiung* 1: 165, 2: 256–62; Vetter, *Kurmärkischer Adel und preussische Reformen*, 137–40; Steffens, *Hardenberg und die ständische Opposition*, 104ff.; Harnisch, "Vom Oktoberedikt des Jahres 1807 zur Deklaration von 1816," 249–53; Klein, *Von der Reform zur Restauration*, 148–49; Simon, *The Failure of the Prussian Reform Movement*, 88–104.

manual labor for their lords. Counterproposals were also advanced by members of the assembly. The most important of these came from Herr von Wistinghausen, who suggested that Lassbauern be compelled to forfeit one-third of their land to the lord; Zeitpächter one-half; and Kossäten all of their land, except house and garden, and that they become daily wage-laborers, earning also a portion of the lord's harvest.

Because Raumer had already left Hardenberg's ministry, Scharnweber became responsible for composing the final draft of the Edict of Regulation, published on September 14, 1811.[123] His formulation represented a compromise between Raumer's draft and the demands of the nobility. In the edict, Scharnweber categorized the peasants differently from the way Raumer had. In the first group he placed only the hereditary Lassbauern; they were to be required to give up one-third of their land to the lord in exchange for the abolition of compulsory labor services. In the second group he placed both the nonhereditary Lassbauern and the Zeitpächter, who were to relinquish half of their lands to their lords and retain half for themselves. Scharnweber's edict contained significant concessions to the estate owners; above all, it acknowledged the principle that compensation should be paid by all peasants and that the most numerous group of peasants in most of Brandenburg, Pomerania, Upper Silesia, and East Prussia, the nonhereditary Lassbauern, would have to give up half of their holdings. But he also pushed through the principle, which went beyond Raumer's draft, that all Zeitpächter were to be "regulated." It was against the regulation of Zeitpächter that the nobility struggled so hard during the next few years.

The significance of the noble opposition to the Edict of Regulation cannot be appreciated without understanding Scharnweber's approach to the problems of Prussian agriculture.[124] Scharnweber had a more comprehensive view of the agrarian reforms than any other reformer. An economic liberal and a disciple of Albrecht Thaer, he saw the elimination of all feudal residues in the countryside as the counterpart of the freedom to pursue a trade (Gewerbefreiheit) in the towns. The objective of agrarian policy, he believed, was "to make landed property mobile, so that it can pass into the hands of those most able to develop it, and to dissolve all the relationships of dependence on the estate owner, which cause agriculture to suffer." He

[123] Knapp, *Bauernbefreiung* 2: 166, 265ff.
[124] This discussion is based on Harnisch, "Vom Oktoberedikt des Jahres 1807 zur Deklaration von 1816," 256–58.

CHAPTER 4

looked forward to the establishment of "colonies of free, strong, and debt-free landowners alongside of the large estates." This required a new attitude toward land, one that viewed land and the production of agricultural products in the same manner that factory owners viewed their production. Scharnweber was "convinced that it is a completely false view . . . that an estate [*Landgut*] is anything other than a factory where material is manufactured as in factories in the towns." This requires "the spirit of the entrepreneur," "the inclination toward one's craft," "operating capital," and "the opportunity to obtain the necessary number of workers." All of these were required in agriculture as in manufacture.

Despite his liberal views, Scharnweber was not doctrinaire. He had no intention of destroying the landowning nobility. Indeed, he believed that the Regulation Edict was its means of preservation, for by providing the nobility with more land, its capacity to command credit improved. In replying to his critics, Scharnweber indicated his primary objectives and the alternatives available for meeting them. "Concern for [the peasants'] preservation, for securing taxes, and for the conservation of the estates required that the lords themselves undertake a thorough alteration of the circumstances from which these troubles originated," he declared. There were only two alternatives: the granting of ownership to peasant leaseholders, as the edict had prescribed, and the division of the large and medium estates and the parcelling of them to peasant renters. The second course would lead to increasing subdivisions and would ultimately impoverish the peasants.[125] It was not necessary for Scharnweber to add that such a course would also lead to the demise of the nobility; its transformation into a rentier class would have deprived it of many of the mechanisms of its Herrschaft on the estate, the foundation of the nobility's political power and style of domination.

Nevertheless, many nobles opposed the Regulation Edict. They used many of the same arguments that had been raised against Raumer's draft and against all of the agrarian legislation since the October Edict—peasant agriculture had been too adversely affected by the war to carry out this regulation, the peasantry was too backward for this kind of emancipation and would become a "class of vagabonds," the edict "unjustly" invaded the property rights of estate owners by making a "gift" of land to the peasants, and noble estate owners would be deprived of the labor necessary to maintain the production on their

---

[125] DZA II, Rep. 74, H. 9, Stände, no. 9, Bl. 63.

estates.[126] The nobles from County Rastenberg, in East Prussia, complained that the edict had been prepared by men of "theory" (Scharnweber) instead of "knowledgeable men of experience." Many officials in the chancellor's office found the complaint so offensive that they demanded that its authors be punished.[127]

Despite noble charges that the Regulation Edict would result in "losing our pleasant existence in the countryside" and that it would "make our estates into a hell for us,"[128] many nobles began to recognize that the edict brought certain advantages. Schön later reported from East Prussia, where the opposition had been the most strenuous, "Some estate owners here have begun to discover from the edict that not they but their small leaseholders ... will suffer, and they have therefore become quieter."[129] Despite the opportunities offered by the Regulation Edict, the nobility continued to try to delay taking any action and worked to alter it to their further advantage. This tactic of delay was assisted by the confusion resulting from the resumption of the war against Napoleon and by the emergence in Berlin of Friedrich von Schuckmann, minister of interior after 1814, who was sympathetic to the position of the nobility.

Between 1811 and 1815, the nobility continued to agitate for a revision of the edict, especially through direct appeals to the king.[130] Shortly after the defeat of Napoleon, Frederick William III ordered Hardenberg to reexamine the principles of the Edict of Regulation. Basically, the nobles wanted three changes: the exclusion of all Zeitpächter from the regulation; the exclusion of all Kossäten and other small holders, regardless of their terms of tenure; and the continuation of the compulsory work obligations of the peasants. Since Hardenberg was preoccupied with foreign affairs, Schuckmann began to exercise a greater influence over domestic policy; he managed to prevent Scharnweber from becoming a member of the commission charged with reexamining the legislation of peasant regulation. Scharnweber, however, still had access to Hardenberg and managed to salvage some of the ideas of the early reform era.

[126] PSK/BD, Provinz Ostpreussen, Rep. 2, *Oberpräsidium*, II, 1916: 11–13, 14, 16–17; DZA II, Rep. 74, H. 9, Stände, no. 3, Bl. 3–7; no. 9, Bl. 56–57; no. 14, Bl. 1–2; no. 19, Bl. 1–3.

[127] Knapp, *Bauernbefreiung* 2: 276–82.

[128] Ibid. 1: 172.

[129] Franz Rühl, *Briefe und Aktenstücke zur Geschichte Preussens unter Friedrich Wilhelm III aus dem Nachlass von F. A. Stägemann* (Leipzig, 1899), 1: 154–55.

[130] Harnisch, "Vom Oktoberedikt des Jahres 1807 zur Deklaration von 1816," 268–69.

CHAPTER 4

The Declaration of May 29, 1816, modified the Regulation Edict in so fundamental a way that it was virtually a new edict. In addition to meeting the requirements of the edict of 1811, peasants were eligible for regulation only if they

1. were *spannfähig*, that is capable of serving and required to serve their lord with a team of draft animals;
2. had their holding listed in the tax records;
3. could show that their family's tenure of the land went back to a fixed date, which varied from province to province;
4. had not previously had their land approved by the authorities for inclusion into the lord's estate, under the provisions of the Ordinance of February 1808 or similar ordinances in the other provinces.[131]

Although the Declaration of 1816 restricted severely the number of peasants eligible for regulation, it was not an unqualified victory for the nobility. Zeitpächter and Kossäten, who were spannfähig and whose land had been in the family for a long time, were eligible for regulation; this included most of the Kossäten in Brandenburg, East and West Prussia, and Pomerania. Still, the law clearly regulated emancipation in the interest of the noble estate owners; fewer peasants qualified for emancipation, and the estate owners retained the compulsory manual labor of their "unregulated peasants." Most important, the Declaration of 1816 formally ended the policy of state protection of peasant holdings (Bauernschutz). All the previous legislation had attempted to prohibit the appropriation of peasant land by the estate owners; after 1816 peasant holders who were not eligible for regulation, that is, who had no acknowledged property rights to the land, could be freed from their work obligations and deprived of their land through a private settlement with their lord. This also permitted the lord to absorb vacant peasant holdings. As had the Regulation Edict of 1811, the declaration permitted cash compensation in lieu of a land compensation for the lord; indeed, article 47 declared that lords were required to accept monetary compensation in those cases in which the division of the peasant holdings would leave the peasant with too little land to support his draft animals. This opened the possibility for peasants to retain all of their lands if they had sufficient capital to pay off the lord.

Two additional statutes completed the framework of peasant eman-

[131] Knapp, *Bauernbefreiung* 1: 188–89.

cipation during Hardenberg's chancellorship.[132] On June 7, 1821, the government issued the Dissolution Ordinance, which provided the terms for the dissolution of the obligations of those peasants with the best property rights to their lands—Erbzinsbauern and Erbpächter—who had been excluded from the previous legislation. These peasants were to retain all of their land and were emancipated from all service obligations or payments in kind to their lords by the compensation payment to the lord of twenty-five times the equivalent of the annual goods and services normally rendered. If they lacked the capital for so significant a payment, it could be transmuted into an annual rent. As with the Declaration of 1816, however, this ordinance applied only to spannfähig peasants; others were excluded. This ordinance gave the opportunity of property rights to a large number of peasants in Brandenburg, Pomerania, Prussia, and Silesia. On the same day, the government issued the Ordinance on the Division of Commons, which prescribed the conditions for the division of common lands. This act was essential for the development of rational agriculture on the lord's lands; it permitted him to claim most of the commons, enclose them, and separate his holdings from those of the peasants.[133]

In the end, it was the nobility that gained from the agrarian legislation of the reform era. An exact accounting of the amount of land gained by the nobility as a result of the reforms is difficult to render. The best estimates indicate that during the half-century after the agrarian legislation was enacted peasants lost approximately 4 million morgen of land to noble estate owners as a result of compensation, free purchase, or simple appropriation by the lords.[134] This does not

---

[132] *Gesetz-Sammlung, 1821*, 53ff., 77ff.

[133] Koselleck, *Preussen zwischen Reform und Revolution*, 496.

[134] The assessment of the amount of land won or lost by the peasantry in the process of emancipation has been controversial. Knapp, in *Bauernbefreiung* 1: 317, concluded that the regulation of the peasants had cost them substantial quantities of land. This was in contrast to the statistics formulated by the Prussian Ministry of Agriculture in 1865, *Zeitschrift des königlichen preussischen statistischen Bureaus*, 5 (1865), nos. 1 and 2, 5. It seems clear that the Ministry of Agriculture manipulated the statistics to put the regulation in the best possible light. Theodor Freiherr von der Goltz, in *Geschichte der deutschen Landwirtschaft* (Stuttgart and Berlin, 1903), 2: 189, concluded that the settlement proved to the advantage of neither the large estate owners nor the peasants. This controversy has been continued more recently in the work of Graf Finck von Finckenstein, *Die Entwicklung der Landwirtschaft Preussen und Deutschland von 1800 bis 1930* (Würzburg, 1960), which considers the regulation to have been a gain for the peasantry. This was effectively refuted by Dietrich Saalfeld, "Zur Frage des bäuerlichen Landverlustes im Zusammenhang mit den preussischen Agrarreformen," *Agrargeschichte und Agrarsoziologie* (1963), 11: 163ff. More recent investigations indicate the substantial loss of land suffered by the peasants. See Hartmut Harnisch, "Statistische Untersuchungen zum Verlauf der kapital-

CHAPTER 4

include the vacant peasant farms seized by the lords during the wars between 1806 and 1815. In addition, through the division of approximately 17 million morgen of common lands, the peasants received only 14 percent, although previously, they had had the use of 52 percent of the commons.[135] The division of the commons was a serious loss for the peasantry; many small peasants could not sustain themselves without a share of common land on which to graze their livestock, so they were forced to sell their holdings and become wage laborers. However, the loss of land does not tell the whole story; in the process of separation, the peasants frequently received the poorest soil on the estate. Small holdings, poor soil, the loss of the commons, all of these factors contributed to the declining number of peasants holding substantial farms and the growing number of poor peasants forced to become wage laborers during the first half of the nineteenth century.[136]

The Impact of the Reforms on the Nobility

The full impact of the reforms on the nobility can be judged only after we have completed an examination of the circumstances of the nobility during the decades after 1815. It seems useful, nevertheless, to pause briefly at this point to consider, if only by means of a superficial recapitulation, how the reforms intersected with the forces of change and continuity with which the nobility was involved. In assessing the impact of the reforms on the Prussian nobility, several interrelated factors should be kept in mind.

1. The reforms were generated not by social and political conflict within Prussia, but by the administrative and economic collapse that accompanied military defeat in 1806. Thus, the reforms came, as Hardenberg said, from above; they were not inspired by protest from below. The reformers wished to lift the burden of serfdom from the backs of the peasantry and to create a society of free citizens, but they did not launch their reforms in response to widespread peasant unrest or the threat of revolution. Indeed, the reforms probably touched off

---

istischen Agrarreformen in den preussischen Ostprovinzen (1811 bis 1869)," *Jahrbuch für Wirtschaftsgeschichte* (1974), part 4, 159ff.; Rudolf Berthold, "Die Veränderungen im Bodeneigentum und in der Zahl der Bauernstellen, der Kleinstellen und der Rittergüter in dem preussischen Provinzen Sachsen, Brandenburg, und Pommern während der Agrarreformen des 19. Jahrhunderts," *Jahrbuch für Wirtschaftsgeschichte*, Sonderheft, 1978, 70ff., Schissler, *Preussische Agrargesellschaft im Wandel*, 109–112.

[135] Koselleck, *Preussen zwischen Reform und Revolution*, 498; Schissler, *Preussische Agrargesellschaft im Wandel*, 109.

[136] Koselleck, *Preussen zwischen Reform und Revolution*, 498–99.

as much, or more, unrest as they quelled. Like all reforms from above, those of the Prussian reformers did not aim at a basic restructuring of the social relations in Prussia. The reforms were to liberate the society, but they were also designed to deal with specific economic and administrative problems; they were intended to improve the productive capacity of the society and to enlarge, thereby, the state revenues. Social change, up to a point, was an acceptable byproduct of these reforms, but none of the reformers anticipated a transformation of Prussian social structure. Even Scharnweber, hated by the nobility for his defense of the small peasants in the debates over agrarian legislation, considered that an objective of the reform was to bolster the position of the nobility. In explaining the Regulation Edict of 1811, Scharnweber declared his intention

> to promote those conditions and thus to establish all those relationships on the land in such a way that the nobleman can more assuredly succeed in discharging gradually his indebtedness, in increasing significantly the value and profitability of his properties, in improving and securing the status of his property so that his existence can retain a solid and unshakable foundation in all pecuniary respects, thus giving to him in his relations to the state and to the other Stände that dignified and effective position that corresponds to his own true interest and to the common good.[137]

2. Because the reforms were prompted by the state's economic and administrative collapse, they were instituted during a time of intense financial pressure on the state and had as an important objective the relief of that pressure. This, the reformers believed, could be achieved through the introduction of a freer market economy. The reformers proposed a new attitude toward land; they were not hostile to large estates and endeavored, as we have seen, to preserve them. But they wanted to free land from the fetters of feudal attitudes and values. Thus, for the first time, noble estates could be legally and freely purchased by commoners in a free market. This opened the door to a more complete capitalist agriculture. Agrarian capitalism meant (a) the reorganization of the system of production, the consolidation of the lord's lands, and the introduction of new methods and crops; (b) the introduction of a labor system based largely on free wage laborers, without the encumbrances of feudal obligations; (c) the development of an agriculture directed toward distant markets, with the willingness

[137] Cited in Harnisch, "Vom Oktoberedikt des Jahres 1807 zur Deklaration von 1816," 259–60.

to concentrate on production for export rather than for local consumption; and (d) the utilization of capital resources and the singular objective of winning a profit with which to build capital. These developments did not come at once; many of them were already visible in Prussian agriculture before the reforms, but they became more pronounced in the succeeding decades. To achieve these objectives, the reformers risked the noble monopoly of landed estates. In subsequent years, they tried to qualify that risk. Theodor von Schön, who in 1807 had argued for the Emancipation Edict on strictly economic grounds, insisting that it was of no concern to the state who owned a particular landed estate, later criticized Hardenberg's agrarian reforms for violating the property rights of the nobility; he considered "the preservation of the most important Stand of the nation" essential.[138]

3. Alongside of the effort to create a free market economy and a society of "free" citizens, the reformers tried to preserve the system of social hierarchy and privilege that gave the nobility a preferred position. Because the reforms did not result from pressure from below, the reformers felt little need to provide a safety valve to popular pressure. Stein shrank from the word *representative* and referred instead to "participation in the administration." He was unwilling to go much beyond the traditional form of ständisch representation. Hardenberg anticipated some form of national representation, but he conceived that body, like the Assembly of Notables or the provisional National Assembly, as having only consultative powers, more a representative of the government to the people than the reverse. The need for some semblance of representation, coupled with the fear of popular assemblies, gave the revived noble assemblies enormous leverage during the reform era. This they continued to exert after 1815. Moreover, the system of noble Herrschaft on the landed estates remained intact after 1815; the effort to set aside the patrimonial courts, police, and patronage rights over the village school and church failed completely. Given the protracted process of peasant emancipation, drawn out over decades, the retention of Herrschaft meant that domination of the peasantry by the noble estate owner changed very little, despite emancipation. The landed estates remained what they had been for the preceding two centuries—the training ground of the nobility and the place where its habitus was formed and its style of domination ac-

[138] See Eduard W. Mayer, *Das Retablissement Ost- und Westpreussens unter der Mitwirkung und Leitung Theodors von Schön*, Schriften des Instituts für ostdeutsche Wirtschaft in Königsberg (Jena, 1916), 43.

quired. The myth of paternalism was more difficult to sustain, for it was less compatible with the system of labor relations that emerged with capitalist agriculture. For that reason, paternalism was given a prominent place in the ideology of conservatism that developed in the early decades of the century.

5

ADAM MÜLLER AND THE GENESIS OF A CONSERVATIVE IDEOLOGY

The Emergence of Formal Ideology

In the early chapters of this book I described the system by which the nobility exercised its domination of the peasantry. The police, the patrimonial courts, and the appropriation of peasant labor were the direct means of control. This was augmented indirectly, I have argued, by the intimate euphemisms of family and paternalism and, at the same time, by a system of symbolic Herrschaft that created social distance between the nobility and the peasantry, naturalizing and justifying the superiority of the nobility. Down to the end of the eighteenth century, the ideological dimensions of this system were never very explicit. When the veil of paternalism was violently torn aside, as in the peasant uprisings of Silesia or in cases of extreme brutality by the lords, the government intervened to reassert the principle that authority ultimately expressed fatherly concern—if not by the noble lord, then by the king. Occasional paternal actions on the part of noblemen or the government served to illustrate the general validity of the system—at least in the minds of the rulers, if not the ruled. Many people recognized that the transformation of agriculture and the unbridled speculation in noble estates had done much to undermine the credibility of the ideology. Still, paternalism functioned as an inexplicit ideology because there did not seem to be acceptable or obvious alternatives.

In the decades that bracketed the end of the eighteenth century, however, a combination of events offered alternative visions of social organization. New economic ideas, trumpeted by the spokesmen of commercial interests, found adherents in Germany, and new political ideas that culminated in the French Revolution found their way into Germany as well. In Prussia the efforts to modernize agriculture and to create a new general law code reflected both the changing economic and political needs of Prussian society and the influence of western European thought. The thrust of these economic and political movements was to separate the public and private sphere, state and society, in ways that had not previously been the case and in ways that were incompatible with the ideology of paternalism.

In this atmosphere, the nature of authority was openly contested and the system of symbolic domination began to break down; the nobility faced what Gramsci called a "crisis of hegemony." It was in order to preserve traditional hegemony that a segment of the nobility, represented by Marwitz and Finckenstein, opposed the reform legislation so vigorously. Although these opponents of the reforms were successful in defeating some proposals that would have restricted the nobility's control over the peasantry, such as the Gendarmerie Edict, and in turning other reforms, such as the agrarian legislation, to their own advantage, they could not resolidify the dissolving structure of cultural hegemony. For someone like Marwitz the measure of this dissolution was to be seen in the "leveling" of all the social distinctions he saw emerging in the world. In one of the final paragraphs of his memoirs, he wrote: "In my youth, a man of my Stand was considered to be foremost wherever he allowed himself to be seen; people tipped their hats to him, they stepped aside for him. Now, in my old age, I cannot, to be sure, say that my personal presence does not command proper respect, but the Stand no longer does. One is lost in the crowd, no one steps aside, no one tips his hat, but they will run over you if you don't get out of the way."[1]

Perhaps such comments deserve to be dismissed as the cranky lamentations of an old man. We know, from an abundance of sources, that Prussian society did not cease to be deferential in the 1820s or 1830s but that the nobility continued to enjoy a privileged position throughout the nineteenth century. Nevertheless, despite his penchant for hyperbole, Marwitz undoubtedly witnessed a perceptible change in the manners and behavior—in short, the culture—through which social relations were expressed. His comment (and there were countless others like it scattered through his papers) reflects a sense of the disappearance of genuine deference. Deference, as anthropologist Gerald Sider has shown us, is an important expression of the cultural ties that bind persons together in a social relationship.[2] The concept of deference combines three of the basic meanings of its root, to defer: to delay or postpone, to submit to the judgment or claim of another, and to pay courteous regard to another. Sider concludes, "Deference

[1] Friedrich August Ludwig von der Marwitz, *Friedrich August Ludwig von der Marwitz: Ein märkischer Edelmann im Zeitalter der Befreiungskriege*, ed. Friedrich Meusel, 3 vols. (Berlin, 1908–1913), 1: 711.

[2] Gerald Sider, "The Ties That Bind: Culture, Agriculture, Property, and Propriety in the Newfoundland Village Fishery," *Social History* 5, no. 1 (January 1980): esp. 21–22.

CHAPTER 5

lies not in the act of tipping one's hat to the lord (to use an example from connections of class inequality), but in the temporal dimensions implied in the act—the invocation of past ties and, especially, the implications for future ties that lie, half-hidden and perhaps still to be negotiated and 'realized,' in the act itself." For Marwitz, the decline of deference meant the disappearance of many of those ties between persons that comprised the nobility's cultural hegemony and on which its ideology of paternalism was predicated. It signaled the emergence of a society in which such personal bonds were of lesser importance.

It is at such a moment in the crisis of hegemony that the need for a formal self-conscious ideology arises. Because the inchoate ideology implicit in the system of cultural hegemony no longer is sufficient, it is necessary to articulate an explicit ideological justification for class rule. Because the system of cultural hegemony no longer automatically commands the "consent" of the dominated groups in the society, it is necessary to justify the coercive powers—all that remains—by logically expressed ideology. And finally, because the attack on those hegemonic structures, which Gramsci calls the "outer fortresses" surrounding the state and the economy, has been carried out by means of a counterideology, it is necessary for the dominant class to arm itself anew with ideological weapons.[3] For the Prussian nobility, this meant developing an explicit definition of authority that would help to conserve its power; it needed a formal and an articulate defense of paternalism with which it could defend its authority in the contested political arena.

Two additional observations need to be made in connection with the emergence of a conservative ideology as a response to the disintegrating cultural hegemony of the dominant class. First, because it represents an effort to reimpose tradition, to restore the "lived experience" that had won consent prior to the crisis of authority, the central features of the conservative ideology reflect those social relations as they had existed prior to the crisis. Conservative ideology is thus deeply embedded in the social relations that have governed production in the past. Second, because that segment of the dominant class which feels most acutely the loss of cultural hegemony and which is least able to adapt the forms of its domination to the new circumstances has the greatest need for an ideological defense, conservatism tends to reflect

---

[3] The notion of consent is Gramsci's. In connection with the collapse of consent and the creation of new ruling-class ideologies, see Antonio Gramsci, *Prison Notebooks* (New York, 1971), 210.

the perspectives of those elements of the class least capable of accepting change.

Ideology, however, is more than the work of people, like Marwitz, directly involved in the struggle for power in society.[4] It is also the creation of intellectuals who cast it in a meaningful framework of universally valid "truths." Karl Mannheim described such intellectuals as "socially unattached," "the typical advocate-philosophers, ideologues who can find arguments in favor of any political cause they happen to serve. Their own social positions do not bind them to any cause, because they have an extraordinarily refined sense for all the political and social currents around them."[5] This notion of social detachment, however, is perhaps exaggerated; it may be, like Plato's "noble fictions," a myth essential to the effectiveness of an intellectual in forming ideologies that appear to transcend class interests and provide universal meaning.

Political theorists are never detached; they are involved in two social dimensions. First, political thinkers communicate their ideas in a language and with symbols that, although they may have a high level of abstraction, are available to and judged by the larger society. As J.G.A. Pocock has said of the political thinker, "He will be communicating with his fellow citizens—as Socrates was judged by them—in terms of what he has done with their publicly-approved paradigms of value and authority."[6] Second, political thinkers compete for recognition with other intellectuals. Thus, they are always engaged in a two-way transaction; their standing in the intellectual community determines in part their ability to influence society's perception of the social and political world, while their ability to influence social perceptions determines in part their position in the intellectual community. Ideology, therefore, is the result of a particular symbiosis of intellectual and social community.

Two features of the intellectual community in Germany at the end of the eighteenth century are important for an understanding of the relationship between the intellectual and the social realms.[7] First, by

[4] Robert M. Berdahl, "Prussian Aristocracy and Conservative Ideology: A Methodological Examination," *Social Science Information* 15, no. 4/5 (1976): 583–99. This represents a somewhat more schematic view than I now hold.

[5] Karl Mannheim, "Conservative Thought," in *From Karl Mannheim*, ed. Kurt Wolff (New York, 1977), 185.

[6] J.G.A. Pocock, *Politics, Language, and Time* (London, 1972), 14–15.

[7] Space does not permit a list of all the important works dealing with the German Aufklärung. A good introduction, complete with an annotated bibliography, is provided by Klaus Epstein, *The Genesis of German Conservatism* (Princeton, 1966), esp. 29–83, 677–710; see also the critical view presented by Reinhart Koselleck, *Kritik und Krise: Ein Beitrag zur*

CHAPTER 5

the end of the eighteenth century, the primary aspects of Enlightenment thought were being subjected to severe criticism in Germany. The German Aufklärung had never become as deeply rooted as was the Enlightenment in the west; the German educated class never developed the level of political and social criticism associated with the Enlightenment in France. Moreover, even major figures of the German Aufklärung endeavored to transcend the assumptions of the Enlightenment. Kant's critical philosophy defined the limits of rationalism; Herder's historicism opened the way to a new view of the world that rejected the doctrine of natural law associated with the Enlightenment; even Lessing, whose thought most resembled the liberating, humanistic qualities of the western Enlightenment, sought to transcend what he considered to be the shallowness of natural religion. By the end of the eighteenth century, enlightened thought was under assault. The *Sturm und Drang* awakened Germans to the existence of human impulses other than the rational, and Germans ultimately reacted to the French Revolution and Napoleonic conquest by repudiating French cultural hegemony. Many early enthusiasts of the French Revolution, such as Friedrich Gentz, turned into bitter opponents; after 1806 many German intellectuals, like Fichte, became ardent German patriots. Eighteenth-century cosmopolitanism was one of the casualties of the Napoleonic wars.

The second feature of the intellectual world in Germany at the end of the eighteenth century is that it was more closely tied to the social system than was the case in France. In short, the legitimizing authority of the intellectual field was more heavily external than elsewhere. Few writers in Germany could support themselves on their earnings as writers; even very distinguished writers could not live from the sale of their writings and most, such as Goethe, Kant, and Lessing, had official positions. The less talented, living on the margin of the intellectual world, had to find a patron if they were to survive. Contemporaries estimated that Germany possessed between three and six thousand professional authors in 1780, many of whom were probably journalists or hack writers. Since the reading public was still small, authors were forced to seek jobs as court poets, librarians, tutors, political secretaries, and other similar positions of dependence.[8] To survive in the world of letters was to compete successfully for these few positions as well as for the attention of those who bought and read books. The

---

Pathogenese der bürgerlichen Welt (Freiburg and Munich, 1959). See also Rudolf Vierhaus, *Deutschland im Zeitalter des Absolutismus*, Deutsche Geschichte, 6 (Göttingen, 1978).

[8] Epstein, *Conservatism*, 51.

prize was a secure life; the cost most often was the loss of a pretense of independent thought.

Müller and His Milieu

Historians have for some time accepted the proposition that the primary patterns of conservative thought emerged prior to the French Revolution and not merely in response to it. Edmund Burke's stunning critique of the revolution, which earned him a preeminent place in the pantheon of conservatives, had been prefaced by earlier political writings and speeches. In Germany, opposition to the Aufklärung produced arguments that were clearly conservative. Justus Möser, an essayist from the small Westphalian state of Osnabrück, offered a view of the state and society that contained many ingredients of a conservative philosophy. After the outbreak of the French Revolution, Hannover, with its Anglophile University of Göttingen, became the center for antirevolutionary ideas in Germany. August Ludwig von Schlözer, editor of the influential *Göttingen Gelehrten Anzeigen*, became an early critic of the revolution, and Ernst Brandes and August Rehberg also developed conservative arguments.[9] And finally, there was Friedrich von Gentz, the latter-day courtier gracing the courts of the rich and the wellborn throughout Europe, who became a powerful pamphleteer and who first translated into German Burke's *Reflections on the Revolution in France*. Adam Müller, as an eighteen-year-old Gymnasium student, impressed Gentz, who became Müller's lifelong friend and patron.[10]

Müller, however, had little in common with these earlier representatives of conservative thought. Rehberg, who retained his basic confi-

[9] On prerevolutionary conservatism see Fritz Valjavec, *Die Entstehung der politischen Strömungen in Deutschland, 1770–1815* (Munich, 1951), and Epstein, *Conservatism*. The essence of Burke's conservatism was already evident in his speech on the reform bill of 1782. See Burke's speech on the reform of representation in the House of Commons, June 16, 1784, in James Burke, ed., *The Speeches of the Right Honorable Edmund Burke* (Dublin, 1865), 405–14. Epstein, *Conservatism*, 297–338, has a long chapter on Justus Möser, as does Friedrich Meinecke, *Die Entstehung des Historismus* (Munich, 1939), 303–54. English trans.: *Historism: The Rise of a New Historical Outlook*, trans. J. E. Anderson (New York, 1972), 250–94. Jonathan Knudsen's *Justus Möser and the German Enlightenment* (Cambridge, 1986) is a major contribution. Epstein, *Conservatism*, 547–94, has a thorough discussion of Rehberg and the Hannoverians.

[10] On Gentz, see Golo Mann, *Friedrich von Gentz: Geschichte eines europäisches Staatsmannes* (Zurich, 1947); Jakob Baxa, *Friedrich von Gentz* (Vienna, 1965); Paul Sweet, *Friedrich von Gentz: Defender of the Old Order* (Madison, Wis., 1941). The correspondence between Gentz and Müller has been published in *Briefwechsel zwischen Friedrich Gentz und Adam Müller, 1800–1829*, ed. Marie von Pilat (Stuttgart, 1857).

dence in rationalism, believed that Müller misunderstood and misused Burke's historical concept of the social contract. A much more systematic thinker than Müller, he criticized the latter's efforts to win an audience by presenting his ideas in the format of public lectures; to hold his listeners, Rehberg charged, Müller resorted to "false ornamentation, dazzling shams of exaggerated assumptions, unfitting expressions, and strident contrasts between strained viewpoints."[11] Even Gentz, Müller's closest friend for more than three decades, did not share his cloudy romanticism; despite Müller's efforts to convert him, Gentz never forsook his rational approach to religion.[12]

Nevertheless, Müller gained considerable influence among the Prussian nobility. He was, beyond doubt, author of the first conservative political ideology that defended the interests of the nobility. His major work, *Die Elemente der Staatskunst*, was a series of lectures delivered in Dresden in 1808 and 1809 on invitation of Prince Bernhard of Saxon-Weimar. His other chief work grew out of a similar set of lectures on Frederick II delivered in Berlin in 1810, at the height of the noble opposition to Hardenberg. Throughout 1810 and the early months of 1811, Müller forged important links to leaders of the noble opposition, especially Marwitz, with whom he corresponded at some length. That connection, however, did not endure, and Marwitz later characterized Müller as a fraud.[13]

Marwitz's harsh ultimate judgment of Müller was shared by many. August Wilhelm Rehberg, as we have seen, was contemptuous of Müller's "pedantic elegance." Friedrich von Raumer, a historian who also worked closely with Hardenberg during the reform era, described Müller during his student days at Göttingen as a poseur who catered to rich Englishmen and who "closed his shutters on bright days and lit candles because it was more poetic and genteel." Wilhelm Grimm asked his brother, "Do you not also feel that a certain falsehood permeates all of his writings?" Friedrich Karl von Savigny, originator of the historical school of law in Germany, wrote that the "deceptive brilliance which he spread through his writings . . . is a remarkable jumble of ideas and I cannot place any confidence in it. His extraordinary talent hangs on him like a coat, encompassing, for me, the most vivid

[11] See Rehberg's critique of Müller, *Sämmtliche Schriften*, vol. 4 (Hanover, 1829), 240ff.; Gunnar Rexius, "Studien zur Staatslehre der historischen Schule," *HZ* 107 (1911): 520–22.

[12] Baxa, *Friedrich von Gentz*, 125, 165–66.

[13] Marwitz, I:624; II/1:263–64; Jakob Baxa, *Adam Müller* (Jena, 1930), 160–61, 167–70. The basis for Marwitz's accusation was false, for he incorrectly believed that Müller had received a pension from Hardenberg in exchange for his silence.

example of the strengths and weaknesses of our time." Goethe, too, had deep reservations about Müller, whose writings, he said, led "in the wrong direction."[14]

Given these views of his intellectual contribution, Müller's effort to establish himself as a man of letters met with little success. He always stood at the periphery of the German intellectual world, never wholly original, often contradictory, always a dilettante, always suspect. He left the University of Göttingen in 1801 as an enthusiast for the economic theory of Adam Smith. On the basis of principles derived from Smith, Müller made his debut in the intellectual arena with a sharp attack on Fichte's essay "The Closed Commercial State." Müller's essay was criticized widely and did little to satisfy his ambition to be regarded as an important young intellectual. Schleiermacher remarked, "The shocking arrogance, completely without reservation, and the empty impudence toward someone like Fichte, I find terribly repugnant in so young a man." Even Gentz was critical: "You have really deserved the criticism. Your haste in the publication of this essay is totally incomprehensible to me; how you could have decided on such a step, without giving me an hour's time to tell you my opinion on the matter, really puzzles me."[15]

In *Die Lehre vom Gegensatz*, an uncompleted work published in 1804, Müller attempted to develop a dialectical philosophy similar to that of Fichte (and later Hegel). But Müller's "theory of polarities" lacked the subtlety of Fichte's ethical idealism and the grandeur of Hegel's historical dialectic of the spirit. Müller referred to the "history of self-consciousness," a phrase borrowed from Schelling, but never developed the idea. His dialectic had no evolutionary dimension; it was static and rigid. He wrote of the contradictions between object and subject, positive and negative, nature and art, science and religion. Everything exists in a tension with its opposite, but these polarities are resolved in a "higher third," or "totality"—his favorite word. He remained fascinated by contradictions; throughout his writings, the phrase that occurs most frequently is that something is "nothing other than" its opposite.[16]

Although *Die Lehre vom Gegensatz* received virtually no notice, Müller's next project, a series of public lectures on German science and

---

[14] The various criticisms of Müller are in Jakob Baxa, ed., *Adam Müllers Lebenszeugnisse* (Munich, Paderborn, and Vienna, 1966), 1: 15, 277, 562, 588, 657; see also Reinhold Steig, *Heinrich von Kleists Berliner Kämpfe* (Berlin and Stuttgart, 1901), 505–6.

[15] Baxa, *Adam Müller*, 7–9; Baxa, *Müllers Lebenszeugnisse* 1: 21, 120.

[16] *Die Lehre vom Gegensatz* (Berlin, 1804); Müller's comments on this essay are in Baxa, *Müllers Lebenszeugnisse* 1: 206–9.

literature, delivered in Dresden in 1806, received some, primarily unfavorable, attention. An anonymous critique by Karl August Böttiger, former director of a Dresden Gymnasium who also lectured in Dresden, stated, "Herr Müller is still a very young man ... he is not yet free of a certain literary and youthful deception, ... despite the talents his friends claim to see in him."[17] In a style characteristic of most of his writings, Müller drew broad generalizations from the juxtaposition of opposites. World history, he maintained, comprised two large epochs: the Greek age of antiquity, which was masculine in character, and the modern German age, which was feminine. Corresponding to these two epochs were two political principles: the idea of urban citizenship (*Bürgertum*), associated with the republican principle of Greece, and the idea of a landowning nobility, associated with the monarchical principle of Germany. In addition, these two epochs and principles were linked with two other sets of opposites: freedom (republican) and law (monarchical), skepticism (republican) and dogmatism (monarchical). Similarly, of German history, he wrote as follows: "Two groups of states stand, in an uncertain balance, opposite one another in their culture, constitution, and morals: the one represents tradition, Catholicism, fidelity to the old; the other represents the desire for the new, Protestantism, the uninterrupted extension of the area of freedom and reason. In the totality of this conflict is to be seen history, its connectedness and its heroes."[18]

By the time of these lectures, Müller had abandoned whatever may have remained of the rationalism and confidence in natural law that he possessed when he left Göttingen in 1801. He had already converted to Catholicism in April 1805.[19] During 1806 he became acquainted with the work of the young Romantic poet Heinrich von Kleist and, when Kleist returned to Dresden in 1807, the two began plans for the publication of a literary journal, *Phöbus*, the following year.[20] Few of the literary giants of the era contributed pieces to the journal and it remained insignificant and floundered. Gentz, dissatisfied with Müller's preoccupation with aesthetic concerns, urged him to turn his attention to politics; in May 1808, he wrote Müller: "Write one of the following two books: either a detailed response to Buchholtz's critical work on the nobility of birth or a collection of political, moral, and historical essays. ... You will make a colossal reputation

---

[17] Baxa, *Adam Müller*, 47–49; Adam Müller, *Vorlesungen über die deutsche Wissenschaft und Literatur*, ed. Artur Salz (Munich, 1920), 145ff.
[18] Baxa, *Adam Müller*, 51–52.
[19] Ibid., 38–39.
[20] Ibid., 64–69.

for yourself—and if you decide to do the former, you will lay the foundation for a highly comfortable existence."[21] The failure of *Phöbus*, the financial difficulties that resulted, and his inability to obtain a university post led Müller to follow Gentz's advice. The result was the lectures in Dresden, published in 1809 as *Die Elemente der Staatskunst*.[22]

In 1809, Müller moved to Berlin, which had become the center of the conflict over social and political reform in Germany. There he proposed to the Prussian ministry that he be subsidized in publishing two newspapers, one openly in support of reform and one anonymously in opposition. The government refused this remarkable offer, and Müller's hope of a post in the Prussian civil service gradually faded.[23]

As the possibility of a government post declined, Müller gravitated toward the noble opponents of the administration. The lectures on Frederick II, delivered in Berlin between January and March 1810 and published later that year, provided the Prussian nobility with a clear-cut ideology.[24] Although the lectures contain little that was not already present in *Die Elemente der Staatskunst*, they concentrated specifically on the Prussian experience. Instead of attacking eighteenth-century statecraft in general, Müller sought to demonstrate how Frederick II had gone astray with a "mechanistic" approach to politics. The lectures comprised a strong indictment of the Frederician state that had collapsed in defeat in 1806; beyond that, however, the attack on Frederick represented a barely concealed critique of the entire reform administration, which, he believed, was inspired by the same mechanistic approach. In what must have been a response to the attitude expressed by reformer Theodor von Schön that the state had no in-

---

[21] Baxa, *Müllers Lebenszeugnisse* 1: 417.

[22] *Die Elemente der Staatskunst*, ed. Othmar Spann (Vienna and Leipzig, 1922), 2 vols. After the failure of *Phöbus*, Müller sought a teaching post at Jena but was unsuccessful. Robert Mühler, *Kleists und Adam Müllers Freundschaftskrise* (Vienna, 1948), 5.

[23] Müller's proposal to Friedrich August von Stägemann was as follows: "A state such as the reorganized Prussian state must also speak out: the viewpoint for a judgment of the new organization, as well as for the extraordinary measures that the shattered position of the state makes necessary, must be published popularly; the opposition that has been aroused by the reform will not be beaten down, but led, or still better, will participate. Above all, the parties that want to demolish the state completely must be led strongly into the official path through a reflective opinion and a reflective opposition. I propose to write: (1) publicly and under the authority of the state council, a governmental newspaper; (2) anonymously, and with the connivance of the authorities, a popular newspaper. In other words, a ministerial and an opposition newspaper." See Baxa, *Müllers Lebenszeugnisse* 1: 483. Müller's later proposal to publish only a governmental newspaper was also rejected (ibid., 488–95).

[24] *Ueber König Friedrich II und die Natur, Würde und Bestimmung der preussischen Monarchie* (Berlin, 1810).

terest in who owned a particular estate, Müller wrote: "What do you say of an era in which the philosophers of state, among others, are disunited over the questions whether the state can be truly indifferent as to whether A, B, or C owns a property?—since it is as clear as anything that, on the whole, the state has only one economic interest and that is that the property owners retain their property."[25]

Frustrated in his bid to become a government publicist, Müller joined with Heinrich von Kleist in publishing Berlin's first daily newspaper, the *Berliner Abendblätter*, which first appeared on October 1, 1810.[26] Almost immediately the paper became embroiled in a controversy arising from Müller's critical review of the work of the late Königsberg economist Christian Jakob Kraus. Since a number of reformers were students and disciples of Kraus, the article was seen as an attack on the reforms themselves. Müller charged that Kraus had possessed little originality and that his writings were derivative of Adam Smith. In a damning phrase, Müller referred to Kraus as "a good, but completely unproductive and dependent head."[27] Throughout November and December 1810, Müller published articles critical of the liberal economic assumptions behind the reforms; shortly after publication of Hardenberg's decree on freedom of occupation (Gewerbefreiheit), Müller attacked the principle of economic freedom.[28] As a result of such comments critical of the administration, the government imposed tighter censorship on the newspaper, forcing Kleist to alter its character. Government pressure forced the paper to halt publication on March 30, 1811.[29]

The failure of *Abendblätter* and his conflict with Hardenberg left Müller with few prospects in Berlin. At the end of May 1811, he left the capital and eventually migrated to Vienna, where he obtained a post in the government of Metternich. Müller published a number of essays over the next decade and a half, primarily on economic questions. He continued his criticism of capitalism and of commercial agriculture, but by the 1820s, when Prussian agriculture was caught in a severe depression, his ideas were no longer pertinent. Müller's ideol-

---

[25] Ibid., 86–87.

[26] Heinrich von Kleist, *Berliner Abendblätter*, ed. Georg Minde-Pouet, facsimile ed. (Leipzig, 1925). See also Reinhold Steig, *Kleists Berliner Kämpfe*.

[27] *Berliner Abendblätter* 11 (12 October 1810).

[28] See Müller's articles on Adam Smith and on national credit, ibid., nos. 40, 41 (15 and 16 November 1810). His attacks on Hardenberg's reform proposals appeared in ibid., no. 55 (3 December 1810), and no. 67 (17 December 1810).

[29] Baxa, *Adam Müller*, 160–79.

ogy was shaped by the conflict over the reforms; the period of the restoration would be dominated by other ideologues.

Müller's Conservative Ideology and the Critique of Capitalism

In *Die Elemente der Staatskunst*, Müller defined the state as the "totality of human affairs, their combination in a living whole."[30] For Müller, there was no division between the state and civil society, between the political and the economic sphere, or between the realms of public and private life; all were integrated into a seamless whole. "Man cannot be conceived of apart from the state," he declared, "and human and civil existence are one and the same."[31] Müller's conservative ideology and critique of capitalism were closely joined, so that one cannot be grasped fully without reference to the other. This brief segment will examine the implications of Müller's integration of politics and economics.

Even more than most intellectuals who formulate explicit political ideologies, Müller operated in the terrain between the interests of a specific social class and the predominant values of the intellectual community. Müller sought to shape a world view that would legitimate the social and political interests of his noble patrons and benefactors. For the wider intellectual community, whose respect he also avidly sought, Müller endeavored to demonstrate his ability to work with, and to reshape, the paradigms of political and social thought. The task was not easy. It required him to defend on grounds of principle a paternalistic social order without even mentioning, much less advocating, serfdom. He had to join in the criticism of rationalism, in all of its manifestations, at the moment when the landowners turned toward scientific agriculture as the means of survival. He had to attack the growing influence of commerce and manufacturing, together with its capitalist ideology, while the fate of the landowning aristocracy of Prussia was becoming inextricably intertwined with the capitalist world economy.

Müller began his effort on behalf of the nobility by validating experience as the proper guide to human affairs.[32] Ever fond of drawing sharp contrasts that were, for Müller, the essence of dialectical thought, he contrasted the theoretician and the practical person. In

---

[30] *Elemente der Staatskunst* 1: 48.
[31] Ibid. 1: 29, 56; Rudolf Kohler, ed., *Adam Müller: Schriften zur Staatsphilosophie* (Munich, n.d.), 178. See also Reinhold Aris, *Die Staatslehre Adam Müllers* (Tübingen, 1929), 23.
[32] *Elemente der Staatskunst* 1: 12–18.

the first of lectures on statecraft, he suggested that the theoretician based theories on "reason" and on "general laws," whereas the practical person based ideas on "experience," "reality," and "locality." "The one floats in the air over all lands and ages, the other stands firmly on his own ground and holds to that which he can grasp with his own hands or survey from his own office," he wrote.[33] This dialectical tension, he maintained, could be expressed philosophically as the conflict between concepts (*Begriffe*) and ideas (*Ideen*), a distinction that had already been drawn before him by both Kant and Fichte.[34] The contrast between concepts and ideas became fundamental for Müller and ran through much of his work. Concepts were derived from reason alone; they were abstract formulations that, according to Müller, were dead. Ideas, on the other hand, were living things, born of the experiences of humankind over centuries. Concepts were mechanical and unnatural; ideas were organic and natural, growing and developing over time. Borrowing heavily from Burke, Müller confirmed that the nobility's understanding of the state, the result of centuries of experience, was natural and healthy; the theoreticians and revolutionaries who tried to build the state from abstract concepts alone were quite wrong. He declared, "There is no concept of the state."[35]

The deadening concept that had intruded upon all true ideas of the state and society in the eighteenth century, Müller believed, was the theory of natural law. "The chimera of natural law, which fifteen or twenty years ago occupied all the minds of Europe, came into the world merely because the idea of the state had never been conceived grandly or magnificently enough," he asserted.[36] This fascination with natural law had produced several fundamental errors. First, it had led to a misunderstanding about the idea of law. Because natural law was "discovered" by reason, it was assumed that positive law could be abstracted from natural law by reason alone. The result was merely another dead concept, not the idea of the law. The idea of the law, Müller insisted, contained two contrasting elements: one was general or universal, the other local or specific. Adherents of natural law the-

---

[33] Ibid. 1: 12–13.

[34] Ibid., 20–25, 40–41. See also Aris, *Staatslehre Adam Müllers,* 17; Jakob Baxa, *Adam Müller: Ausgewählte Abhandlungen* (Jena, 1921), 111. Baxa also has a long note on the distinction between concepts and ideas in his appendix to *Elemente der Staatskunst* 2: 292–94.

[35] *Elemente der Staatskunst* 1: 20. See the many citations of Burke, ibid. 1: 19ff. Burke, Müller believed, represented the perfect fusion of theory and practice, thought and experience.

[36] Ibid. 1: 40.

ory separated the two, concentrating only on the first, the general aspect of the law, believing it to be universally valid and everywhere applicable. But the true idea of the law also possessed "locality" and manifested itself as the "higher third" only when the general, universal aspect of law was fused with or applied to local circumstances. "The state is a large, specific locality and its legislation is the mass of formulas that belong to it. Whoever considers both, the locality and the formulas, within one another, and thus in movement, has grasped the idea of the state."[37]

A second error of the emphasis on natural law was that it offered a thoroughly mechanistic view of the state. The state came to be viewed as a machine that operated according to certain abstract principles; only an "engineer" was required to run it. The state was not seen as an organism that grew and changed and therefore required a living personality at its head. This was, above all, the failure of Frederick II, who, despite his genius, bore a responsibility for the subsequent collapse of the Prussian state, for his successors in administration were "educated in the mechanistic school of Frederick."[38] Precisely this mechanistic approach to statecraft was what Müller objected to in Hardenberg's policies.

The third error, the infection of natural law with its emphasis on universals, had led, Müller believed, to cosmopolitanism and undermined the sense of patriotism necessary for survival of the state. Here the intellectuals had played an especially devastating role in destroying the feeling of "nationality." "They, more than any other group [*Stand*], have helped to splinter and scatter the holy capital of our ideas of fatherland," Müller charged; "they have introduced a certain universal arrogance into our social life: claims that our patriotic efforts cannot sufficiently achieve, that thus must lead to a complete indifference toward the fatherland."[39] But Frederick II bore some responsibility, too, for he helped introduce French manners, customs, and education into German courts and noble society, giving them a cosmopolitan flavor.[40]

Closely related to these errors, which made law exclusively a product of reason, the state an artificial mechanism, and people free of any sense of national identity or obligation, Müller found an additional misconception in the eighteenth-century political theorists: they believed that individuals existed prior to society and that the state re-

[37] Ibid. 1: 41–42.
[38] Ibid. 1: 14; *Ueber Friedrich II*, 178–79, 239–40.
[39] *Ueber Friedrich II*, 235.
[40] Ibid., 137–40.

sulted from a social contract that could be set aside or reformulated according to the will of the collection of indvididuals. Müller repeatedly rejected the notion that individuals could exist outside the framework of society. He attacked the theories of social contract with a logic borrowed from Burke. The state, he insisted, was not an ephemeral institution, but eternal. It was not formed by individuals to achieve specific ends and could not be dissolved by them to suit their purposes. It was composed of moral bonds that transcended generations and linked people together with mutual rights and obligations.

The proper point of departure for an understanding of the state, according to Müller, was not the individual, but the family. "All theories of the state . . . must begin with the theory of the family," Müller asserted.[41] The family formed the model for the state; within it were reconciled those polar opposites whose parallels were to be found also in the state. The family possessed a temporal dimension, a past and a future, represented in the immediate family by youth and age, but linked as well to the generations of the past and those yet to be born. The state also was built upon the claims made by past and future generations on the present. Müller believed, moreover, that two central aspects of the state, the law and the economy, stood as polar opposites, homologous to age and youth, past and future. Law was rooted in the past, in tradition; it endeavored to provide the state with continuity. The economy, on the other hand, was oriented toward the future; it endeavored to provide the state with new wealth.[42]

The metaphor of the family as the marriage of the sexes also served for Müller's elaboration of the state. The family had its origin in the union of the two other polar opposites, with the male representing movement and change, the female representing conservation and endurance. The state, too, was formed by the higher union of the masculine forces of change and movement, representing commerce, and the feminine forces of conservation and endurance, representing agriculture. So also the sexes represented the two Stände in the state: the masculine impulse for change found in the middle class, the feminine impulse for conservation located in the nobility. The organic state, like the true family, was a union of the two Stände. Therefore, Müller concluded, the nobility must be preserved. "The nobleman represents the invisible, the force of custom and spirit in the state, and

---

[41] *Elemente der Staatskunst* 1: 100; Jakob Baxa, *Einführung in die romantische Staatswissenschaft* (Jena, 1931), 167. Müller believed that Frederick II had failed to grasp the organic essence of the state because he lived an isolated life without a family. *Ueber Friedrich II*, 181.

[42] *Elemente der Staatskunst* 1: 89, 99, 69.

thus he is, in the larger marriage that is the state, what the wife is in the usual understanding of marriage."[43]

These two sets of polar oppositions, youth and age, male and female, formed the axes of the family and provided Müller with the metaphors from which he built the homologies and axes in his theory of the state. At the intersection of the axes between the two opposites, balancing and reconciling both, stood the prince, who, as Müller said, "is to his people as the Hausvater is to his family."[44]

Müller maintained that the corollary of the pernicious political philosophy of natural law in the economic sphere was the teaching of Adam Smith, whose universal laws governing the economy were based on individualism and private property. Müller believed that the dissolution of what he called the feudal economy, in which personal bonds of mutual obligation formed the fundamental exchange, not merely a cash nexus as Adam Smith would have it, brought about the disintegration of the organic state and society. The "universal despotism of money" had depersonalized human relations.[45] Under the domination of capitalism, Müller charged, the state became "nothing more than an ugly warehouse"; Adam Smith made the state into a mere appendage of industry and proposed to "turn all occupations into trades, all service into wage labor, because he acknowledges only one form of community, namely the market."[46] But the market provided no model for community. It was based on competition and conflict, an extension of the possessive individualism upon which Smith's society was built. "The civil society [*bürgerliche Gesellschaft*] is the conflict, the totality of buying and selling; if I ask too high a price for my wares today, I must offer too low a price for those of my neighbor tomorrow: I am unjust, my neighbor is unjust."[47] The law of supply

---

[43] Ibid. 1: 101ff., 109.

[44] Ibid. 1: 146–47; see also Kohler, *Schriften zur Staatsphilosophie*, 185.

[45] Baxa, *Ausgewählte Abhandlungen*, 21. Müller referred to the individualism of the liberal economists as "Egoismus," which in German means more than *egotism* does in English. It is not merely a personal quality, but a social one as well. The German meaning comes close to what C. B. MacPherson has called "possessive individualism," which, he says, characterizes the political theory of the market society in the early stages of capitalism. See C. B. MacPherson, *The Political Theory of Possessive Individualism: Hobbes to Locke* (Oxford, 1962).

[46] Baxa, *Ausgewählte Abhandlungen*, 92, 75.

[47] Ibid., 91. The phrase "*bürgerliche Gesellschaft*" is difficult to translate, for it has two meanings in English: "civil society" and "bourgeois society." To avoid imposing the connotations that "bourgeois society" carries, which he may not have intended, I have generally used the more neutral translation, "civil society."

and demand had become in the economic sphere what the *vox populi* had become in the political sphere. In a sharp and prescient criticism of the conflict between labor and capital under capitalism, Müller wrote of England:

> The observation has already been made that England, as a result of its tax and debt system, which is based on the principle of the alienability of all things, resembles the nature of a beehive and that it is dissolving into one taxpaying, working nation and into another idle, capitalist and profit-taking nation, with the former paying the lion's share of the taxes on behalf of the latter. This largely true observation, translated into languages of the present framework, would be: both forms in which each individual citizen appears—as head of a state or capital, and as a member of a state or worker—have separated from one another in England and are placed in a certain condition of dissolution. . . . Capital and labor, which should everywhere support and reinforce one another as materials and tools, have been separated in England and are, to a large extent, hostile masses.[48]

In his attack on capitalism, Müller evoked warm images of the mutual caring and concern that presumably prevailed in the workshop of a guild master or on the estate of a paternalist landlord. Here he joined arms with the Prussian nobility to forge an ideological defense of paternalist social relations. The personal relations of the traditional system could not be called slavery, as its critics maintained; far more accurately the new system could be called monetary slavery, for it contained none of the warmth and sense of mutual obligations present in the old. He wrote: "Instead of the heartfelt association of the master and the second estate [Stand] of the working journeymen and the third estate [*tiers-etat*] of manually assisting and casting apprentices in the old workshop, a cold, calculating entrepreneur stands at the head of the new manufacture, thinking only of profit. Science normally thinks of princes as state-entrepreneurs: the manufacturer-entrepreneur stands like an emperor over an absolute *tiers-etat* of robotlike wage laborers—and such a dead essence they call: Freedom! I do not."[49]

Müller believed that the primary cause of this modern form of monetary slavery was the division of labor in capitalist manufacturing, and the enormous increase in the circulation of money that the market

---

[48] Adam Müller, *Gesammelte Schriften* (Munich, 1839), 1: 275–76.
[49] *Elemente der Staatskunst* 1: 313; see also Baxa, *Ausgewählte Abhandlungen*, 65; for Müller's description of monetary slavery, see *Schriften zur Staatsphilosophie*, 230–33.

society necessitated.[50] The division of labor, lauded by Adam Smith for its remarkable increase in productivity, was contrary to human nature. "If labor is subjected to division, it must be more mechanical and more manual," Müller reasoned, "and since all absolutely mechanical and manual labor is improper and unnatural, the division in a factory into men and machines, or into living or dead cog wheels, will not succeed. If one makes the division of labor into the principle of national wealth, men will be degraded into pure machines and slaves," Müller continued.[51] In addition, the increased circulation of money, brought about by the growth of trade and manufacture, threatened to impose the wage-labor system into all aspects of the economy, including agriculture, and thereby to transform all relationships into monetary ones. But the relationship of a Hausvater to his subjects must be personal, for "the peasantry is, according to the nature of things, nothing else than the wider family of the nobleman; only as such can it work and belong to the state."[52] Legislation such as the servants' ordinance (Gesindeordnung), however, threatened that personal bond between the Hausvater and his dependents. "A personal bond between the servant and the family, which the nature of things requires, can almost no longer be conceived. According to the present views, servants are those who perform certain carefully measured duties that recur daily or hourly, in exchange for money, but who stand outside the family whom they serve in all other respects."[53] As a result, Müller lamented, the true meaning of freedom was being lost. For freedom did not consist in the absence of personal bonds of obligation or in having the right to sell one's labor; true freedom, he maintained, was to be found in fulfilling one's duties within the framework of personal bonds of mutual obligation and affection. "Man is obedient in order to be free, and in his obedience is his freedom, in this reality, his individuality."[54]

The individualism of the age also subscribed to the concept of private property, a concept that was, according to Müller, derived from Roman law and foreign to the German tradition. There was no such

---

[50] On the division of labor, see ibid., 175–76; *Elemente der Staatskunst* 2: 24; Baxa, *Ausgewählte Abhandlungen*, 18, 46–47. He discussed the increased circulation of money in several places. See, above all, *Versuche einer neuen Theorie des Geldes*, ed. Helene Lieser (Jena, 1922); Baxa, *Ausgewählte Abhandlungen*, 29–34; Müller, *Gesammelte Schriften*, 126–29.

[51] *Elemente der Staatskunst* 2: 24–25.

[52] *Ueber Friedrich II*, 103.

[53] *Schriften zur Staatsphilosophie*, 229.

[54] Ibid., 231.

thing as private property, Müller maintained, especially as it pertained to land. Because a noble estate owner was obligated by invisible bonds to both the preceding and the succeeding generations of his family, he could not regard his estate as his individual property. To do so was to misunderstand the nature of capital and to ascribe to property a purely market definition of value. An "invisible" half of the value of an estate resided in the family; it could not be alienated. The other, "visible" half of the value of an estate resided in the land itself; it could be alienated. If simply placed on the market to be bought or sold as any commodity, land lost the invisible half of its value, for the value of a family's personal bonds to an estate and the estate's subjects, acquired over centuries of inheritance, could not be transferred. The sale of noble estates thus reduced the sum total of national wealth. The same held true for peasant holdings within a village, although Müller's concern was chiefly with noble landholdings. The treatment of property as personal and private, to be bought and sold in speculation, Müller believed, was one aspect of the spirit of mechanization that had permeated the Prussian state by the end of the eighteenth century.[55]

More significant, Müller believed, this emphasis on private property and individual satisfaction reflected the unfortunate separation of private and public life that characterized his era. The "privatization" of life, as he called it, had begun several centuries earlier. It was caused by the acceptance of Roman legal concepts of private law and private property, by the spread of the concept of private pleasure and the "privatization of all the concerns of life," and by the Protestant Reformation which, especially in Germany, had produced the idea of "private religion."[56] The effects of this long process had reached their climax in the "Roman-French Revolution." Now the "worship of private property" was everywhere, and likewise the "unconditional quest for the increase of income" and the "aversion for everything that resembles a corporate entity," including the fatherland—except for those institutions in which can be found "a certain bourgeois arithmetic, such as that in account books."[57] But most important, the separation of private and public life had weakened the principle of authority, for genuine authority grew out of personal contact and

---

[55] *Elemente der Staatskunst* 1: 157, 162; *Ueber Friedrich II*, 99–100; Friedrich Lenz, *Agrarlehre und Agrarpolitik der deutschen Romantik* (Berlin, 1912; reprint Scientia Verlag, Aalen, 1979), 23–25; Alexander Lewy, *Zur Genesis der heutigen agrarischen Ideen in Preussen* (Stuttgart, 1898), 30–31; Baxa, *Einführung in die romantische Staatswissenschaft*, 177.

[56] *Elemente der Staatskunst* 1: 298–99.

[57] Ibid. 1: 267.

relationships. Private life was inclined toward "republican" principles; its primary objective, the acquisition of money, had nothing to do with the organic state.[58]

Such circumstances of our political world, where the public has been separated from the private life, and each pursues its own special objectives, I have called the interregnum. No one can serve two masters: public life demands generous sacrifice of special appetites and properties to the common good. The private life demands exclusive pleasures, a completely isolated, most opulent, independent, enriched existence. No one can serve these two disparate lords. When, therefore, private and public life are separated, no one serves; likewise, no one really rules. An interregnum takes place.[59]

For Müller, the hope for bringing this interregnum to an end, for reestablishing the union of public and private life, lay in the preservation of feudal agriculture.[60] Market agriculture, which prevailed in England and was trumpeted in Germany by Albrecht Thaer and his disciples, was oriented exclusively toward producing a profit in the marketplace. It was based on a wage-labor system and represented the intrusion of the trade or "mercantile" mentality into the countryside. Müller referred to this as "nomadic agriculture," for it assumed that estates could change hands regularly and that wage-earning farm laborers could move freely about, from estate to estate. Market agriculture functioned best in regions located close to urban markets.

"Isolated" agriculture was based on entirely different assumptions. Because its purpose was not primarily economic but political, Müller also referred to it as "national" agriculture. This form of agriculture was not a trade, but an "office," a "duty." It was not directed toward winning a great profit in a distant market, but toward feeding the population of a locality and providing a framework of authority and community. Because agriculture was the most important activity of the state, it required the greatest security and protection. That such security was not to be found in dependence on an uncertain and volatile world market had been amply demonstrated, Müller pointed out, by the effects of the continental system on grain exports to the British market. Although market agriculture might be suitable for England,

[58] *Ueber Friedrich II*, 106–7.
[59] Ibid., 28.
[60] Baxa, "Agronomische Briefe," in *Ausgewählte Abhandlungen*, 71–94. The second edition of this collection (Jena, 1931) contains an additional essay on agronomy. See also Lenz, *Agrarlehre und Agrarpolitik*, 36–45, 67–68; Lewy, *Zur Genesis der heutigen agrarischen Ideen*, 27–36, 46–49.

which was one "large city," it was not right for Germany. The choice, as Müller stated dramatically, was "either feudalism or indebtedness. Dependence cannot be avoided, but the choice remains between dependence on a feudal lord or dependence on a creditor. Either a noble, personal, mutual obligation, as the Christian law teaches, or a Roman obligator, which is slavery."[61]

In defending "feudal agriculture," Müller made his most direct defense of the ideology of paternalism. The village community, he believed, combined the private and public spheres when the noble estate owner became "father, friend, and educator of his workers." These bonds could never be replaced with money, for the essence of agriculture required personal service.

Agriculture, whose prosperity is coupled with changes in the seasons and alterations of very sensitive and almost incalculable elements, requires unpayable, neighborly, mutual assistance which cannot be replaced by money; coins lose their power in many agrarian circumstances. A higher form of money—the loving aid that one extends to another, in short, the personal support of neighbors—steps into the place of precious metals.[62]

The introduction of rational agriculture posed a twofold threat to the monarchical state. Müller maintained the paternalist system of personal relationships, found in the estate and its village, was monarchical in essence. He even referred to noble estates as small "states." By joining the public and private basis for authority, the estate produced a "discipline, the subordination of all efforts under one another and the common good," that offered a "living and natural representation of the monarchical interest." The wage-labor system of the urban manufacturers, on the other hand, was "republican" in essence; rootless, individualistic, without any sense of subordination to a larger good, the system's introduction into the countryside threatened to weaken the monarchical foundation of the state.[63] In addition, Müller declared, the increase in the number of agricultural wage laborers was dangerous. It increased poverty, vagrancy, and social division. Wilhelm von Schütz, one of Müller's avid disciples and among the most reactionary of nobles in the Mark Brandenburg, went even further in portraying the dangers of the growing numbers of agricultural wage laborers. In the *Deutsche Staats-Anzeigen*, a journal edited by Müller be-

[61] Baxa, *Ausgewählte Abhandlungen*, 2d ed., 184.
[62] *Ueber Friedrich II*, 98.
[63] Ibid., 102.

tween 1816 and 1818, Schütz declared that growth in the number of agricultural wage laborers was threatening because they tended to drift toward the towns, where they became factory workers—"the most unfortunate of all classes of men who also have no firm bond to the state," and who "in their moral-political views are the most dangerous for the state."[64]

SOME FINAL THOUGHTS ON MÜLLER AND THE NOBILITY

Much of the literature dealing with Adam Müller and the genesis of conservatism in the early nineteenth century categorizes Müller as a representative of German "political Romanticism."[65] His writings are lumped with those of Friedrich Schlegel and Novalis as characteristic expressions of the Romantic mood. Indeed, his prose is murky and his thought often obscure; to analyze his political thought is to run the risk of presenting him as more systematic than he actually was; however, to label Müller a Romantic is not very helpful, for it raises the old, much debated problem of Romanticism's definition and tends to overemphasize his intellectual origins and connections. Müller's role in history can be understood only if we situate his thought within the social framework that generated it and see how his ideology addressed specific problems confronted by the Prussian nobility from 1807 to 1815.

Müller wrote at a time when the self-confidence of the Prussian nobility had been deeply shaken. The French Revolution had called into question the entire institution of a nobility of birth. Not only had the Prussian army been defeated by the French, but the actions of the reformers in the aftermath of that defeat seemed to suggest that the state's recovery required the setting aside of the social system through which the nobility had practiced its domination. Müller served the Prussian nobility at this time by providing an ideological framework that justified—one is tempted to say, sanctified—its traditional role. He offered a world view that corresponded to much of the nobility's experience on its landed estates. By rejecting the idea of the state as an artificial creation of a social contract, and stressing, instead, its or-

---

[64] Baxa, *Ausgewählte Abhandlungen*, 64–65; Lenz, *Agrarlehre und Agrarpolitik*, 113–16.
[65] The most prominent of these treatments is Carl Schmitt, *Politische Romantik*, 2d ed. (Munich and Leipzig, 1925); Paul Kluckhohn, *Persönlichkeit und Gemeinschaft: Studien zur Staatsauffassung der deutschen Romantik* (Halle, 1925); Sigmund Neumann, *Die Stufen des preussischen Konservatismus*, Historische Studien, 190 (Berlin, 1930). Jakob Baxa, *Gesellschaft und Staat im Spiegel deutschen Romantik* (Jena, 1924), is a much less satisfactory collection, as is his *Einführung in die romantische Staatswissenschaft*.

ganic origins in the family, he helped confirm the paternalist ideology implicit in the nobility's claim to rule. He attacked the "mechanistic" princely absolutism of the eighteenth century that had curtailed the local power of the nobility and, in its newest form under the reformers, threatened to restrict the nobility further. He criticized the infusion of natural law and Roman law, an explicit objective of the Allgemeines Landrecht, into Prussian legal thought. He attacked the disintegrative force of capitalism in society and argued that agriculture, more important than commerce to Prussia, should avoid being drawn into the capitalist world economy. Although he did not defend serfdom per se, he did stress that paternalist social relations required a personal bond between lord and peasant that precluded a system of wage labor.

Despite his efforts, Müller never succeeded in providing a closely integrated, logical analysis of the state, economy, and society that would not only defend the interests of the nobility, but also provide a guide to future conservative statesmen. His criticisms were harsh and direct, his solutions vague and imprecise. He spoke frequently of the necessity of a "ständisch constitution" and of the resuscitation of "ständisch relationships" but never clearly defined how such a constitution or such relationships could be established. He spoke of the need for "ständisch representation" in the state, but he feared that any institutionalized form of representation would be artificial and mechanistic instead of organic. For Müller, representation meant a kind of fusion in the spirit and impulse of the two Stände, the nobility and the middle class, or agriculture and trade.[66] He delivered a sharp, and at times insightful, critique of capitalism, but he understood little of its dynamics and none of its economics. When wrestling with the problem of how to prevent the spread of wage labor, his only recommendation was to create savings banks so that workers could save enough money to buy land and return, at least partially, to agriculture. He wrote, "In short, the chief concern in the creation of savings banks must be to help that part of the nation that has lost the roots of its existence through the monetary and factory system . . . not merely to acquire a little capital, but to enter into the condition *in natura*."[67]

Some aspects of Müller's conservative ideology did not fit perfectly the interests of all segments of the Prussian nobility. His attack on rational agriculture found a few adherents—his disciple Wilhelm von

[66] See his discussion of "ständische Repräsentation," *Ueber Friedrich II*, 151ff., 243ff.

[67] Baxa, *Ausgewählte Abhandlungen*, 68–69. Savings banks "should offer to the individual workers what they have lost through the factory system, namely, an authentic Stand in civil society."

Schütz defended the three-field system as based on the Holy Trinity—but most noble estate owners felt few qualms about improving their profits through new scientific methods. Müller's national feeling often went beyond the provincialism of the Prussian nobility of that era, and his sweeping definition of the state as the "totality of all affairs" went perhaps further than many nobles, suspicious of the state and jealous of local prerogatives, would have gone. But, as I suggested at the outset of this chapter, an ideology is often forged by one faction of a class, in this case, the most alienated, with the remainder of the class subscribing only to those parts of it that seem appropriate or useful. One did not need to accept all of Müller's ideas in order to condemn the impersonal cash nexus of capitalism and extol the personal bonds of paternalism. Müller's general world view offered a useful ideological point of departure for the Prussian nobility on the eve of the restoration.

6

THE POLITICS OF RESTORATION

Historians generally refer to the period of German history between 1815 and 1848 either as the restoration or as *Vormärz* (pre-March). Each of these terms implies a certain historical evaluation of the era. *Restoration* suggests an emphasis on the recovery of the conservative elements of the society after the tumultuous years of the wars and the reforms and points to the strength of the forces of continuity and preservation. The term *Vormärz*, on the other hand, is forward looking. It views the era as a prelude, a preparation for the revolutionary days of March 1848, and suggests the irrepressible force of social change. Both terms are, of course, equally valid; like all epochs, the period from 1815 to 1848 contained a residue of the past and a hint of the future. Old social forms were revived, but never fully; old concepts and words were used, but acquired new meanings. But it is truer for the period after 1815 than for most eras that the Prussian nobility made a self-conscious effort to preserve the old; the nobility viewed this era as a time for restoration.

This chapter will attempt to trace the manner in which the Prussian nobility fought, with some success, to rescue its social position threatened by the reforms. It will try to point out how cultural symbols of the past were carried forward into the new era and then changed.

BETWEEN ADMINISTRATION AND CONSTITUTION, 1815–1822

On May 22, 1815, King Frederick William III announced to his subjects that Prussia was to become a constitutional monarchy, complete with a "written document as a constitution for the Prussian state" and representative bodies at both the provincial and the national level for "consultation over all aspects of the legislation."[1] The announcement was generally well received. Liberal supporters of the reform movement viewed it as the capstone of the reform era; conservatives may

---

[1] DZA II, Rep. 74, H. 9, Stände, no. 19, Bl. 7–8. *Gesetz-Sammlung für die Königlich preussischen Staaten, 1815*, 103ff.; also in Wilhelm Altmann, *Ausgewählte Urkunden zur Brandenburgisch-Preussischen Verfassungs- und Verwaltungsgeschichte* (Berlin, 1897), 2: 87–89.

have objected to the idea of a written constitution, but they took solace in the phrase "ständisch representation," which they interpreted as a reconfirmation of the ständisch social structure, dominated by the nobility. Although this "promise of a constitution" declared that a constitutional commission would begin deliberations on September 1, 1815, no commission was formed until March 1817; during the subsequent five years, five different commissions dealt with the issue of a constitution without producing such a document. By the time of the death of State Chancellor Hardenberg in 1822, it was clear that no constitution would be forthcoming. The king's failure to honor his promise clouded the remainder of his reign;[2] indeed, the question of a constitution hovered on the periphery of Prussian politics throughout the period of Vormärz. When Frederick William IV ascended the throne in 1840, he was immediately greeted by demands that the promise be fulfilled.[3]

The history of "Prussia's first constitutional conflict," from 1815 to 1822, is complex. This is so not only because its outcome was determined, in part, by circumstances outside of Prussia—especially the policies of Metternich in combatting liberal and radical thought throughout Germany and Europe—but also because the question of the proper constitutional structure for Prussia was very much entangled with Hardenberg's administrative reforms. The task here, then, is to examine how the nobility's response to the constitutional issues involved an assault on Hardenberg's administrative policies as well.

As already shown, Hardenberg considered administration to be the central agent in liberalizing society. One Prussian reformer, B. G. Niebuhr, put it succinctly: "Freedom depends much more on administration than on constitution."[4] Hardenberg had consistently given higher priority to the administrative and social reforms than to the idea of a constitution. He had delayed convening a constitutional commission in September 1815 because he wished to complete the administrative reforms first, believing that the careful reorganization of the administration must precede the creation of a constitutional system. Thus, he wrote to the liberal governor (Oberpräsident) of Posen, Zerboni di Sposetti, in 1817, two years after the king's promise of a constitution:

[2] Reinhart Koselleck, *Preussen zwischen Reform und Revolution* (Stuttgart, 1967), 286; Ernst R. Huber, *Deutsche Verfassungsgeschichte seit 1789* (Stuttgart, 1960), 1: 304.

[3] See chapter 9.

[4] Cited in Leonard Krieger, *The German Idea of Freedom* (Boston, 1957), 217; Koselleck, *Preussen zwischen Reform und Revolution*, 217; Herbert Obenaus, *Anfänge des Parlamentarismus in Preussen bis 1848* (Düsseldorf, 1984), 90ff.

CHAPTER 6

It is indeed the constant purpose of the government to set up a representation appropriate to the nation, but we have believed that we must allow the organization of the administrative authorities to precede it and that, given the great variety of the provinces—in part, entirely new—constituting the Prussian monarchy, we must approach the problem deliberately and cautiously. The State Council [*Staatsrat*], whose establishment is at hand, will be the keystone. Simultaneously, a beginning at representation will be made.[5]

Hardenberg insisted on viewing the constitution as an integral part of the administration. His own preference for a constitutional structure, finally presented in 1819, essentially was a proposal for the reorganization of local government—village, county, and provincial—that would enhance the administrative chain of command at the same time that it introduced representative institutions standing beside, and supporting, this reinforced administrative authority.[6] This insistence on the priority of administrative reorganization was, in part, tactical, for he needed to have well-established, centripetal government agencies in place to counteract the centrifugal force that local and provincial ständisch representation would produce. Indeed, given the fact that the Prussian monarchy after 1815 comprised a large number of new and socially divergent territories, the centralistic emphasis resulting from the primacy of administrative authority was imperative. Even minor modifications in the boundaries of the old provinces, amalgamating some parts with the newly acquired territories, touched off protests in 1815 that revealed how deeply provincialism remained in Prussia, despite the effort to engender nationalism during the reforms and the wars of liberation.[7]

---

[5] Paul Haake, *Der preussische Verfassungskampf vor hundert Jahren* (Munich and Berlin, 1921), 79. Krieger cites a portion of the statement in *The German Idea*, 220. The best treatment of the various plans for a constitution is in Obenaus, *Anfänge des Parlamentarismus*, 89ff.

[6] The document is printed in Heinrich von Treitschke, *Deutsche Geschichte im neunzehnten Jahrhundert* (Leipzig, 1882), 2: 635–37; for Treitschke's discussion, see 589ff.; see also Treitschke, "Der Erste Verfassungskampf in Preussen," *Preussische Jahrbücher* 29 (1872): 425–28.

[7] The proposal to change the location of a county capital caused one noble to complain that if police authority were removed farther from his estate, vagabond peasants would steal all the cabbage and potatoes from his fields. Such admissions reveal the efficacy of the paternalism claimed by the nobility. More significant, the nobles from the Brandenburg county Beeskow-Storkow protested the proposal to include their county in the new boundaries of the province of Prussian Saxony. "We should remain Brandenburgers and retain our tradition," they declared. Their request was honored. Treitschke, "Verfassungskampf," 315–16.

Hardenberg's emphasis on administration as the crux of government, however, was more than a tactical effort to head off provincialism; it was fundamental to his entire conception of the state. He remained, to the end of his life, the rational bureaucrat, wedded to the centralized absolutism of the eighteenth century. He made no concessions even to the organic vocabulary of his opponents, which had gained a wide acceptance by the second decade of the century; he continued to speak, almost defiantly, of the "machine of state." Ständisch representative bodies were useful insofar as they contributed to the strength of the central state, but they had little importance beyond that. This conception of the state, and not merely the petty jealousy and bureaucratic infighting, was the basis of the conflict between Hardenberg and Wilhelm von Humboldt. The constitutional principles enunciated by the two men, although similar, had different meanings. For Humboldt, institutions such as the representative Stände were not merely instrumental for state power, but essential to the nature of the state as the framework for individual development. Thus, he objected to the Carlsbad Decrees severely limiting individual freedoms as a violation of the nature and purpose of the state, whereas Hardenberg supported them as essential to the state's preservation of control.[8]

Hardenberg's administrative centralization, against which the conservative nobility struggled, revolved around two agencies of government: the ten (later eight) provincial governments and the twenty-five subprovincial governmental districts (*Regierungsbezirke*) of the monarchy. The cornerstone of this organization lay in the Ordinance for the Creation of Provincial Authorities, issued on April 30, 1815, just prior to the announcement promising a constitution.[9] Hardenberg designed the balance of power between these two levels of administration, the provinces and the governmental districts, in such a way as to maximize the control of the central government while offering a focal point for provincial identity.

Although the structure of administration made it appear as though provinces were the essential units—the provincial governor was called the *Oberpräsident*, whereas the head of the governmental district was merely a *Präsident*—in fact, the critical aspects of local and regional

[8] Krieger, *The German Idea*, 222–23.
[9] *Gesetz-Sammlung, 1815*, 85–92; Altmann, *Ausgewählte Urkunden* 2: 82–87. Originally, the Rhineland was divided into two provinces and Prussia was separated into East and West Prussia. When each of these regions was later consolidated, the number of provinces was reduced from ten to eight: Prussia, Posen, Pomerania, Silesia, Brandenburg, Saxony, Westphalia, and the Rhineland.

CHAPTER 6

administration were in the hands of the governmental districts.[10] Officials of the districts did not receive their instructions from the provincial governor, but directly from the ministry in Berlin. In many cases, the provincial governor was not even informed of the directives forwarded from Berlin to the governmental districts. The authority of these districts was substantial. Each district had two departments: one department, responsible to the ministers of foreign affairs, internal affairs, and war, dealt with matters relating to security, police, social welfare, and local government; the second department, responsible to the minister of finance, dealt with taxes, tariffs, commerce, royal domains, and trade guilds. In addition, the districts had wide-ranging powers of administrative justice. In order "to ensure their respect for the constitution, uniformity of proceedings, liberality, and nonpartisanship,"[11] officials of the governmental districts originally operated with a collegial system in which all officials discussed policy and assumed a collective responsibility for its execution. This system gave the districts a certain advisory role in the legislative process as well; as long as no genuine system of representation developed, the officials served as an important source for ascertaining public opinion. After the creation of the provincial diets in 1823, their advisory role declined. In 1825, new instructions to the governmental districts reduced their collegial character and delegated greater power to the district president and to the directors of the two departments. None of the changes, however, limited the power of these governmental districts; throughout Vormärz, they remained the essential agencies of Prussian administration. Hardenberg fended off all efforts to reduce their authority. In response to criticism in 1817, he let it be known that it was the king's will "that the purview of authority attached to the governmental districts should not be curtailed."[12]

With most of the business of administration flowing past the provincial governors from the ministry to the governmental districts, and with little responsibility to oversee the actions of the districts, the authority of the provincial governor was necessarily restricted. The governor's exclusion was explicit in the ordinance of April 30, 1815: "The

[10] On the role of the governors, see especially Fritz Hartung, "Der Oberpräsident," *Staatsbildende Kräfte der Neuzeit* (Berlin, 1961), 275–308; Koselleck, *Preussen zwischen Reform und Revolution*, 221–37. On the governmental districts, see Koselleck, ibid., 237–64.

[11] *Gesetz-Sammlung, 1815*, 85; Altmann, *Ausgewählte Urkunden* 2: 82.

[12] Hartung, "Der Oberpräsident," 292. For an example of the conflict that occurred between the provincial governornd the governmental districts, see Rolf Engels, *Die Preussische Verwaltung von Kammer und Regierung Gumbinnen (1724–1870)* (Cologne and Berlin, 1974), 32, 35.

provincial governors do not form an intermediate stage between the ministry and the governmental districts, but they conduct the business entrusted to them under their special responsibility as permanent commissars of the ministry."[13] They were to deal with the ständisch affairs of the province, with the important exception of the credit institutes, the Landschaften, which remained under the supervision of the minister of internal affairs; they were responsible for security measures in the extraordinary cases that extended beyond the boundaries of the governmental districts; they were the liaison with the military commanders of the province; and they had responsibility in some cultural affairs, including medicine, higher education, and the church consistory of the province. In many respects, the governor occupied a position in the province not entirely unlike that of the king in the state, except that his ultimate authority was much more limited. He was not really within the administrative hierarchy so much as adjacent to it. His power was largely moral, growing from his ability to understand and articulate the needs of his province. Zerboni, for example, referred to himself as the Hausvater of his province.[14] Several of the early provincial governors—Schön in Prussia, Sack in Pomerania, and Vincke in Westphalia—were able to use this moral authority to develop considerable influence.

But the early provincial governors complained of their limited authority. Friedrich von Motz, governor of Prussian Saxony from 1821 to 1825, commented that the position had been created as a "pensioner's post" (*Versorgungspost*) for deserving senior civil servants.[15] Governors launched at least two substantial efforts between 1815 and 1822 to alter the system and increase their power. In June 1817, a petition written by Schön and signed by six other governors argued that the intense centralization of administration, "of the French variety," had transformed the governmental districts into departments and crippled the public spirit within the provinces. The result was that the reform impulse had become stalled; public confidence, gained during the wars of liberation, was evaporating, the governors complained, because the government had failed to move forward with a constitution and representative assemblies that would bring a degree of provincial self-government.[16]

---

[13] Altmann, *Ausgewählte Urkunden*, 83.

[14] Koselleck, *Preussen zwischen Reform und Revolution*, 225.

[15] Hermann von Petersdorff, *Friedrich von Motz* (Berlin, 1913), 1: 231.

[16] Hartung, "Der Oberpräsident," 288; Koselleck, *Preussen zwischen Reform und Revolution*, 226–27; Ernst Klein, *Von der Reform zur Restauration*, Veröffentlichungen der Histo-

CHAPTER 6

Hardenberg responded by issuing new instructions to the provincial governors that merely restated the areas of competence previously outlined and broadened them only to include roads, canals, and other minor matters that were of provincial, not merely district, interest. The chief responsibility of the governor, stated the instructions, was to see that "the life and spirit of the administration are not lost in paperwork" (*Schreiberei*). Each governor was to tour his province at least once a year to acquaint himself with its conditions.[17]

Again, in 1821, a group of provincial governors complained of their lack of authority. Ludwig Freiherr von Vincke, a member of a committee appointed by Hardenberg to examine the administration, proposed a partial return to the pre–reform system of administration by suggesting that the ministry be altered to comprise four provincial ministers, replacing the governors, and four specialized ministers—war, finance, foreign affairs, and justice.[18] This would elevate the influence of the provincial authorities by placing them at the center of government. The existing system, with only specialized ministries, he charged, led to a "superfluity of paperwork," to "slowness and unwieldiness," to the exaggeration of theory and the underestimation of experience. Worse, in every province, "the unknown state officials are considered to be forces hostile to the provincial interests." Several other provincial governors on the committee supported Vincke's plan, but officials representing the governmental districts vigorously opposed it. They charged that such a plan, by eliminating the Ministry of Internal Affairs, would seriously weaken the unity of the state. Even Hardenberg's antagonist, Wilhelm von Humboldt, whose opposition to the chancellor on other issues had led him into an unlikely alliance with the conservative provincial nobility, did not go along with Vincke's plan for decentralization.[19] Hardenberg rejected the proposal as he had the one from Schön four years earlier. Nevertheless, it demonstrated the tug of war between provincial and central administration that surrounded the conflict over the constitution.

A highly centralized administration, of course, was anathema to the conservative Prussian nobility. Throughout the constitutional discussions, conservative nobles worked to restore provincial hegemony in the state; working with the notion of "the old Prussian ständisch con-

---

rischen Kommission zu Berlin, 16 (Berlin, 1965), 190; Treitschke, *Deutsche Geschichte* 2: 199ff.

[17] Hartung, "Der Oberpräsident," 290–99.

[18] Ibid., 295–96; Koselleck, *Preussen zwischen Reform und Revolution*, 233–34; Treitschke, *Deutsche Geschichte* 3: 234.

[19] Bruno Gebhardt, *Wilhelm von Humboldt als Staatsmann* (Stuttgart, 1899), 2: 422–23.

stitution," it seemed logical that the restoration of provincial diets should be accompanied by the establishment of provincial ministers. In 1823, Marwitz wrote a long memorandum to the crown prince advocating the creation of provincial ministers.[20] The memorandum is significant both because it was addressed to the crown prince, who had emerged as an important link between the conservative provincial nobility and the government, and because it employed many of the symbolic metaphors that were becoming central to the conservative ideology. The existing "hierarchical organization" of the state, Marwitz declared in language reminiscent of Adam Müller, "pushes things [*Sachen*] into the foreground, while persons disappear." "This hierarchical organization is pure demagogy and has been known only since the revolution." It is intended to "destroy the possibility of personal service"; it gives positions to the "rootless" (*Heimatlosen*) and "opens to them a leisurely existence, while it excludes from the administration the local residents." If one accepts the idea, Marwitz reasoned, that "the circumstances and needs of the province are the plumb line of its administration, then it follows that it may not be administered by rootless intellectuals [*Heimatlos Studierte*], but by residents of the province." If the Landräte should be selected from among the landowners of the county which they administer, so, too, should the provincial ministers. Marwitz's memorandum encompassed most of the arguments of the conservative ideology, insisting that government should consist of personal relationships, that it should not be drawn from abstract theories by intellectuals but be based on concrete realities by those with experience, and that its cornerstone was locality, not universality. Although his proposal had no apparent impact, a year later, after the provincial diets had been established, he again proposed that the administration and the representation be organized on the same local basis.[21]

The other aspect of Hardenberg's plan to reorganize the administration before enacting a constitution—reorganizing it in such a way that the administration would control the centrifugal effects of provincial and national representation—was the construction of the State Council (*Staatsrat*).[22] As we have already noted, Hardenberg described the State Council as the "keystone" of the administrative reform, com-

---

[20] Friedrich August Ludwig von der Marwitz, *Friedrich August Ludwig von der Marwitz: Ein märkischer Edelmann im Zeitalter der Befreiungskriege*, ed. Freidrich Meusel, 3 vols. (Berlin, 1908–1913), II/2:285ff.

[21] DZA II, Rep. 92, v. Rochow, A III, no. 6, Bl. 139, Marwitz to Rochow, 23 March 1824.

[22] Hans Schneider, *Der preussische Staatsrat, 1817–1918* (Munich and Berlin, 1952), 47–60; Koselleck, *Preussen zwischen Reform und Revolution*, 264ff; Herbert Obenaus, *Anfänge des Parlamentarismus in Preussen bis 1848* (Düsseldorf, 1984), 95ff.

CHAPTER 6

pleting the foundation on which constitutional representation could be built.[23] The State Council, created by a royal decree on March 20, 1817, formed "the highest advisory authority" of the state. Composed of the princes of the royal family, high civil and military officials, and other officials in whom the king had "special confidence," the State Council was to offer advice on "all laws, constitutional and administrative norms, plans concerning administrative matters through which the principles of administration will be altered."[24] Under Hardenberg's chairmanship, that proved not to be the case; important decisions of the ministry were not discussed in the State Council, which by 1821 and 1822 considered only about one-third of the laws that were enacted by the state. After Hardenberg's death, even fewer measures were brought to the council for consideration.[25]

The importance of the State Council lay not only in the manner in which the chancellor could utilize it in support of measures he wished to impose, but in the fact that it could be used as a counterweight to a future national diet. In fact, it came to be viewed as a parliament of officials, whose representative character was even partially acknowledged by provincial groups who protested against legislation that had been enacted without the consultation of the State Council. Moreover, by providing consultative representation, albeit only with state officials, the State Council could be seen as lessening the need for additional national representation. Reinhart Koselleck has stressed this aspect of the council: "The tendency toward inner-administrative constitutionalization was driven forward by the solution of 1817, and, to be sure, at the cost of the national representation yet to be created."[26]

Support for the idea of a national diet had already waned considerably by the time the first constitutional commission met in July 1817. Secretary of State for the State Council Wilhelm von Klewitz, who subsequently became an important member of the first commission, advised Hardenberg prior to the commission's first meeting that provincial assemblies were preferable to a national diet. "These lands—the old as well as the new—expect nothing more than that to which they have been accustomed and which they once had, insofar as it can be accommodated to the present. . . . A constitution for the ständisch structure of the provinces will, in part, satisfy this desire and also be more advisable than a constitution for the kingdom, which, in its

[23] See p. 184.
[24] *Gesetz-Sammlung, 1817*, 67ff.; Altmann, *Ausgewählte Urkunden* 2: 99–110.
[25] See Schneider, *Der preussische Staatsrat*, 60–63.
[26] Koselleck, *Preussen zwischen Reform und Revolution*, 266.

drafting and execution, may not be free of difficulty and objection for the Prussian king." Klewitz went on to recommend that representatives of the commission interview notables in the provinces rather than convene an assembly of notables in Berlin.[27] Hardenberg's experience with the Assembly of Notables of 1811 had not been a happy one; the king accepted Klewitz's recommendation. Although Hardenberg looked forward to a constitution and some form of national, ständisch representation, he too was cautious. "History teaches us," he warned the commission at its first meeting, "that the old Prussian provincial diets [Landstände] did not work to the good of the state but were really only guardians of the privileges of individual groups of the population and were genuine hindrances to the machinery of the state." The present situation required a constitution and representation, but the representative assemblies would have only an advisory, not a legislative, role.[28]

The decision against convening an assembly of notables in Berlin was crucial. It seriously compromised the cause of a national diet. Without any systematic representation from the various classes in the monarchy, which an assembly might have occasioned, the three ministers who made the provincial tours were free to interview whomever they chose and to filter the results of their interviews through their own perspectives. Invariably, they sought the advice of officials and nobles. Peasants were rarely consulted.[29]

Two questions were central to the inquiries of the three ministers who toured the provinces: how, and to what extent, should representation be organized on a provincial or a national level; and to what extent should the peasantry be represented in these assemblies.[30] Predictably, the western provinces of Westphalia and the Rhineland, toured by Minister of Culture Karl Freiherr zum Altenstein, were the most liberal and favored some form of national representation. The provinces east of the Elbe, where the conservative landowning nobility was heavily represented in the consultations, were more cautious. Most recognized that some form of national representation was re-

---

[27] Treitschke, "Verfassungskampf," 349–50; see also his *Deutsche Geschichte* 2: 286–87; Alfred Stern, "Die preussische Verfassungsfrage im Jahre 1817 und die Rundreise von Altenstein, Klewitz, und Beyme," *Deutsche Zeitschrift für Geschichtswissenschaft* 9 (1893): 64ff.

[28] Treitschke, "Verfassungskampf," 350–51; Walter Simon, *The Failure of the Prussian Reform, 1807–1819* (Ithaca, N.Y., 1955), 125; Obenaus, *Anfänge des Parlamentarismus*, 96ff.

[29] Koselleck, *Preussen zwischen Reform und Revolution*, 290–91.

[30] Treitschke, "Verfassungskampf," 351–52.

CHAPTER 6

quired because, as Field Marshal von York put it, "a constitution and representation have been promised to the country, and the promise must be kept,"[31] but few were enthusiastic. Most preferred provincial representation and believed that no national representation should be created without prior experience at the provincial level. The young leader of the conservative nobility of the Mark Brandenburg, Gustav von Rochow, spoke for many when he recommended that national representation be delayed by twenty years. Only 2 of 128 persons consulted by Klewitz in Brandenburg, Saxony, Silesia, and Posen objected to provincial diets as divisive of the monarchy. One was the liberal president of the governmental district of Erfurt, Friedrich von Motz; the other was Count Itzenplitz, of Brandenburg, a vigorous proponent of scientific agriculture. Itzenplitz believed that only a modern constitution with full representation based on population and not on the "residue of the Stände" would suffice. The highest priority should be given to national representation. Rochow concluded that although Itzenplitz may have been a nobleman in his disposition, he was, "in his judgment, a bourgeois businessman."[32]

Most of those consulted from the eastern provinces also agreed that some form of representation of the peasantry was necessary.[33] Except for East Prussia, however, consultations with nobles revealed a measure of fear and hostility toward the peasantry that necessitated limitations on its political representation. Some declared that the peasantry should be represented by the large landowners because it was "not yet mature enough" to represent itself. Others used the consultations as an occasion to criticize the effects of the previous reform measures on the peasantry. A Major von Winterfield, from the Mark Brandenburg, complained that "the old constitution has been shot full of holes and trodden underfoot." "Who can describe the misfortune that out of the old, demolished constitution, no new one has emerged," he wrote. But clearly what he meant by a constitution was little more than respect for order. He continued, "My little village, where once quiet and harmony prevailed, where each knew what he

[31] Stern, "Die preussische Verfassungsfrage im Jahre 1817," 81–82.

[32] For a summary of the consultations, see Koselleck, *Preussen zwischen Reform und Revolution*, 290–94. For Rochow's role in the consultation in the Mark Brandenburg, see Ernst Müsebeck, "Die märkische Ritterschaft und die preussische Verfassungsfrage von 1814 bis 1820," *Deutsche Rundschau* 174 (1918): 158–82, 354–76. His description of Itzenplitz is on p. 359. On Motz, see Petersdorff, *Motz* 1: 152.

[33] The group that most wanted to be excluded were the intellectuals. Koselleck, *Preussen zwischen Reform und Revolution*, 293; on the manner in which the radical movement complicated the constitutional plans, see Obenaus, *Anfänge des Parlamentarismus*, 90ff.

was to do, and legal action and police coercion were unheard of, has become, since this unfortunate edict [Peasant Regulation of September 14, 1811], a place of discord and strife."[34]

The late summer and early autumn of 1817, the time of the ministerial tours, was probably the moment at which it would have been most possible for Prussia to have enacted a constitution. Thereafter the chances for a constitution declined steadily. In October 1817, the radical, nationalist student group, the *Burschenschaften*, held its famous *Wartburgfest*, celebrating the tercentenary of the Lutheran Reformation by burning the books of conservative, antinationalist authors.[35] A few months later, in January 1818, a democratic publicist from the Rhineland, Joseph Görres, circulated a petition reminding the king of his unfulfilled promise of a constitution; he followed his petition with an inflammatory pamphlet criticizing the government for its failure to produce one. These events strengthened the position of the conservatives who had access to the king: Johann Friedrich Ancillon, Prince Wittgenstein, and the crown prince.[36] Frederick William III found the Görres petition an affront to his sovereignty: "I will determine when the promise of a constitution shall be fulfilled, and I will not be swayed by untimely remonstrances. ... The duty of the subjects is to await, with confidence in my sovereign discretion, ... the time which I, guided by my grasp of the whole situation, shall find suitable for its fulfillment."[37]

While the king denounced the demands for a constitution from the liberal flank in the west, Hardenberg attacked the activities of the conservative flank in the east. The provincial nobility in several of the eastern provinces organized themselves in 1816 and 1817 to demand a constitution that would guarantee their old rights. The nobles in Upper Silesia, always less organized than nobles elsewhere in the monarchy (Frederick II had denied them the right to select their Landräte), began to organize themselves through their provincial landcredit institute. They claimed to speak for the province against the effects of the agrarian legislation of 1811 and 1816. Hardenberg denounced the group as representing "only one part of the inhabitants, ... the owners of noble estates," but in no way the whole province. Undaunted, seventy-one noble estate owners petitioned the king in 1817 for a constitution that would reestablish their rights. They com-

---

[34] Stern, "Die preussische Verfassungsfrage im Jahre 1817," 78.
[35] Treitschke, *Deutsche Geschichte* 2: 424–44.
[36] See pp. 204–6.
[37] Simon, *The Failure of the Prussian Reform*, 130–32; Koselleck, *Preussen zwischen Reform und Revolution*, 302–3.

CHAPTER 6

plained that the legal basis of the state, the Allgemeines Landrecht, had been set aside by the reforms after 1806, but that no new basic law had replaced it. In the resulting void, "a situation of legal uncertainty," the administration had acted unilaterally as a legislative agency, altering and interpreting old and new laws as it saw fit. To curb the administration, these Silesian nobles called for the government to proceed with a constitution and "not to permit any new organic laws before the introduction of the promised constitution." Hardenberg could not accept this attack on the administration.[38]

Led by Marwitz's brother-in-law, Gustav von Rochow, who traveled widely through the province in 1817 and 1818 circulating letters and petitions, the nobility of the Kurmark and Neumark of Brandenburg also pleaded for the restoration of its traditional rights.[39] A petition to the king on March 17, 1818, declared that "the most important concern of the province and the pressing wish of the Stände" was reestablishment of the old constitution of Brandenburg, by which it meant the Recess of 1653. Significantly, these opponents of Hardenberg also petitioned the State Ministry at the same time to forbid the sale of noble estates to peasant communes; such communes, they reasoned, would be unable to exercise the patrimonial jurisdiction and should be forbidden. Tantamount to a reversal of the October Edict, which was predicated on the free sale of estates, this petition and the one submitted to the king made it clear that the nobility looked upon a constitution as a means of undoing some of the reforms of the previous decade.[40]

The Committee of the Stände from East Prussia also collided with Hardenberg on a number of issues in these same years. East Prussia was a strange anomaly, for nowhere else in the monarchy were liberal-constitutional ideas more entangled with conservative defenses of ständisch rights. The committee was led by Count Alexander von Dohna, who, it will be recalled, had warned in 1811 that the Stände

---

[38] Koselleck, *Preussen zwischen Reform und Revolution*, 306–10.

[39] For the activities of Rochow, see Caroline von Rochow, *Vom Leben am preussischen Hof, 1815–1852* (Berlin, 1908), 116ff.

[40] DZA II, Rep. 74, H. 9, Stände, no. 20. This petition to the king declared the following: "We are animated by no spirit of opposition to the determinations of our regent; we have, on the contrary, viewed with regret and deep pain the confusion of the Stände in other lands. No, if we know our old rights and are animated by the spirit of permanence and conservation, so also do we understand the demands of the times and the needs of the state; therefore, we would no more cling to everything old and inherited merely in our own interest than we would attempt to build the future structure of our ständisch constitution merely out of new theories." See also the discussion in Müsebeck, "Die märkische Ritterschaft," 176ff., 358ff.

"would merely advance their corporate interests in the fashion of a party." Now, Dohna himself became the head of the East Prussian party. He flooded the government with letters and petitions complaining about Hardenberg's policies but objecting especially to the actions of the General Commissions in Prussia. These General Commissions had been set up to carry out the "regulation" of the peasants by separating their lands from those of the lords according to the prescriptions of the laws of 1811 and 1816. Because the General Commissions exercised enormous discretionary powers in interpreting the disputes between peasants and lords, they frequently antagonized the nobility, even though most of the decisions favored noble estate owners. After ignoring many of Dohna's appeals, Hardenberg finally attacked the committee much as he had the group of nobles in Upper Silesia. He denied the legality of the committee; it did not represent the population of East Prussia, he declared, but only the "private opinions" of a minority of the land. Dohna interpreted Hardenberg's description of the Stände dominated by the nobility as representing only a "minority" of the province to be a veiled reference to representation by head count and not representation in the "true ständisch sense."[41]

The struggle over the constitution between 1817 and 1819 reveals the fundamental dilemma that confronted Hardenberg and the reason that Prussia received no constitution in Vormärz. Hardenberg faced, on the one hand, the problem that had plagued all of his attempts at representation since 1811: any form of ständisch representation was liable to give the nobility a powerful voice that would jeopardize many of the previous reforms. On the other hand, the demands of liberals for a constitution had aroused the vigorous opposition of the king, who now began to gravitate toward the conservatives in the court and the countryside. Suspended between these two poles, the constitution remained uncompleted.

After 1819, until Hardenberg's death in 1822, the complicated development of the constitutional question produced increasing confrontation between the chancellor and his conservative opponents within the government. Although, as we shall see, important connections developed between the landowning nobility of the provinces and the conservative circle in the court, the fate of the constitution during this period was determined largely within the central government. As

[41] Koselleck, *Preussen zwischen Reform und Revolution*, 312–17; Theodor von Schön, *Aus den Papieren Theodor von Schön* (Berlin, 1875), 6: 653. For evidence of the political actions of the East Prussian Stände at this time, see: PSK/B-D, *Provinz Ostpreussen*, Rep. 2, Oberpräsidium, Tit. 23, no. 19; DZA II, Rep. 74, H. 9, Stände, no. 9, Bl. 69–70.

CHAPTER 6

this story involved the landowning nobility less directly, we need concern ourselves here with only a brief summary of events.

In January 1819, Wilhelm von Humboldt entered directly into the process of constitutional planning when appointed to the newly created post of minister of ständisch affairs.[42] Humboldt's ideas on a constitution, contained in a lengthy memorandum dated February 4, 1819, illustrate how closely interrelated the questions of administration and constitution had become. The "objective purpose" of a constitution, he declared in the opening paragraphs of the memorandum, was to render the administration "more successful," "more consistent," "simpler and less costly," and "more just and orderly." However, Humboldt had less confidence in an administrative state than Hardenberg. He viewed ständisch representation as a kind of constitutional check on the administration, "for according to the natural order of things, the Stände represent the principle of preservation, whereas the administration represents the striving for improvement."[43] Yet the details of Humboldt's approach differed little from Hardenberg's. Both based the right of representation on ownership of land; both foresaw representation resulting from the reorganization of the communal, county, and provincial levels of government and culminating in a national diet; and both allowed the representative bodies advisory power only. Nevertheless, tension developed immediately between Hardenberg and Humboldt. Humboldt resented Hardenberg's meddling in the constitutional question, which he considered to be within the competence of his ministry; he moved to reduce Hardenberg's role in the ministry to that of a *primus inter pares* instead of that of a dominant chancellor.[44] But Humboldt lasted less than a year. After opposing the Carlsbad Decrees, he was forced to resign, along with Beyme and Boyen, the other liberal members of the ministry.[45]

The departure of three liberal ministers strengthened the conservatives in the court and further set back the constitutional movement. A new constitutional commission, appointed in August 1819, was already more conservative than its predecessor; when introduced in the following year, Hardenberg's plan for a new communal and county

---

[42] Gebhardt, *Wilhelm von Humboldt* 2: 333–60; Obenaus, in *Anfänge des Parlamentarismus*, 105ff., has an excellent discussion of Humboldt's views on the constitution in 1819.

[43] See Humboldt's memorandum in Wilhelm von Humboldt, *Gesammelte Schriften* (Berlin, 1904), 12: 380–467. See especially "Zur ständischen Verfassung im Preussen," 3, 16, 17, 34, 56, 82–94.

[44] Gebhardt, *Wilhelm von Humboldt* 2: 355; Simon, *The Failure of the Prussian Reform*, 218.

[45] Karl Friedrich von Beyme was minister of legislative affairs; General Hermann von Boyen was minister of war.

organization touched off determined opposition within the government and another round of complaints from the provinces. This plan for a new county ordinance (*Kreisordnung*) would have transformed the Landrat into a state servant, a kind of prefect over whom the county assembly would have no influence. Moreover, Hardenberg proposed to eliminate the right of each noble estate owner to appear personally in the county assembly (*Virilstimme*) and substituted in its place the election of representatives from among the noble estate owners who would, like each of the other two Stände, have one-third of the representation.[46] One member of the State Council referred to the proposal as "a firebrand to revolution."[47]

While Hardenberg attended the international conference at Troppau, his opponents seized the opportunity to persuade Frederick William III to appoint a new constitutional commission. Composed of the crown prince, Ancillon, Schuckmann, Wittgenstein, and Albrecht, this commission was thoroughly conservative.[48] It set aside the chancellor's plans for the constitutional organization of communal, county, and provincial assemblies. Grasping that the intent of the commission was to lead the king to abandon all plans for a written constitution, Hardenberg warned him: "In my view, the royal order of May 22, 1815, as a publicly expressed royal promise, must be kept."[49] Wittgenstein, representing the commission, struck back, outlining the differences between the chancellor's views and those of the commission. The commission, he declared, opposed a written constitution and advocated provincial assemblies instead of a national diet.

> The constitution of the Prussian state stands firm as a purely monarchical one, so there is no need for a new document.... The most recent experiences prove that in the negotiations with representatives, there soon develops everywhere a vigorous conflict and the most intense differences between the representatives and the government about the scope and the interpretation of the rights of the assembly

---

[46] See Hardenberg's constitutional plans in Ernst Klein, *Von der Reform zur Restauration*, 195–96; Treitschke, *Deutsche Geschichte* 2: 589ff., 3: 112; Treitschke, "Verfassungskampf," 425–28, 441–43. For the plans of a new communal and county reform supported by Hardenberg, see Obenaus, *Anfänge des Parlamentarismus*, 128–36.

[47] Cited in Treitschke, *Deutsche Geschichte* 3: 114.

[48] Friedrich Ancillon, former tutor to the crown prince, in 1818 was named director of the political department in the ministry of foreign affairs; Friedrich von Schuckmann, minister of internal affairs; Wilhelm Prince von Wittgenstein, minister of the royal household; Daniel Ludwig Albrecht, member of the State Council. For a discussion of this commission, see Obenaus, *Anfänge des Parlamentarismus*, 141ff.

[49] Treitschke, "Verfassungskampf," 450; Klein, *Von der Reform zur Restauration*, 205–6.

CHAPTER 6

given in the constitutional document. There remains, therefore, where a constitutional document is to be promulgated, only the choice between either holding firmly to the pure monarchical principle and thereby allowing only advisory provincial diets or, in reality, adding the democratic principle.[50]

The king accepted Wittgenstein's position instead of Hardenberg's. His decision settled the fate of the constitution; there would be no written document, no national assembly. On October 30, 1821, he appointed a new commission, charged with drafting the legislation creating provincial diets. He instructed this new commission to "take into consideration local circumstances, while holding constantly in mind the monarchical principle."[51] The king's decision represented a triumph for the provincial nobility, for localism over centralism. This final constitutional commission forged the essential link between the landowning nobility and the conservative elements within the central government. With its creation, the politics of the Prussian restoration entered a new phase.

THE RECONQUEST OF LOCAL AFFAIRS

The final constitutional commission charged with drafting legislation creating the provincial diets was, in reality, not a new commission at all. It included all the members of the previous commission who had torpedoed Hardenberg's constitutional proposals—the crown prince, Ancillon, Schuckmann, Wittgenstein, and Albrecht. Three new members were added: Vincke, from Westphalia, Minister Otto von Voss-Buch, and President Schönberg, from the governmental district of Merseburg.[52] Voss-Buch was an old conservative from the Mark Brandenburg who exercised considerable influence over the crown prince. His growing power is seen in the fact that he was chosen to succeed Hardenberg after the chancellor's death in November 1822. Vincke and Schönberg were the only relatively liberal members of the commission. The commission's conservative character was evident in the fact that it invariably selected some of the most outspoken conserva-

---

[50] Cited in Treitschke, "Verfassungskampf," 452–54; see also Schuckmann's memorandum to the king, criticizing Hardenberg's plans, in Klein, *Von der Reform zur Restauration*, 204–5; see Obenaus, *Anfänge des Parlamentarismus*, 147.
[51] Treitschke, "Verfassungskampf," 456.
[52] Obenaus, *Anfänge des Parlamentarismus*, 151ff.

tives from the provinces for consultation.⁵³ Among the notables brought to Berlin for advice, nobles far outnumbered commoners and only occasionally—never from most of the eastern provinces—was a peasant invited to offer his opinions.

On some fundamental issues, the commission readily agreed and even resisted efforts of the provincial nobility to twist the diets completely to its advantage. For example, the commission agreed early that some form of representation from the peasantry was unavoidable. That assumption was disputed by some notables. Gustav von Rochow argued that peasants should not participate in any discussions in the diets that touched on the exclusive rights of the nobility, such as patrimonial police and justice. Von Quast, a nobleman from the Mark Brandenburg who had fought beside Marwitz against Hardenberg's reforms, was even more outspoken. He delivered a long, written brief against peasant representation. Except in East Friesland, peasants had never been represented in provincial diets under "the old German constitutions," he argued. That they had participated in the Assembly of Notables in 1811 and in the subsequent provisional assembly did not give them a claim for permanent representation in the provinces. They were not well enough educated, he insisted, to be discerning, and bad advice would be all too prevalent now that "demagogues can easily buy noble estates and find their way into the assemblies." Peasants should be consulted only on the issues that touched them directly.

---

⁵³ Werner J. Stephan, *Die Entstehung der Provinzialstände in Preussen, 1823* (phil. diss., Berlin, 1914), 19–22; Treitschke, "Verfassungskampf," 457. The nobles consulted from Silesia wanted all commoners who owned noble estates excluded from the first estate. Richard Röpell, "Zur Geschichte der Ersten Einrichtung der heutigen Provinzialstände Schlesiens," *Uebersicht der Arbeiten und Veränderungen der schlesischer Gesellschaft für vaterländische Kultur im Jahre 1846* (Breslau, 1847), 276–312. Gustav von Rochow also wished to exclude non-noble owners of noble estates from the first estate. He placed great hope in the provincial diets. On February 21, 1821, he wrote the following to Marwitz:

> You are right to trace the sickness of our time solely to the dominance of theories and of money . . . and the subsequent undermining of experience and custom. As long as men lived without need of money, they lived without theories. . . . In the seventeenth century, the pace became unfortunately faster, in the eighteenth century, its victory was determined, and in the nineteenth century, the modern constitutions completely bar the way to a reversal. This final gallop is not yet completed here and therefore I so zealously push the reestablishment of the constitution of the provincial Stände, because hereby can at least the final keystone of the revolution still be held back. In addition, these institutions are, by their nature, the means to work against the power of theories and money in that through them the remaining authority and discrimination can be built and fortified in the other Stände and finally set against that which is valued by the aristocracy of money and learning. (DZA II, Rep. 92, v. Rochow, A III, no. 9, Bl. 31–33)

CHAPTER 6

Quast's extreme position was not shared by many of those consulted. Peasants were to be included in the diets.⁵⁴

The question of how much representation should be allowed the peasantry was more difficult. Schönberg took the most liberal approach, arguing for equal representation from each of the three Stände: nobles, burghers, and peasants. The majority of the commission recommended a ratio among the three Stände of 3:2:1. Rochow asked for a much larger representation of noble estate owners, for they provided the monarchy's primary bulwark "against ideology and the mania for innovations."⁵⁵ Although he favored permitting all noble estate owners to sit in the provincial diet, thus granting them the *Virilstimme*, Rochow recognized that to be unrealistic; a more proper ratio, indicating the importance of the nobility, he thought, would be 6:2:1. But Rochow's substitute motion failed and the commission's recommendation was sustained.

The notables from the old provinces, especially Brandenburg, requested that the old boundaries of the province, which had been altered by the administrative districts established with the acquisition of the new territories, be used to constitute the basis for membership in the diet. The commission was not unanimous, but the request for the recognition of the old territorial boundaries was granted.⁵⁶

The commission also disagreed on whether legislation creating the provincial diets should be presented as partially fulfilling the royal promise of a constitution and "popular representation" (*Repräsentation des Volks*). Ancillon and Voss opposed any reference to the royal promise and objected to the reference to popular representation. Ancillon wrote: "Since not all national or popular representation is ständisch, and since these days the expression is coupled with a completely different concept, I would not like to apply it to a document when this expression is used with a completely different preference." Ancillon argued that because the commission proposed to limit representation to landowners, it could not be considered a genuine system of popular

---

⁵⁴ Stephan, *Die Entstehung der Provinzialstände*, 23–25. See also: STAP, Pr. Br., Rep. 37, von Quast/Garz, nos. 5 and 95; Klaus Vetter, *Kurmärkischer Adel und preussische Reformen*, Veröffentlichungen des Staatsarchivs Potsdam, 15 (Weimar, 1979), 71–76. If the peasants were to be included in the diets, the nobility insisted that they be peasants living on the land and tilling their own fields. DZA II, Rep. 92, v. Rochow, A III, no. 9, Bl. 111.

⁵⁵ See Stephan, *Die Entstehung der Provinzialstände*, 28, and Obenaus, *Anfänge des Parlamentarismus*, 180, for a discussion of ratio of the Stände.

⁵⁶ Ibid., 23. The nobility in the various provinces had better contact with each other than had been the case during 1811. See the letter from the Silesian leader von Lüttwitz to Rochow, May 15, 1822, DZA II, v. Rochow, A III, no. 8.

representation as promised by the king in 1815. Schönberg, on the contrary, thought it important to refer to the royal promise. "A ständisch representation remains, nevertheless, a representation of the people." The fact that actual representation was limited to landowners made no difference, he insisted, for the landless would be represented as well by property owners. "Were this not the case, then all subjects of the crown who are not fortunate enough to own land would, to a certain extent, be placed outside the law, which is certainly unacceptable."[57] As usual, Ancillon's viewpoint carried. Indeed, the commission ultimately decided that to avoid any confusion as to whether the establishment of the provincial diets was to be interpreted as the promised constitutional document, the royal order establishing the diets should be very brief. Individual laws would be drafted for each province, further emphasizing the local nature of representation.[58]

On June 5, 1823, the king issued the royal order setting forth general principles for the establishment of provincial diets. One month later, he issued the first decree setting up the diet in the Mark Brandenburg and Lower Lusatia; with a few variations, it formed the model for the establishment of other provincial assemblies.[59] Eligibility for election to the diet from each of the three Estates was limited to those who (1) owned land in the province for at least ten years, or who inherited it from someone who had owned it for that length of time, or who were exempted from this requirement by a royal dispensation; (2) were members of a Christian church; (3) were thirty years old; and (4) possessed an "irreproachable reputation." Election to the first Estate, the *Ritterschaft*, was open to anyone, regardless of birth, who had owned a noble estate for the specified length of time. The election of representatives to the diet from the first two Estates, the Ritterschaft and the towns, was direct; from the Third Estate, the peasants, it was indirect, through electors. The presiding officer of the diet was the marshal (*Landtags-Marschall*), who was appointed by the king from among the members of the First Estate; he conducted the meetings of the diet and set the agenda.

The authority of the diets was only consultative. They could advise the government on all legislation that affected their province specifically and, in the absence of any national diet, on any general legislation that altered personal or property rights or taxes. The diets had the right to submit petitions and complaints to the crown. Finally, the

[57] Treitschke, "Verfassungskampf," 459–60.
[58] Ibid., 461–62.
[59] *Gesetz-Sammlung, 1823*, 129–30, 130ff.; *Gesetz-Sammlung, 1824*, 101ff., 108ff., 144ff.

CHAPTER 6

diets were to offer specific advice concerning proposals to reorganize communal and county governments in the provinces.

The organization of the provincial diets received mixed reactions from all shades of the political spectrum. Dohna was displeased with the decree because it did not exclude deputies who were heavily in debt, which contradicted, he believed, the principle of representation based on landownership.[60] Marwitz, on the other hand, welcomed diets based on old provincial boundaries, because they moved toward the "setting aside of the new, arithmetic administrative divisions."[61] They restored authority to the "residents" of the province instead of leaving it merely to "rootless" administrators. Schön referred to the decree as a "miscarriage," which employed the concept of "Stände" instead of "representation," although "the earlier meaning of this concept [personal nobility] can no longer be upheld." Nevertheless, he welcomed the diets as providing a vehicle for the development of public opinion in the provinces.[62] Similarly, Karl A. Varnhagen von Ense summarized the event: "The anchor has been dropped into the feudal system, but the sails on the high seas are filled with popular representation; it remains to be seen which is stronger, the anchor or the wind."[63]

In fact, the establishment of provincial diets was not an unqualified triumph for the provincial nobility. The diets did, as Marwitz understood, restore some vitality to the old provincial structure; they represented, as Humboldt had foreseen, a counterpoise to the centralistic tendencies of the bureaucracy. Koselleck has referred to the "double net" that now covered the monarchy—the one organized according to the administrative structures introduced by the reforms, the other according to the ständisch structures of the old provinces.[64] Still, the provincial diets were weak compared with the bureaucracy; only after the reorganization of county government, which the provincial diets helped facilitate, did the ständisch structures offer a counterweight to the administration in the manner in which they affected the daily lives of the citizens.

The edict creating the provincial diets must be seen as a confirmation of reforms that had altered Prussian society over the previous fif-

[60] Cited in Stephan, *Die Entstehung der Provinzialstände*, 59.
[61] Marwitz, 1: 686.
[62] Schön, *Aus den Papieren* 3: 73.
[63] Cited in Stephan, *Die Entstehung der Provinzialstände*, 59.
[64] Obenaus, *Anfänge des Parlamentarismus*, 171–72, discusses the mixture of ständisch and property qualifications that were part of the system of representation; see also Koselleck, *Preussen zwischen Reform und Revolution*, 472.

teen years. The definition of the Stände was an arbitrary one, imposed by the state. It was no longer possible, as Schön understood, to defend the Stände as purely "natural" divisions of society. The *Allgemeines Landrecht* had contained a mixed definition of the Stände; while proclaiming the ständisch divisions as artificial and the product of social necessity, it nevertheless had divided society into Stände based on birth and occupations.[65] These distinctions were partially natural. Now, the royal decree declared bluntly, "landownership is the condition for membership in a Stand." Property, not birth or occupation, became the primary basis for the distinctions in society. This confirmed the assumption with which Stein had approached the reforms a decade and a half earlier, that property should form the basis for representation. By admitting non-noble estate owners to the first estate, the provincial legislation confirmed the Emancipation Edict of 1807, which had permitted the sale of noble estates to commoners. Although in practice the nobility continued to dominate provincial affairs in the eastern provinces, in theory that monopoly was now broken.

The legislation establishing provincial diets thus confirmed the fact that many reforms had instituted irreversible changes in the society. But it also indicated that the interests of conservatives high in the administration were not always synonymous with those of the provincial nobility. However much they may have wished to serve and preserve the nobility on the land, those at the center of government were not inclined to relinquish too much power. The perspective from the center is always different from that on the periphery. For example, Gustav von Rochow, as we have seen, worked during the early 1820s to maximize the influence of the nobility in the diets. His vigorous defense of the provincial nobility led his brother-in-law, Marwitz, to view him as an ideal candidate for a provincial minister. By the end of the decade, however, after he had made his way up the ranks in the government to become, in 1834, minister of internal affairs, Rochow lost his confidence in the Stände as the safeguard of the monarchy; he now viewed the bureaucracy as the backbone of the state, its bulwark against revolution.[66] It is important, therefore, as we consider the politics of the nobility and the genesis of its conservative ideology, that we not simply lump all conservatives together or consider the differences that distinguish them to be variations of an "ideal type," but

[65] See chapter 3.
[66] Ludwig Dehio, "Wittgenstein und das letzte Jahrzehnt Friedrich Wilhelms III," *FBPG* 25 (1923): 229–30.

CHAPTER 6

that we locate them, as well, in relation to the center of power. In this respect, it is instructive to consider the thought of Johann Friedrich Ancillon, who, as a member of the commission designing the provincial diets, exercised considerable influence among conservatives in the court during the early 1820s.[67]

Ancillon was one of the few commoners to achieve ministerial status in Prussia during the first half of the nineteenth century. Ironically, he was an important figure in bringing about the political restoration that later made it virtually impossible for commoners to rise to so high a station. At the time of Ancillon's death in 1837, Varnhagen von Ense, a perceptive observer of Prussian politics, commented that "it can be said with certainty that no commoner will be seen in such a high post again."[68] Ancillon owed his rise to power to the fact that after 1808 and 1810 he had been the tutor of the crown prince and gained, through him, access to positions of influence. Born in 1767 into a family whose forebears were French Huguenots forced to migrate to Prussia by the Revocation of the Edict of Nantes, Ancillon had studied theology and served briefly as pastor to the French Protestant community in Berlin. Through the crown prince, he gained a government post in 1814. A year later, he was alarmed when the king announced his intention to issue a written constitution and convene a national diet, for Ancillon had traveled in France during the revolution and believed that convocation of the Estates-General had been a mistake. He therefore wrote a pamphlet, *Ueber Souveränität und Staats-Verfassungen*, in 1815, opposing national representation. The pamphlet earned him a modest reputation in the court circles as a political thinker, so he proceeded to write several more books on political theory during the 1820s. In 1817, he was appointed to the State Council; he served, as we have noted, on the constitutional commissions that blocked Hardenberg's plans for constitutional reform and that drafted the ordinance creating provincial diets; in 1818, he was appointed director of the political section of the Foreign Ministry, and he served from 1832 until 1837 as minister of foreign affairs.

Although Ancillon's thought often showed traces of the influence of other conservatives, such as Müller (Ancillon also spoke in terms of a dialectic in which extremes were "mediated" [*vermittelt*]) he was much

[67] On Ancillon, see Paul Haake, *J.P.F. Ancillon und Kronprinz Friedrich Wilhelm IV. von Preussen*, Historische Bibliothek, 42 (Munich and Berlin, 1920); *Allgemeine Deutsche Biographie* (Leipzig, 1875), 1: 420–24. Treitschke, very critical of Ancillon, calls his memoranda "by far the worst that I know of the official work of a Prussian statesman of any age." "Verfassungskampf," 448–49.

[68] K. A. Varnhagen von Ense, *Tagebücher*, 2d ed. (Leipzig, 1863), 1: 43–44.

more of a rationalist. He admired Montesquieu above all other political thinkers and, like Montesquieu, believed that human reason was always coupled with experience.[69] He rejected the concept of a state of nature, from which the natural-law theorists of the eighteenth century embarked, but he did not reject the idea of natural law altogether. He wrote: "The laws [*Gesetze*] of freedom are ethical. They assert duties that are based upon rights [*Rechte*] and rights that originate in duties. These ethical laws have often been called natural laws, and the duties upon which they are based have been called natural rights, both in contrast to positive laws and rights. It is far more accurate to call the ethical laws, laws drawn from reason [*Vernunft-Gesetze*] and the natural rights, rights drawn from reason [*Vernunft-Rechte*]."[70]

This natural law and these natural rights are not learned from nature; they are acquired only "when a person achieves a certain degree of education" (*Bildung*). This education takes place within the family, first as one becomes aware of external coercion, the legislative authority to which one is subjected, and second as one becomes aware of the inner compulsion for freedom and morality, which is self-discipline. The third level of understanding arrived when this self-discipline led to the "drive toward perfection" in the realization of that freedom by fulfilling one's duty.[71] The function of the state was to complete the liberation begun by education within the family. It was to create the conditions in which "moral freedom" could be achieved, in which "men will do that which they should." Ancillon's ideas resemble the liberal idealism of Immanuel Kant, although he never directly acknowledged Kant. Like Müller, Ancillon considered the family to be the essential model for the state, but, unlike Müller, he chose to stress not the patriarchal and authoritative structure of the family, but the family as the framework for moral development.

Ancillon did not carry this premise to a liberal conclusion with an emphasis on freedom, however, for his chief concern was to assure the sovereign power of the prince. He borrowed phrases from the liberal vocabulary, such as "general will," but used them to buttress the authority of the monarch. The monarch embodied the general will; without him, no general will existed, only "a mass of individual wills."[72] A people (*Volk*) did not relinquish its sovereignty to a prince, for the

[69] Haake, *Ancillon*, 26, 98–99.
[70] Friedrich Ancillon, *Ueber den Geist der Staatsverfassungen und dessen Einfluss auf die Gesetzgebung* (Berlin, 1825), 7.
[71] Ibid., 9–11, 20.
[72] Friedrich Ancillon, *Ueber Souveränität und Staats-Verfassungen*, 2d ed. (Berlin, 1816), 12.

sovereignty of a prince was prior to the existence of a people. A people is created by the sovereignty of a prince. Therefore, the legislative sovereignty of a monarch, embodying the general will, "is the living principle of the state."[73]

Although absolute, Ancillon maintained, the prince's power was mediated by the nobility to prevent despotism. The nobility "stands nearer to the people than the king and nearer to the king than the people." The monarchy thus depended on the nobility for its preservation; "without nobility, there is no monarchy, but only western despotism or monarchical democracy."[74] But the monarchy was also tied to the nobility by the principle of birth and inheritance, so it was essential that the monarch secure the rights of the nobility. "Without landed property, there is no nobility, for without this form of property the nobility would become beggars at the door of the king and the nation, or else it would have to engage in trades and in commerce. If the nobility does that, it loses its characteristic spirit."[75] This justification of nobility was far different from that offered by Müller; for Ancillon, the importance of the nobility was its instrumentality. It was not a natural development, but a political necessity. Ancillon put it this way: "The nobility is a political creation that simultaneously limits the monarchy and gives it stability."[76]

The nobility could best fulfill its function of preventing despotism and stabilizing the government, Ancillon believed, through a system of ständisch representation. As it was essential for the nobility to own landed property to be a true nobility, so was the ownership of property the basis for representation. "There are in the present European states, and especially in Germany, two elements of a true ständisch representation, namely two chief types of property, . . . immobile property . . . and mobile property."[77] The one represented preservation, the other change. In much the same way, Müller had argued for two Stände, agriculture and commerce. Representation should be based only on property ownership, Ancillon insisted; occupations did not constitute Stände. The propertyless required no representation. "Those who possess no property are really strangers in the land and can be regarded as travelers, here today and gone tomorrow."[78] Few

[73] Ibid., 15, 17.
[74] Ibid., 35–36; *Ueber den Geist der Staatsverfassungen*, 86.
[75] Ibid., 86.
[76] Ibid., 87.
[77] Friedrich Ancillon, *Ueber die Staatswissenschaft* (Berlin, 1820), 101; see also *Ueber den Geist der Staatsverfassungen*, 127–38; *Ueber Souveränität*, 33–36.
[78] *Ueber die Staatswissenschaft*, 103.

ideologists have made blunter defenses of the state as the sole preserve of the propertied classes.

Many of Ancillon's views on Prussia's constitutional future were drawn from his observations of the French Revolution. His perceptions of the long-range causes of the French Revolution were relatively profound, and they resembled, in some fundamental ways, the explanation later offered by Tocqueville. The roots of the revolution lay in the destruction of the nobility's political power in the seventeenth century, Ancillon maintained. The Estates were destroyed, and with them the only institutions that could both limit and support the monarchy. "Richelieu founded the despotism upon which Louis XIV built."[79] Moreover, the nobility retained many social and economic privileges while losing its political raison d'être. Instead of issuing a constitution and beginning the revival of provincial estates, the crown made the mistake of convening the Estates-General. Ancillon drew the appropriate lessons for Prussia: no national assembly should be convened, but only provincial assemblies with purely consultative authority; if a constitution were to be forthcoming, it should be promulgated by the king.

Both Stein and Hardenberg, as we have stressed, conceived of representation as closely integrated with the administration; Stein spoke repeatedly of representatives as "participants in the administration," and Hardenberg considered consultative representatives primarily as an extension of the administration. For Ancillon and the conservative opponents of Hardenberg on the commission planning the diets, it was important that the provincial diets be free of the influence and control of the bureaucracy that they considered too liberal. Although they did not wish to grant the diets more than consultative power, these conservatives wished to secure their independence from the administration. This independence was ensured with the creation, on November 5, 1824, of the Commission for Ständisch Affairs directly under the king (*Immediatkommission für die ständischen Angelegenheiten*).[80] This commission stood between the ministry and the king, advising the king on all matters pertaining to the Stände, and was composed of members of the previous constitutional commission with the exclusion

---

[79] Friedrich Ancillon, *Zur Vermittlung der Extreme in den Meinungen* (Berlin, 1831), 1: 258; for his general discussion of the French Revolution, see 247–322.

[80] This discussion of the Immediatkommission is based on the informative article by Herbert Obenaus, "Die Immediatkommission für Ständischen Angelegenheiten als Instrument der preussischen Reaktion im Vormärz," in *Festschrift für Hermann Heimpel*, Veröffentlichung des Max-Planck-Instituts für Geschichte (Göttingen, 1971), 36/1:410–46; see Obenaus, *Anfänge des Parlamentarismus*, 233ff.

CHAPTER 6

of the two liberals, Schönberg and Vincke, who were not appointed on the ground that they did not reside in Berlin. Thus, the commission was thoroughly conservative in its composition—the crown prince, Ancillon, Schuckmann, and Wittgenstein.

From its creation in 1824 until its dissolution in 1847, the commission served as a primary link between conservatives in the government and the conservative provincial nobility. Its membership was always drawn from the most conservative elements of the state; most members were from the inner circle of advisers to Frederick William III or the crown prince. Vincke and Schönberg were replaced immediately by Count von Lottum, a member of the king's immediate advisers in the civil cabinet, and General von Müffling, a close friend of both the king and the crown prince and a person who also had the trust of Marwitz. A year later, Friedrich von Motz, newly named minister of finance, joined the commission; he may have been its most liberal member, although he grew increasingly conservative after the death of Hardenberg. Subsequent appointments during the reign of Frederick William III included Rochow, who became minister of interior in 1834, and Count von Alvensleben-Erxleben, one of the wealthiest noble landowners in Prussia, an admirer of the Swiss conservative ideologist Karl Ludwig von Haller, and a close friend of the conservative associates of the crown prince, Leopold and Ludwig von Gerlach. In 1841, the ultraconservative Karl von Voss-Buch joined the commission.[81]

The commission had full responsibility supervising all activities of the provincial diets. Although initially it carried out this responsiblity quite independently of the ministry, by the early 1830s, when the ministry itself was again safely conservative, the commission worked more closely with the ministry. The commission exercised wide latitude in dealing with the provincial diets. It received their petitions and requests and it alone prepared the king's response to them. When the credentials of persons elected to the diets were in question or when a royal dispensation was requested to exempt a member-elect of a diet from the requirement of ten-year ownership of land, the commission investigated the case and rendered a decision. Invariably, the Commission's political perspective weighed heavily in such decisions. For example, the towns of Zeitz and Weissenfels had elected a von Ponikau to the diet, although he did not fulfill the qualifications for member-

[81] Karl von Voss-Buch said of the peasant regulation on his estate: "I don't wish to have peasants, I want subjects" (*Untertanen*). Cited in Obenaus, "Die Immediatkommission," 424.

ship in the Second Estate, because he neither had a trade nor was an urban magistrate. Nevertheless, his election was approved by the commission because of his "personality." In another case, Leopold Freundt, a Königsberg pharmacist, asked for exemption from the ten-year property-ownership requirement. The subsequent investigation showed that his political reliability was "not free of doubt," for he had left the official church and joined a free religious community and, more damning still, he was a friend of the Königsberg liberal Johann Jacoby. The commission denied the requested exemption.

Two other cases, involving interpretation of the requirement that persons elected to the diets be of "unblemished reputation," also show how political were the decisions of the commission. One case involved a Landrat von Ziegler elected to the Silesian diet. Ziegler had served a sentence of house arrest because he had "mistreated a woman" in the course of his official duties. The commission, after investigating the case, concluded that Ziegler's reputation was not sufficiently damaged by the incident, despite his sentence, for his actions had merely been the result of "ill-considered official zeal." He was allowed to take his seat in the diet. The other case involved a man named J. F. Brust, who had been elected to the diet of the province of the Rhine. Brust had criticized the government openly and demanded the establishment of a national diet. He was, stated liberal representative David Hansemann, "one of the most able, legally learned, and liberal members" of the diet. For his offensive criticism, the commission considered him unworthy of membership and excluded him from the provincial diet.[82]

Although the commission was clearly intended to shield the provincial diets from intrusion by the bureaucracy, it never attempted to broaden the authority of the diets in ways that would have enabled them to check bureaucratic power. The royal order of June 5, 1823, creating the diets' assured that they would be consulted on general legislation that would have the effect of "altering personal and property rights and taxes," but, in fact, countless laws were promulgated during the next two decades that were of general significance without the diets' ever having been consulted. The law framing railroad construction issued in 1838 was not presented to the diets, for it was assumed to be of limited importance; the first factory legislation, limiting child labor in 1839, was not discussed with the diets; the same was true of a series of measures in the criminal code that certainly affected personal rights. None of the laws creating the customs union (*Zollver-*

[82] Ibid., 434–36.

CHAPTER 6

ein) came before the diets, despite its implication for state taxes; moreover, between 1838 and 1840, several new taxes on agricultural products were introduced without consultation by the diets. With merely a consultative capacity, and without being consulted on major legislation passed by the government, the provincial diets remained powerless and largely symbolic throughout Vormärz.[83] Tight censorship prevented publication of any of the discussions within the diets, which as a result never succeeded in becoming focal points of public political opinion, as liberals such as Schön had hoped. The inherent weakness of the diets, their unrepresentative character, and their failure to evolve into some form of national representation led, as we shall see, to a confrontation during the early years of Frederick William IV's reign.[84]

Nevertheless, the positions taken by the diets on the issues on which they either were consulted or submitted petitions to the king provide some indication of the chief political concerns of the nobility and how it sought to utilize the diets to shape official policy to its advantage. Especially during the late 1820s and early 1830s, when Prussian agriculture suffered from a severe depression, appeals were made through the diets for increased governmental support. Some of those requests were for aid to noble estate owners, others involved aid for a beleaguered rural population. At its first meeting, the diet of Mark Brandenburg requested that the government purchase a large amount of grain in the province for military magazines to support the price.[85] The Pomeranian diet called for import tariffs on agricultural products to protect domestic producers; it further asked the government to support the price of mortgage notes (Pfandbriefe), issued by the provincial rural credit institute (Landschaft), because their value

[83] Adolf Arndt, "Der Anteil der Stände an der Gesetzgebung in Preussen von 1823–1848," *Archiv für Oeffentliches Recht*, vol. 17 (1902), 570–88; see anonymous article "Ueber Provinzialstände," *Deutsche Vierteljahres Schrift*, Heft 1 (1841), 245–72. Caroline von Rochow believed that the provincial diets were powerless but that they, nevertheless, helped to "awaken again in a younger generation of nobles an awareness and an interest for the concerns affecting them." *Vom Leben am preussischen Hof*, 213. Obenaus, in *Anfänge des Parlamentarismus*, 230, argues that the actions of the diets were "restorative." They were active advocates of certain policies, especially in opposition to the division of peasant holdings.

[84] See chapter 9. The criticism of the diets as unrepresentative began shortly after their establishment. See the anonymous pamphlet *Königthum und Freiheit: Ein Wort an der preussischen Provinzial-Landstände* (Ilmenau, 1832).

[85] J.D.F. Rumpf, *Die Gesetze wegen Anordnung der Provinzial-Stände in der preussischen Monarchie* (Berlin, 1826), 1: 31–32. For an excellent survey of the issues that came before the diets, see Obenaus, *Anfänge des Parlamentarismus*, 213ff.

had fallen precipitously.[86] In the province of Prussia, hardest hit by the agricultural crisis, the diet called for direct relief of the poor by the distribution of grain from the military magazines and the issuing of seed grain to estate owners from the magazines. It also asked that the government foster the development of spinning and weaving in Prussia to aid the poor rural population.[87] The Silesian diet reported in 1830 that its taxes were the highest in the monarchy and that its economic development was severely depressed; between 1816 and 1825, the diet claimed, the Silesian population had increased by 19 percent, although the number of dwellings had increased by only 7 percent, the number of horses by 7 percent, and the number of cattle by 11 percent.[88] Repeatedly, the diets requested compensation for the loss of the noble monopoly on milling and brewing.[89]

When consulted regarding possible new legislation on Jewish civil rights, which would modify the Jewish Emancipation Edict of 1812, the provincial diets revealed their deep fear of Jews' purchasing noble estates. Since the law creating the provincial diets did not allow Jewish owners of noble estates to be members of the First Estate in the diet, Jews should be prohibited from buying estates altogether, they claimed. Moreover, "according to the unanimous opinion" of the Brandenburg diet, Jews should not be permitted to acquire peasant holdings as well unless they agreed to give up all commercial enterprises, to work the land themselves, together with their children, and agreed not to take on any Jewish dependent laborers (*Miethsleute*). "If these conditions have not been fulfilled within six months of the purchase, the farm must be sold again," declared the Brandenburg diet.[90] Even in the towns Jews should not be allowed to own more land than their own house and garden. In addition, Jewish schools should be dissolved, Jewish children should be required to attend Christian schools, and Jews should fulfill their military obligation. The fear that the open market for noble estates would result in many estates' falling into the hands of Jews continued throughout Vormärz. In 1840, the Ministry of Internal Affairs requested the provincial governors to report the number of estates in their province that were held by Jews. If

---

[86] Ibid., 70–72; see also 138ff.

[87] J.D.F. Rumpf, *Landtags Verhandlungen der Provinzial-Stände in der preussischen Monarchie* (Berlin, 1828) 4: 124–26. (This is a continuation of the series in footnote 85.)

[88] Ibid. 5: 49–54.

[89] Ibid. 1: 149, 4: 18, 146–47.

[90] Ibid. 1: 16–25, 74–77, 133–38. See also Horst Fischer, *Judentum, Staat, und Heer in Preussen im frühen 19. Jahrhundert*, Schriftenreihe Wissenschaftlicher Abhandlungen des Leo Baecks Institutes, 20 (Tübingen, 1968), 67–83.

CHAPTER 6

the report from Prussia was at all typical, it indicates that the fear was vastly exaggerated. Of the fifty-five counties in East and West Prussia, embracing more than two thousand noble estates, fifty-two counties had no Jewish noble estate owners; in the other three counties, there were five estates in Jewish hands.[91]

Through the diets, the nobility also appealed for the restoration of some of the instruments of domination that it had lost through the reforms. In 1827, for example, the diet of the Mark Brandenburg requested that the government reimpose restrictions on the marriages of agricultural servants and day laborers, for, since the lord's permission was no longer required to marry, early marriages had led to too many children and increasing rural poverty.[92] A petition from the Prussian provincial diet several years later called for an expansion of the estate owners' rights of disciplinary punishment over servants and wage laborers. At the same time that the estate owners requested the means for greater disciplinary control over their servile population, they acknowledged that the paternalist structure of social relations was disintegrating and that consequently the police power of the state needed to be enlarged. In a statement revealing the nobility's perception of the disintegration of its paternalist claims, the Prussian provincial diet called on the state to assume the costs of criminal investigations on the land:

> The position of the noble estate owner, whose possession has been endowed with the rights of criminal jurisdiction, has been completely changed by the recent legislation. The nearly domestic relationship of the noble estate lord and his subjects has been dissolved; the estates have, to a certain degree, been opened up for settlement, and, because of progressive agricultural methods and successive parcellization [of peasant holdings], a large number of persons have moved onto the estates who have no close connection with the estate lord.[93]

If the provincial diets remained relatively inconsequential and primarily of symbolic importance to the nobility, control of county government did not. County government was by far the most important aspect of the political power of the nobility.[94] It had far more impact on the everyday lives of the overwhelming majority of the population than did the provincial diets, provincial governors, and officials in the governmental districts. By tradition, all village police were subordinate

[91] PSK/B-D, *Provinz Ostpreussen*, Rep. 2, Oberpräsidium, Tit. 36, no. 15.
[92] Rumpf, *Landtags Verhandlungen* 4: 30–31.
[93] Ibid. 12: 28–30, 33.
[94] Carl W. Lancizolle, *Ueber Königtum und Landstände in Preussen* (Berlin, 1846), 383.

to the Landrat, the chief official in the county. The Landräte were selected, usually upon the recommendation of the county assembly dominated by the nobility, from among the local noble estate owners; they worked closely with the estate owners in maintaining order in the county. Hardenberg had threatened to change all of this. First came the Gendarmerie Edict of 1812, which, as we have noted, was largely suspended by 1815.[95] In 1816, in order to clarify the confusion over local government after the suspension of the Gendarmerie Edict, new instructions were issued to the Landräte that generally restored their traditional responsibilities; nevertheless, it was clear that the reorganization of county government would take place within the context of a constitution or, at least, within the framework of provincial and national representation.[96] Hardenberg's constitutional plans of 1819 and 1820 indicated that he still intended to draw county government more tightly within the web of the central administration. He proposed to transform the Landrat into a civil servant whose appointment came solely from the king and who would not participate in any significant way in the county assembly. In Hardenberg's proposal, representation in the county assembly was to be drawn equally from each Ständ, so that the nobility lost its absolute control.[97] With the defeat of Hardenberg's plans in 1821 and the establishment of the provincial diets in 1823, the way was cleared for a reconsideration of county government. This was one of the primary issues on which the king sought the counsel of the provincial diets during their first meetings.

Discussions on the reorganization of county government produced substantial disagreements in the provincial diets. The draft proposal of a county ordinance discussed by the Brandenburg diet, written by the conservative "notables" of the province, called for the Virilstimme for noble estate owners, permitting each a seat in the county assembly.[98] It proposed to grant each town with more than two thousand

[95] See pp. 141–43. Although the bulk of the Gendarmerie edict had been suspended, some aspects remained. The nobility of East Prussia, for example, submitted numerous requests for suspension of the remaining aspects of the edict. It was clear that, during the discussions of a constitution in 1819 and 1820, there was great concern, as one petition put it, "that a new communal organization threatens to tear the last bond between us and our subjects."

[96] H. von Gräff et al., *Ergänzungen und Erläuterungen der Preussischen Rechtsbücher durch Gesetzgebung und Wissenschaft unter Benutzung der Justiz-Ministerial-Akten und der Gesetz-Revisionsarbeiten* (Berlin, 1864), 6: 191ff.

[97] See p. 197.

[98] Klaus Vetter, *Kurmärkischer Adel und preussische Reformen*, 78–81. For Marwitz's materials on the county organization, see STAP, Pr. Br., Rep. 37, Marwitz/Friedersdorf, 584; Marwitz, II/2:342–62.

CHAPTER 6

residents a representative in the assembly, as well as a representative for each town with fewer inhabitants that nevertheless owned a noble estate; towns of less than two thousand inhabitants with no noble estates would have a collective representative. The proposal would limit peasants to three representatives in each county assembly, although many nobles felt a single representative was sufficient. Marwitz explained why the peasantry did not require greater numerical representation: "We consider the admission of peasants to the Kreistag more as a process of educating them than as an express necessity to attend to their advice and insight. We believe that their presence there should far more serve to open to them the insight into the discussions and to produce in them the conviction that nothing that transpires there is to their disadvantage."[99] The diet could reach no agreement on the formula for representation, nor could it agree with the noble recommendation that only the first estate of noble landowners in the county vote in the selection of candidates for the post of Landrat. Each estate submitted its own recommendation to the king.[100]

Debate in the Silesian diet followed much the same lines as in Brandenburg. The draft recommendation there was written by the conservative spokesman for the nobility, Freiherr von Lüttwitz.[101] It followed the noble recommendations that had already been submitted by the Brandenburg diet. In addition, it called for measures to restrict the freedom of peasants to move about the province; the increased mobility resulting from peasant emancipation, Lüttwitz claimed, had resulted in vagabondage and widescale begging. He recommended some system of registration that would prevent free movement of persons. When representatives of the peasantry complained that the peasantry would be underrepresented by such a scheme of representation, the nobility answered that the interests of the peasantry would be protected by noble landowners. One town representative observed that with such a reply, the nobility itself had undermined the principle of ständisch representation. As in Brandenburg, no agreement could be reached, so each Estate submitted its own proposal to the king. The appeal from the Fourth Estate, the peasantry, showed that it was well aware of what was at stake.

We have gained all the rights of happy citizens and have obtained, thereby, for the first time, a fatherland. . . . And what of the critics of

[99] STAP, Pr. Br., Rep. 37, Marwitz/Friedersdorf, 584, Bl. 124–25.
[100] Vetter, *Kurmärkischer Adel und preussische Reformen*, 80.
[101] Willy Klawitter, *Der erste schlesische Provinziallandtag im Jahre 1825* (phil. diss., Breslau, 1909), 60–76.

our Stand? Can they prove that we are unworthy of the good that has been granted us, that we are ungrateful and insubordinate? Empty declamations about moral depravity and the lack of culture resound, to be sure, in the prominent circles, although it seems to us that we are not so bad as that and that the people of Prussia are not yet so degenerate that the soft authority of religion and the reins of existing law are not able to hold them in check. . . . Such accusations, however, must be put forward if one wants to create bound serfs [Knechte] once again. The author of this draft of the law wished to show us, in a long speech, that it was disadvantageous for us to stand immediate to the king, to be able to receive our blessings directly from him, that the subordinate relationship of our Stand must be reestablished and that the Fourth Estate must again become bound serfs as before. . . . The king will not concede that out of false pretenses a way is to be built in order to lead us out of the bright sunlight of the throne and back into the dark night of hereditary subjection and bondage.[102]

The government issued the ordinances for county government in the various provinces of the monarchy between 1825 and 1828.[103] With slight variations, the provisions for counties in the six eastern provinces were essentially the same: the First Estate of each county assembly included the owner of each noble estate in the county, insofar as he was twenty-four years of age, was of the Christian faith, and had an "unblemished reputation"; in Pomerania, Saxony, Silesia, and Posen every city had the right to send a delegate to its respective county assembly, whereas in Brandenburg and Prussia only the larger towns had their own representatives, and the smaller towns had a collective representative; the Third Estate of the peasantry had three representatives in each assembly. In Prussia, the owners of larger kölmische estates also had the right to appear in person in the First Estate of the assembly. Except in Brandenburg (including Lusatia) and Pomerania, where the traditional exclusive right of the First Estate to nominate candidates for Landrat was maintained, each county assembly had the right to nominate three candidates for Landrat, from whom the king would select one. With these county ordinances, the landed nobility recovered the essential instruments of local domination. The county

[102] Cited in ibid., 69.
[103] Brandenburg and Pomerania, *Gesetz-Sammlung, 1825*, 203ff., 217ff.; Prussia, Saxony, Silesia, Rhineland, and Westphalia, *Gesetz-Sammlung, 1827*, 34ff., 54ff., 71ff., 117ff.; Posen, *Gesetz-Sammlung, 1828*, 3ff. For a discussion of the ordinances, see Georg-Christoph von Unruh, *Der Kreis* (Cologne and Berlin, 1965), 105–15; Heinrich Heffter, *Die Deutsche Selbstverwaltung im 19. Jahrhundert* (Stuttgart, 1950), 131–32; Gräff et al., *Ergänzungen und Erläuterungen* 6: 173ff.; Obenaus, *Anfänge des Parlamentarismus*, 492–500.

CHAPTER 6

assemblies became secure again as the singular preserves of noble estate owners; they were to remain so, despite another reform of county government in 1872, for the remainder of the century. A later advocate of reform, Rudolf Gneist, decried the monopoly exercised by the noble estate owners in the county assemblies: "I know of counties in which, for example, 163 noble estate owners have 163 votes, one town of 10,583 persons 1 vote, and the rural population (62,000 souls) 3 votes. Or a still nearer county where 65 noble estate owners, 3 peasants, and 3 townsmen represented a population of 29,000 urban and 27,000 rural inhabitants."[104]

Aside from the important right of nominating candidates for the office of the Landrat, the authority of the county assemblies was limited largely to local affairs—maintenance of roads, dikes, drainage systems, fire societies, hospitals, and poor relief. For the nobility, however, the significance of the county assemblies lay not in whatever material advantages could be gained through control of the assemblies but in the symbol of authority they communicated. Because each noble estate owner in the county was a member of the county assembly, each held a public office by virtue of a private possession. The significance of the conservative triumph in the restoration of the old order of county government lay in the fact that it confirmed the private exercise of public authority. The essence of the conservative ideology of the Prussian nobility during the early period of the restoration was the effort to rejoin the public and private origins of authority.

In many ways, the Landrat epitomized this fusion of public office and private station.[105] Although appointed by the king, he was a noble estate owner in the county; if he lost his estate through foreclosure or disposed of it through sale or partition, he lost the right to serve as Landrat.[106] His appointment came from above but was contingent on his commanding the respect of his fellow noble estate owners in the county. His position occupied the sometimes disputed terrain between the government officials and the local nobility, but it also provided him with considerable independence. His success was frequently more the result of his personal ability than his official authority. The instructions for Landräte of 1816, which remained the official set of instructions through most of Vormärz, provided a paradigmatic state-

[104] Cited in Heffter, *Die Deutsche Selbstverwaltung*, 131.
[105] Georg-Christoph von Unruh, *Der Landrat: Mittler zwischen Staatsverwaltung und Kommunaler Selbstverwaltung* (Cologne and Berlin, 1966), 49ff.; Koselleck, *Preussen*, 452–57; see also Gräff et al., *Ergänzungen und Erläuterungen* 5: 175ff.
[106] Cabinet order, March 23, 1839: Gräff et al., *Ergänzungen und Erläuterungen* 6: 187.

ment of paternalist rule.[107] The Landrat was to treat the residents of his county with "gentleness, moderation, and patience," but, when duty required it, also with firmness and authority. "Most especially must the Landräte direct sympathetic attention toward the lower classes of town and country laborers, and be everywhere at hand for them with instruction, encouragement, and good advice. ... [The Landräte] must, by the awakening of personal trust, bring the county residents to consider the Landrat as their natural adviser." To do this, they must travel regularly throughout the county and "avoid paperwork." In order to be equally accessible to all the residents of the county, the Landrat should keep his office in the primary town of the county.[108]

Hans von Kleist-Retzow, who was appointed Landrat of County Belgard in Pomerania in 1844, wrote a vivid description of the difficulties, tasks, and power of the office to his friend Friedrich Ranke.

The office which God has entrusted to me is truly excellent and beautiful. Independent from above, from the governmental districts, as from the county residents below, the living contact that I establish with these residents is my responsibility alone. I can and must work with them more through my personality than through the administration of the laws. There are, indeed, in this a multitude of very small things that I have to settle and put in order. Such a Landrat will scarcely find a place in your brother's history books; however, the more that he has the opportunity to be faithful in the little things, the more will his memory be revered in future generations. ... I undertake to do everything myself and wherever possible, on the spot. Seldom am I home more than two or three days in the week, often none at all; then there comes this or that visit, here a menial servant, there a peasant or a drifter who needs advice and help from me and leads me out into his field, to the mowing and baling. Still, the Landrat has an authority that often frightens me, and since I was earlier a jurist, people often come to me from afar in order to get advice on some matter related to my office or on some unrelated legal concern. When the children are told that the Pope is not allowed to marry, they ask whether the Landrat has forbidden it.[109]

[107] Ibid. 6: 191–99. For a description of the tests required to become a Landrat, imposed after July 10, 1838, see ibid., 188–90.

[108] Karl Albert von Kamptz, ed., *Annalen der preussischen inneren Staats-Verwaltung* (Berlin, 1813–1839), 11: 598–99, 12: 902.

[109] Cited in Hermann von Petersdorff, *Kleist-Retzow: Ein Lebensbild* (Stuttgart and Berlin, 1907), 84. For an indication of the relationship of the Landrat to the other nobles of the county, see ibid., 15.

CHAPTER 6

That this "frightening" authority of the Landrat had occasionally an aspect to it other than the idyllic paternalism portrayed by Kleist-Retzow can be seen from the case of Landrat von Wittenburg, of County Neustadt in the predominantly Polish-speaking region of Upper Silesia.[110] In the late summer of 1844, the police in the county apprehended three young men suspected of being responsible for a number of thefts in the region. According to the account later given by the men, one, Michael Zimolka, was bound to a bench and beaten by two policemen constantly for a half-hour until he lost consciousness. The officials revived him by splashing him with water and beat him again until he confessed. The second man, Gottlieb Hoose, confessed more readily but was severely beaten the next day and "kicked in the side" by the Landrat himself for having "lied." The third man, Joseph Gutsfeld, was also beaten by officials, including the Landrat, with a leather whip. The mother of one of the young men took the step, unusual for someone from the lowest rung of society, of bringing charges in the superior court in Ratibor against the Landrat for "gross mistreatment." The court initiated an investigation of the case. Immediately a jurisdictional dispute broke out between the judiciary officials and the officials of the bureaucracy. Wittenburg's superiors in the governmental district of Oppeln claimed that the case was not criminal at all and did not belong in the courts; it should be handled, they maintained, administratively, for Wittenburg was guilty, at the most, only of "overstepping the bounds" of his authority. Moreover, the bureaucratic officials claimed that the case needed to be judged within the overall context of the problems of local administration, which in this case involved a band of thieves committing frequent crimes in the county. In an appeal to the Ministry of Internal Affairs that the case be dealt with administratively, the officials of the district warned that it would set a bad precedent to allow criminal proceedings to take place against officials, including noble estate owners, for minor transgressions of their police powers. Such action could "cripple" the authorities if they had to stand "in constant fear of investigation and punishment," they warned.

In a subsequent investigation of the case, the official investigator for the governmental district, Count Eulenberg, found that Landrat Wittenburg had been "overzealous" in carrying out his duties and had violated several procedural regulations, such as that against forced

---

[110] I am indebted to Alf Lüdtke for bringing this incident to my attention. For a fuller account of it, from which this description is drawn, see Lüdtke, 'Gemeinwohl,' Polizei un 'Festungspraxis': Staatliche Gewaltsamkeit und innere Verwaltung im Preussen, 1815–1850, Veröffentlichungen des Max-Planck-Instituts für Geschichte, 73 (Göttingen, 1982), 184–90.

confessions. Nevertheless, although "the end does not justify the means," the fact remained that Wittenburg had broken up the band of thieves that had been operating in his county. The other investigator in the case, Ewald, also justified Wittenburg's actions in terms of its results: "That he thereby achieved the useful objective of public security has itself been acknowledged by the thanks of the superior court." Despite the appeals from the government officials, the Ministry of Internal Affairs, in discussions with the Ministry of Justice on the matter, decided that the case had become too well known to be handled merely administratively and that it should be treated as a criminal matter. At the same time, but without knowing of this decision, Wittenburg asked to be relieved of his duties as Landrat; the president of the governmental district persuaded him to remain in office pending a final decision of the court and the ministry.

A year later, nearly two years after the incident, the court announced its verdict. Wittenburg was found guilty of criminal "mistreatment while carrying out his office" and fined 100 taler, which represented nearly the minimal punishment prescribed for such a case. Despite the verdict, Minister of Internal Affairs von Bodelschwingh requested that Wittenburg retain his position and wrote the following:

The punishment of a transgression of official authority, which proceeds out of too much professional zeal, [appears] not to be at all a defamation of honor, so I can only wish that, because of the otherwise good service and the completely unblemished nature of his [Wittenburg's] character, he will wish to withdraw his earlier offer of resignation . . . [for] it would be regrettable if he were to abide by his intention to give up his office.

Wittenburg withdrew his letter of resignation and remained Landrat.

The case reveals the complex nature of public authority in Prussia at its most basic level. On the one hand, the requirements of the state bound by public law, the *Rechtstaat*, were satisfied: in the courts, Wittenburg was found guilty of criminal behavior and fined. On the other hand, the extreme and arbitrary brutal power of public officials was confirmed: in the administration, Wittenburg was guilty of being merely "overzealous" and encouraged to remain in office. The operative phrases in Bodelschwingh's memorandum requesting that Wittenburg remain Landrat were that he had suffered no "defamation of honor" and that his character remained "unblemished." Honor, a private attribute, determined whether he could retain a public office. Honor thus became a public and legal category as well, just as only persons of "unblemished reputation" were allowed to sit in county or

CHAPTER 6

provincial diets. It was probably true that Kleist-Retzow could succeed as a paternalist Landrat because of his "personality," but that personality was endowed with both private and public aspects; behind it stood the fully sanctioned coercive force of public authority. The measure of the nobility's success in conserving its position through Vormärz was the fact that despite the reforms the fusion of public office and private interest remained somewhat intact.

The Changing Concept of Stand

Through the recovery of its control of local institutions and the important positions in the central government during the 1820s and 1830s, the nobility seemed to have halted the erosion of its position caused by the flood of reform legislation under Stein and Hardenberg. This was, of course, only partially the case, for the fragile layer of the restoration barely covered the subterranean currents of change that would lead to the collapse of 1848. The fundamental causes of these changes lay in the developing European and world economy over which the Prussian nobility had little control. I will describe the manifestations of those changes in Prussia, particularly as they affected agriculture and the control of land in the eastern provinces, in the next chapter. The purpose of this section is to analyze one manifestation of the change by examining the concept of Stand, so central to the nobility's efforts at restoration that I have just described.

As noted in the discussion of symbolic Herrschaft, the concept of Stand played a central role in the symbolic system through which the nobility exercised its cultural hegemony throughout much of the early modern period of German history.[111] Positing a differentiated and hierarchical society, with the nobility in the preeminent position, the concept of Stand was the primary category through which people perceived their social order. The concept penetrated so deeply into popular consciousness that it became impossible to think of society in other categories; even the peasantry thought of itself as organized into Stände. The struggle to establish a system of ständisch representation in the 1820s thus involved more than simply the preservation of a structure that would allow the nobility to dominate the representation; it was also an effort to sustain cultural hegemony, that is, control over the popular perceptions of society. Ancillon had this in mind when he claimed, "The Stände have grown with the society and are rooted in

[111] See chapter 2.

it, so that one cannot think of society without the Stände."[112] The idiom was so pervasive that even liberal thinkers were compelled to work within it. Thus, Rotteck and Welcker's *Staats-Lexikon* declared, "The Stände form the skeletal structure of society."[113] Ultimately, most liberals tried to bend the concept to their purposes by defining the Stände on the basis of two principles: personal ability and material possessions. The effort to retain old meanings in the concept of Stand, therefore, also formed an essential part of the nobility's strategy of conservation during the restoration.

Although both Stein and Hardenberg endeavored to retain the ständisch categories in society, as, for example, in their plans for a system of representation, they ultimately undermined those categories by changing the basis of the relations between Stände. The daily life of most peasants did not change dramatically as a result of the agrarian reforms; they still fell under the lord's police and judicial authority, and most lords undoubtedly continued to be as kind or as brutal as before. But the basis of the lord's hegemony did change. The peasants were no longer personally bound to the estate; gradually, they became contractually bound, and because of that, the lord's authority assumed a more public, less private character. It was, for example, drawn more closely under the supervision of the public law of the state. After 1810, all patrimonial courts were explicitly bound by the prescriptions of state law, and the punishments they could administer were increasingly restricted by the state. The appeal of noble estate owners in 1833 for the state to assume the costs of criminal investigations, because the "nearly domestic" relationship between the lord and his subjects had been dissolved, indicated that the private legal bond between nobles and peasants was being replaced by public law.[114]

The most far-reaching impact of the reforms on the concept of Stand, however, resulted from the removal of legal restrictions on the purchase of noble estates by commoners and the subsequent transfer of many noble estates into the hands of non-nobles. By law, the new owner, whether common or noble, acquired all the privileges associated with the estate. Ständisch rights ceased to be personal rights and became property rights. The most obvious manifestation of this change in the meaning of *Stand* came in 1823 with the establishment

[112] Ancillon, *Ueber die Staatswissenschaft*, 96.

[113] Carl von Rotteck and Carl Welcker, *Staats-Lexikon; oder, Encyclopädie der Staatswissenschaft* (Altona, 1843), 15: 128. See also Martin Schumacher, *Gesellschafts- und Ständesbegriff um 1840: Ein Beitrag zu sozialen Bild des süddeutsche Liberalismus nach dem Rotteck-Welckerschen Staats-Lexikon* (phil. diss., Göttingen, 1955).

[114] See footnote 93.

CHAPTER 6

of the provincial diets; "natural" definitions of *Stand* were set aside and ownership of land, rural and urban, became the sole criterion for defining the Stände. The First Estate continued to be called the Ritterschaft, the "knights," but it included commoners as well as nobles. These social, legal, and institutional changes emptied the concept of Stand of its traditional meaning. Eduard Gans, the philosopher of law, saw this most clearly.

The laws of 1807 dissolved the three Stände by permitting a nobleman to pursue a trade and a tradesman to own a noble estate. The provincial diets have called these Stände back from the dead. Stände, however, are only truly present when an individual can belong to only one Stand; if he can simultaneously belong to various Stände, the ständisch principle is merely an artifice, the acceptance of it arbitrary, and its inner truth is stripped away.[115]

The loss of what Gans here calls the "inner truth" of the ständisch principle was apparent in the disintegration of the noble symbols of privilege and domination. Some nobles were upset by the fact that non-nobles wore the same uniform in the diets as noble members of the First Estate; they wished for some visible difference that would distinguish nobles from commoners. Nobles complained bitterly of others of noble birth disgracing themselves with unscrupulous business activities but retaining their noble titles.[116] They objected to high civil servants' or distinguished burghers' being addressed as *Hochwohlgeboren* (high-, wellborn) although they lacked the requisite title. By 1840, differences over the forms of address in the army had become such that the government ruled that officers of non-noble birth should be addressed simply as *Wohlgeboren* (wellborn), while nobles alone should be addressed as *Hochwohlgeboren*.[117] Another irritant for the nobility was the use by commoners of the term *Fräulein*, a form of address previously reserved for the daughters of nobles.[118] Another common complaint involved the use of coats-of-arms, to which they had no right, by commoners' purchasing noble estates; one angry nobleman reported a commoner on an estate near Königsberg decorating his "coaches, buildings, and tableware" with such symbols of nobility.[119]

---

[115] Cited in Gräff et al., *Ergänzungen und Erläuterungen* 6: 147.
[116] Schön, *Aus den Papieren* 3: 56, 4: 426.
[117] Gräff et al., *Ergänzungen und Erläuterungen* 5: 27.
[118] For noble complaints on forms of address see also Karl Adam, "Stände und Berufe in Preussen gegenüber der nationalen Erhebung des Jahres 1848," *Preussischer Jahrbücher* 89 (1897): 288–89.
[119] Schön, *Aus den Papieren* 4: 426.

THE POLITICS OF RESTORATION

These incidents are perhaps not as insignificant as they may appear. They indicate, on the one hand, how the concept of Stand was being emptied of its cultural content, how the nobility was losing a monopoly of the symbols through which its hegemony had been expressed and found particular meaning. The noble Stand was quite literally being "demeaned," that is, deprived of its meaning. One worried noblemen wrote the following in 1826: "The time that has elapsed since 1807 is still too short for us to have already noble shoemakers, cabinetmakers, and other craftsmen. We have only to wait. It can also come to pass that we will have noble farm hands [Knechte] and noble servant girls [Mägden], when not only will all previous distinctions between the nobility and the other Stände disappear, but the nobility itself will also cease to exist."[120] On the other hand, these incidents also reveal the pervasive quality of ständisch culture, for upwardly mobile commoners sought to appropriate the symbols traditionally associated with domination. This was a significant aspect of the "feudalization" of the bourgeois in Prussia, forming the basis for a landed aristocracy of both noble and non-noble origins.

The discussion over the meaning of *Stand* that emerged in Vormärz took place, therefore, at a time when the symbols of ständisch culture were being devalued on the one side and reaffirmed, though with different content, on the other. The natural response of some nobles was to build what bourgeois liberals charged was a "castelike spirit" within the nobility. The nobles in the Rhineland, for example, formed an exclusive party within the First Estate of the provincial diet, calling themselves with the purposefully redundant title the "nobly born noble Estate of the Rhineland" (*Rheinische ritterbürtigen Ritterschaft*).[121] In Westphalia the nobility formed a "club," which functioned as "a kind of parliament adjacent to the provincial diet." In 1826, elaborate plans for a "noble chain" (*Adels Kette*) circulated in East Prussia.[122] Built on the premise that monarchy and nobility are tied together by the principle of birth, the proposal declared: "The nobleman is of value. He is of high value, for through his being and the heredity of his Stand, the people's belief is strengthened and solidified that no one may possess the throne except he who is born to it." The purposes of the organization were to guard jealously the use of noble symbols, especially coats-of-arms, against their abuse by commoners; provide private sup-

[120] Ibid.
[121] Koselleck, *Preussen zwischen Reform und Revolution*, 374ff.
[122] For Westphalia, see Heinz Reif, *Westfälischer Adel, 1770–1860*, Kritische Studien zur Geschichtswissenschaft, 35 (Göttingen, 1979), 398–431. The comment is Reif's, page 429. For the East Prussian Adels Kette, see Schön, *Aus den Papieren* 4: 420–67.

CHAPTER 6

port for the training of younger sons of the nobility so they would not be forced into "common" occupations; work to locate noble buyers of estates that had to be sold to prevent them from falling into the hands of commoners; and maintain genealogical records for proof of noble ancestry.

Conservative nobles in the government joined in the effort to restore the "inner truth" of the nobility by setting it apart from the other Stände. Throughout the early 1820s, they circulated memoranda among themselves offering prescriptions for the preservation of the nobility of birth. Some of these suggestions also included building exclusive clubs and associations for the nobility alone. General von Müffling believed that only nobles should be "eligible for presentation at court" (*Hoffähig*). He also called for the creation of "courts of honor" for the nobility, similar to the military courts of honor, which would examine charges of violations by nobles of the unwritten code of noble honor; these courts would be fully empowered to deprive a nobleman of his title, and "such judgments would be sanctioned by the state without an explanation of the grounds." Müffling also wanted to tighten the prohibitions against marriages between nobles and non-nobles. To prevent young nobles from being contaminated by bourgeois attitudes, he wanted to restrict the early education of noble children to exclusive schools for nobles.[123] Gustav von Rochow developed more fully the idea of a special education for nobles. Private tutors, he argued, were too costly and beyond the means of many nobles; to prevent noble children from submitting to an education intended for commoners, he proposed the endowment of schools for young nobles designed to educate them for careers proper to the nobility: estate ownership, civil service, and the military.[124]

Rochow also strongly opposed permitting commoners who owned noble estates to exercise all the privileges accorded to nobles. He wanted to deny non-noble estate owners membership in the First Estate of the county and provincial assemblies; if membership was granted, however, he called for the king to "declare openly and publicly that the nobility shall continue to exist and that it will be newly constituted." Distinctions had to be drawn, he believed, between noble and non-noble and an order of knights should be established that would devote "all its efforts to the elevation of its Stand."[125]

All commentaries on the preservation of the nobility agreed that

---

[123] DZA II, Rep. 92, v. Müffling, no. 29, Bl. 7–10.
[124] DZA II, Rep. 92, v. Rochow, A III, no. 10, Bl. 11–30.
[125] DZA II, Rep. 92, v. Rochow, A III, no. 10, Bl. 1–10.

ownership of landed estates was essential to its survival. Therefore, noble estates should be entailed, all claims against the inheritance by children other than the eldest son should be restricted, and the estates should not be encumbered with any significant debt. Prince Carl von Mecklenburg blamed the plight of the nobility on the inheritance system. In a long memorandum, written shortly after he became president of the State Council, Mecklenburg wrote, "The division of the inheritance necessarily led to alienation, which made land into a mobile commodity, thereby extinguishing all historical memories and the related religious desire to preserve and maintain, and put in their place the spirit of speculation and of profit or loss."[126] Both Rochow and Mecklenburg urged the state to assist noble families in setting up endowments, separate from the estate itself, that would provide an income for the sons and daughters excluded from the inheritance and enable them to have lives appropriate to their Stand.

All of the commentaries were marked with pessimism about the chances of restoring and preserving the old nobility. Typically, the old Marwitz was the most pessimistic of all. He wrote the following to his brother-in-law, Rochow:

> The nobility is not an aggregate of individual noble persons, or of "Herrn von," or of rich landowners, but is the totality of those landowners who have a special relationship to the state, who exercise special rights and bear special duties.
>
> Now, I ask, where is this totality? Where is this relationship to the state? Where are these rights and obligations? I see nothing other than a confused phantasy of empty shadows. Instead of the totality, I see isolation. Instead of an ordered relationship, I see a motley of noble and non-noble landowners and of real and artificial noble persons without land. . . . Instead of rights, I see partially well-founded and partially unfounded and constantly contested claims; instead of duties, only the striving for the greatest possible profit for each individual.[127]

Rochow, too, believed that "the nobility in the Prussian state is to be considered as politically annihilated."[128] Mecklenburg bluntly commented that he believed "the smaller portion of the old nobility that still exists can be preserved." Mecklenburg, however, was one of the first willing to sacrifice the older nobility in order to build a new aristocracy. He agreed that all noble estates should be entailed and re-

---

[126] DZA II, Rep. 92, v. Rochow, A III, no. 20, Bl. 3.

[127] DZA II, Rep. 92, v. Rochow, A III, no. 9, Bl. 45–47. Marwitz to Rochow, 20 March 1821.

[128] DZA II, Rep. 92, v. Rochow, A III, no. 10, Bl. 5.

CHAPTER 6

main free of debt, that noblemen who did not pursue careers suitable to their Stand should forfeit their titles, and that endowments should be established to prevent inheritance claims from draining the wealth of the land-owning nobility. But he went further than the others were willing to go. He insisted that all persons granted a hereditary title of nobility own an entailed estate; otherwise the title was for the individual only and ceased with his death. More important, he believed that every non-noble who acquired a noble estate should be granted privileges identical to those of a noble. After ten years of estate ownership, the non-noble estate owner would be evaluated by the nobility of the province and, if found worthy, be granted a title upon the entailment of his estate.[129] In short, if the nobility's monopoly of noble estates could not be maintained, those who acquired the estates would be ennobled. If the old Stand could not be sustained, a new noble Stand would be created. This was a conscious effort to build a new aristocracy of landowners; it was an idea that would be taken up again by Frederick William IV after 1840.

The issue of noble honor arose repeatedly during these discussions. As already noted, the notion of honor became the central symbol for the nobility through all of its history. By suggesting that the nobility would sacrifice all, save honor, the nobility was elevated above self-interest and thereby justified its privileges and its paternalistic domination. The notion of honor was closely associated with the ownership of land and avoidance of careers motivated chiefly by profit and self-interest. Mecklenburg believed that the nobility "must be based on the one hand on honor and glory, and on the other hand on land ownership; accordingly, the noble spirit will be retained only if those careers and those occupations are open to it that are based on honor and glory, and, conversely, those are denied and closed to it which are based merely on profit and acquisition."[130] Rochow wrote similarly: the nobleman "is driven by his knightly spirit, without hope of gain; he does everything solely for honor."[131] The survival of the state required a nobility committed solely to the preservation of honor, which was inconsistent with the quest for profit or personal gain replacing honor. Therefore, Rochow recommended virtually the reversal of the thrust of the reform legislation—the nobility should be excluded from commerce and the trades, and commoners should not be allowed to serve as officers in a peacetime army. "The title of noble should never be

[129] DZA II, Rep. 92, v. Rochow, A III, no. 20, Bl. 1–4.
[130] Ibid., Bl. 1–2.
[131] DZA II, Rep. 92, v. Rochow A III, no. 10, Bl. 2.

granted because of wealth or civil service; the sword, and only the sword, ennobles."

The symbolic importance of honor to the nobility may be seen in the changes in the government policy toward duels of honor fought by members of the officer corps during Vormärz. The duel had always been viewed by the nobility as an essential means of defending personal honor. Although prohibited by a royal order as early as 1652, private duels were not halted.[132] Duels of honor were frequently tolerated within the army and, even when one party was killed, the winner was not severely punished. In the conflict between the public law of the state and the private code of the nobility, the nobility adhered to the latter; the punishment for dueling was less severe than the punishment of dishonor for refusing to duel. Prince Carl von Mecklenburg summed up the conflict accurately: "The law of the land forbids the duel. . . . The law of honor commands the duel."[133]

The conflict between these two commandments became a substantial problem after the military reforms admitted a large number of commoners to the officer corps after 1813. The nobility opposed the loss of its monopoly of the officer corps; resentment grew as the ratio of noble to commoner in the officer corps became increasingly less favorable to the nobility. The tensions led to frequent duels.[134] The government was eager to repress such conflict and to build an esprit de corps within the army transcending differences of birth. Accordingly, Frederick William III countermanded the recommendation of dismissal reached by a court of honor against a young lieutenant who had refused to fight a duel although insulted and physically abused. The commanding general of Königsberg, Carl Heinrich von Borstell, in whose command the incident had taken place, supported the king's decision. But he was also critical of the lack of clarity in government policy toward dueling. "It is not to be denied that dueling has actually been encouraged by the present uncertainty of the law and by the widespread conviction that the supreme authorities in the state connive to countenance the duel when it takes place among officers, despite the advance of civilization." Borstell therefore recommended the creation of "honor commissions" for each division of the army whose

---

[132] Karl Demeter, *Das Deutsche Offizierkorps in Gesellschaft und Staat, 1650–1945* (Frankfurt a.M., 1962), 114. See also A. von Boguslawski, *Der Ehrbegriff des Offizierstandes* (Berlin, 1897).

[133] DZA II, Rep. 92, v. Müffling, B, no. 11, Bl. 55. See the entire memorandum on dueling, Bl. 55–58.

[134] Demeter, *Offizierkorps*, 121; see also *Handbuch der Militärgeschichte 1648–1939*, part 4, *Militärgeschichte im 19. Jahrhundert*, vol. 2 (Munich, 1979), 43.

CHAPTER 6

purpose would be to settle disputes before they reached the dueling field.[135]

Frederick William III responded to this recommendation by issuing two cabinet orders in 1821 that broadened the authority and sanctions of the military courts of honor.[136] These courts, established in 1808 in order to rid the army of officers negligent in their duties or leading unsuitable lives, now acquired authority to investigate matters of duels. In 1828 and 1829, the king, observing that the number of duels had increased instead of diminished, instructed these courts to deal more decisively with officers involved in duels. He stated unequivocally his own abhorrence of the practice: "An officer corps that bans duels through the suitable handling of such matters of honor will acquire a claim to my good will and demonstrate that a true spirit of honor lives in it."[137]

These efforts to curb dueling had no effect. The percentage of noble officers increased again during the 1820s and 1830s, and the noble concept of honor penetrated the army more fully. A commission established in 1837 to draft new instructions for courts of honor found that the practice of dueling continued with "remarkable vitality." It concluded that the feeling of honor was something that naturally and necessarily did not submit to external judgment or control. A revised ordinance, based on these conclusions, was rejected by the king in 1839.[138]

As in so much else, Frederick William IV reversed the course taken by his father on matters of military discipline, as they related to the honor courts and dueling. In this he was assisted by the former liberal Hermann von Boyen, whom he recalled as minister of war. Boyen did not object to the duel as a means of satisfying honor; indeed, he had himself fought a duel with Wilhelm von Humboldt and believed the duel could be ethically justified. The fact that the state had once severely punished persons violating the prohibition against dueling but subsequently meted out increasingly milder punishments was taken as "a clear proof that the struggle of public opinion against the law on this point has had some success."[139] Duels were not only unavoidable, but advantageous to the state in that army officers regarded their honor more highly than their lives. Boyen hoped to extend the con-

---

[135] The document is printed in Demeter, *Offizierkorps*, 260–66.

[136] *Handbuch zur deutschen Militärgeschichte*, 2: 48.

[137] The documents are printed in Demeter, *Offizierkorps*, 266–68.

[138] See Friedrich Meinecke, *Das Leben des Generalfeldmarschalls Hermann von Boyen* (Stuttgart, 1899), 2: 513–14.

[139] Ibid., 514.

cept of honor through the creation of additional honor courts, especially for the landed nobility as well as for noncommissioned officers and enlisted men. Although this wish was not fulfilled, he did alter the structure of the existing military courts, broadening their scope and redefining their responsibility in duels.

Two ordinances issued on July 20, 1843, broadened the competence of the military courts of honor until they intruded into virtually all aspects of an officer's life.[140] In addition, the punitive sanctions available to the courts were enlarged. They were also given jurisdiction over officers of the reserve, the *Landwehr*, who were predominantly non-noble; Friedrich Meinecke characterized this extension of the military courts as the military's "dropping its anchor also into the civilian life."[141] The ordinances created honor councils in each battalion, empowered to investigate charges of violations of the honor code by officers, to attempt to settle disputes that threatened to result in duels, or to bring such disputes before the divisional honor court. If no settlement were possible and the offended party was still determined to proceed to a duel, the honor council was to be present at the scene of the duel to attempt a final settlement or, failing that, to supervise the ensuing duel. In short, the ordinances virtually legalized dueling.

The ordinances of 1843 marked a victory for the nobility in its struggle to win recognition for the symbols of its Stand. Meinecke concluded of Boyen's ministry under Frederick William IV: "Thus his entire work served only to fortify the aristocratic-military spirit of the Stand."[142] If the officer corps could not be kept free of bourgeois contamination, it would instead be infused with a noble sense of honor. The effort of the government to develop a collective sense of honor, an esprit de corps in the army, did not fail; but neither did it succeed in displacing the older belief that honor ultimately was a private affair, one that could be satisfied only personally, on a dueling field. Honor remained a personal attribute of the nobleman. In this the nobility succeeded in allowing its private authority to triumph over public law.

The nobility was less successful in sustaining other symbols associated with domination. For example, it had traditionally veiled the mixture of public authority and private interest that characterized its rule of estate and village with the claim of being honorably above self-interest, dispassionately filling the role of a Mittelstand between the crown and the peasantry. This notion of the nobility as Mittelstand

[140] *Handbuch zur deutschen Militärgeschichte* 2: 49–54.
[141] Meinecke, *Boyen* 2: 517.
[142] Ibid., 516.

had figured prominently in both Marwitz's and Ancillon's defenses of the nobility. Since at least the late eighteenth century, however, the bureaucracy had also laid claim to the role of Mittelstand; that claim was partially recognized when the Allgemeines Landrecht had identified the bureaucracy as a separate Stand.[143] In an effort to deny that claim, the nobility successfully opposed granting to the bureaucracy or the intelligentsia any separate status or representation as a separate Stand in the provincial diets. But the veil of being above self-interest, always rather transparent, was torn away as the market society steadily clipped the remaining threads of the fabric of paternalism and as the regulation of the peasantry after 1816 often pitted lords and peasants against one another. The bureaucracy, educated in Humboldt's humanistic ideal, successfully claimed to be the Mittelstand in Vormärz, administering in a fair and disinterested fashion between the competing interests of society. The bureaucracy, of course, was hardly disinterested, especially after the late 1830s, when more noblemen obtained positions in the administration.[144]

These examples show that the nobility fought on many fronts in the period of the restoration. Some of its victories, such as the establishment of the provincial diets, proved to be relatively hollow; others, such as the retention of control over county government, were more significant. But the lines of those battles were clearly drawn; advance and retreat could be easily measured and new alliances struck to recover ground lost during the reforms. On other fronts, the lines were less clear, the opponents only faintly discernible. Obviously the concept of Stand was important to the nobility as a means of differentiating society and as a primary category for shaping popular social perceptions. But it was more difficult for the nobility to recover ground lost as the concept of Stand was emptied of its meaning or permutated by events over which it had little control. The attempt to reimpose meaning into the concept of Stand called for the further development of a conservative ideology.

[143] The development of the *Beamtenstand* after the *Allgemeines Landrecht* is one of the central themes of Koselleck, *Preussen zwischen Reform und Revolution*. On the later development of the bureaucracy, see John R. Gillis, *The Prussian Bureaucracy in Crisis, 1840–1860* (Stanford, 1971).

[144] Gillis, *Prussian Bureaucracy*, 37–38; Koselleck, *Preussen zwischen Reform und Revolution*, 433–34. A most interesting article on the development of the bureaucracy as an elite educated in the system designed by Humboldt is by Ulrich K. Preuss, "Bildung und Bürokratie: Sozialhistorische Bedingungen in der ersten Hälfte des 19. Jahrhunderts,"*Der Staat: Zeitschrift für Staatslehre, Oeffentliches Recht, und Verfassungsgeschichte* 14, Heft 3 (1975): 371–96.

7

THE IDEOLOGY OF RESTORATION

The conservative ideology that emerged in Prussia prior to 1815 had developed largely in response to the reforms of Stein and Hardenberg. As shown, however, it also reflected the "crisis of hegemony" that had afflicted the landowning nobility in Prussia since the late eighteenth century.[1] New crops and methods of tillage, rising prices for grain and land, the expansion of credit and subsequent speculation, the deeper penetration of the rules and values of the market into rural society, all of these developments had conspired to loosen the bonds of paternalism long used to justify the nobility's domination of the peasantry. After 1807, reformers threatened to sever those bonds completely. Conservatism thus emerged as a defensive reflex. Its leading early spokesmen, Marwitz and Müller, attacked both the reforms and the emergent social system of developing capitalism. They objected to the centralizing and universalizing tendencies inherent in the growth of state power and the extension of public law; they called for the preservation of the local Stände and the "private" jurisdiction of local estate owners as the basis for a paternalist social ethic. Nevertheless, their writings exhibited a profound pessimism. Their criticisms of the present were clear and specific, their prescriptions for the future vague and uncertain.

The conservative ideology that emerged in Prussia after 1815 was different. Although the "crisis of hegemony" had certainly not been resolved, its intensity was felt less acutely after Napoleon's defeat and the enervation of the reform impulse in Prussia. By the 1820s, conservatives had recaptured the important posts in the government; they had succeeded in bending the agricultural reforms to the advantage of the nobility, they had blocked the promulgation of a constitution, and they had initiated legislation that reasserted the ascendancy of noble estate owners in provincial and county affairs. The mood was no longer one of pessimism; if it had not turned to optimism (conservatives are rarely optimists), the mood had at least become one of deter-

[1] See chapter 5.

mination. Conservative ideologues were no longer an isolated minority; their posture was no longer largely defensive, but offensive. They were determined to articulate a conservative ideology that would lead in the "restoration" of the traditional structure of authority in society. For the conservative nobility of Prussia, this found its most persuasive formulation in the theory of the patrimonial state developed by the Swiss thinker Carl Ludwig von Haller.

Haller's Theory of the Patrimonial State

Carl Ludwig von Haller (1768–1854) was born into a family that had belonged to the ruling patriciate of the Swiss city-state Bern for several centuries.[2] Despite extended periods in exile, during which he entered the service of foreign governments, Haller remained loyal and devoted to his native Bern. In the introduction to the first volume of his major work, he acknowledged the influence of Bern on his thought. "I not only loved my father city," he wrote, "but I was, through a wide variety of relationships, deeply rooted in it."[3] The prosperous, small city-state, ruled by a paternalistic patriciate, provided Haller with a model for the patrimonial state he developed in his political theory. His father had risen to a high post in Bern; the young Haller entered civil service at age nineteen. When he began his career, he was a staunch adherent of the political ideas of the Enlightenment; his first publication, written as secretary to Bern's economic commission, was a vigorous defense of free trade. During several trips to Paris in the revolutionary 1790s, Haller developed reservations about the course taken by the French Revolution, but he remained committed to liberal political ideas. In February 1798, after a revolution overthrew the ruling aristocracy of Bern, the provisional government asked Haller, despite his own aristocratic connections, to draft a constitution for the

---

[2] Biographical treatments of Haller are K. Guggisberg, *Carl Ludwig von Haller: Die Schweiz im deutschen Geistesleben*, vol. 87/88 (Frauenfeld, 1938), and Ewald Reinhard, *Karl Ludwig von Haller: Ein Lebensbild aus der Zeit der Restauration*, Görres Gesellschaft, 2 (Cologne, 1915). For discussions of Haller's political thought, see H. von Sonntag, *Die Staatsauffassung C. L. Von Hallers, ihre metaphysische Grundlage und ihre politische Formung* (Jena, 1929), and Heinz Weilenmann, *Untersuchungen zur Staatstheorie Carl Ludwig von Hallers* (phil. diss., Bern, 1955). See also Sigmund Neumann, *Die Stufen des preussischen Konservatismus: Ein Beitrag zum Staats- und Gesellschaftsbild Deutschland im 19. Jahrhundert* (Berlin, 1930), 8off.; Heinrich O. Meisner, *Die Lehre vom monarchischen Prinzip im Zeitalter des Restauration und des Deutschen Bundes*, Untersuchungen zur Deutschen Staats- und Rechtsgeschichte, 122 (Breslau, 1913), 133ff.; Friedrich Meinecke, *Weltbürgertum und Nationalstaat*, 7th ed. (Munich, 1972), 192ff.

[3] Carl Ludwig von Haller, *Restauration der Staatswissenschaft* (Winterthur, 1816), 1: xxxi.

new republic. Haller's draft constitution, though never enacted, was thoroughly liberal. It proposed a state based on the universal rights of humankind; it called for political freedom, popular sovereignty, equality before the law, and freedom of religion, thought, and the press. Haller joined the new government briefly early in 1798, but he quickly developed disagreements with it and resigned his post. In April of that year, he began publishing a journal, the *Helvetische Annalen*, but his open criticism of the government led to the suspension of the journal seven months later. Haller's rapid disillusionment with the revolutionary government in Bern produced a complete reversal of his political position; he became a conservative critic of all the liberal assumptions of the Enlightenment.

In 1799, Haller left Bern and went into exile in Austria, where he obtained a position in the Ministry of War. After the aristocratic faction regained control of Bern four years later and founded an academy that would later become a university, Haller was offered the chair in political theory and Swiss history. By the time of his return to Bern in 1806, he had already developed the main lines of his conservative political thought. In 1808, he published the *Handbuch der Allgemeinen Staatenkund* (Handbook of the general study of the state), which contained an outline of his later writings.[4] The first volume of his major work, *Restauration der Staatswissenschaft* (Restoration of the science of the state) appeared in 1816. Haller gave up his professorship in that year in order to devote himself to the completion of the *Restauration*; three more volumes were published by 1820 and the last two volumes in 1834. His conversion to Catholicism in 1820 resulted in his being forced to relinquish all his public offices in Protestant Bern, so again he left in exile, emigrating to Paris in 1822. There, he was eventually given a post in the Foreign Ministry, which he held until the July Revolution of 1830. He then returned to Switzerland, taking up residence in the small Catholic town of Solothurn, in the valley of the Jura north of Bern. Haller entered the town council of Solothurn in 1834 and remained involved in its politics until 1840, when a liberal government came to power. During the final two decades of his life, he remained in close touch with conservative groups throughout Germany, but most especially with the group of Prussian conservatives that clustered around the weekly newspaper *Das Berliner Politische Wochenblatt*.[5]

Haller began his *Restauration* with a lengthy critical review of all the theories that had dominated European political thought since the be-

---

[4] Carl Ludwig von Haller, *Handbuch der Allgemeinen Staatenkund* (1808).
[5] Minecke, *Weltbürgertum und Nationalstaat*, 203ff.

ginning of the seventeenth century. He concluded that all these theories relied on four essential principles: (1) human beings were born into a state of nature in which all enjoyed the natural rights of freedom and equality; (2) in this natural state, their natural rights were not completely secure; (3) to secure these rights, they formed social contracts according to which they delegated their power to one or to several persons; and (4) through this social contract creating a state, the freedom of the individual was more secure than it had been in nature.[6] These theories had developed, Haller believed, because of the strong influence of Roman law on recent European thought. He also blamed the Protestant Reformation, which had unleashed a "great hatred" against hierarchical authority and, in some cases, had introduced the principle of a "spiritual democracy" in which the religious community elected its own spiritual leaders. And finally, he believed the theory of the social contract emerged in England during the conflict between the king and Parliament in the seventeenth century.[7]

The most pernicious aspect of social contract theory, according to Haller, was the assertion that all authority originates from below, from the people, and is delegated to those above who rule. This teaching had spread throughout Europe "like an epidemic" in the eighteenth century, with detrimental effects everywhere.[8] In Prussia, for example, this doctrine caused Frederick II to refer to himself as "the first servant of the state." Frederick's General Law Code, the *Allgemeines Landrecht*, reflected the language of the contract theory. It "usurped" the real authority of the king by referring to him as the "chief of state" (*Oberhaupt des Staates*), never a king; his officials were called "servants of the state," and his own private demesne lands were declared to be the property of the state (1: 181ff.). The language of such law codes depersonalized the ruling prince, robbing him of his "moral power." Haller despised the "chancellery style" of such law codes that disguised the personal and private power of the ruler. "Instead of the old and hearty, paternal (hausväterlich) or lordly language, which was animated with a feeling for his own and others' rights, during the last three decades of the eighteenth century, one hears, in the princely laws and publications, increasingly of civil unions, of delegated power of the people, of legal and executive authority, of state servants or public servants, of state finances, and so on. These expressions and forms of speech, which proceed from the school of new wisdom, nec-

---

[6] Haller, *Restauration* 1: 283.

[7] Ibid. 1: 84ff.

[8] On the impact of contract theory on the practices of the states according to Haller, see ibid. 1: 173ff. Subsequent references in the text are from this edition.

essarily abet the general confusion of the concepts and thereby gradually exterminate the memory of the old and true relationships" (1: 214–15). Ultimately, these teachings produced an arrogance among "servants of the state" that led to absolutism and to the French Revolution, which failed because the principles it expressed were "false, impossible, unreasonable, and contrary to nature" (1: 276).

The principles of the social contract were false, Haller maintained, because they were not drawn from experience and history but were based solely on an initial idea that is a "juridical fiction" (1: 285). The state of nature posited by contract theorists never existed; human beings never lived in a state of freedom and equality. They did not originally form communities because of fear or a quest for security, but because of mutual needs and the instinct to form families. The family was the initial social experience and from it all forms of community developed. Because of natural human inequality—the weakness of some (women and children) who depend on the stronger for protection—the family did not originate in natural freedom and equality. Even the contract theorists implicitly recognized this, Haller observed, for they excluded women and children from participation in the social compact on the grounds that they were in a dependent status. If the social contract involved only those who are truly independent, that is, the heads of households (Hausväter) who owned property, then the theory already comprised its principle of freedom and equality by recognizing that some were independent, others dependent (1: 300–301). Moreover, Haller added, contract theory was based on a further absurdity. It assumed that the social compact would delegate power to persons who are strongest and wisest, otherwise it would not succeed in providing the security of rights that was its raison d'être. From the outset, therefore, contract theory recognized the inequality of strength and wisdom among people (1: 308). Finally, Haller pointed to the logical contradiction involved in the contract theorist's notion that, once a social contract had been formed, one ceased to live in a state of nature. Nature, Haller declared, was the creation of God; it was as unchanging as God, so that one could not merely set nature aside (1: 327ff.).

In fact, Haller declared, "the state of nature has never ceased to exist. This natural condition of men, this divine order, which still exists as it did originally, is not the total absence of society, a general independence, freedom, and equality; but it comprises in its necessary arrangements some nonsocial and a wide variety of social relationships, and in each of the latter, there is superordination and subordination, freedom and servitude, domination and dependence" (1: 327).

When one speaks of the "origin of social relationships, one implies that there was a moment in which such relationships did not exist," Haller commented. They have always existed just as they do now, he insisted. "Society is a phenomenon of the entire nature. ... Every newborn child already exists in a social relationship with his parents" (1: 331–32).

Authority, thus, was not a human creation; it did not originate in the social contract and was not delegated by any act of popular will. Authority was rooted in nature; it was an expression of the will of God. "None of those who rule has received his power from those beneath him, but he possesses it from nature itself, that is, by the grace of God; he is either born to it or he acquires it" (1: 338–39). All authority originated in the human condition of inequality. "Thus the father rules over his wife and children, the experience of age over youth, the lord over his servants, the leader over his followers, the teacher over his pupils, the master over his apprentices. ... No one suggests that in these simple relationships there is something unjust or contrary to reason" (1: 343). All social relations embodied strength and dependency: "Where strength and need meet, a relationship develops in which the former acquires domination and the latter dependence. It is therefore the eternal law of God that the more powerful dominates, must dominate, and will always dominate" (1: 361).

Despotism developed, according to Haller, when this natural order is reversed, when those who are in positions of power are weakened and become dependent on those whom they ruled. "They seek to maintain themselves while the power which they lack lies with those beneath them" (1: 370). Genuinely strong rulers did not become despots; "cruelty is always only the error of the weak, who cannot count on personal respect and must turn to the awful use of force in order to win obedience to commands" (1: 371). Historically, Haller concluded, the tendency toward despotism, inherent in the absolutist monarchies of Europe in the eighteenth century, developed with the princes' need for larger tax revenues. This requirement weakened the princes and forced them to become more dependent on their diets and parliaments, which were reluctant to grant new taxes. The result was the absolutist inclination to rule without reference to the diets (1: 371n).

Although all legitimate authority originated in the natural domination of the weak by the strong, Haller believed that a natural check against the despotic abuse of such power was contained in the "law of duty" (*Pflichtgesetz*), the quintessence of the paternalist ideology (1: 383). With authority came responsibility; a natural law bound every relationship of power—the commandment of God, written on every person's conscience to "do good and avoid evil." "Do unto others as you would have done unto you."⁹ This law of duty, Haller asserted, was really the only obstacle to the misuse of power. It was a surer safeguard than any written constitution or expression of the general will. Moreover, because a ruler who commanded the respect of his subjects was stronger than one who did not, failure to observe this law of duty was actually a manifestation of weakness.

Nevertheless, in those instances in which the prince abused his power over his subjects, Haller ultimately recognized the right of resistance.¹⁰ The subject should first appeal to his superior's sense of duty. If that were insufficient, he was justified in "resistance, permissible self-help—that is, the use of his own understanding and strength, which God has given him for his own protection" (1: 401). This is simply the natural law of self-defense. A corollary was the subject's right to appeal to others for assistance. Like all manifestations of power, however, the right of resistance was limited by the law of duty: in resisting a superior, the subject was not permitted to violate the fundamental rights of his superior. Although Haller believed that armed resistance to an unjust prince was rarely justified and almost never successful, he did not exclude it altogether (2: 414–46). If all appeals failed and the subject was not strong enough to protect himself from his superior, he was justified in fleeing and seeking protection elsewhere (1: 416).

Society, for Haller, thus comprised a nearly infinite number of private relationships of superordination and subordination. These extended from the lowest level of the social hierarchy to the highest. At each level, people exercised domination over those below them and dependency on those above them; only at the top, where an independent prince ruled without any obligation to anyone above him, except God (or in a republic, where a large number of men are thus free of obligations to any superior), were sovereignty and freedom total. Haller explained: "Power and superiority, domination and servitude, freedom and dependence are relative concepts, which are not to be seen as things in themselves, but only in a relationship to another" (1: 433–34). In Haller's system, therefore, there were many "gradations" of independence and dependence; yet each was to some extent free, for each reigns supreme and sovereign in some sphere, however small, into which no superior may rightfully intrude. "Sovereignty does not

⁹ Haller, *Handbuch*, 37.
¹⁰ Haller, *Restauration* 1: 398ff.

exist in the size of the realm . . . but only in the independence" (1: 438–39). But all aspects of sovereignty were encompassed in each realm of independence, even at the level of the family. "Every family forms a small monarchy. . . . Every individual man is king and monarch in the circle of his realm, only smaller and less powerful, more or less subordinated, by nature or contract, to a higher authority" (2: 2). "In every family, considered from the standpont of its independence, there is to be found a likeness of a monarchical state. The Hausvater or Hausherr is in his own home independent . . . and even the entire household is not set above him" (2: 22). As a small sovereign, the Hausvater had legislative authority, the right to formulate the rules; judiciary power, the right to judge infractions of the rules and to punish them, as well as to adjudicate disputes between subjects under his authority; and the right to the income from his possessions and the free disposition of his property. Even the adherents of social-contract theory, Haller argued, did not wish to challenge the essentially monarchical authority of the Hausvater (2: 27).

Two important conclusions can be derived from this. First, the state was not a public institution at all. It existed solely in the multitude of private contracts for domination and service; it had no purpose in itself apart from the wide variety of purposes contained in the private relationships of which it was composed. A state, Haller declared, possessed no general will or purpose; "it is, in its essential character, a private existence, a large household" (*magna familia*).[11] Second, because the state was not a public institution, the prince was "nothing other than the wealthier, the more powerful person who is subordinate to no one."[12] What political theorists called the state was merely the dependent private domain of the independent ruler. In such a hierarchy of dependence and independence, Haller believed, monarchy was the "first, most natural, most numerous, and most durable form of the state."[13] It grew naturally from the family.

Haller delineated three forms of monarchy: a patrimonial monarchy, based on the control of land; a military monarchy, based on a monopoly of military power; and a spiritual monarchy, based on intellectual or religious control. The most important and durable of these was the patrimonial monarchy, so that, to ensure survival, each of the other two forms had an inclination to transform themselves into a state based on land.[14]

[11] Haller, *Handbuch*, 49.
[12] Haller, *Restauration* 2: 1.
[13] Haller, *Handbuch*, 51.
[14] Ibid., 129ff.

Haller's description of the patrimonial state followed from the premise that the state was nothing more than the private domain of the prince. For example, the right of the prince to wage war was an extension of his natural right of self-defense. But war was merely the private affair of the prince; it was not a matter of public concern. There was no such thing as a "peoples' war" (*Volkskrieg*), for "the people [*Volk*] of a prince is a scattered mass of men, an aggregate of dependent or voluntary serving people with an endless variety of obligations; they have nothing in common other than their common overlord; they do not form a whole, they do not constitute a community, and therefore they cannot *in corpore* be injured."[15] As a result, the subjects of a prince did not have an unlimited obligation to serve him in time of war. Their military obligation could be based on three grounds: the moral obligation they might feel for a prince who had defended their rights in the past, their evaluation of their own private interest in the outcome of the war, and the contractual obligations they might owe the lord as his vassals. Except for those who were contractually bound, however, there was no legitimate compulsory military service, for "the body of the subject is not the property of the prince." Even in a republic, only those "independent members of the sovereign corporation" were obligated to serve; the subjects were not. Military conscription, Haller concluded, was a "revolutionary principle of the state" introduced by the "pseudophilosophers of the eighteenth century." Not only did the prince not have the right to conscript his subjects in wartime, but he also did not have the right to seize their property; he should conduct war "at his own cost" (2: 80–90).

Similarly, in Haller's private patrimonial state, the power to legislate resided with the prince alone, for law was merely "a binding expression of the will" of the prince (2: 168). It was absurd, Haller declared, to speak of the separation of the legislative, executive, and judicial powers, as had Montesquieu, for the will and sovereignty of a prince were indivisible. This emphasis on the separation of powers, he judged, had been the "first step toward a revolutionary system" (2: 177). Because legislative power was sovereign, it could not be limited by a constitution or shared with a parliament without rendering the prince dependent and thus no longer sovereign and free. Nevertheless, princely legislative power was not capricious or arbitrary; it was bound to conform to the laws of nature and the commandments of God. It might not intrude on those sovereign rights of persons subservient to the prince. To assume, moreover, that all laws issued by a

---

[15] Haller, *Restauration* 2: 70. Subsequent references in the text are from this edition.

prince had to be universal and apply to all subjects equally was incorrect. The prince had the right to extend his grace to individuals at will; he had the power to suspend or to grant dispensations to the laws, just as a Hausvater might differentiate among his children and subjects in applying the rules of his household. Moreover, because of the wide variety of gradations of independence and dependence, such inequality before the laws of the prince was natural and essential (2: 207ff.).

Judicial authority was also an expression of sovereign power, a manifestation of "paternal [*väterlich*] Herrschaft." In this context, Haller offered an explicit defense of patrimonial courts. They were essential to the preservation of the independence of those lords who were above the people but below the princes. Without patrimonial courts, the gradations of independence would disappear and only an undifferentiated mass would stand below the prince. To those who argued that patrimonial courts were partisan and an abuse of power, Haller replied that placing the courts completely under the control of the prince was no guarantee against the misuse of power or against partisanship. Again the paternal law of duty was for Haller the only safeguard against the abuse of power (2: 229–30).

In his treatment of the finances of the prince, Haller again stressed the private nature of the patrimonial state (2: 262–305). The royal demesne lands were private, not state, property. The prince derived his income primarily from these properties, as well as from whatever industries he possessed, and from tariffs and excise taxes. Normally, the prince did not have the right to confiscate the property of his subjects by means of taxation. In some instances, he had contractual claims on some of the property of his vassals that amounted to taxes. Any special need for additional revenue, as in war, required that the prince obtain the consent of those immediately dependent on him, who acted through the Landstände to approve new taxes (2: 323–27).

The Landstände were composed of those persons who exercised their sovereign power immediate to the prince. They did not constitute a "popular representation" (*Volks-Repräsentation*), for they represented only themselves. The Landstände, Haller argued,

were not and cannot be formed arbitrarily but are made through the natural relationships; they are called Stände because they enjoy a self-sufficient (*selbständige*) existence on their allodial lands or estates held in fief, and, except for the prince, they are dependent on no one. Naturally, therefore, in the period in which there were no cities, the Landstände comprised only the nobles and the priests, as immediate vassals or free landowners, for the remainder of the inhabitants were dependent on them and had no relationship with the prince. Peasants or rural people were not included because they were only servants or Knechte of their lords and possessed no free property.... In the eleventh and twelfth centuries, free cities developed which were granted privileges and favors by the king and were subordinated to no one but him.... Thus it developed that deputies of the towns, or the so-called *Bürgerstand*, were later admitted to the Landstände, and that thereby the Landstände in all lands were composed of the nobles, the priests and the towns, an order that is completely in accord with nature and justice. (2: 324–25)

Because the authority of the prince was private and not derived from the approval of his subjects, it, like his private property, could be alienated according to his will (2: 449). Territories changed hands in a number of ways: through purchase, exchange, gift, marriage, treaty, settlement, and even conquest. Whatever the means, the new possessor acquired all authority and obligations previously held by his predecessor. This right of alienation formed the legal basis for inheritance, for inheritance was merely the alienation of a property to an heir by means of a family testament. Princes also occasionally acquired territory through illegal means—confiscation, usurpation, secularization, and invasion. This represented a violation of power, an abuse of proper authority; nevertheless, Haller declared that the long, undisturbed possession of a territory, even that which originated in an illegal usurpation, was legitimized by time and occupation (2: 549).

Haller believed that all states experienced periods of development and decline. He traced at length the history of patrimonial kingdoms because he believed they were the most enduring form of the state. Being the private property of the prince, nevertheless, the patrimonial state rose and fell with his fortunes, with his ability to sustain his independence. The patrimonial prince could lose his sovereignty in a number of ways (2: 555–74). Some patrimonial states disappeared as a result of the divisions of an inheritance, the voluntary alienation of freely held land, or the dying out of the royal family. Others were lost as a result of foreign conflicts. Defeat often stripped the prince of his power through treaties that rendered him subservient to someone else. Still others declined because the prince undertook too many obligations or acted unjustly. In a lengthy section of his third volume, which reads like a primer for princes, Haller discussed the "*Makrobiotik* of patrimonial states"—the means for securing their survival (3: 8–172). He considered the establishment of a system of primogeniture to be essential. He also stressed the importance of "good economy," for which it was important that the royal demesne not be alienated or mortgaged, for it was essential to the independence of the prince. The alienation of royal estates, he declared, "is the most dangerous operation; it undercuts the principality at its roots, dissolving the most natural bond that binds the subjects to their lord, and also sacrificing the most solid . . . and most independent income" (3: 19). Too much debt or too much luxury also weakened the prince, for it forced him to press his subjects for taxes, producing internal discord.

The patrimonial prince should also take care in selecting his servants, choosing for higher positions men of property and outstanding reputations. He should do nothing that would in any way injure his "moral power," the respect and honor he commanded from his subjects. He should avoid treaties and alliances when possible, for they often deprived him of independent action.

Haller concluded his discussion of the patrimonial state by extolling the virtues of the paternalist social system it produced.

> Finally, in conclusion, we should repeat what we are reminded of so often and in so many circumstances: that the lordly paternal bond is the mildest and friendliest that can be imagined, that human freedom has not suffered the slightest damage from it, and that all that one calls Herrschaft or servitude consists only of voluntary private contracts, of mutual assistance, and of an exchange of mutual charity. Nature has founded the state through this bond and generally joined men together in a clear form of love. . . . Everything is free, humane, and reciprocal; an exchange of charity, a relationship of pure justice and love, completely similar to that of the private family. (3: 159–61)

Such statements are found throughout Haller's writings and offer the most complete expression of the ideology of paternalism. The very phrase "patrimonial state," to which Haller gave new meaning, evoked an image of paternalist social relations.[16] The family provided Haller with the original framework for society, and fatherhood offered the original form of authority. He felt no need to impose limitations on the authority of kings, princes, or noble landlords other than the "law of duty," which bound them to respect the rights of their subjects and to treat them with paternal charity.

The most noteworthy aspect of Haller's political system was his denial of the public nature of the state. As I have stressed throughout the preceding chapters, a primary tendency of the modern state and society was the separation of the public and private spheres of author-

---

[16] Georg von Below, *Der deutsche Staat des Mittelalters* (Leipzig, 1914), 6.

ity, with the expansion of the former and the limitation of the latter. It was against this tendency that conservative ideologues struggled. Adam Müller had sought to reintegrate the public and private realms by insisting on the retention of feudal agriculture and the rejection of a capitalist economy. Müller tried to bridge the growing gap between the public and private spheres by turning all essential social relationships, even the disposition of landed property, into public relations. Only the restoration of corporate and family life would restore the "grandeur" of the "idea" of the state as "the totality of human affairs, their combination into a living whole." Haller followed an opposite course. He hoped to reunite the public and private realms by denying completely the existence of the public and by insisting that all social relationships were essentially private. The state was merely the private property of the prince.

Haller's radical solution, which denied even the existence of public law, had important implications. First, it left Haller with an intensely individualistic approach to society. Müller had emphasized the corporate framework of life and denounced the emphasis on private property as having dissolved the sense of corporate existence. He insisted, for example, that landed estates were not private property, but family property, and could therefore not be alienated by the individual. He had located the idea of "freedom" within the corporate entities of family and Stand. Haller, by contrast, had no sense of social interest or corporate existence. In denying the existence of any single social contract and insisting, instead, on the existence of a multitude of individual private contracts of domination and subordination, he eliminated the basis for a corporate, ständisch society as envisaged by Müller. Nothing bound the subjects other than their subjection to a common prince. Freedom was experienced not within any corporate entity, but in the degree of independence one possessed. The individual had absolute freedom to dispose of private property however he chose.

A second implication of Haller's denial of public authority was that it required that all power be exercised as private power. No distinction was to be drawn between public and private morality. There was no "interest of state" that dictated behavior for the prince different from that for a private person; the prince was merely a private person. He was bound by the same moral constraints as the father; even his wars were private affairs that did not concern his subjects. Conservatives welcomed this principle as a guarantee against absolutism and as a restraint on the actions of the prince. A half-century later, for example, Ludwig von Gerlach, one of Haller's devoted disciples, complained bitterly about Bismarck's differentiation between the commands of private morality and those of the interest of the state.

Haller has usually been considered to have been the most reactionary of conservative ideologists. Friedrich Meinecke dismissed his political thought as based on "highly naive and emotional arguments" that represented an entirely false image of medieval feudalism.[17] Friedrich Julius Stahl, who succeeded Haller as the leading ideologist for the Prussian conservatives, referred to his thought as a "caricature of the Middle Ages."[18] Undoubtedly Haller distorted the nature of feudalism and idealized feudal society. But in important respects, he stood closer to liberal theorists than at first appears. His intense individualism, to the point of defining freedom as an individual attribute and not an attribute of the Stand, brought him nearer to the liberal definition of freedom than was true of most conservatives. His system was essentially rationalist. He argued from the premise of natural law—the natural domination of the strong over the weak—so that his reference to the divine origin of that law and the divine grace that imparted strength to some did not vitiate the essential rationalism of his approach. Despite his conversion to Catholicism, his system was not fundamentally Christian.

In other particulars as well, Haller reflected a less reactionary outlook than is usually assumed. He justified the system of inherited power, but not on the basis of any sacred right of nobility or kingship or on the basis of any assumption of ständisch superiority. Inheritance was an expression of the individual right any property owner had to alienate his property. Haller also offered a very "loose construction" of the principle of legitimacy, for he recognized the right of princes, who acquire lands by illegitimate means, to become legitimate rulers. He considered domination and servitude to be the elemental forces in social relations; the particular forms of domination did not concern him. He did not, for example, criticize as improper the wage-labor system of domination in capitalism, as Müller had done. Although his patrimonial state presumed that land constituted the major source of wealth, he did not explicitly exclude or attack other forms of wealth. He merely assumed that all forms of domination were subject to the same rules and limitations—the law of duty and paternal charity. And finally, he even justified resistance to unjust authority, in extreme cases to the point of armed conflict.

---

[17] Meinecke, *Weltbürgertum und Nationalstaat*, 194.
[18] Friedrich Julius Stahl, *Die Philosophie des Rechts*, 5th ed. (Tübingen, 1878; facsimile ed., 1963), 1: 560–68; quotation, 567.

All of these aspects of Haller's thought were important to the development of a conservative ideology for the Prussian nobility during the period of restoration. His recognition of the alienability of landed estates was important to the nobility which, during the 1820s, was forced to sell much of its land. He permitted a more relaxed definition of the noble Stand by stressing simply that its essential feature was the control and domination of its subjects; this opened the possibility for broader definitions of the Stände, such as that given to the provincial Landtage after 1823: membership in the noble Estate was dependent solely on the ownership of a noble estate. And Haller's outlook allowed conservatives to apply the essential elements of their ideology— the paternalist approach to social relations—to a wider context than merely the landlord-peasant connection, for it was implicit in all forms of domination. Although no one carried the conclusion this far, paternalism could also provide an ideology for the relationship between factory owner and worker.

Few of these features of Haller's thought, however, were immediately apparent. What attracted the Prussian conservative nobility to Haller was his belief in the indivisibility of sovereignty. This meant that the Herrschaft of the noble estate owner should continue to comprise its legislative, judicial, and executive unity: the noble rights of patrimonial justice and the police were fundamental elements of the independence and sovereignty of the nobility. They could not legitimately be altered by the monarch. Conservatives welcomed Haller's rejection of the notion that power emanated from below, as a result of the social contract; authority came from above, from God. They found in Haller's patrimonial state, composed of a multitude of individual and local forms of domination, an explicit defense of provincialism and a safeguard against monarchical centralism. Haller's definition of the Stände simply as those who exercised authority and were dependent only on the monarch was clear and logical; his claim that the Stände represented only themselves constituted a defense of the Virilstimme in the county assemblies. And finally, by demonstrating the relationship between royal absolutism, which in the eighteenth century expanded the public office of the monarch as the "servant of the people," on the one hand, and the development of revolutionary ideologies, on the other, Haller provided conservatives with a formal ideology that could be used against both absolutism and revolution.

Haller was by no means the only important conservative political theorist during the restoration in Germany.[19] Indeed, it is probable

[19] Hartwig Brandt, in *Landständige Repräsentation im deutschen Vormärz* (Neuwied and

CHAPTER 7

that some of his critics, such as the leaders of the historical school of law, Carl von Savigny and Karl F. Eichhorn, contributed more in the long run to the development of German conservative thought in the nineteenth century.[20] Nevertheless, Haller was of paramount importance for the articulation of a conservative ideology within the ranks of the Prussian nobility. His ideology, unlike Müller's, was not designed especially to win the allegiance of the Prussian nobles but corresponded closely to their interests and buttressed the paternalist ethic which they had long used to justify their dominance.

THE GERLACH CIRCLE AND *DAS BERLINER POLITISCHE WOCHENBLATT*

Shortly after the first volume of Haller's *Restauration* appeared, it became a central topic of discussion within a small group of young army officers, aspiring public officials, and literati that called itself the *Maikäferei* (May bugs), after the name of the restaurant owner, Mai, where the group held weekly meetings.[21] The Maikäferei began meeting in 1816. The group was organized by Clemens von Brentano and included the three Gerlach brothers (Wilhelm, Leopold, and Ludwig), Carl von Voss-Buch, Friedrich Karl von Bülow, Gustav von Below, Carl von Rappard, Count Cajus von Stolberg, Count Alvensleben-Erxleben, and Karl von Lancizolle. Others occasionally joined the group, but about twelve members were usually present. Originally, the Maikäferei discussed a wide variety of literary, cultural, and philosophical topics, but after 1817 the discussions focused increasingly on politics and religion. The political discussions were prompted by Haller's *Restauration*, which quickly won the approval of several members. Leo-

---

Berlin, 1968), 59, writes: "The Bern patrician Carl Ludwig v. Haller can scarcely be considered as the protagonist or the schoolmaster of German conservatism." See also Heinz Gollwitzer, *Die Standesherren*, 2d ed. (Göttingen, 1964), 211.

[20] For contemporary criticisms of Haller, see K. Guggisberg, *K. L. von Haller*, 100ff. Savigny considered Haller's theory to be a form of crass materialism. See Hans Joachim Schoeps, *Aus den Jahren Preussischer Not und Erneuerung: Tagebücher und Briefe der Gebrüder Gerlach und ihres Kreises, 1805–1820* (Berlin, 1963), 232.

[21] For a description of the Maikäferei, see Ernst Ludwig von Gerlach, *Aufzeichnungen aus seinem Leben und Wirken, 1795–1877* (Schwerin, 1903), 1: 94–95; Leonie von Keyserling, *Studien zu den Entwicklungsjahren der Brüder Gerlach*, Heidelberger Abhandlungen zur mittleren und neuern Geschichte, 36 (Heidelberg, 1913), 63–64; Hans Joachim Schoeps, *Das Andere Preussen*, 2d ed. (Honnef/Rhein, 1957), 15; Sigmund Neumann, *Die Stufen des preussischen Konservatismus*, 79; Friedrich Wiegand, "Der Verein der Maikäfer in Berlin," *Deutsche Rundschau* 160 (1914): 273–85; Robert M. Bigler, *The Politics of German Protestantism: The Rise of the Protestant Church Elite in Prussia, 1815–1848* (Berkeley and Los Angeles, 1972), 127–30.

pold von Gerlach suggested to his friends, for example, that they pledge themselves never to attend a social occasion without mentioning Haller's teaching at least once.[22] The religious discussions were prompted by the fact that several members of the group began attending the church services of pietist clergymen in Berlin.[23] A religious "awakening" began to spread across Germany after the wars, and several members of the Maikäferei underwent religious conversions. In 1816, Lancizolle and Adolf von Thadden, a close friend of several of the Maikäfers, traveled to Bavaria to observe a religious revival taking place there.[24] As the religious issue became predominant, the old Maikäferei gradually dissolved; by 1819, many of its original members had left Berlin.[25] Nevertheless, out of the Maikäferei there developed lifelong friendships and alliances among persons who exercised considerable influence in Prussia in the following decades.

The pietist movement that spread through Germany in the years after 1815 had much in common with the ideas of the restoration. The wars of liberation came to be seen by many as a great spiritual victory over the godless forces of rationalism and revolution.[26] As a result, the new pietists were not content to be merely "the quiet in the land," as their precursors in the seventeenth and eighteenth centuries were called; rather, they saw themselves engaged in a battle that often carried them into the arena of public politics. Theologically, however, they differed little from their predecessors. They believed that the religious practices of the state church had become sterile and perverted with rationalism; human reason was, as Luther maintained, an unre-

[22] Gerlach, *Aufzeichnungen* 1: 101.

[23] Schleiermacher had earlier been influential, but he was too rational and not sufficiently evangelical to suit many of the "born-again" pietists. Adolf von Thadden wrote Ludwig von Gerlach in 1818 that he was pleased that "you and your older brothers have already been free of Schleiermacher's heresy for some time." See Schoeps, *Aus den Jahren Preussischer Not*, 594. More popular with the young pietists were the sermons of J. G. Hermes in the Saint Getraud Church (popularly known as the *Spittelkirche*), and Johannes Jänicke, at the Bethlehem Church of the Moravian Brethren. Bigler, *Politics of German Protestantism*, 128.

[24] Eleonore Reuss, *Adolf von Thaden-Trieglaff* (Berlin, 1890), 15ff.; Friedrich Wilhelm Kantzenbach, "Ausstrahlung der bayrischen Erweckungsbewegung auf Thüringen und Pommern," *Zeitschrift für Ostforschung* 5, Heft 1 (1956): 257–58; Bigler, *Politics of German Protestantism*, 128.

[25] Gerlach, *Aufzeichnungen* 1: 115; Keyserling, *Studien zu den Entwicklungsjahren der Brüder Gerlach*, 64.

[26] Hellmuth Heyden, *Kirchengeschichte Pommerns*, vol. 2, *Von der Annahme der Reformation bis zur Gegenwart* (Cologne and Braunsfeld, 1957), 179; Friedrich Wiegand, "Eine Schwärmerbewegung in Hinterpommern vor hundert Jahren," *Deutsche Rundschau* 184 (1921): 326.

liable and a dangerous guide, for faith alone provided the proper means of righteousness and salvation. Pietists laid great stress on the conversion experience and the inner development of the individual's religious belief. They took seriously the doctrine of the priesthood of all believers, which justified their refusal to attend the regular church services of pastors they considered "nonbelievers"; instead, they held their own services, called "conventicles." In many instances, pietist laymen, unwilling to receive the sacraments from "rationalist" pastors, administered baptism and communion themselves within the conventicles.[27]

Pietism prospered among the Pomeranian nobility, particularly during the 1820s and 1830s. One of its centers was located on the estates of Reddentin, Gatz, and Seehof, owned by the brothers Gustav, Karl, and Heinrich von Below.[28] All three had served in the wars of liberation. Afterward, Gustav von Below was stationed at Berlin, became a member of the Maikäferei, and underwent a religious conversion. He gave up his military career in 1818 and returned to Pomerania, where he married a Puttkamer, a prominent pietest family. Karl and Heinrich von Below also returned to Pomerania after their military service and also became devout pietists.[29] The extreme religious beliefs and practices of the Belows resulted in a conflict with the established church. Gustav von Below, for example, was convinced that the teachings of the regular church would lead souls to damnation and that "rationalist" pastors were agents of Satan. With Heinrich he denounced their pastors to the consistory and asked to have them removed. Owing to a reform of the Patronatsrecht, estate owners could no longer dismiss village pastors without approval from the head of the provincial consistory. When the request was refused, Heinrich publicly denounced the head of the consistory as a false prophet and urged other pietists not to follow the consistory's teaching. The Belows organized their own worship services and encouraged their followers to abandon the official church. The movement spread to other villages. Not only did these pietists administer the sacraments themselves, but often they performed their own marriage ceremonies, although the state refused to recognize such marriages and declared their children illegitimate. Disturbances and threats of violence against clergymen were reported when the state refused to remove rationalist pastors. The authorities became alarmed. In 1820, the state placed the

[27] Bigler, *Politics of German Protestantism*, 131.
[28] Heyden, *Kirchengeschichte Pommerns* 2: 181ff.; Wiegand, "Eine Schwärmerbewegung," 324ff.
[29] Wiegand, "Eine Schwärmerbewegung," 324–30.

Belows under police observation and punished some of the extreme practices of pietists with fines and even jail sentences. Such actions had little effect; the pietists merely became even more fanatic. They held their conventicles in the woods or barns, wherever they could escape police surveillance, often with the cooperation of village officials.[30]

A less extreme form of pietism centered on the estate of Adolf von Thadden at Trieglaff. After the war, Thadden organized the Trieglaff conferences together with his pastor, Dummert, at which a group of pietist laymen and clergy met annually from the late 1820s until the early 1840s. The conferences were intense religious experiences for those who participated, and they returned to their homes more zealous than ever. Although Thadden always remained within the framework of the official church, the conferences concerned the consistory, and in 1838 Bishop Ritschl advised Thadden to discontinue them. Thadden refused, and the meetings were held for several more years.[31]

Pietist conventicles, often held in the manor houses of nobles, appeared to possess democratic tendencies. Lords and day laborers, peasants and Knechte, all prayed together and experienced the camaraderie of "true believers." Heinrich von Below reported having spent a half-day discussing the Bible and Luther's writings with his gardener; his woodcutter became a close spiritual brother and consultant to the family; and he was once moved to tears by the preaching of a shepherd.[32] Adolf von Thadden was praised by his peasants because he considered them his brothers in Christ. As a result, some of the opponents of pietism denounced its "Jacobin" tendencies.[33] In 1825, Minister of Culture Karl von Altenstein complained that the conventicles encouraged "complete disrespect for the social relationships that have previously existed."[34] Despite its apparent egalitarianism, however, pietism never threatened to alter any perceptions of the social order. These pietists were faithful adherents of Luther's doctrine of the two kingdoms: although all were equal before God in the realm of grace, inequality was necessary in the kingdom of this world.

[30] Heyden, *Kirchengeschichte Pommerns* 2: 181–83.

[31] See Hermann Theodor Wangemann, *Sieben Bücher preussischer Kirchengeschichte* (Berlin, 1860), 3: 66–94, for a detailed description of these conferences. Thadden did not move away from the official church as had the Below brothers. Nevertheless, the authorities were concerned with the Trieglaff conferences, and the head of the consistory for Pomerania, Bishop Ritschl, urged Thadden in 1838 to stop holding the meetings. See Reuss, *Thadden-Trieglaff*, 50, 167–78, about the exchange between Thadden and Ritschl.

[32] Wiegand, "Eine Schwärmerbewegung," 326–27.

[33] Wangemann, *Sieben Bücher* 3: 67.

[34] Neumann, *Die Stufen des preussischen Konservatismus*, 86.

CHAPTER 7

The worldly kingdom was one of authority and order, established by God to control the sinful nature of human beings. God ordained each to a particular station in life; an attempt to rise from that station or to deviate from it was a sin.

Pietist theology in Prussia generally supported conservative political assumptions and stressed the primacy of the individual relationship between God and people, who assume personal responsibility for their actions, for their sins, contrition and acceptance of God's grace. What happens is God's will. To suffer misery and injustice in this life was the consequence of sin and divine justice, not of an inequitable social system or of the landlord's avarice. Pietism did much to reinforce the paternalist ideology of domination that was disintegrating in these years. Pietist noblemen insisted not only on the preservation of the divinely ordered structure of worldly authority, but also on the tempering of that authority with paternal charity. This explains, in part, their enthusiasm for the political thought of Haller. Thadden, for example, firmly believed in the right of a noble estate owner to rule over his peasants. In words reminiscent of Haller, he declared: "The king is a large estate and landowner, the estate owner a small king. . . . We say a small king, even when he is so small that his crown, scepter, and imperial orb are only a fur cap, a walking stick, and a potato! Whoever denies this is a Jacobin!"[35] Thadden, however, was perturbed by the fact that many noble estate owners took their responsibility lightly, for they should be the embodiment of Christian charity for their subjects. "How is the lordly and paternal [väterliche] relationship between a lord and his peasants to be preserved with the continual sale of estates?" he asked. Those unwilling to take their responsibilities seriously should sell their estates to someone who would, he declared.

Whoever considers his noble estate solely as a source of profit, who visits his barns daily, but his village school never, the livestock market always, the county assembly never; whoever squeezes the bitter sweat from his day laborers, but then never pays them their rightfully earned wage on time; whoever willingly sends his faithful worker over the border because he is fifty years old; whoever directly and indirectly forces his people to work on Sunday, and so on—even if he bears a noble title—he would do well to sell his estate and buy a plantation in that part of North America where even the women constantly carry a whip (for the slaves) instead of a fan."[36]

---

[35] Reuss, *Thadden-Trieglaff*, 220–21.
[36] Ibid., 245–46; see also Bigler, *Politics of German Protestantism*, 147.

THE IDEOLOGY OF RESTORATION

The pietists made significant headway during the 1820s and 1830s. Gradually, pietist pastors began to replace the rationalists in the village churches of nobles. By 1841, Thadden's old Maikäfer friend Rappard marveled at the number of pietist neighbors who gathered at the Trieglaff conference, whereas, he noted, twenty years earlier, when Thadden's daughter, Marie, was to be baptized, "one had to search twenty to thirty miles away to find a believing pastor" for the ceremony.[37] In addition, by the late 1820s, the state relaxed some of its efforts to control the spread of pietism. Pietists themselves had become somewhat less zealous, while the state's efforts to fuse the Reformed and Lutheran churches into one state church with a common liturgy, which had produced considerable initial dissension, had largely succeeded. By the tercentenary of the Augsburg Confession in 1830, the union of Reformed and Lutheran churches had gained wide acceptance throughout Prussia.[38]

Much of the strength of pietism during the following decades grew from the fact that Pomeranian nobles were also bound by kinship. The nobility in Prussia, as elsewhere, generally married within its own ranks; pietists also married within the faith.[39] As a result, many of the young Maikäfers came to be related by marriage as well as by friendship, religion, and politics. Adolf von Thadden, Ernst von Senfft-Pilsach (later governor of Pomerania and a leading conservative politician), and Ludwig von Gerlach married three sisters from the Oertzen family. Gerlach's wife, Auguste, died only four months after their wedding; three years later, he married the cousin of his first wife, Luise von Blanckenburg, the aunt of Moritz von Blanckenburg, who later also became an important conservative politician. Ludwig von Gerlach's younger brother, Otto, married Luise's sister, Pauline. Moritz von Blanckenburg married Marie von Thadden, who had introduced Otto von Bismarck to his future wife, Johanna von Puttkamer. Marie von Thadden's early death had a profound impact on the young Bismarck and led to his religious conversion. The kinship circle of the Pomeranian pietists could be extended further, but the point

[37] Reuss, *Thadden-Trieglaff*, 53.

[38] Bigler, *Politics of German Protestantism*, 38; Wangemann, *Sieben Bücher* 1: 3–118; Erich Foerster, *Die Entstehung der preussischen Landeskirche unter der Regierung Friedrich Wilhelms des Dritten* (Tübingen, 1906), vol. 2, is entirely devoted to the controversy surrounding the union. For the differences over the union among Pomeranian pietists, see Heyden, *Kirchengeschichte Pommerns* 2: 189–90.

[39] Frau von Thadden wrote of her joy that Blanckenburg was a "believer," adding, "You certainly understand, however, that we would never have given our child to anyone other than a believing Christian." Reuss, *Thadden-Trieglaff*, 63.

CHAPTER 7

seems clear: kinship supplemented the religious and political bonds linking these young men and women to one another.[40]

Prussian pietists had acquired sufficient strength by 1827 to sponsor a newspaper, the *Evangelische Kirchen-Zeitung*, to express their views. The newspaper was planned and launched by two former Maikäfer, Ludwig von Gerlach and Adolf Le Coq.[41] For its editor, they selected a young philologist and theologian in Berlin, Ernst Wilhelm Hengstenberg, largely because he had openly criticized the government's efforts to dampen the newly awakened evangelical spirit in Prussia. Although Hengstenberg was not completely within the pietist camp, Karl von Altenstein, the minister of culture, distrusted the group surrounding the newspaper, and, so long as he was in power, the newspaper suffered at the hands of censors. Hengstenberg insisted that the newspaper not be attached to any party and that it avoid getting involved in political issues. It was a position that was impossible to maintain, for theological differences inevitably involved fundamentally different views of humanity and the world. Moreover, because the church was a state institution, politics and religion could not be neatly separated.[42]

The inseparable entanglement of politics and religion was evident in the controversy in which the *Evangelische Kirchen-Zeitung* became embroiled in 1830.[43] The controversy was touched off by Ludwig von Gerlach, who had moved to Halle in 1829 as the director of the district court. The theological faculty at Halle was overwhelmingly rationalist in orientation. Gerlach decided to expose the heresy of these theologians in articles published in the *Evangelische Kirchen-Zeitung*. From notes taken by students, Gerlach concluded that two theologians, Julius August Wegscheider and Friedrich Wilhelm Gesenius, taught students to disbelieve the Scriptures by casting doubt on the authenticity of the miracles of Jesus. He called for their dismissal. The articles unleashed a furor, not only over the issues raised by Gerlach, but also over the issue of academic freedom and the somewhat underhanded

[40] For a description of these ties of kinship, see Hellmut Diwald, *Von der Revolution zum norddeutschen Bund: Aus dem Nachlass Ernst Ludwig von Gerlach*, Deutsche Geschichtsquellen des 19. und 20. Jahrhundert, no. 46, vol. 1 (Göttingen, 1970), 13.

[41] Gerlach, *Aufzeichnungen* 1: 159–60; Johannes Bachmann, *Ernst Wilhelm Hengstenberg: Sein Leben und Wirken* (Gütersloh, 1880), 2: 65ff.; Marshall K. Christensen, *Ernst Wilhelm Hengstenberg and the Kirchenzeitung Faction: Throne and Altar in Nineteenth Century Prussia* (diss., University of Oregon, 1972), 30ff.

[42] Christensen, *Hengstenberg and the Kirchenzeitung Faction*, 34.

[43] Gerlach, *Aufzeichnungen* 1: 180–82; Bachmann, *Hengstenberg* 2: 178ff.; Christensen, *Hengstenberg and the Kirchenzeitung Faction*, 56–60; Bigler, *Politics of German Conservatism*, 101–7.

method Gerlach had used in obtaining his information. Not even all the conservatives approved Gerlach's method. The public debate compelled the government to appoint a commission to investigate "the actual limits of the freedom to teach ... and to interpret theological truths." Conservatives at the court, including the crown prince and his friends, wanted to restrict the academic freedom of professors; liberals rose in defense of the rationalist theologians. The case provided an issue in which the major political factions in Prussia could state their views on the nature of freedom. It emerged at just the moment that the July Revolution in Paris overthrew the Bourbon monarchy, chilling conservative circles throughout Europe. Ultimately the state took no action against the professors, although the king declared that candidates for the theological faculties must accept the dogmas of the Evangelical Church.

Ludwig von Gerlach was a frequent contributor to the pages of the *Evangelische Kirchen-Zeitung*; indeed, he took a public position on almost every religious or political issue in Prussia during the half-century after the mid-1820s. Although not an original thinker, Gerlach was an effective propagandist; it is impossible to consider the development of a conservative ideology in Prussia in the nineteenth century without giving attention to the role of Gerlach.

Ludwig von Gerlach was one of four brothers who were active in Prussian politics and religion during Vormärz.[44] Two of the brothers, Wilhelm and Otto, died relatively young and were consequently less prominent. Ludwig's older brother, Leopold, was a trusted confidant of the crown prince and later king, Frederick William IV. Leopold's influence was based on his personal relationship with the king, and it lasted only as long as Frederick William remained in power. He played a significant role in the *Kamarilla*, the band of private counselors who surrounded the king during the revolution of 1848 and intrigued against the liberal ministry that came to power in the wake of the revolution.[45] Leopold was inclined to view politics as a matter of personal connections. Ludwig, on the other hand, did not enjoy a close relationship with Frederick William; as a public official climbing the bureaucratic ladder, he spent much of his time away from Berlin. His influence derived from being the spokesman for a larger group of conservative nobles; he helped found the *Evangelische Kirchen-Zeitung*, the major conservative religious newspaper; in 1831, he was closely

[44] Keyserling, *Studien zu den Entwicklungsjahren der Brüder Gerlach*, 6–21; Schoeps, *Das Andere Preussen*, 14–15.

[45] See especially Diwald, *Von der Revolution zum Norddeutschen Bund*, vols. 1 and 2. See Epilogue.

involved in the founding of the *Berliner Politisches Wochenblatt*, and he helped found the *Neue Preussische Zeitung* (*Kreuzzeitung*) in 1848, which became the major conservative political newspaper.[46] Ludwig was also one of the founders of the Prussian Conservative Party in the summer of 1848. His views on politics were always more theoretical than Leopold's. Leopold once wrote in his diary, "Ludwig, with whom I had a long conversation yesterday, belongs to a different generation than I. He cannot grasp what it means to be personally loyal to the king. . . . For him, the reality, the concrete, the personal is phantomlike, because he sees the reality only in the idea." When Ludwig stressed the concept of kingship, Leopold replied, "I do not want to serve a concept, or be the subject of some ideal kingdom."[47]

The Gerlach brothers grew up in a political family. Their father had been Lord Mayor of Berlin but had resigned in 1810 because of differences with Hardenberg. In 1811, he was called to the Assembly of Notables, where he joined the opposition to Hardenberg.[48] The political consciousness of the young Gerlachs thus developed in an atmosphere of controversy produced by the reforms. In 1811 Leopold wrote to a friend, "It can already be reckoned that Hardenberg has cost the country more and destroyed more than the French. No form remains standing, no right, no property, all is appearance."[49] The Gerlachs objected especially to the reforms for dissolving the bonds of mutual obligation between lords and peasants. Ludwig was at the family estate of Rohrbeck in 1818 when representatives of the General Commission arrived to supervise the separation of peasant lands. He recorded in his diary his sadness at the "shattering of all the bonds of the community," the dissolution of the "holy, indeed heavenly, relationship between a lord and his subjects in the village community." Inspired by "the good conservative doctrine for which I had become even more enthusiastic because of Haller," Ludwig proposed a paragraph for the separation agreement that would have preserved the old "law and constitution of Rohrbeck" unless explicitly altered by the agreement. The General Commission rejected the paragraph, declaring that all relations between lords and peasants had been fundamentally altered by the reform edicts.[50]

Although Gerlach spent his entire career in the bureaucracy and was never a country squire, his political conservatism was grounded in

---

[46] Gerlach, *Aufzeichnungen* 1: 159–60, 199, 524–37. See Epilogue.
[47] Leopold von Gerlach, *Denkwürdigkeiten aus dem Leben* (Berlin, 1891), 1: 576, 423.
[48] Keyserling, *Studien zu den Entwicklungsjahren der Brüder Gerlach*, 41.
[49] Ibid., 42.
[50] Gerlach, *Aufzeichnungen*, 1: 115; see also Schoeps, *Aus den Jahren Preussischer Not*, 284.

the social relations of das ganze Haus. In 1819, he wrote Thadden, who had just returned to Trieglaff: "I consider this profession, estate lord, to be very important and holy for a servant [Knechte] of the Lord—perhaps the more so, the less it is recognized as such by most others. All external relationships and constitutional structures still carry the imprint of a large family."⁵¹ Gerlach remained critical of Stein and Hardenberg for having destroyed the paternal basis of society. They had utterly failed to recognize, he wrote, "that these fetters were also the bonds of morality and discipline, that they guaranteed honor, law, and freedom, and that through their mild and earnest influence, they regulated the morals, honor, and discipline of the subjects, as well as marriage, property, and family relationships of the entire rural population."⁵²

The Gerlachs were originally drawn to Haller because of his rejection of absolutism, his refutation of all social theories that conceived of the state as originating in a social contract, and his assertion that all authority originated from above. Ludwig believed that "all absolutism is the service of idolatry."⁵³ Like Marwitz and Müller, he blamed Prussia's problems on the absolutist policies begun under Frederick II. On more than one occasion, Gerlach earned for himself opprobrium for his refusal to recognize Frederick II as "the Great."⁵⁴ Absolutism led inevitably to revolution, he believed, because it robbed authority of its mystical power, its symbols of superiority. "There is no more vexatious enemy of legitimate rulers, . . . no more able and fearful ally of revolution than absolutism. . . . Absolutism robs the king of the brilliance of his majesty, for it strips his office of that which exalts it: that he is the servant and swordbearer of Almighty God, His first subject and executor of His holy will."⁵⁵

However, the Gerlachs found Haller's system lacking a proper appreciation for God's direct involvement in the creation of the state. When the fourth volume of Haller's *Restauration* appeared in 1820, Otto complained to his brother Ludwig, "It is completely without a trace of Christian convictions and is actually neological in that he wishes to base the whole of Christendom on natural origins."⁵⁶ Ludwig insisted on a much more Augustinian view of the relationship of God

---

⁵¹ Ibid., 600.
⁵² Cited in Max Wildgrube, *Die politischen Theorien Ludwig von Gerlachs* (phil. diss., Heidelberg, 1914), 64.
⁵³ Schoeps, *Das Andere Preussen*, 31.
⁵⁴ Gerlach, *Aufzeichnungen* 2: 376.
⁵⁵ Cited in Wildgrube, *Theorien Ludwig von Gerlachs*, 99.
⁵⁶ Gerlach, *Aufzeichnungen*, 1: 127. "Neological" referred to rationalist religion.

to the world and the state. The Fall necessitated the creation of the state. Before the Fall, a sinless humankind had lived in harmony with God; the advent of sin, however, splintered the unity of the spiritual and material worlds, necessitating the creation of the state, which came into being to control sinful humanity. The state, therefore, played a role in the reconciliation of people and God by curbing sin. Its purpose was essentially religious.[57] Haller had not appreciated this. He attributed no general purpose to the state other than maintenance of the multitude of private contracts of which it was composed. He believed that the state was the domination and protection of the weak by the strong, which was, to be sure, a manifestation of God's grace and will, but he did not see this relationship as originating to control sin or as an instrument assisting in salvation. His was essentially a rational, deductive system, whereas Gerlach's was fundamentally theological.

For Gerlach, the ideal state was a feudal theocracy. He considered God to be the feudal overlord whose vassals were the kings and princes of this world. The state and the church, throne and altar, were thus joined in the common purpose of the salvation of humanity. "The state is the kingdom of the law of God among men."[58] Gerlach shared with Savigny and the historical school the idea that the state developed its own personality and that states thus differed in the manner in which they expressed the laws of God. But he sought to avoid the relativism implicit in the historical school by insisting that states, like individuals, were "liable also for their sins."[59]

The state and church corresponded to each other as the law does to the gospel, "the realm of law" and "the realm of grace." Because the state was the product of sin, "natural man belongs to the state" and was bound by its laws. The church, "the community of saints," also needed the state but had loyalties that transcend it. "The born-again belong to the state only insofar as they do not yet live completely in the realm of the spirit, and therefore, they need the state's laws as a discipline until they die and are freed by God's grace."[60] Because the state existed to provide the framework in which people could more easily avoid sin, it was constantly judged by the "community of saints" and was subordinate to the church. It could not fulfill its role in hu-

---

[57] Eugen Jedele, *Die Kirchenpolitischen Anschauungen des E. L. von Gerlachs* (phil. diss., Tübingen, 1910), 18ff.; Wildgrube, *Theorien Ludwig von Gerlach*, 20ff.
[58] Schoeps, *Das Andere Preussen*, 21; Wildgrube, *Theorien Ludwig von Gerlach*, 44.
[59] Ibid., 44–45.
[60] Cited in ibid., 38.

man salvation unless directed by Christian people toward Christian objectives.

Although Gerlach differed from Haller in his assumptions about the origin and purpose of the state, he agreed with him that the process by which states came into existence originated in the family. The family was the original social unit shaped by God; to it was added the servants and other dependents in das ganze Haus, so that families gradually became tribes and tribes became states. The Old Testament, Gerlach believed, revealed this process.[61] The patrimonial state was the proper biblical form. He accepted from Haller that the state was a product of the will of God, working through nature, but he went even further than Haller in stressing that, as a product of nature, the state was an organism with living parts fulfilling different functions. From this he derived his central concept of the Stände as the vital organs of the state. The tragic error of absolutism and revolution, he declared, was that they led to the "atomistic pulverization" of the people, and the subsequent destruction of the organic life of the state. Gerlach blended his emphasis on the organic Stände with his belief in the paternal structure of social relations in a way that both accepted the private relationships central to Haller and provided the prince with a public function as well. He wrote: "Woe to the statesman who wishes to consult or to govern the masses as masses! To find the organism in them, to awaken and fertilize the seeds, even if they are so small as a mustard seed, of this organism with a devotion that comes from above, with a devotion that is not merely that of kings, but also of masters for apprentices, of peasants for stablehands, a devotion that is not haughty but humble—that is what it means to govern, that is the task and high calling of the statesman."[62]

Ludwig von Gerlach played an important role in the development of a conservative ideology for the Prussian nobility during the period of the restoration. His steady advancement through the ranks of the bureaucracy reflected the recovery of a conservative element within the government after the death of Hardenberg. The contacts of the two Gerlachs with the crown prince were significant in shaping the attitudes and values of the future king. Ludwig von Gerlach's tireless efforts to found new organs for the dissemination of conservative ideas and his attacks on theological rationalism signaled the counteroffensive launched by conservative ideologues in the 1820s and 1830s. He brought the abstract, general political thought of Carl Ludwig von

[61] Ibid., 54–57.
[62] Ibid., 58.

Haller into contact with the concrete experiences of the landowning nobility, providing an explanation of the origin and development of the state that shored up the eroding foundations of paternalism. He added the dimension of pietism to the ideology of paternalism, insisting that all authority reflected the fatherhood of God.

The ideas of Gerlach and Haller were repeated frequently in the pages of *Das Berliner Politische Wochenblatt*, the conservative weekly that began publication in October 1831 and continued through the following decade. Plans for the newspaper first developed in the circle of the crown prince during the summer of 1830, when the first news of the July Revolution in Paris shocked conservatives in Berlin.[63] Carl von Voss-Buch described the scene at the court when the news of the revolution reached the Prussian capital as follows: "As usual, Ancillon was there and read aloud the incoming dispatches and the newspaper articles, while a most unusual gloomy silence fell upon the group, so that I have a very unpleasant memory of that evening. Both of the Berlin newspapers, which were of a liberal character, did not directly take the side of the revolution and the new citizen-king, but their leading principles favored the revolution."[64] Concern over the lack of a countervailing, conservative newspaper for Berlin grew more acute and ultimately led to the founding of the *Wochenblatt*. Published under the slogan "We do not propose a counter-revolution but oppose the revolution," coined by de Maistre, the *Wochenblatt* represented a joint effort of Catholic and Protestant conservatives to offer a "German-Christian" point of view. Joseph Maria von Radowitz, one of the driving forces behind the founding of the newspaper, and K. E. Jarcke, its first editor, were both Catholics; other frequent contributors, such as the Gerlachs and the historian at Halle, Heinrich Leo, were Protestants.[65]

The political posture of the *Wochenblatt* was essentially that of Haller, although it added a more decisively religious dimension. Many of its articles seemed to be inspired directly by Haller's writings, and some acknowledged his influence; some were written by Haller. The newspaper commonly viewed the state as a collection of private contracts that guaranteed the private rights of each Hausvater over his

---

[63] Varentrapp, "Rankes Historisch-politische Zeitschrift und das Berliner Politische Wochenblatt," *HZ* 99 (1904): 35–119; Robert Arnold, "Aufzeichnungen des Grafen Carl v. Voss-Buch über das Berliner Politische Wochenblatt," *HZ* 106 (1911): 325–40; Paul Hassel, *Joseph Maria von Radowitz (1797–1848)* (Berlin, 1905), 1: 43, 60, 212ff., 248; Gerlach, *Aufzeichnungen* 1: 199.

[64] Arnold, "Aufzeichnungen des Grafen Carl v. Voss-Buch," 331–32.

[65] Meinecke, *Weltbürgertum und Nationalstaat*, 205–6.

particular sphere of authority. "Family fathers and property holders are in a small circle what princes are in a larger one," it read in 1834.[66] The newspaper maintained that the absolutist state had obliterated these private contracts by intruding upon them with public law and by making the state the focal point of all life, to the extent that if the public demanded the sacrifice of some right, it was forfeited. Thus absolutism led inevitably to revolution, first in 1789 and also, unfortunately, in 1830, for the restored Bourbon monarchy had mistakenly pursued once again the absolutist policies of its predecessors. "Unfortunately, the restoration bitterly disappointed the hopes of all Europe," wrote the *Wochenblatt*, "for in this land from which had emerged the Jacobin rapture over the republic and the lust for the conquest of Europe by the emperor, there appeared a new and more dangerous form of absolutism—more dangerous because it was veiled and measured. This came in the form of liberal constitutionalism."[67] The "German-Christian" state—"the dominance of unlimited, legitimate private freedom on the one hand, and the subordination of all freedom to the supraworldly Christian law on the other hand"—stood as the major bulwark against this revolutionary threat.[68]

In effect, the *Wochenblatt* translated the abstract principles of Haller's ideology into the concrete political situation in Germany and Europe. For example, Wilhelm von Gerlach wrote the article "What Is Law?" in 1833, using Haller's conception of the state to justify the continuation of patrimonial courts.[69] The family, he insisted, was the wellspring of all authority: "The first Hausvater was the first superior authority, the first head of state. . . . Out of the first family there developed more Hausväter, more authorities and superiors, partially standing beside one another, partially standing above or beneath one another, so that the highest authority united all other powers beneath him." From this perspective, Gerlach defended patrimonial courts. "Patrimonial jurisdiction is the point of departure for all jurisdiction, the patrimonial relationship is the genetic and static basis of the state; indeed, it is a miniature state. The most recent history has offered ample proof that the principle that deprives estate owners or town authorities of their courts eventually destabilizes the throne."

Similarly, the *Wochenblatt* defended the ständisch basis of provincial diets against the demands for a popular system of representation and against the growing demand that the deliberations of the diets be re-

[66] *Das Berliner Politische Wochenblatt*, 1834, 45. (Hereafter cited as *BPW*.)
[67] *BPW*, 1832, 190.
[68] *BPW*, 1832, 173.
[69] *BPW*, 1833, 49ff., 60ff., 67ff.

ported in the public press. The ständisch constitution, the *Wochenblatt* insisted in an article probably written by Jarcke, was "no artificial discovery, but a natural and necessary institution that developed from the living concepts of law and freedom contained in the sum of all social relations."[70] The representative system, on the other hand, was an artificial creation that presupposed that sovereignty resided with the people. The Stände comprised the individual and collective authorities of the nation; they did not draw their authority from below, from the people, for they did not represent the people, but themselves. They were responsible only to the king, their only sovereign. Thus, the king convened the Stände to seek their advice; they did not have the right to convene themselves, as a representative system insisted. If the deliberations of the diets were to be published, the diets would be subjected to pressure from the people, thereby reversing the real basis of their authority.

This series of articles on the ständisch system of representation, however, went beyond Haller in one important respect. Whereas Haller blamed the dissolution of the traditional structure of authority largely on rationalism, absolutism, and revolution, the *Wochenblatt* also recognized the impact of the capitalist market society. Because the representative system acknowledged only numerical representation, "the atomistic masses of the crumbling nation," it, in fact, recognized only the representation of money. The *Wochenblatt* declared the following:

Where, in the life of a people, aside from political opinion, only one power is recognized and revered by the state—namely, that of money—where every other form of property is put in question, every other right is accorded minimal esteem and subordinated to the interest of money; where the entire property of the population, even the most stable and unassailable, is placed on the market; where nothing is inaccessible to monetary wealth and it alone receives the highest respect—there, in the inevitable nature of things, no matter how the form of representation may vary, nothing other than the power of money and the power of political opinion will be represented.[71]

One significant article, "The Railroads," which appeared in 1839, not only captured all of the *Wochenblatt*'s aversion to the modern age of capital and industry, but also revealed the newspaper's pessimism about the future. "Where money tinkles, the bells of heaven cannot be

---

[70] For this long series, see *BPW*, 1833, 303ff., 310ff., 321ff., 325ff.; 1834, 2ff., 15ff.
[71] *BPW*, 1833, 304.

heard," it warned.[72] The current age was characterized by "sensual lust and the joys of the flesh." "The means of achieving these is money, so money becomes the goal of all strivings and efforts." Many believed that the advent of steam power would solve human problems, that "steam is the universal solution for all political, religious, moral, and physical misfortunes." But the *Wochenblatt* did not agree, arguing that the rise of factory industry had resulted in moral deterioration. Advocates of liberalism had welcomed the elimination of serfdom as a great step forward; they had considered serfdom to be virtual slavery. But the misery to be found around the new factories was far greater than that produced by serfdom, for the "monetary slaves of heartless speculators," the factory workers, had none of the protection offered to serfs. "The bound serfs of our forefathers were tied to their lord as a piece of his heart," the newspaper asserted. The factory system was destroying the entire artisan Stand, "one of the most solid foundations of the life of our state."

The spread of railroads, the newspaper continued, only enhanced the power of the factory system and the monetary aristocracy. But the railroad would have other pernicious effects: it would "intensify the abstract nature of life" by centralizing and further depersonalizing the structure of authority in the state. The uniqueness and individuality of each local area will be obliterated, the newspaper prophesied. "Undeniably the railroads will expand into a complete system, bringing the people into a proximity that now can be scarcely conceived, and destroy all nationality. Indeed, the centralization of the administrative apparatus of the state will become tighter, easier, and more mechanical. In the shortest possible time, a command can be delivered from the capital to the farthest corner of the state. The large state will be as easily governed as is now a small county."

In the late 1830s, the *Wochenblatt*'s criticism of capitalism intensified. Capitalism had much in common with rationalism, it maintained, for both denied the personal nature of domination. "They bring only material and external effects to bear; in a word, their connection with and influence upon the governed lack any internal nexus and are merely indifferent relationships."[73] In the "modern finance economy," as the *Wochenblatt* referred to the capitalist economic order, everything assumed a monetary character. "Even those goods that God has given us through nature—land, forests, and so on—have no immediate relationship to men, but only one mediated through money; things have

[72] *BPW*, 1839, 82ff.
[73] *BPW*, 1836, 245.

value only through their monetary price." "So-called mystics, enthusiasts [*Schwärmer*], and conservatives" were not alone in "recognizing the pernicious influence of money," observed the newspaper; so also did the radicals, "who call the army of the proletarians into the field."[74] The July monarchy exemplified the triumph of money for the *Wochenblatt*; its liberal constitutional structure provided only a veil for an aristocracy of money. Unlike the old aristocracy, however, this new aristocracy of money possessed no honor, loyalty, or family traditions. It could not provide the warmer bonds of paternal rule that had once been given by the nobility; as a result, the lower orders in France were beginning to claim the promises of the liberal ideology for themselves. Guizot's only answer was to give them work.[75] But this was not an adequate answer. "True security is preserved only with the reins that lie in the moral feelings and convictions of men. But these reins are absent from the present circumstances of the lower classes in the society." The only means to restore those "moral feelings and convictions," asserted the *Wochenblatt*, was through "the return to the true, natural order of things, to the pure, original basis of all Herrschaft."[76]

The *Wochenblatt* endeavored to adapt Haller's feudal view of society and the ideology of paternalism to the modern industrial state. It insisted that employers and employees in a factory enter into the kind of private contract that marked the relationship between lords and peasants. Employers should have the same rights over their subjects that lords had over theirs; but so, too, should they assume the same obligations toward them. Workers should not be dependent solely on monetary wages, which fluctuated unpredictably, but should also be paid *in natura*, which would underscore the enduring paternal obligation an employer had toward his workers. This article, perhaps written by Radowitz, anticipated the political efforts conservatives would later make to win the support of the working classes. "The government will not be able to do anything against the storms that threaten the immediate future," warned the *Wochenblatt*, "unless it has the courage to make a common cause with the people against the aristocracy of money."[77]

The question of how to preserve the traditional, landowning nobility in the face of the growing economic power of industrial and finance capitalism—a question of burning importance to the Prussian nobility during the 1830s, when hundreds of noble estates were pass-

[74] *BPW*, 1837, 202.
[75] *BPW*, 1837, 131.
[76] *BPW*, 1837, 223.
[77] Ibid.

ing into the hands of commoners—concerned the *Wochenblatt* throughout its entire existence. The preservation of landed estates was of paramount importance to the nobility, the newspaper declared, because from its ties to agriculture and the land, with claims on both the past and the future, the nobility developed its ständisch self-consciousness. Therefore, the estates should be entailed and retained within the family. Landownership comprised "nearly all forms of Herrschaft," the newspaper affirmed; thus, the preservation of the nobility and its possessions was also essential to the survival of monarchy.[78]

By the early 1840s, the ideology articulated in the *Wochenblatt* no longer captured the imagination of all conservatives. The politics of restoration no longer sufficed to cope with all the problems created by social changes wrought by the agricultural depression of the 1820s and early 1830s. This conservative political ideology was insufficient to deal with the increasing capitalization of agriculture, the growing discontent among the lower classes, and the need for the state to assert its authority in terms of the public power of monarchy instead of the ideas of private law that were inherited from the past. Before turning to the emergence of a newer conservative ideology, it is necessary to explore carefully the economic and social changes of the 1820s and 1830s.

[78] On the preservation of a landed nobility, see *BPW*, 1833, 266; 1834, 54; 1835, 258ff., 300ff.; 1836, 125. On the necessity of preserving a ständisch consciousness, see especially *BPW*, 1836, 126.

8

NOBLE AND PEASANT BETWEEN REFORM AND REVOLUTION

The Depression of the 1820s: Crisis for the Nobility

On March 24, 1822, as the agrarian crisis that had begun two years earlier showed signs of deepening, Theodor von Schön, then governor of West Prussia, wrote a troubled and prescient letter to Chancellor Hardenberg. "Everyone considers it to be a momentary market conjuncture, builds plans upon plans, and asks for help in averting a quickly passing danger," he wrote.

> The estate owners of this province have held on and, up to the present, no estate has been forced into sale; but one can see trouble coming and, especially in East Prussia, there is spreading concern of a total transformation of landownership. . . . The trouble is near, a great trouble is near, and a much greater misfortune is to be feared for the people on the land than for the business people, for . . . with the transformation of landownership, bonds are torn and relationships dissolved that are very important morally and politically; the sudden shearing of those bonds must bring with it incalculable moral and political damages.[1]

Schön's prognosis was largely correct. The searing agricultural depression of the next decade led to profound changes in the pattern of social relations in rural Prussia. If the Stein-Hardenberg reforms opened the door to capitalist agriculture, the depression of the twenties pushed the nobility over the threshhold.[2] The depression hastened the process by which large numbers of noble estates passed out of the hands of nobles into the hands of commoners. Overburdened with debts reaching back into the closing decades of the eighteenth century, many noble estate owners simply went bankrupt. Those who

---

[1] Theodor von Schön, *Aus den Papieren Theodor von Schön* (Berlin, 1875), 1: 205–6.
[2] This is the contention of Hanna Schissler, *Preussische Agrargesellschaft im Wandel*, Kritische Studien zur Geschichtswissenschaft, 33 (Göttingen), 145, with which I agree. Reinhart Koselleck, *Preussen zwischen Reform und Revolution* (Stuttgart, 1967), 487ff., is more inclined to stress the effect of the reforms.

survived the crisis did so by cultivating entrepreneurial instincts and employing the methods of rational agriculture. As Schön predicted, the depression led to the severing of old bonds between noble families and their estates and peasants. But it also produced many of the "moral and political damages" he feared. For the depression came at precisely the time that the "regulation" of the peasantry, prescribed by the reforms, was getting under way. Their precarious existence made the lords especially grasping in the settlements with their peasants. The depression deprived the new landowning peasantry of the monetary credit it required for the maintenance and improvement of its holdings, now reduced by the settlements with the lords. As the market for grain collapsed, the landless peasants had trouble finding work, even at seriously reduced wages; their misery deepened. Bitter and disillusioned over the meager and sour fruit they had obtained from the reforms, the poorer peasants found themselves slipping into the status of daily wage laborers, or what was coming to be called the rural proletariat. Their rage increased as their subsistence declined over the next two decades until, with the harvest failures of the mid-1840s, their situation became desperate. The "incalculable moral and political damages" caused by the depression of the twenties could first be calculated only in the revolution of 1848.

Although the agricultural crisis of the 1820s had a number of causes, its most immediate source lay in the Napoleonic wars.[3] The wars had affected European grain production in two fundamental ways: first, they had produced a high military demand for grain at the same time that they interrupted production, not only through direct war damage, which was considerable in some areas, but also through the indirect damage of taking men and draft animals away from agricultural labor. For example, in 1813, East Prussia lost an estimated 40 percent of its horses and 30 percent of its cattle, a loss estimated at 23 million taler. Other provinces less affected directly by the war also lost

---

[3] Schissler, *Preussische Agrargesellschaft im Wandel*, 145–46; Arnold Ucke, *Die Agrarkrisis in Preussen während der zwanziger Jahre dieses Jahrhunderts* (phil. diss., Halle, 1887), 10–17; Johannes Ziekursch, *Hundert Jahre schlesischer Agrargeschichte* (Breslau, 1927), 322–34; Anna Neumann, *Die Bewegung der Löhne der ländlichen "freien" Arbeiter im Zusammenhang mit der gesamtwirtschaftlichen Entwicklung im Königreich Preussen gegenwärtigen Umfangs vom Ausgang des 18. Jahrhunderts bis 1850* (Berlin, 1911), 126–29; Hans Liebaug, *Die Ursachen der Agrarkrisis der zwanziger Jahre des 19. Jahrhunderts im Urteil der Zeitgenossen* (phil. diss., Giessen, 1924); Siegfried von Ciriacy-Wantrup, *Agrarkrisen und Stockungsspannen: Zur Frage der langen "Welle" in der wirtschaftlichen Entwicklung* (Berlin, 1936), 17ff.; Wilhelm Abel, *Agrarkrisen und Agrarkonjunktur*, 3d ed. (Hamburg and Berlin, 1978), 225ff. Herta Westphal, *Die Agrarkrise in Mecklenburg in den zwanziger Jahren des vorigen Jahrhunderts*, Mecklenburgische Landwirtschaftliche Mitteilungen, Heft 6 (Rostock, 1925).

livestock put to military uses.⁴ The subsequent decline in production forced prices upward.

Second, especially as a result of the continental system, the wars interrupted the normal flow of international trade in grain, forcing up the prices of grain in those countries, such as England, which were large grain importers. The high prices and reduced imports encouraged the cultivation of marginally productive lands. After the war, the agricultural interests in the western European states demanded protection from cheaper imported grain from central and eastern Europe. In 1815, England enacted the Corn Laws; a year later, France also imposed a grain tariff. The effects of these tariffs were not immediately felt in Prussia, for the crop failed in England and was poor throughout most of western Europe in 1816, so the demand for grain pushed prices to near-record highs. There was a brief flurry of land speculation in Prussia in 1817 because of the high prices, and everywhere new lands were put under the plow to take advantage of the opportunity. After 1818, however, prices began to fall. Then France in 1819 and England in 1822 raised tariff levels so high that they virtually prohibited the importation of grain. Grain prices plummeted—by 1823 in Prussia to 48 percent of what they were in 1817 and still lower in 1826.⁵ Thereafter, they rose again slowly. In 1827 and 1828, England introduced a sliding scale of duties that allowed more imports. Moreover, Prussian producers met the crisis by diversifying their crops; after 1833, the depression gradually abated and Prussian agriculture entered a period of prosperity that lasted more than forty years.

The depression hit the Prussian noble estate owners especially hard because of their high level of indebtedness. Although many blamed the war, much of the debt was inherited from the late eighteenth century, when easy credit made available by the Landschaften had touched off a speculation boom.⁶ As the value of land had soared,

⁴ Ucke, *Die Agrarkrisis in Preussen*, 13.

⁵ Ibid.; Rudolf Schäffner, *Zur Geschichte der Agrarkrisen im neunzehnten Jahrhundert* (phil. diss., Heidelberg, 1933), 11–14; Schissler, *Preussische Agrargesellschaft im Wandel*, 149–50.

⁶ Discussion of the indebtedness of noble estate owners naturally arose in connection with proposals to extend the capital moratorium on debt that had been introduced in 1807, modified in 1811, reintroduced in 1816, and ultimately renewed for East and West Prussia until 1832. It was defended by an official of the Landschaft, Manitius, in the essay "Was hat der Landwirt in Preussen zu thun, um auch unter den heutigen Umständen zu bestehen und die Zinsen seiner Gläubiger zu berichten" (Königsberg, 1813). Manitius maintained that debtors and creditors were citizens of the same state and should share the burdens of the wars equally. This was answered by the essay "Ueber die unglückliche Verhältnisse der Grundeigenthümer und Geldeigenhümer in Ostpreussen" (Königsberg,

more debt had been contracted against it, often without improvements in productivity; now, when the price of grain collapsed and with it the value of land, many estates owed more than their market worth. Thus, for example, the estate of Wensöwen in County Oletzko, East Prussia, had an appraised value of 60,000 taler and was mortgaged for 48,000; when put up for sale, the highest offer was 27,000. Another estate, appraised at 50,000, owing 39,000, was ultimately sold for 22,000 taler.[7] In 1827, the noble estates of the Kurmark Brandenburg, with a total value estimated at 27 million taler, were indebted for 21 million— 78 percent. This level of indebtedness was typical for the monarchy.[8] So much back interest was owed that estate owners used relief funds received from the state—intended to rebuild their lands after the war or for agricultural innovation—to pay off creditors. This happened, for example, with the money distributed in East and West Prussia after 1816.[9]

Although the depression touched all of Prussia's provinces, some were more deeply affected than others. The territories located on the shores of the Baltic Sea—Pomerania, West and East Prussia—always more dependent on the export of grain to western Europe, suffered the most. The statistics of the grain export from the Baltic ports of

---

1814), by the historian L. von Baczko. Baczko maintained that most of the debts had little to do with the war but were from the speculation boom of the late eighteenth century. Many estate owners, he claimed, were virtually bankrupt before 1806 and were now asking the state to assist them because of the war. In 1823, the officials of the governmental district of Marienwerder examined the origins of the noble debts and concluded the following: "The larger portion of the debts, which currently oppress the estate owners, grew from the years form 1798 to 1806, during a prosperous time for agriculture in Prussia, when capital was obtained with ease." Eduard Mayer, *Das Retablissement Ost- und Westpreussens unter der Mitwirkung und Leitung Theodors von Schön*, Schriften des Instituts für ostdeutsche Wirtschaft in Königsberg (Pr.) (Jena, 1916), 25–27. The most thorough and careful study of the indebtedness of East Prussian estates is being undertaken by Bernd Ristau. I am grateful to Ristau for sharing with me his thoughts on the manner in which the East Prussian nobility shamelessly manipulated the Landschaft and the government for its advantage. Ristau's study will be a major contribution to our understanding of the economic strategies of the nobility.

[7] Robert Stein, *Die Umwaldung der Agrarverfassung Ostpreussens durch die Reform des neunzehnten Jahrhunderts* (Königsberg, 1934), vol 3, *Durchführung und Wirkung der Agrarreform*, 123. See also Ucke, *Die Agrarkrisis in Preussen*, 20–21.

[8] Erich Jordan, *Die Entstehung der konservativen Partei und die preussischen Agrarverhältnisse von 1848* (Munich and Leipzig, 1914), 21. A survey taken later compared the indebtedness of estates in six eastern counties in 1837 and 1847. The average level was 78 percent in 1837 and 83 percent in 1847. Much of the debt increase between 1837 and 1847, however, was not the result of speculation, but of investment and improvement of the land.

[9] Mayer, *Das Retablissement Ost- und Westpreussens*, 23–24.

CHAPTER 8

Danzig and Elbing offer a measure of their decline. Between 1801 and 1805, these two ports shipped a yearly average of 76,547 *Last* (6,336,043 bushels) of wheat and rye; between 1821 and 1825, the yearly average had fallen to 10,591 Last (876,651 bushels).[10] Silesia also faced grave difficulties. In 1830, the president of the governmental district of Oppeln in Upper Silesia, Theodor von Hippel, described the situation as the worst in his memory, except for the war year of 1812. He appealed to the ministry for public works projects to support needy rural wage laborers; he asked that the tax burden be eased for those unable to pay; and he called for more credit for large landowners, whose "entrepreneurial spirit" was being crippled for lack of capital.[11] On various occasions during the depression, the government supported the price of grain by large purchases through the military grain magazines; at other times, it distributed seed grain from the magazines to those who had none. Other provinces, where production had always been directed toward a local market as well, suffered somewhat less.[12] The Rhineland and Westphalia, for example, did not witness the level of land transfers that took place in the eastern provinces.[13] Because East and West Prussia were most profoundly affected by the depression, the government's policies toward the estate owners in these territories show how the government worked to preserve the nobility.

The agrarian crisis began earlier and spread more rapidly in East Prussia than elsewhere. While good harvests in most of Europe after 1817 led to an oversupply of grain and depressed market prices, East Prussia had "three unprecedentedly poor harvests" beginning in

[10] A Last was a cubic unit of measure. One Last equaled 30.0996 hektoliters, or 82.77 bushels. Thus, the weight of a Last varied with the density of the material measured; one Last of rye equaled roughly 2,190 kilograms, and one Last of wheat equaled roughly 2,400 kilograms. See Czeslaw Biernat, *Statystyka Obrotu Towarowego Gdansak w Latach 1651–1815* (Warsaw, 1962), 62. The statistics from Danzig and Elbing cited here are found in Ucke, *Die Agrarkrisis in Preussen*, 15. In 1800, the shipping from three ports, Danzig, Elbing, and Königsberg, amounted to nearly one-third of the entire international grain trade. Jerome Blum, *The End of the Old Order in Rural Europe* (Princeton, 1978), 243.

[11] DZA II, Rep. 2.2.1, no. 30435, Bl. 35–38.

[12] DZA II, Rep. 2.2.1, no. 30435, Bl. 27. The administrative reports in Brandenburg do not bear the same intensity of concern shown in the reports from East Prussia and Silesia. The governor's reports on agriculture from Brandenburg, for 1829, 1830, and 1831, for example, are fairly routine. Each begins with the identical sentence: "With regard to agriculture, the previous year was not as favorable for the inhabitants of the province as would be wished." STAP, Pr. Br., Oberpräsidium, Bd. 356, Bd. 357 (Tit. 12: Geschäftsverwaltung), Bl. 19.

[13] Heinz Reif, *Westfälischer Adel, 1770–1860*, Kritische Studien zur Geschichtswissenschaft, 35 (Göttingen, 1979), 213ff.

1819.[14] As a result, its share of the grain market declined at the same time that prices dropped, compounding the effects of the depression. Under the vigorous leadership of Count Alexander zu Dohna, the Committee of the East Prussian Stände, already actively bombarding Berlin with petitions opposing Hardenberg's tax and administrative reforms, began to agitate for relief measures by the government for the landowners in the province. In a report on November 16, 1822, the committee called for a delay in the execution of the agrarian reforms, for the "regulation" of the peasantry added burdens to the estate owners at the moment of their greatest financial difficulties. Because peasants lacked the capital to transmute their service obligations into rents, the lords were forced to accept land as compensation for the dissolution of the peasants' service. This meant that the lords had more land to cultivate at a time when they were becoming more dependent on hired labor; but they, too, lacked the capital necessary to improve their lands or pay wage labor. The report declared, "Many estate owners who still stand in a most favorable situation, who could be aided by the results of the regulation, now find themselves in the greatest difficulties and the greatest danger during the current period of transition, and, without speedy and effective help during this transition, they will go under."[15]

The government responded to this appeal of the noble estate owners. On December 20, 1822, the Ministry of Internal Affairs instructed the General Commission in Königsberg, responsible for the regulation of the peasants under the terms of the reforms, to slow its work. The General Commission was ordered to reduce its staff and to plan intentionally for a slower pace of work. Aware of the effects that this order might have on the peasantry, the ministry instructed the commission to keep it secret. "To avoid misunderstanding and unrest among the great mass of the peasantry, the wider circulation of these instructions is not permitted; the commission will therefore take all earnest steps to prevent this from happening," wrote the ministry. Within a month of Hardenberg's death, therefore, tempering of the moderate reforms had begun in the interest of the landowning nobility.[16]

On November 21, 1822, the Committee of the Stände also appealed to the crown prince for assistance, reminding him that the impoverish-

[14] PSK/B-D, Provinz Ostpreussen, Rep. 2, Oberpräsidium, Tit. 40, no. 15, Bl. 8.

[15] Ucke, *Die Agrarkrisis in Preussen*, 12; see also Rolf Engels, *Die Preussische Verwaltung von Kammer und Regierung Gumbinnen* (Cologne and Berlin, 1974), 104.

[16] Stein, *Die Umwandlung der Agrarverfassung Ostpreussens* 3: 117–18. On the inability of peasants to pay compensation with money, see Hartmut Harnisch, *Kapitalistische Agrarreform und Industrielle Revolution* (Weimar, 1984), 169.

CHAPTER 8

ment of the noble estate owners signified a weakening of the monarchical principle.[17] Numerous other requests for assistance flowed in from individual nobles and county assemblies throughout East Prussia. After the committee submitted yet another request for help in February 1823, three delegates of the Stände, led by Count Dohna, traveled to Berlin in April to present the case personally to Ministers Schuckmann and Lottum. The delegates requested 3,300,000 taler from the central government to support the landowners and Landschaft of East Prussia. Of that amount, 300,000 would go to cover some of the immediate costs incurred by noble estate owners as a result of peasant regulation. The remaining 3 million would go to the Landschaft to be used in two ways: to offset losses suffered by the Landschaft through numerous defaults by debtors, thus strengthening its ability to attract investment; and to allocate loans to estate owners enabling them to improve their estates and diversify production, especially through the introduction of sheep farming.[18] Unwilling to authorize so large an expenditure without closer investigation of the situation in East Prussia, the king approved an advance of 100,000 taler to enable the Landschaft to pay the interest on the mortgage notes (Pfandbriefe) held by investors, and he instructed an economic adviser, August Heinrich von Borgstede, to tour East Prussia and report his recommendations for assistance to the province.[19]

Borgstede made a fact-finding tour of East Prussia during the summer of 1823 and painted a grim picture of the conditions of noble estate owners in the province.[20] The crisis, he believed, was caused by the losses suffered during the war, which he set at a total of 98,547,737 taler, against which compensation given the province totaled only 21,972,584 taler. In addition, the crisis was exacerbated by recent poor harvests, the lack of cash, and indebtedness. The Landschaft had lent 10,552,900 taler on 551 estates appraised at 17,317,729 taler. Their net profit, not counting the amount necessary to service their debt, was currently only 824,773 taler, while the interest on their mortgage notes (4 percent) was 422,116 taler, more than half their annual income. Since 1816, 94 of the mortgaged estates had been foreclosed, and 57 of them had been auctioned off for less than

---

[17] Stein, *Die Umwandlung der Agrarverfassung Ostpreussens* 3: 116.

[18] Ibid., 129–30; Mayer, *Das Retablissement Ost- und Westpreussens*, 34; see also Dohna's letter to Schön, *Aus den Papieren* 4: 486–89.

[19] Stein, *Die Umwandlung der Agrarverfassung Ostpreussens* 3: 130; Mayer, *Das Retablissement Ost- und Westpreussens*, 35.

[20] The entire report, dated November 19, 1823, which Mayer was unable to locate, is in the PSK/B-D, Provinz Ostpreussen, Rep. 2, Oberpräsidium, Tit. 40, no. 5, Bl. 16–74.

their appraised value, a loss to the Landschaft of 469,408 taler in capital and interest. In order to avoid even greater losses, the Landschaft had assumed ownership of 8 of these estates. Since 1806, at one time or another, almost half of the estates in the governmental districts of Königsberg and Mohrungen and more than a quarter of those in Angerburg had been sequestered by the Landschaft. By 1823, 103 were sequestered and 714,157 taler in back interest were owed to the Landschaft. The value of the notes (Pfandbriefe) sold by the Landschaft had fluctuated wildly and currently stood at 79.5 percent of their face value.

Borgstede's lengthy report gave scant attention to the problems of small landowners and landless peasantry in East Prussia. Like the government, he was concerned about the fate of large estate owners. If deprived of its wealth, the nobility, he believed, could not perform its proper function in the monarchy. "The landowners, especially large landowners, have had to promote the well-being of almost all other classes of citizens at the sacrifice of their own fortunes, through their own ruin: the well-being of the money holders through high rates of interest . . . ; the well-being of small landowners, peasants, and those bound to service through the elimination of serfdom, payments in kind, and through limitations on all kinds of claims to rents. . . . If these changes have their good side and the most splendid effects—as is certainly the case—it is not just to demand that the large landowners should be impoverished by them, as now is vividly the case."[21] To preserve the large landholders, Borgstede recommended that the government underwrite the Landschaft's payment of interest on mortgage notes for a period of ten years and that the interest collected from noble estate owners be used to enable those who received land in compensation for the dissolution of peasant service to improve their properties. He also recommended a general moratorium on mortgage and interest payments.

Borgstede's recommendations were never acted upon. They encountered substantial criticism, especially from Schön, who believed that Borgstede had underestimated the costs of his program and that no blanket policy of helping floundering estate owners would work; decisions had to be made on an individual basis. Moreover, he believed that a general moratorium on mortgage payments would destroy the credit of the Landschaft and the province.[22] Schön was given the op-

[21] Ibid., Bl. 49–50, 60.

[22] Schön's commentary on Borgstede's report is found in ibid., Bl. 75–77; additional comments are in Bl. 78–81a. See also Mayer, *Das Retablissement Ost- und Westpreussens*, 107–11.

CHAPTER 8

portunity to formulate his own proposals, for he was named governor of the unified province of Prussia (both East and West Prussia) on April 21, 1824.

Schön's career offers a commentary on the vicissitudes of Prussian politics from the pre–reform era through most of Vormärz.[23] A brilliant student, Schön entered the University of Königsberg in 1788 at the age of fifteen. He studied with Kant and Kraus and acquired from them a liberal perspective that he retained throughout his life. He also was heavily influenced by Fichte, a friend from his early years. Schön's politics were a fusion of freedom and authority that typified the moral sense and the demand for order that lay at the core of the political thought of German idealism. His motto, "You must do that which you ought," was an abbreviation of Kant's categorical imperative. He had little time for the patrimonial theory of the state; the task of the monarchy and administration, he believed, was to make "a true community out of a heretofore shapeless mass of the people." The Prussian disaster of 1806 served as a constant reminder of the weakness of a cold and indifferent administration; in 1838, he commented, "Of how little value is a lukewarm people that has been neutralized by a bureaucracy and by lordly rights was shown by the year 1806, when the enemy went from one end of Prussia to the other."[24]

After entering state service, Schön rose quickly; Stein recognized his keen intelligence and drew him into the upper ranks of policy advisers. Schön, it should be recalled, drafted the outline for the Emancipation Edict of 1807; he also wrote Stein's *Political Testament*, outlining the statesman's political ideas for the reform.[25] That Schön never obtained a high ministerial post was due in part to Frederick William III's lack of confidence in him; he considered Schön intellectually arrogant and too independent.[26] After the conservatives gained control of the court in the early 1820s, there was little chance of Schön's being called to Berlin. That he did not attain a position commensurate with his ability embittered Schön and made him privately critical of the reformers with whom he had worked so closely. Although socially conservative, Schön always remained politically liberal, occupying the liberal edge of the political mainstream. As the mainstream moved to the right in the 1820s, he moved with it, but always stayed on the left edge.

[23] See the article on Schön, *Allgemeine Deutsche Biographie* (Leipzig, 1891), 32: 781–92; Hans Rothfels, *Theodor von Schön, Friedrich Wilhelm IV und die Revolution von 1848* (Halle, 1937). See also Leonard Krieger, *The German Idea of Freedom* (Boston, 1957), 167.

[24] Cited in Rothfels, *Theodor von Schön*, 12.

[25] See chapter 4.

[26] *Allgemeine Deutsche Biographie* 32: 783.

When Prussian political opinion grew more liberal in the 1840s, Schön emerged as a liberal spokesman within the administration. His liberal views brought him into conflict with Frederick William IV, and he resigned his governorship of the province of Prussia in 1842.[27]

The serious economic crisis of the 1820s in Prussia gave Schön the opportunity he had long sought to liberate himself from the many shackles of the bureaucratic system developed by Hardenberg. He had always chafed at the weak position of the provincial governors in this system; on more than one occasion, as we have noted, he worked to win approval for a system of provincial ministers, men who were familiar with the provinces they directed, not merely cogs in the bureaucratic machine. Confronted with the task of guiding the combined provinces of Prussia through the agrarian crisis, Schön acquired the freedom he believed provincial governors should have. In writing of his appointment and his handling of the crisis, he stated the following:

> The control of the administrative authorities must be secondary for him [the provincial governor]; they will be led to a great extent by the ministerial departments and, if the provincial governor limits himself merely to these, he will be only "a tinkling cymbal and a sounding brass." He will be thoroughly poisonous for the province, however, if he does not oppose with all his strength ministerial orders that are not appropriate for the province or which would cripple its good spirit. ... The provincial governor is obliged above all other servants of the king to keep the faith of the inhabitants of his province. He is called and duty bound above all other royal servants to appeal directly to the throne and to risk his own political existence when he sees some measure that is contrary to his task. The lack of personal independence is not good in any public servant and can never bear good fruit for the sovereign, but with a provincial governor, it is a sin against the Holy Ghost that can never be forgiven in this life or in the hereafter.[28]

Schön, who had declared in 1807 that it was a matter of indifference to the state who owned a particular estate, was not at all indifferent to the impending transfer of landownership in Prussia. It was his purpose, he declared, "to ameliorate the threatening misfortune of a significant transfer of landownership" and "to preserve the most important families of the nation." In appealing to the ministry for 3.5 million taler to support Prussian landowners, Schön admitted, "The purpose of the support is less economic than political: it is to sustain, wherever

---

[27] Rothfels, *Theodor von Schön*, 108ff.; see chapter 9.
[28] Schön, *Aus den Papieren* 3: 80.

possible, the old families of estate owners." According to Count Dohna, the director of the Landschaft in 1824, it was quite possible that two-thirds (about 370) of the estates mortgaged through the Landschaft would go under unless given assistance. The danger, he declared, was that unsalvageable estates would destroy the credit of the Landschaft and thereby damage the estates that remained relatively healthy. Schön formulated his plans accordingly. Assistance would go only to estates that were mortgaged at less than three-quarters of their assessed value, unless "political considerations" dictated otherwise. He would try to save only those that could be rescued. Families whose estates could not be rescued would be given pensions to allow them to maintain a minimal standard of living appropriate for their station. Determined that "no one would receive something as a gift," Schön insisted that the money advanced to estate owners be used to improve agriculture, especially through the purchase of high-quality merino sheep.[29]

The government approved Schön's plan and authorized 3 million taler for support of the Landschaft and the landowners of the Prussian province.[30] Actually, more than that was spent. At the final accounting, in 1834, Schön reported spending a total of 3,889,297 taler, of which 1,521,715 taler went directly to estate owners in the form of 4 percent loans whose repayment was to begin five years after they were granted. An additional 101,458 taler were granted for pensions for noble families who lost their estates. After the first year of the program, Schön reported that assistance had been given to 189 estate owners; only 22 estates were judged to be beyond saving. By the end of 1827, he reported assistance to 595 landowners in East Prussia and 48 in West Prussia. Of those who received assistance in West Prussia, 38 were nobles; in East Prussia about 400 were owners of kölmische estates. The figures are misleading, however; all of those receiving help in West Prussia owned noble estates, whereas only the largest kölmische estates qualified for support—more than 2,000 were excluded. Even then, the grants to these large peasant holdings were small, averaging 150 taler, with some as small as 20 taler. Important nobles received enormous sums: Farenheid, 46,000 taler; Count Dohna, 51,250 taler; and Borke, 61,424 taler. In some doubtful cases, Schön

[29] It was already the policy of the government to assist noble estate owners with the cost of peasant regulation. See PSK/B-D, Provinz Ostpreussen, Rep. 2, Oberpräsidium, II, 3472, Bd. 2, Bl. 7a, 8, 15–17, 122. For Schön's comments and recommendations, see Mayer *Das Retablissement Ost- und Westpreussens*, 43–47, 107–11; Schön, *Aus den Papieren* 3: 79; Stein, *Die Umwandlung der Agrarverfassung Ostpreussens* 3: 135ff.

[30] Mayer, *Das Retablissement Ost- und Westpreussens*, 111–14.

allowed the estates to be foreclosed, then provided the family with the means of repurchasing their property. Some nobles, unable to persuade Schön that they could survive, won the intercession of the king; thus the Countess von der Groeben received 30,000 taler over Schön's objection. Schön was correct; by 1838, the family had lost all of its estates.[31]

Despite all of this support, a significant number of noble families lost their estates. In his study of Schön's rebuilding of the East Prussian economy, Edward Mayer claims that between 1824 and 1834, 320 estates in East Prussia were foreclosed.[32] This would indicate that roughly 40 percent of the 551 estates Dohna had reported as mortgaged in the Landschaft in 1824 went under. Although less than the two-thirds that Dohna had feared, the number was still significant. The archives contain statistics for East Prussia that deal with a somewhat different time frame, although they seem to verify Mayer's information. The figures in table 2 show that in 1806 the Landschaft held mortgages on 888 estates, of which 195 had been forced into sale and 249 sold voluntarily. In addition, 66 estates were currently being forced into auction, so that a total of 510 (57.4 percent) estates had changed hands during the twenty-three-year period. Only 42.6 percent remained in the hands of the family who had owned them in 1806.

Table 3 shows that the chief beneficiaries of this transfer of landownership were commoners. These statistics, too, are broken down by administrative districts of the Landschaft; unfortunately, the report from Angerburg fails to distinguish between the large peasant, kölmische, estates and the noble estates owned by commoners; so these

---

[31] Ibid., 50–52, 115–17. Schön's decisions were made individually, according to his estimate of the family. He opposed giving assistance to the Groebens because some of their debt came from recent purchases of estates, not as a result of war damage or costs incurred in the regulation of peasants. DZA II, Rep. 2.2.1, no. 30404, Bl. 125. The pensions he approved averaged 300 to 400 taler annually and were granted usually on the basis of the family's standing and reputation. About a von Schleinitz, for whom Schön recommended no direct support to preserve his estate and only a modest pension, Schön wrote: "The reputation of the man is not very favorable because of the various ways he has endeavored to become rich, and that of his wife is very poor because of major immorality." For a full record of the support offered noble familites and Schön's comments, see DZA II, Rep. 2.2.1, nos. 30355, 30356, 30402, 30404, 30405, 30406; for the similar support offered to noble estate owners in the other provinces, although nowhere on the scale of Prussia, see DZA II, Rep. 2.2.1, nos. 30382 (Brandenburg), 30415 (Pomerania), 30420 and 30422 (Posen), 30432 and 30435 (Silesia).

[32] Mayer, *Das Retablissement Ost- und Westpreussens*, 57. In the period from 1829 to 1831, 111 estates in East and West Prussia were forced into sale. See Koselleck, *Preussen zwischen Reform und Revolution*, 512; Jordan, *Die Entstehung*, 26.

TABLE 2
Changes of Ownership of Estates Mortgaged through East Prussian Landschaft, 1806–1829

Landschaft district	Estates mortgaged in 1806	Estates mortgaged in 1806 and in different hands in 1829		Estates facing auction in 1829	Total number of estates with changed ownership	Number of estates under original ownership
		Through forced auction	Through voluntary sale			
Königsberg	382	77	85	31	193	189
Mohrungen	261	59	87	16	162	99
Angerburg	245	59	77	19	155	90
TOTAL	888	195	249	66	510	378

SOURCE: PSK/B-D, Province Ostpreussen, Rep. 2, Oberpräsidium, Tit. 22, no. 46, Bl. 51.

TABLE 3
Transfer of East Prussian Estates to Commoners, 1806–1829

	Estate ownership in 1806		Estate ownership in 1829	Newly registered estates, 1829	Total estate ownership in 1829	
	No.	%			No.	%
Landschaft Königsberg						
Noble	249	75.7	177	9	186	48.3
Burgher	41	12.5	111	29	140	36.4
Kölmer	39	11.8	37	20	57	14.8
Possessed by Landschaft	—	—	2	—	2	0.5
TOTAL	329	100.0	327	58	385	100.0
Landschaft Mohrungen						
Noble	157	74.8	106	—	106	40.6
Burgher	26	13.3	73	—	73	28.0
Kölmer	25	11.9	25	49	74	28.4
Possessed by Landschaft	—	—	8	—	8	3.0
TOTAL	210	100.0	212	49	261	100.0
Landschaft Angerburg						
Noble	84	57.9	48	6	54	22.4
Burgher	61	42.1	83	92	175	72.6
Possessed by Landschaft	—	—	12	—	12	5.0
TOTAL	145	100.0	143	98	241	100.0

SOURCE: PSK/B-D, Provinz Ostpreussen, Rep. Oberpräsidium, Tit. 22, no. 46.

figures are misleading and render a composite picture of the province impossible. The only conclusion one can draw from the Angerburg figures is that, in 1829, the nobility owned 36 percent fewer estates registered in the Landschaft than in 1806. The figures from the districts of Königsberg and Mohrungen are more revealing. If one ignores the kölmische estates, the statistics show that in 1806, nobles owned 85.9 percent of estates mortgaged in the Königsberg district of the Landschaft and 84.9 percent of those mortgaged in Mohrungen; by 1829, the share of estates owned by nobles had fallen to 57 percent in Königsberg and 59.2 percent in Mohrungen.

The transfer of landownership in the other provinces was not as sudden or dramatic but as inexorable as in East Prussia. The rural credit institute of the nobility in Posen received 200,000 taler in assistance from the king; nevertheless, of the 1,405 noble estates in the province, 172 had been forced into sale by 1828. In Pomerania, the situation of the noble estates was so bad between 1817 and 1829 that at one time or another more than one-third were sequestered and administered by the Landschaft.[33] Between 1811 and 1831, 369 Silesian estates failed and had to be sold at auction.[34] A significant number of these estates were purchased by commoners; as Schissler concluded, "Never before and never again were the chances so favorable for a wealthy bourgeoisie to buy its way into the possession of landed estates."[35] Even after the agrarian crisis, the shift of land toward nonnobles continued. By 1857, only 7,023 (56.9 percent) of the noble estates in the monarchy remained in the possession of nobles.[36]

[33] Koselleck, *Preussen zwischen Reform und Revolution*, 512.

[34] Ziekursch, *Hundert Jahre*, 327, 343, 385ff. See also "Ueber den gesunkenen Preis schlesischer Güter," *Schlesische Provinzial Blätter* 97 (1833): 15–34; for a more liberal response to this article, advocating modern methods of agriculture, see ibid., 288–96.

[35] Schissler, *Preussische Agrargesellschaft im Wandel*, 166.

[36] Jordan, *Die Entstehung*, 26. Jordan also shows in the following table that the average estate changed hands twice during the thirty-year period:

Total Transfers of Estates in the Years 1835–1864

Province	Number of Estates	Number transferred hereditarily	Number sold voluntarily	Number of forced sales	Total of ownership transferred	Percentage of total
Brandenburg	1,852	1,176	1,916	135	3,227	174
East Prussia	1,707	1,042	2,335	121	3,498	204
Pomerania	1,802	1,272	2,299	160	3,731	207
Posen	1,548	1,185	1,816	442	3,443	222
Silesia	3,085	1,904	4,777	407	7,088	229
Saxony	1,287	947	1,144	69	2,160	167
Westphalia	490	377	117	13	507	103
TOTAL	11,771	7,903	14,404	1,347	23,654	200.9

CHAPTER 8

Although it is clear that the nobility's monopoly on the ownership of landed estates was broken during these years, it does not follow that its control of land declined proportionately or that its influence on the countryside was passing rapidly into the hands of the middle class. Commoners purchased a large number of estates, but they tended to be small. For example, as late as the 1880s, the nobility still controlled 68 percent of the estates of more than 1,000 hectares and almost all of the large latifundia of more than 5,000 hectares. Of the 159 such large estates in the eastern provinces in the 1880s, only 10 were owned by commoners.[37] Moreover, it would be equally misleading to assume that all commoners who purchased noble estates were typically middle class. The data are very incomplete, but of 59 cases of land transfers in East Prussia between 1806 and 1829 in which the occupation of the commoner buying a noble estate can be ascertained, 12 were military officers, 20 were former managers of royal estates, 18 were civil servants, 1 had been the owner of a smaller, non-noble estate, and 2 had formerly leased smaller non-noble estates. Only 3 of the 59 were businessmen.[38] Although the pattern for provinces such as Brandenburg, with their proximity to Berlin, might reveal a higher percentage of businessmen, a fair assumption would be that most of those commoners who purchased noble estates early in the century were those whose style of life and values differed very little from those of the Junkers whom they displaced. Yet the nobility's fear that the noble estates, with all of their privileges, would fall into unworthy hands could not be overcome. Even a fairly moderate noble like Ernst von Bülow-Cummerow harbored exaggerated fears about the transfer. "If someone is a chimney sweep today, tomorrow a noble estate owner, and the day after tomorrow appoints the village pastor, then something is very wrong," he charged.[39]

Despite the resentment, at times open hostility, of the nobility toward new, non-noble estate owners and efforts to differentiate itself from them, by the 1830s a new aristrocracy on the land, noble and non-noble, was coming into existence. The "pseudo-feudalization" of

[37] Hans Rosenberg, "Die Pseudodemokratisierung der Rittergutsbesitzerklasse," in his *Machteliten und Wirtschaftskonjunkturen*, Kritische Studien zur Geschichtswissenschaft, 31 (Göttingen, 1978), 88.

[38] PSK/B-D, Provinz Ostpreussen, Rep. 2, Oberpräsidium, Tit. 22, no. 46. Not all commoners had an easy time acquiring a noble estate. For the sad tale of two estate purchasers, see Robert M. Berdahl, "Junker and Burgher, Conflicts over the Purchase of *Rittergüter* in the Early Nineteenth Century," in *Mentalitäten und Lebensverhältnisse, Festschrift für Rudolf Vierhaus* (Göttingen, 1982), 160–72.

[39] Ernst von Bülow-Cummerow, *Preussen, seine Verfassung, seine Verwaltung, sein Verhältniss zu Deutschland* (Berlin, 1842), 96.

the non-noble estate owners was often accompanied, as noted, by pretentious appropriations of some symbols of nobility. On the other hand, the *"embourgeoisment"* of the nobility also advanced in these years with the progress toward capitalist agriculture. An uneasy alliance began to form between the two groups. In the 1840s, the government tried to encourage it; the revolution of 1848 strengthened it; and the depression of the 1870s and 1880s confirmed it. Just as the new aristocracy was built from a fusion of the old nobility and the new estate owners, so too were the governmental policies toward this class a mixture of traditional, ständisch attitudes and liberal economic assumptions. An estate could be created by combining peasant lands or by purchasing either a part of a former noble estate or a royal estate. When, for example, a commoner applied to have his newly acquired estate registered as a noble estate (a *Rittergut*, with all associated privileges), he was personally investigated to ascertain whether he was *Standesfähig*, worthy of being a member of the First Estate. To ensure that persons of poor reputation did not easily acquire access to the First Estate, any estate designated as a noble estate after such an investigation generally received this designation only for the lifetime of the purchaser or for as long as he owned the estate. Since the value of a noble estate was greater than one lacking such a privilege, this proviso also discouraged estate speculation. Thus, the decision was made on personal and ständisch grounds. On the other hand, no estate could be designated as a noble estate unless it had a minimum net profit of 500 to 2,000 taler per year, depending on the province.[40] Old noble estates remained noble as long as they were not subdivided, regardless of their size or annual profit; new estates could be designated as noble only if they were of a certain size and income. The decision thus was also made on economic grounds. These criteria were used in drawing up the lists of estates eligible for membership in the First Estate of the provincial diets. Reinhart Koselleck, who has so brilliantly described this borderland between feudalism and capitalism in the Prussian Vormärz, succinctly summarized the process as follows: "The origins were determined by ständisch norms, the future by economic norms."[41]

---

[40] In Posen, where small estates were to be discouraged, and where the Germanization of the class of estate owners was favored, the king rarely granted requests to have an estate acknowledged as a noble estate. See Irene Berger, *Die Preussische Verwaltung des Regierungsbezirks Bromberg (1815–1847)* (Cologne and Berlin, 1966), 94–96.

[41] Koselleck, *Preussen zwischen Reform und Revolution*, 516–21; quotation from 520. In his administrative report of 1829, Schön reported that the fusion of commoners and nobles in East Prussia was facilitated by the presence of kölmische estates. "East Prussia has the advantage, above all other provinces of our state, that the kölmische Stand is a

CHAPTER 8

The government's policy toward its rural population during the depression can also be seen as a mixture of traditional mercantilism and new economic liberalism, for it provided massive protective aid to large landowners while it generally followed a laissez-faire policy toward the small holders and landless peasants. Of the 3.9 million taler pumped into East Prussia during the depression, only slightly more than 50,000 were used for public works projects for poor relief.[42] In some regions of the monarchy, the condition of lowly farm laborers was desperate. In the northeast corner, with its heavily Lithuanian population, an exceptionally cold winter in 1822–1823 froze one-third of the potato stocks; a warm spell in February was followed by bitter cold, with snow and freezing weather lasting until late April. The shortage of fodder forced peasants to feed seed grain to their livestock. According to one report, "in many places, the roofs have been dismantled in order to save the lives of the animals with old straw."[43] The landowning peasantry could not provide employment for the landless. Finally, the government offered assistance by putting men to work building roads. A portion of the earnings from such public works was usually paid in grain from the military magazines.

At least one instance of peasant unrest as a result of deprivation during the depression took place. The provincial report for East Prussia in 1829 contained the following comment:

> The landless peasants [Instleute], who became unruly as a result of their impression that they were to receive 14 morgen of land as their own property, were quieted by the measures undertaken. According to the opinion of the Landrat, the basic reason for this arrogant demand lay in the unemployment of this class, for the impoverished estate owner is unable to give any employment and the peasants whose land has been separated are unable to help, for they need less service; meanwhile the population of this class is constantly growing.[44]

The plight of the peasant with a small plot of land was also severe. He could not afford to pay taxes without selling part of the land at a depressed price. Small holdings became smaller. Landräte and other officials frequently called for a reduction in taxes or the deferring of

---

means of connecting the noble and the non-noble. The 'good gentry' of England is brought in East Prussia by the kölmische Stand." PSK/B-D, Provinz Ostpreussen, Rep. 2, Oberpräsidium II, 1969, Bl. 52–53.

[42] Mayer, *Das Retablissement Ost- und Westpreussens*, 116.

[43] Cited in Engels, *Die Preussische Verwaltung*, 106.

[44] PSK/B-D, Provinz Ostpreussen, Rep. 2, Oberpräsidium, Tit. 40, no. 10, vol. 4, Bl. 288. The measures undertaken were not described.

their collection.⁴⁵ Schön, with the pure logic of economic liberalism, considered such proposals unsound; they constituted a "handout" that would weaken the moral fiber of the peasantry. He insisted that they work off their tax debt through employment in public works. The landlords themselves opposed this because it would draw the peasantry away from tending the fields, so agriculture would suffer. Finance Minister Friedrich von Motz also objected to Schön's policy of compelling peasants to work on public projects in lieu of taxes; with some irony, he referred to this policy of the author of the Emancipation Edict as tantamount to the reintroduction of serfdom.⁴⁶ Similarly, Schön opposed all efforts to provide small peasants with cheap credit to hold on to or improve their holdings. When a proposal for a credit institute for small peasants reached the provincial diet in 1832, Schön opposed it, saying: "Educated people propose to exclude the small and uneducated landowner from real credit because without this exclusion, he would soon be overburdened with too much debt and ruined; it would be much better to limit the credit of the small landowners far more than has been heretofore the case." Similarly, the efforts to launch Landschaften for peasants in Pomerania and Silesia were beaten back in 1833.⁴⁷

In 1818, when the General Commissions first began the work of settling conflicting claims between lords and peasants in Prussia, Count Dohna protested to the king that such officials would intrude upon the "happy patriarchal relationship" that existed on the land. Dohna insisted that the settlements be left for the lords themselves to work out with their peasants. Drawing once again from the arsenal of the paternalist ideology, Dohna continued:

> For we are filled with great inner distress as we see that an alien system increasingly endeavors to dissolve those old bonds of these honorable relationships that we have inherited from our forefathers and to set in their place the machinery of lower civil officials. We confidently believe that even the most noble and just official . . . will never be able to perceive the interest of the common man with the warmth and vital sympathy which he has found so often in his lord through the centuries.⁴⁸

---

⁴⁵ See the requests for assistance, ibid., Bl. 4–8.

⁴⁶ Mayer, *Das Retablissement Ost- und Westpreussens*, 90–92.

⁴⁷ Cited in ibid., 96; on Pomerania and Silesia, see Jordan, *Die Entstehung*, 97; Helmut Bleiber, *Zwischen Reform und Revolution: Lage und Kämpfe der schlesischen Bauern und Landarbeiter im Vormärz, 1840–1847* (Berlin, 1966), 28–30.

⁴⁸ Cited in Stein, *Die Umwandlung der Agrarverfassung Ostpreussens*, 56–57.

CHAPTER 8

Acts of paternalism were rare during the depression of the 1820s. Freiherr von Lüttwitz wrote graphic descriptions in the *Schlesische Provinzialblätter* of the suffering of the wage laborers in Silesia and urged lords to clear new lands to employ the growing numbers of landless poor and to build housing for them. "Only in this way can the noble estate owners enter upon the second stage of patriarchal life," he admonished.[49] Few appear to have followed his advice. Many estate owners, themselves about to go under, were undoubtedly incapable of offering much help to their peasants, even if so inclined. Moreover, the large-scale transfer of estate ownership, coupled as it was with the free-market ideology of the reforms, virtually completed the process of dissolution of the basis of paternalism, which had already begun during the estate speculation boom of the late eighteenth century. New estate owners everywhere felt few obligations toward the peasants on the estates they purchased. The peasants of one village, Wachow, wrote the king to praise the charity of their lord, a Franz von Wallhofen, who distributed free grain to ease their hunger.[50] Still, the documented cases of paternalist generosity during this period of hardship were rare for a nobility that had for so long justified its domination with an ideology of paternalism.

The large-scale transfers of landownership broke down more than the basis for the traditional paternalistic ideology of the nobility. The new estate owners, less dominated by tradition, more willing to introduce new agricultural methods, and above all, equipped with fresh capital, led the way in the transformation of Prussian agriculture. In his 1829 report on agricultural conditions in the governmental district of Marienwerder, West Prussia, President Eduard von Flottwell stressed this point. "The numerous noble estates that have been forced into sale," he wrote, "are already to be found in the hands of owners who combine sufficient capital with insight and good intentions; they hold the promise of bringing about a much better status of agriculture on these possessions in the course of a few years."[51] Gradually, the traditional three-field system began to give way to more complex and productive systems of crop rotation. The first stage was usually the introduction of an "improved three-field system," accord-

[49] "Staats- und Landwirtschaftliche Bemerkungen," *Schlesische Provinzial Blätter* 88 (1828): 550. See Lüttwitz's other articles on similar themes, ibid. 89 (1829): 3–9, 135–44, 236–45, 315–24, 413–21.

[50] DZA II, Rep. 2.2.1, no. 30435, Bl. 50–51. I found no other case of outstanding charity mentioned in the archives.

[51] PSK/B-D, Provinz Ostpreussen, Rep. 2, Oberpräsidium, Tit. 40, no. 10, vol. 4, Bl. 25–28.

ing to which fallow fields were planted with forage crops; later, more sophisticated rotation plans were undertaken. It did not happen simultaneously everywhere, and peasants everywhere, lacking the capital or the education, lagged far behind the large estate owners in adopting new methods.[52] Brandenburg was relatively advanced; by 1818, the agronomist Albrecht Thaer reported that most estate owners in the Kurmark had already abandoned the three-field system.[53] In East Prussia, on the other hand, most estates still employed the three-field system as late as 1830, although during the 1830s, the improved three-field system made great headway. Silesia was about as far behind as East Prussia. A report from Posen in 1844 declared that the three-field system was still common there on large estates.[54]

The modernization of Prussian agriculture during Vörmarz was a complex process that involved much more than abandoning most of the three-field system. It depended on a number of highly interrelated factors. For example, the elimination of fallow and planting of "green fallow" crops, such as clover, required a shift to the stall-feeding of cattle, which in turn depended on adequate capital for construction of barns and stalls for the livestock. The shift away from the heavy dependence on cereal grains, whose market had collapsed during the depression, to alternative forms of production, especially high-quality sheep, also required substantial amounts of capital to build up the herds. The shift toward animal husbandry depended on the division and enclosure of the commons, through which the lords received the lion's share of the land, in order to provide fields for the grazing of sheep. Sheep production and wool export increased enormously during the 1820s and 1830s; many saw it as the primary means of surviving the depression.[55] The extensive cultivation of root crops, such as

[52] There were frequent complaints about the backwardness of peasant agriculture. In 1839, for example, in an effort to educate the peasantry on the virtues of modern crop rotation, the government established fifteen model peasant farms in the governmental district of Marienburg, West Prussia. DZA II, Rep. 2.2.1, no. 30168, Bl. 5–10, 12.

[53] *Möglinsche Annalen der Landwirtschaft*, II/3 (1818), 568.

[54] Schön reported that the three-field system still predominated in the late 1820s. DZA II, Rep. 2.2.1, no. 30168, Bl. 1–2. See also Stein, *Die Umwandlung der Agrarverfassung Ostpreussens*, 326–27, 330ff.; Ziekursch, *Hundert Jahre*, 359; Bleiber, *Zwischen Reform und Revolution*, 86–88. In the early 1840s, a specialist on agriculture toured Silesia and reported that it was well behind the other provinces in its methods. See Beckedorff, "Schlesien: Auszüge aus einem Reiseberichte des Directors des Landes-Oeconomie-Collegiums," *Annalen der Landwirtschaft in den Königlich Preussischen Staaten* 6 (1845): 188–266, 366–74. The same volume contains a report on the backward status of agriculture in Posen. Ibid., 161–87.

[55] By far the best and most detailed account of the process by which Prussian agriculture was transformed is Harnisch, *Kapitalistische Agrarreform und Industrielle Revolution*. On

CHAPTER 8

sugar beets or potatoes, was possible only after facilities were developed to process them on the land. The bulkiness of sugar beets or potatoes prohibited their transport over long distances, so sugar refineries and distilleries had to be built in rural areas to transform the produce into transportable and marketable commodities. This, too, required both capital and an entrepreneurial spirit. Between 1841 and 1848, the number of sugar refineries in Prussia increased from 99 to 125; between 1840 and 1850, the amount of sugar beets refined grew from 160,714 tons to 390,845 tons.[56]

Although the age of mechanized and chemical agriculture came primarily after 1850, some mechanization was already under way in Vörmarz. Horse-driven threshing machines, reapers, and some crude sowing machines were utilized. Steam-driven machinery appeared first in the distilleries and sugar refineries before 1848. In addition, improved plows and better draft animals increased the productivity of the soil.[57]

Improved agriculture also depended on indirect assistance from the state. A report on the backward status of agriculture in Posen in 1844 stressed that the shortage of decent roads for the transport of produce had hampered market incentives and retarded the province's development; in many parts of the monarchy, roads were impassable through much of the year.[58] Thus, road construction during the 1820s was not only a means of poor relief, but also a direct contribution to the recovery of agriculture during the depression. Theodor von Schön launched an ambitious program of road construction in East Prussia. Throughout the monarchy, state-built roadways increased be-

---

the introduction of sheep, see Schissler, *Preussische Agrargesellschaft im Wandel*, 169; Ziekursch, *Hundert Jahre*, 323; Jordan, *Die Entstehung*, 18ff. For an example of investment in sheep that paid handsome dividends, see the case of Schön's brother-in-law, Magnus von Brünneck, in Paul Herre, *Von Preussens Befreiungs- und Verfassungskampf: Aus den Papieren des Oberburggrafen Magnus von Brünneck* (Berlin, 1914), 25–27, 460–61. For reports on the increase of sheep farming, see STAP, Pr. Br. Oberpräsidium, Tit. 12, Bd. 356, Bl. 8082. Schön encouraged sheep farming: PSK/B-D, Provinz Ostpreussen, Rep. 2, Oberpräsidium, II, 1969, Bl. 54–55. One official urged the state to support the establishment of woolweaving factories for the wool produced in East Prussia, rather than export it all. Ibid., Rep. 2, Oberpräsidium, II, 3475, 26–47.

[56] A. Kotelmann, *Die preussische Landwirtschaft nach dem amtlichen Quellen statistisch dargestellt* (Berlin, 1853), 186ff.; August Meitzen, *Der Boden und die landwirtschaftliche Verhältnisse des preussischen Staates* (Berlin, 1869), 2: 378–420.

[57] Heinz Haushofer, *Die deutsche Landwirtschaft im technischen Zeitalter*, Deutsche Agrargeschichte, vol. 5 (Stuttgart, 1972), 111–17; Jordan, *Die Entstehung*, 11–13; Meitzen, *Der Boden und die landwirtschaftliche Verhältnisse* 2: 25–86.

[58] See the report on Posen, *Annalen der Landwirtschaft in Königlichen Preussen*, vol. 6 (1845), 178; Jordan, *Die Entstehung*, 19.

tween 1816 and 1846 from 419.75 to 1466.4 Prussian miles (1 Prussian mile equals 7.53 kilometers). By 1844, an additional 113.4 miles of railway had been completed, and 200 miles were under construction.[59] The state endeavored to improve the quality of agricultural education and the dissemination of knowledge of rational agriculture. Scattered throughout the monarchy were five higher technical schools for agriculture and fourteen smaller training schools; these institutions were intended to train persons to farm large estates. For peasants, forty-five model farms taught the application of modern techniques on small holdings. The Edict of September 14, 1811, had ordered the creation of agricultural associations throughout the state; these associations published information on new agricultural techniques, diagnosed problems, and gathered data on agriculture for the government. By 1847, 136 official associations existed, 51 of which had been established since 1841. These were centralized in 17 associations located in almost every governmental district of the state. They had 29,650 members by mid-century.[60] It seems evident that the "culture" that surrounded agriculture in Prussia had become increasingly technical, specialized, and organized in the first half of the century.

All of these efforts succeeded in improving the agricultural yield considerably. Beginning in 1816, the production of grain and potatoes in Prussia climbed steadily. The amount of land devoted to agriculture increased, and the gradual elimination of the three-field system meant that a larger portion of the agricultural land became productive. Moreover, the yield per acre increased impressively, so that the total grain production of Prussia grew from 44 million *Scheffel* in 1805, to 58 million in 1831, and to 68 million in 1843—despite the fact that more land was devoted to other crops.[61]

Although we are accustomed to thinking that agriculture modernization becomes less labor-intensive and therefore releases a labor force to be employed in industrial development, the first stages of such an agricultural transformation are actually much more labor-intensive. Only when agriculture became relatively mechanized did it require less labor. A labor supply became available for industrial work as a

[59] Jordan, *Die Entstehung*, 19–20.
[60] Kotelmann, *Die preussische Landwirtschaft nach den amtlichen Quellen*, 320–25; Meitzen, *Der Boden und die landwirtschaftlichen Verhältnisse* 2: 18–24.
[61] Schissler, *Preussische Agrargesellschaft im Wandel*, 153–57: Ciriacy-Wantrup, in *Agrarkrisen und Stocksspannen*, 52–60, offers statistics on the growth of grain production. On two West Prussian estates, he shows that wheat production increased by 13 percent, rye by 51 percent, barley by 24 percent, and oats by 73 percent per morgen between the first and fifth decades of the century, with the largest jump taking place in the latter period.

result of the agricultural revolution because the increased productivity allowed for a rapid population increase, not because the new methods immediately released large numbers of people from agricultural occupations. Simply abandoning the three-field system, in which roughly one-third of the fields were left fallow each year, increased the amount of land under cultivation by 50 percent. But most other innovations, with the exception of sheep farming, were labor-intensive as well. Stall-feeding of cattle involved much more work than had been the case when livestock were merely allowed to graze on the fallow; fodder had to be brought to the stalls, the dung removed and delivered to the fields. The cultivation of root crops involved much more labor; turnips, used to feed livestock, required much hoeing; potatoes were not grown extensively until an adequate supply of cheap labor, mostly women and children, was available for the arduous job of harvesting them. Clover had to be cut twice per season, dried, and stored. As stall-feeding made straw more valuable, greater care had to be taken in the cutting of grain stalks. Thus, the first stages of the transformation of agriculture required a large supply of labor, often employed quite differently than in the past. All of these changes formed the background for the tense lord-peasant relations of Vormärz and for the growth of the rural proletariat. It was not a radical, but a prominent conservative, who complained in 1846 that the more estate lords "are transformed from small rulers into technicians and chemists," the more the human dimension is lost from work and "socialist and communist ideas" reign among the rural workers. "Rational agriculture threatens the relationships with the working and serving men as these relationships are apparently less important and more and more obscured by machines, by the technical and mercantile operations, and also by the prevailing mercantilism, which inclines men more and more toward the highest profit as the most essential objective."[62]

Lords and Peasants in the Emergence of Capitalist Agriculture

The process of peasant "regulation," as prescribed by the legislations of 1811, 1816, and 1821, was an extremely complicated undertaking, fraught with difficulties and conflicts. It was not yet completed when the revolution of 1848 gave new urgency to the program for emancipating the peasantry. The reasons for the protracted process were numerous. Some nobles, of course, opposed emancipation as an invasion

[62] Carl W. von Lancizolle, *Über Königtum und Landstände in Preussen* (Berlin, 1846), 482.

of traditional rights and dragged their feet about bringing it into effect. Still more aristocrats became alarmed at the prospect of losing their bound labor force at a moment when money required to hire wage labor was in short supply because of the depression; so they, too, worked to delay the settlements. At least in East Prussia, as we have seen, they persuaded the government to move slowly on the process of peasant regulation.

Not all delays, however, were due to the ill will of large landholders. Many legal problems also complicated the negotiations. Peasants existed in many legal categories and they had to demonstrate that their rights as spannfähig, hereditary or nonhereditary leaseholders, reached from a certain date (it varied in the different provinces) in order to be eligible for regulation. These rights were frequently contested by the lords, and all too often written records, reaching back in some cases three-quarters of a century, were sparse. Even when neither political opposition nor legal barriers existed, the technical problems involved in distinguishing the lord's lands from those of the peasants were not inconsiderable. With peasant holdings scattered in dozens of strips in the various large, open fields, exact measurements of the property belonging to each were not a simple matter; surveying the fields of large estates consumed time. Then, too, when all of these matters were no longer contested, disagreements often arose over the translocation of peasants on new lands. Although it can hardly be seen as a social revolution, for so much remained the same in the relationships between dominant landowners and dominated peasantry, the process was, nevertheless, wrenching for Prussian rural society. In 1846, the conservative Carl von Lancizolle commented: "For all concerned it was a morally and economically difficult and troublesome task to surmount, with patience and with undisturbed peaceful harmony, the confusion and uncertainty of the most cumbersome provisions in the still uncompleted process of transforming and dissolving the old relationships."[63]

The "difficult and troublesome task" of peasant regulation was to be the work of nine General Commissions established in 1817. Hardenberg had planned for the establishment of these special authorities, separate from the regular bureaucracy, since 1811. At first composed of three, then four members each, the commissions, as Hardenberg had insisted, comprised "experienced and intelligent men," some of whom would be legal experts and others who would be knowledgeable

[63] Ibid., 326.

CHAPTER 8

"in rational and practical agriculture."⁶⁴ If no amicable settlement could be arrived at voluntarily between a lord and his peasants, the General Commissions had the power to intervene and impose a settlement. The authority of the General Commissions was awesome. They were to examine the disputed rights and claims of lords and peasants on an estate and determine the amount of compensation due the lord for the abolition of compulsory peasant services; they were responsible for deciding how the commons should be divided according to the provisions of the Ordinance of 1821; they were responsible for the execution of all decisions regarding peasant regulation; and, finally, as authorities of the state, they were to assess the new tax liabilities accruing from the new distribution of land.⁶⁵ Because of the substantial authority of the General Commissions and the peasants' innate suspicion of outsiders and persons of authority, the peasants commonly viewed the commissioners as agents of the noble estate owners. Moreover, drawn from the ranks of society far removed from the peasantry, in some cases nobles themselves, the commissioners were most often favorably inclined toward estate owners. As proponents of modern agricultural methods, they often favored larger landholdings and, especially in the division of the commons, distributed the land in a manner they considered most useful to "rational agriculture." The nobility was the chief beneficiary of this distribution. Indeed, the nobility soon learned that it had little to fear from the General Commissions; it grew impatient to have the commissions complete their business. In 1829, Governor Schön spoke of the slow work of the General Commission in East Prussia. "In regard to the division of the commons," he wrote, "this is good, for the awareness here, the knowledge of better methods of farming, and the means of bringing them about as a rule are very limited among the common man. However, with regard to peasant regulation, it is extremely advisable that these matters be completed soon. This is now even the wish of those who earlier were among the strongest opponents of the measures."⁶⁶

The actual process of regulating the peasants of a village was conducted by the special Economic Commissions and their staffs, working under the direction of the General Commission of the province. Gen-

---

⁶⁴ For the instruction to the General Commissions, see Johann Karl Kretschmer, *Concordanz der königlichen preussischen agrarischen Gesetzen* (Danzig, 1840), 267.

⁶⁵ For a discussion of the General Commissions, see Koselleck, *Preussen zwischen Reform und Revolution*, 493–97. Heinz Paul, *Zur Frage der Uebereinstimmung der Produktions-Verhältnisse mit dem Charakter der Produktivkräfte beim Uebergang vom Feudalismus zum Kapitalismus in der Landwirtschaft Preussens* (Wirtschaft. diss., Leipzig, 1957), 191ff.

⁶⁶ PSK/B-D, Provinz Ostpreussen, Rep. 2, Oberpräsidium II, 1969, Bl. 53–54.

erally, the commissioners began by ascertaining which village lands were not liable for regulation: those of Erbzinsbauern or Erbpächter whose better rights gave them proprietary claims to their lands; the lands designated for the school and for the church; and in some cases, those lands allocated to the taverner, the smith, or other artisans in the village. They then examined the peasant claims of eligibility for regulation. The lords frequently challenged the claims of individual peasants or, in some cases, of whole villages, asserting that they were not spannfähig, for example, by claiming that although they served the lords with a span of horses or oxen, they did so not in exchange for their land tenure, but merely as wage laborers; hence, they had no claim to their land as property under the rules of regulation. Or the lords might contest a peasant's claim to hereditary tenure, asserting that his tenure was nonhereditary, so that he would be required to give up one-half of his land instead of one-third of it under the terms of the regulation legislation. Since the norm year for tenure status lay in most cases in the distant past (in East Prussia, for example, it was 1752), and because the lords had often forced hereditary peasants into nonhereditary status since that time, it was difficult for the peasants to prove their cases. In addition, since the division of common lands frequently accompanied the regulation, both lords and peasants submitted their claims to the commons to the special commissions. The lord was also given the opportunity to make his demands for the settlement to the commissioners. He could determine whether the compensation paid by the peasants would be in land or money or both. He did not have the right to demand full monetary compensation from the peasant in a single payment, but, if he wished monetary compensation, he could demand annual rent. In addition, he could demand the consolidation of his holdings, which forced the translocation of the peasants to other lands. He had the right to demand continued service from the peasants during a transition period and in exchange for continued use of his woods by the peasants to gather firewood. Finally, if the peasant died before the regulation was completed, the lord had the right to determine which son would inherit the new proprietary holding.[67]

Obviously, enormous potential for conflict and disagreement surrounded each step of the process. The General Commissions made the initial decisions in all cases of disagreement, but appeals could be made to a review panel and, above that, to a tribunal in Berlin. Ap-

---

[67] This discussion is drawn from Stein, *Die Umwandlung der Agrarverfassungs Ostpreussens* 3: 75–97.

CHAPTER 8

peals were expensive, however, and often beyond the means of peasants. Nevertheless, in 1834 alone, 5,673 appeals of the decisions of the General Commissions were filed.[68] Some of these appeals, of course, came from the lords. For example, Schön's brother-in-law, Magnus von Brünneck, one of the most innovative estate owners in West Prussia, who led the way in sheep farming there during the 1820s, became embroiled in a bitter conflict with the General Commission over the settlements in one of his villages; ultimately, he served fourteen days of fortress detention as a result of the conflict. His peasants, who bitterly resented compulsory resettlement on different lands, requiring them to move to different villages, refused to perform the services they still owed under the terms of the settlement.[69]

As the Brünneck case demonstrates, both lords and peasants were sometimes dissatisfied with the outcome of the regulation process. Peasants were more frequently unhappy with the process, for the commissioners commonly sided with the lords in the disputes. The influence of the lords on the commissioners was immeasurably greater than that of the peasants. While conducting their investigations, the commissioners and their staff generally had to take up residence in the manor house, for there were rarely other suitable accommodations. They ate the lord's food and drank his wine and spent their evenings in his company. "We are betrayed and sold out before they have finished with the soup," was an expression common among the embittered peasants.[70] In a polemic written against the Silesian nobility, Wilhelm Wolff, a son of a Silesian peasant who joined the communist revolutionary movement in 1848, portrayed the behavior of the commissioners in terms that undoubtedly corresponded to the perceptions of many peasants. "If the application for regulation was submitted," he wrote, "the Herr Commissioners and company appeared in the village in order to take up the first negotiations. The lord of the estate, who always understood good business, invited these officials, who now had become the most important of all, to their manor houses, where they were entertained and cultivated. Often the cultivation had begun earlier, and since the nobleman did not spare the champagne when it would achieve something, these patrimonial endeavors were usually successful."[71]

---

[68] Kosselleck, *Preussen zwischen Reform und Revolution*, 495.
[69] Herre, *Von Preussens Befreiungs- und Verfassungskampf*, 30.
[70] Cited in Jordan, *Die Entstehung*, 49.
[71] Wilhelm Wolff, *Die schlesische Milliarde* (Berlin, 1954), 66. On Wolff's early life and conversion to communism, see Walter Schmidt, *Wilhelm Wolff: Sein Weg zum Communisten* (Berlin, 1963).

If the subtle persuasion of the comforts of the manor house were not sufficient, outright bribery sometimes worked. Although the peasants could not hope to compete with the lords in any contest to win the favor of the commissioners through bribes, they sometimes tried. A small holder, a blacksmith with fifteen morgen of land, for example, was reported by Wolff to have given the surveyor a gift of thirty quarts of honey and gained, in return, an extra half-morgen of land.[72] Much of the injustice may have resulted from incompetence as well as dishonesty. This was the judgment of Ludwig Jacobi, a government official in Silesia, who believed that both lords and peasants suffered in the settlements primarily because of the incompetence of the commissioners. He wrote, in a stinging indictment of the settlement process, in 1860:

Whoever has had the opportunity to become acquainted with a large number of cases of peasant regulation by studying the documents will be amazed at the relatively large number of incompetent people who were appointed to the Economic Commissions during the first two decades after the organization of the authorities for the settlements, who were to bring into effect and carry out the most significant legislation in recent history. One can scarcely believe his own eyes when one reads, in the documents, of the manner in which they carried out their offices, chiefly, it appears, to achieve the highest possible fees for themselves. Many believed they satisfied the duties of their offices by holding fruitless, useless, and often completely improper and illegal sessions; of the judicial role of a commissioner, they had, in most cases scarcely any notion.[73]

The process of peasant regulation helped to shatter whatever may have remained of the myth of paternalism in the relationships between lords and peasants. It produced a set of circumstances in which the self-interest of the lords could not be masked by any softening metaphors such as *das ganze Haus*. The lords stood clearly on one side of the issue and the peasants on the other; the lords could not persuade the peasants, or probably even themselves, that their demands for peasant lands, their maximizing of rents, or their plundering of the commons were somehow expressions of fatherly concern. Bitter-

---

[72] Ibid., 68. The inaccuracy of many of the surveys was discovered later when the railroads were being built. Jordan, *Die Entstehung*, 49; Bleiber, *Zwischen Reform und Revolution*, 51.

[73] Ludwig Jacobi, *Der Grundbesitz und die landwirtschaftlichen Zustände der preussischen Oberlausitz in ihrer Entwicklung und gegenwärtiger Gestaltung* (Gorlitz, 1860), cited in Ziekursch, *Hundert Jahre*, 356.

CHAPTER 8

ness grew among peasants who felt cheated in the process, were uprooted, and moved onto new lands and into new villages, whose lords made little effort to provide them with suitable housing or whose lands were too small or too poor to support them independently. A Pomeranian noble estate owner, on signing the regulation document for his village, lamented that he had been forced to regulate his peasants in this manner. One of his peasants replied, "It all comes as a result of Jena, Your Grace. Now you have settled with us; who knows whether our sons will not someday again settle with you Junkers."[74]

These confrontations were important to the developing self-consciousness of the peasantry. Although most were denied, the enormous number of appeals that were filed shows that the peasants had become bolder, more assertive, and more willing to risk the displeasure of the lords. The process revealed to them the arbitrariness of the lords and the one-sided nature of the law, and it left the peasants less awed by authority. An example from Silesia in the early 1840s illustrates this point. The peasants from a village in County Oels signed a petition requesting permission to shoot wild game on the estate for food. The lord summoned the sexton and several other signers of the petition and prevailed upon them to withdraw their signatures; similar efforts with the rest of the signers, however, failed, and the lord forwarded the petition to the Landrat. He in turn, summoned the peasants and reproached them for their effrontery. They responded dryly, apparently unimpressed by his authority, that he need not trouble himself any further with the matter, for they had already filed suit in a court of law.[75]

Newly regulated, proprietary peasants encountered a number of difficulties that threatened their independent existence. Most lords chose to take land from peasants in compensation for the dissolution of the servile bonds, preferring that to a fixed rent, which might lose its value quickly. Rents, however, were calculated on the average income of the land, based on grain prices, over the previous ten years, so that the rents claimed by lords in the early 1820s, on the basis of grain prices ten years earlier, when they were extraordinarily high, had to be paid when prices were exceedingly low. Faced with high rent

---

[74] This is the original of the statement, in dialect: "Dat kummt noch alles van Jena her, Ihr Gnaden. Nu hebben Se sick met us regelirt, wer weet, of sick use Junges nich mal wedder mit Ere Junkers regeliren." Cited in Hartmut Harnisch, "Probleme junkerliche Agrarpolitik im 19. Jahrhundert," *Wissenschaftliche Zeitschrift der Universität Rostock—XXXI Jahrgang* (1972), Gesellschafts- und Sprachwissenschaftliche Reihe, Heft 1, part 2, 100. Also cited in Jordan, *Die Entstehung*, 57.

[75] This case is recounted in Bleiber, *Zwischen Reform und Revolution*, 139.

payments and low grain prices, many peasants fell into arrears and lost their land to the lords anyway. As a result, an increasing number of lords elected to receive their compensation in rents.[76] Moreover, the lords welcomed the monetary payments as a means of transforming all labor on their estates to a wage system.

The absence of cheap credit made it difficult for peasants to pay a lump-sum compensation to the lords. If compelled to borrow money to pay back rents, they had to go to private lenders, whose interest rates averaged 7 to 8 percent, in contrast to the 3 to 4 percent the lords paid the Landschaften. Often peasants borrowed small sums, on which rates were significantly higher; an official of the agricultural department (*Landesökonomiekollegium*) reported that a peasant in Prussia might have to pay up to 35 taler in interest and fees on a loan of only 100 taler. One Landrat reported that it was not at all uncommon for peasants to lose their farms because of debts on only 10 or 20 taler.[77] In the face of government opposition to admitting peasant landowners to the Landschaften or to creating government credit institutes for them, some Landräte worked to establish savings banks that could lend small sums to peasants at reasonable rates; but before 1848, little progress was made.[78]

Agricultural modernization hurt the small, garden-holding peasants and the landless peasants even more. The division of the commons, for example, deprived them of pasture to graze their cows. In 1847, the East Prussian estate owner Farenheid reported that forty years earlier nearly every small holder or landless peasant had owned a cow, but now, not more than one in forty did.[79] The abolition of the three-field system and the introduction of new crops also hurt these small peasants, some of whose income had traditionally been paid as a portion of the harvest. Sheep farming not only took land out of cultivation altogether but required little labor, another blow to agrarian workers. Many new crops were cash crops in which the peasants' share declined or was translated into a lesser cash wage. Machinery also reduced the income of these small peasants; under traditional arrangements, some peasants in West Prussia received $1/11$ of the harvested

[76] Stein, *Die Umwandlung der Agrarverfassung Ostpreussens*, 90; Ziekursch, *Hundert Jahre*, 342, reported the same phenomenon in Silesia.

[77] Jordan, *Die Entstehung*, 50–51.

[78] The East Prussian Landschaft finally approved extending credit to some peasants in 1847. Only those peasants who had achieved "full property rights" and who had land worth 500 taler or more were eligible. PSK/B-D, Provinz Ostpreussen, Rep. 2, Oberpräsidium, Tit. 22, no. 36, Bl. 97ff.

[79] Jordan, *Die Entstehung*, 74; Bleiber, *Zwischen Reform und Revolution*, 48, 68.

grain; when machine threshing was introduced, this portion fell to $1/21$ or $1/22$.[80]

The experience of the Dreschgärtner in German Silesia provides a hint about the fate of such peasants under the pressures of capitalistic agriculture.[81] The Dreschgärtner, it will be recalled, had small plots of land, really only gardens of between four and ten morgen; they performed considerable service for their lord: each was obligated to provide the labor of two persons daily and three persons during the harvest. They received a small daily wage for their work for the lord and, in addition, a portion of the harvest, normally every tenth or fourteenth Scheffel. Some were spannfähig, while many were not. So long as the three-field system existed, the number of Dreschgärtner on an estate was controlled by the amount of land under cultivation by the lord, for an increase in the number of Dreschgärtner would diminish the share that each received for the portion of the harvest allocated to them. Because of the important labor they performed for the lord, noble estate owners in Silesia won, in 1827, a ruling that severely restricted the right of spannfähige Dreschgärtner to apply for regulation.

So long as the traditional system of cultivation continued, especially during the depression when money was short and the grain with which Dreschgärtner were paid was cheap, the lords had little reason to change this arrangement. However, as the harvest yield increased due to improved methods, the earnings of the Dreschgärtner increased correspondingly; when, in the early 1830s, the price of grain also improved, owners chafed at having to give up between 7 and 10 percent of their harvest yield to these peasants. Moreover, as the stall-feeding of cattle was introduced, the harvested straw became more important to the lords, and they resented that portion taken by the Dreschgärtner. By 1838, 153 estates in German Silesia had abandoned the practice of paying Dreschgärtner primarily from the harvest.

Other changes in the system of cultivation brought new problems. When the three-field system was abandoned and fallow fields cultivated, estate owners demanded that Dreschgärtner undertake the cultivation and harvesting of the new fields. The same was true of the new lands added to the lord's domain by the process of peasant regulation or through the clearing of new land. However, the Dreschgärtner were given no part of the harvest from these new lands. They

[80] Jordan, *Die Entstehung*, 65–66.
[81] See the discussions of the Dreschgärtner in Ziekursch, *Hundert Jahre*, 358ff.; Bleiber, *Zwischen Reform und Revolution*, 43–47.

considered this an increase in their work obligations without increase in their income; moreover, they resented the cultivation of fallow fields, which robbed them of valuable grazing rights for their livestock. They responded with passive resistance to the commands of the lords and initiated numerous suits and appeals to the authorities. In 1845, the lords pushed through a decree that made all Dreschgärtner eligible for regulation. Henceforth, they would not receive their traditional portion of the harvest but would be paid largely with daily wages. This represented a significant deterioration in their position; one estate owner in County Oels declared that under the old system, his Dreschgärtner had cost 480 taler per year; after shifting to a wage system the same work was performed for only 370 taler per year.[82] It is significant to note that the ruling of 1845, allowing for the transformation of the Dreschgärtner into wage laborers, applied only in German Silesia; in the Polish region of Silesia, where the peasants had fewer rights and where the old system was still profitable for the lords, the law did not apply.

The situation of similar garden-holding peasants throughout the eastern provinces of Prussia deteriorated during Vormärz. Although their daily wages had always been somewhat less than those received by the day laborers who had no land and no claim on a portion of the harvest, they had been better off because of their garden plots and because the estate owners usually provided them with work throughout the year, in contrast to those daily wage earners who had no assurance of work except during peak seasons. Now, with the estate owners no longer formally bound to provide paternal protection for the peasants in their villages, and because estate owners were interested primarily in maximizing profits and minimizing costs, the small peasants gradually began to slide into the ranks of the daily wage laborers. Even in those areas where they still received a portion of the harvest, their earnings declined. Farenheid reported in East Prussia that the average summer earnings of a Dreschgärtner and his wife had declined from 12 taler and 12 Scheffel of grain in 1805 to only 8 or 10 taler and 8 or 10 Scheffel of grain in 1847.[83]

The conditions of "free" rural workers—those with no land and no long-term contractual relationship with a large estate owner—also worsened during this period. In the late eighteenth century, the population of the landless peasantry was already increasing faster than that of other groups. In the period after 1815, it grew even more rap-

[82] Ziekursch, *Hundert Jahre*, 362.
[83] Jordan, *Die Entstehung*, 66.

CHAPTER 8

idly. To the population's natural growth were added those peasants who had slipped from a position of better status—"regulated" peasants who could not hang on to their new proprietary holdings or small holders who were forced to a poorer existence as wage earners. The swelling numbers of this rural "proletariat" kept wages at a minimum; indeed, the real income of wage laborers in the eastern provinces declined steadily through the 1830s and improved only slightly during the early 1840s.[84] This large mass of rural poor lived a marginal existence. One official commented: "Morally destroyed, lazy, given to drink, mired in stupidity, one must rightly number these unfortunates among the dregs of society." Vagabondage, begging, and crime increased perceptibly among those living on the margin of rural society.[85]

The concern of government officials over the problem of the subdivision of peasant farms must be viewed in the context of this growing body of impoverished, landless farm laborers. Throughout Vormärz, officials worried that the process of peasant regulation would lead to the partitioning of peasant farms with the result that the farms would eventually become too small to support a family and the class of peasant proprietors would disappear. The Edict of September 14, 1811, had expressly granted peasants the right to dispose of their lands as they pleased, once they had undergone the process of regulation and their lands had been separated from those of their lord. In 1823, Minister of Internal Affairs Schuckmann initiated consultations with officials, lessees of royal estates, and ultimately the new provincial diets, on the issue of the parcelling of peasant lands.[86] With the excep-

[84] Anna Neumann, *Die Bewegung der Löhne der ländlichen "freien" Arbeiter im Zusammenhang mit der gesamtwirtschaftlichen Entwicklung im Königreich Preussen gegenwärtigen Umfangs vom Ausgang des 18. Jahrhunderts bis 1850* (Berlin, 1911), especially table 1, opposite p. 400.

[85] See Jordan, *Die Entstehung*, 69. The growth of crime and vagabondage was commonly reported. See, for example, Friedrich August Ludwig von der Marwitz, *Friedrich Ludwig von der Marwitz: Ein märkischer Edelmann im Zeitalter der Befreiungskriege*, ed. Friedrich Meusel, 3 vols. (Berlin, 1908–1913), II/2:446–75. On the growth of crime in Vormärz, see Dirk Blasius, *Bürgerliche Gesellschaft und Kriminalität*, Kritische Studien zur Geschichtswissenschaft, 22 (Göttingen, 1976). For administrative reports on the problem, see STAP, Pr. Br., Oberpräsidium, Bd. 356, 357, Bl. 146, 13.

[86] See Harnisch, "Probleme junkerliche Agrarpolitik," 104. Officials constantly reported their concern over the parcelling of lands. See STAP, Rep. 2, Reg. Potsdam, I Kom, no. 982, Bl. 6–7; see similar reports, ibid., nos. 975, 976, 977, 978, 979. STAP Pr. Br., Rep. 2A, Reg. Potsdam, Abt. I. I P, no. 138, Bl. 195ff., 250, 292, 302, 360ff., for the annual reports of officials constantly concerned with parcelling. DZA II, Rep. 2.2.1, no. 30113, offers an enormous number of documents on the problem. See especially Bl. 3–7, 10–11, 12–14, 17, 19, 27–44, 135–38, 146.

tion of representatives of the peasantry in the provincial diets, everyone favored legislation that would prevent the partitioning of peasant farms below a certain minimal size. Their reasons varied somewhat according to their own interests and their own perceptions of the problems associated with the transformation through which Prussian rural society was passing. Landräte were concerned that the decline of a landowning peasantry would weaken the state by depriving the army of a class from which it recruited its noncommissioned officers; they feared that, in wartime, the absence of prosperous peasants would complicate quartering troops or providing them with adequate forage. Many noble estate owners worried that the subdivision of peasant farms would soon wipe out all of the peasants capable of supporting a team of draft animals, so the entire burden for raising such livestock would fall to the noble estate owners. Three lessees of royal estates, who were active supporters of the agrarian reforms and the modernization of agriculture, offered reasons for restrictions on the subdivision of peasant lands that touched on the deeper concerns that many shared. They blamed the noble estate owners for the problem because the nobles were buying up peasant holdings; they suggested legislation to limit such purchases. But above all, they stressed the dangers for rural society posed by a landless proletariat. As one wrote, "The misery is great, and the decline of the state is certain where the land and soil are held in the hands of a few individuals and the masses are without bread."[87] The prospect of a direct confrontation between rich and poor on the land aroused anxieties that reveal the perceptions of large landowners about the transition of rural society: the continuation of their domination was enhanced by a class of middling peasants serving as a buffer between them and the landless masses. Just as the differentiation of the peasantry had, in the past, worked to prevent the easy development of a common class consciousness, so now was the preservation of a landowning peasantry essential to the continued differentiation of rural society. Observing these divisions in rural society, the social economist Karl Rodbertus wrote in 1849, "These changes in the situation of the landless worker in the peasant villages are the chief reasons for their present agitation. The expression is common among them: 'The division of the commons made the full peasants into noblemen and us into beggars.' "[88] The landowning peasants were still too suspicious and their interests too distinct to make common cause

[87] Cited in Harnisch, "Probleme junkerliche Agrarpolitik," 104.
[88] Cited in Georg F. Knapp, *Die Bauernbefreiung und der Ursprung der Landarbeiter in ältern Preussens*, 2 vols. (Leipzig, 1887), 1: 306.

CHAPTER 8

with noble estate owners, but their interests were also very distinct from those of the landless poor.[89]

As some nobles realized, peasant proprietors were conservative props for the sanctity of landed property. In 1842, an article in *Die Schlesischer Provinzialblätter* stressed this role of the landowning peasant: "If one compares the larger peasant enterprise with those of the smaller noble estates, one finds that the true conservative element is much more sharply expressed in the peasantry than in any other class. The striving of this class to acquire landed property, to hold on to what it has acquired, to enlarge it, and some way to pass it on to a member of the family, is widely acknowledged by everyone."[90]

Despite widespread concern for the parcelling of peasant farms and the repeated demands by officials and estate owners for its limitation, the government did not act immediately. Instead, during the 1830s and 1840s, it constantly collected data on the question. Actually popular perceptions and fears differed widely from reality. The statistics demonstrated that partitioning was not a serious problem.[91] Subdivision was apparently counterbalanced by reconsolidation, producing a relatively constant number of peasant farms. Nevertheless, acquiescing to the demands of noble estate owners, the government issued a decree on January 3, 1845, that imposed some limitations on the subdivision of peasant holdings.[92]

Most of the legislation issued during the 1830s and 1840s corresponded to the interests of the landholding aristocracy. A measure promulgated on January 31, 1845, for example, undermined the Dissolution Ordinance of 1821, providing for the abolition of the service of those peasants with the best proprietary claims to their lands, the Erbzinsbauern and the Erbpächter. According to the ordinance, their service obligation could be terminated either by a rent settlement paid over a number of years or by a lump-sum settlement. The 1845 amendment eliminated the option of rent payments as compensation.[93] Since few peasants possessed the capital necessary for a single

---

[89] Harnisch suggests a deliberate effort of the noble landowners to seek the alliance of peasant proprietors as early as the 1820s. I think the mutual suspicions were too great for that to have been a very widespread consideration among the Junkers.

[90] E. Heinrich, "Der schlesische Bauer," *Schlesische Provinzial Blätter* 116 (1842): 516–26. Heinrich declared that the daily wage laborers brought "all the dangers of the factory workers with them and are therefore not to be wished for."

[91] See the report from 1837, STAP, Pr. Br. Rep. 54, Bd. 23, Bl. 14ff. See also Harnisch, "Probleme junkerliche Agrarpolitik," 106.

[92] At least one administrative report claimed that the law put an end to subdivision. STAP, Pr. Br., Rep. 2A, Reg. Potsdam. Abt. I, I P, no. 138, Bl. 360.

[93] *Gesetz-Sammlung, 1845*, 93. Koselleck, *Preussen zwischen Reform und Revolution*, 523–24.

cash payment, the measure effectively curtailed the abolition of service by these peasants.

Throughout this period of the restoration, the nobility retained most of its traditional "feudal rights" over the peasantry. Indeed, its exploitation of these rights in the transformation of agriculture was a characteristic feature of the Prussian transition to capitalism. For example, despite the bitter opposition of peasants, the Silesian nobility retained the *Laudemien*, the obligation of each new peasant owner to pay the lord a fee, usually 10 percent of the value of the land, whenever acquiring new land, whether through purchase or inheritance.[94] As land transfers became more common and the price of land increased again after the depression, this became an onerous burden for the peasantry and the source of capital for the nobility. Other fees caused similar irritations.[95] The *Sporteln*, court costs associated with every form of transaction that required a legal registration or certification, enriched the patrimonial judges and hurt the peasants; *Schutzgeld*, paid by the poorest peasants to offset the police and judicial costs of criminal investigations, not only was an oppressive tax, but, as one critic said, "it made an entire class of citizens into presumptive criminals."[96] New burdens fell on the peasants also as a result of the agrarian legislation; with the division of the commons, for example, many peasants lost their rights to gather firewood from the lord's woods, except in exchange for a fee. As the value of wood increased substantially during this period, so did the fees, and, it should be added, the cases of "wood theft."[97]

Equally hated by the peasantry, and of little economic value to the lords, was the preservation of the lord's hunting privilege. As suggested earlier, its preservation acquired symbolic importance for the lords as a residue of the feudal past as well as a source of pleasure. But in Vormärz, the hunting privilege also acquired great symbolic significance for the peasants; for them, it was a flagrant example of oppressive privilege. They had difficulty in recovering adequate compensation for damage to their crops caused by the lords in pursuit of game, so the hunting privilege actually posed a threat to the survival of the marginal peasant. In addition, because the peasant could be punished for killing wild game that foraged in his fields, the exclusive hunting privilege offered evidence that the lord cherished his game and his pleasure more than he did his peasants.

The retention of these "feudal rights" by the owners of noble estates

---

[94] See chapter 2.
[95] Bleiber, *Zwischen Reform und Revolution*, 34.
[96] Ibid., 64–65.
[97] Ibid., 45. See Blasius, *Bürgerliche Gesellschaft und Kriminalität*, 46–49.

CHAPTER 8

points up the contradiction that characterized Prussian society from the reforms to the revolution of 1848 and, to some extent, even after. The reforms were ostensibly based on the principles of freedom of property and freedom of persons. But neither principle was achieved by the 1840s, and their application had always been carried out differentially in the interest of the large estate owners. Most of the peasantry, though free persons, obtained no property rights whatsoever; moreover, they no longer had any claim on the paternal protection of their lord and lost their rights to a share of the commons, although most of their service obligations remained intact. Their traditional forms of compensation—which had included housing, food, firewood—were gradually replaced by seasonal wages; as a result, they slipped steadily into the ranks of a marginal rural proletariat. Those peasants who did acquire property rights to their land found those rights hedged about by the residue of feudal obligations. Many still owed their lords an assortment of services and rents that inhibited the free transfer of land; and in an evident violation of the principle of free property rights, they even had to watch helplessly as their crops were destroyed to satisfy the lord's exclusive sport of hunting. The state contradicted the principle of free property when it crippled the peasants' ability to borrow against their land, while, in a time of crisis, it provided substantial financial assistance to the owners of large estates. The freedom of property and of person implied the free exchange of property among persons. But that was never achieved because neither persons nor property was considered equal before the law; certain categories of persons were not allowed to own some categories of property, while a few forms of property, namely noble estates, were endowed with privileges such as police and judicial power that not only added to their market value, but gave them an edge in the process of agricultural modernization. By the 1840s, these contradictions between the structure of authority on the land, still largely in the hands of the landowning nobility, and the thrust of rural society, generated by capitalist agriculture, became difficult to overcome.

Lord and Peasant Confrontations in the "Hungry Forties"

The disparity between the capitalist impulse, reflected in the reforms and the subsequent transformation of agriculture, and the survival of the precapitalist, personal forms of authority was most obvious in the village community. Although the land-holding aristocracy dominated the institutions of the county, province, and the central government, the cutting edge of social change in rural Prussia was felt more keenly in the village community, and it was there that the confrontations between lords and peasants took place in the 1840s. In order to understand the basis of this conflict, it is necessary to examine how the social and economic changes interacted with the structure of the village.

As we know, Stein had intended to reform village government in a way that would complement the Emancipation Edict, similar to the manner in which the City Ordinance corresponded to the changing social and economic conditions in the towns. But neither he nor Hardenberg succeeded in doing so.[98] Several drafts of a new village ordinance (*Gemeindeordnung*) were circulated between 1815 and 1820, but nothing came of them. It was decided to postpone the introduction of a new village ordinance first until the provincial and county ordinances had been secured, then until the regulation of the peasantry was completed. Changes were made in the structure of village government in the western provinces, but in the eastern provinces everything remained as before. This meant that the power of the estate owner remained completely intact; he controlled village affairs through his patrimonial police and courts. During the 1830s, several drafts of communal ordinances circulated through the government, but they encountered important opposition, especially from Minister of Internal Affairs Gustav von Rochow, and they remained stillborn. During the following decade, the issue was discussed frequently, but without resolution before the revolution of 1848.[99]

Changes in agricultural production altered the fundamental structure of social relations in the village community. The elimination of the three-field system and the separation of the estate lands from those of the peasants did away with the *Flurzwang*, according to which all the strips of the large open fields had to be farmed in unison. In a long memorandum, written in 1847, Wilhelm Adolf Lette, one of the most liberal Prussian officials and an expert on agricultural affairs, wrote of the changes in village structures: "The common interests

---

[98] See chapter 4.

[99] For a general consideration of communal governance, see Friedrich Keil, *Die Landgemeinde in den östlichen Provinzen Preussens und die Versuch, eine Landgemeindeordnung zu schaffen*, Schriften des Vereins fur Sozialpolitik, 43 (Leipzig, 1890); Dorothee Mussgnug-Stürner, *Landgemeinde und Untertänigkeit: Zur preussischen Verfassungsentwicklung vom Erlass der Allgemeinen Landrecht bis zum Jahre 1842* (phil. diss., Heidelberg, 1971). For evidence of the discussion of the communal structure in the government during Vormärz, see STAP, Pr. Br., Rep. 2A, Reg. Potsdam, 1 P, no. 137, Bl. 242–43; ibid., no. 138, Bl. 65–68, 141ff., 233ff.; STAP, Pr. Br. Rep. 2 A, Reg. Potsdam, 1 Komm, no. 53, esp. Bl. 149–50, 159, 167, 168–69, 184, 249–64, 325, 332; STAP, Pr. Br., Oberpräsidium, Bd. 993, Bl. 1–4, 22–35.

CHAPTER 8

which held the community together, the subject of its common counsels and decisions, resided in the communal economy and its attributes: protecting the common fields and meadows, the common pastures . . . , often even the relationship of communal service and dues of members of the village community or also entire classes of the community with the noble landlord." Now these relationships as well as the village community's own economic forms, together with those forms of common life that had developed out of them for more than a thousand years, Lette maintained, were partly changed, partly in the process of dissolution.[100]

With peasant holdings separate and estate lands consolidated, the communal nature of agriculture gave way to a more individualized form of production. With the division of the commons, another communal interest disappeared. Regulation forced some of the peasants to move to new villages; the increase of individualized, private holdings weakened a sense of communal interest. The shifts of property rights, the movement of people, the growth of the numbers of the propertyless, the decline of some villages and the rapid growth of others, all these factors created confusion in the organization of authority in the village.

Lette advocated a revision of village government. He argued that changes in the social and economic relationships in the villages necessitated a new communal organization.[101] As long as serfdom existed, he reasoned, "it seemed natural" that in the "private-law relationships" between a lord and his village subjects, the same person who supervised the labor services in the village would also be responsible for "protecting property and maintaining order." The arbitrary nature of this private authority was tempered by patriarchal concern. With the dissolution of serfdom, however, "the noble estate owner's private-law authority acquired a completely different functional legal shape. It appeared now for the first time . . . most decisively as a purely public law, as part of the political, governmental authority of the state." For this reason, Lette pointed out, the police and judicial powers of estate own-

[100] For the long Lette memorandum, see STAP, Oberpräsidium, Bd. 993, Bl. 59ff. Similarly, the annual report from the office of the governor of Brandenburg in 1841 recognized the disappearance of any true patriarchal relationship, which had been the foundation of the traditional communal governance. STAP, Pr. Br., Oberpräsidium, Rep. 1, Bd. 360, Bl. 25.

[101] See Lette memorandum, STAP, Oberpräsidium, Bd. 993, Bl. 59ff. Lette also wrote *Die ländliche Gemeinde und Polizeiverfassung in Preussens östlichen und mittleren Provinzen* (1848). On Lette himself, see *Allgemeine Deutsche Biographie* 18: 459–60; Harnisch, "Probleme der junkerliche Agrarpolitik," 108.

ers had been drawn more tightly under the control of the state. Nevertheless, abuses often resulted from these important changes. "If we consider the matters objectively and generally," Lette wrote, "experience teaches that estate inspectors, administrators, accountants, and so on all too frequently misuse for the satisfaction of private injuries . . . the public authority that has been delegated to them and that those people who stand in a purely private relationship, as, for example, in the job of supervising wage laborers and servants, all too often mix that relationship with the administration of police authority in an outrageous fashion." In addition, the frequent transfer of estates and "the industrial tendency of the times" had worked "to weaken the moral force of traditions and those patriarchal elements" that provided lords with a common interest in their subjects. As a result of the changing nature of authority, there was "animosity, injustice, and hatred" in the villages; "never before had so many lawsuits and complaints between lords and peasants" developed. Lette found it imperative, therefore, to impose greater constraints on the exercise of police powers in the villages or to sever completely the mixture of public and private authority that was exercised there.

Lette's memorandum was written in the midst of a vigorous public debate about the continuation of the patrimonial authority of noble estate owners. He identified the problem more accurately than most, however, by seeing that it lay in the disparity between traditional institutional forms and new social circumstances. Some defenders of the patrimonial powers of noble estate owners still did so in terms of the patrimonial function of the Hausvater, but such terminology more frequently than not aroused cynicism and ridicule.[102] In response to

---

[102] Carl von Mutius, *Die Patrimonialgerichtsbarkeit als Grundlage einer festen Landescommunalordnung* (Breslau, 1837), 3: "As the rational understanding [*Wissenschaft*] had not yet established the modern concept of the police alongside the originally all-inclusive word *justice*, the lord of an estate ruled as a Hausvater in the midst of his subjects." Despite Mutius's moderate approach, he was attacked for his paternalistic assumptions by Eduard Pelz, writing under the pseudonym Treumund Welp, in *Die Patrimonial-Gerichtsbarkeit: Bruchstück aus den Memoiren eines schlesischen Bauern* (Leipzig, 1834). The debate was evident in the pages of the *Schlesische Provinzial Blätter*. See, for example, C. von Koschutzki, "Ist die Fortdauer des bisherigen sogenannten Priviligien und Berechtigungen der Dominialbesitzer . . . in Schlesien zu wünschen?" vol. 120 (1844): 546–65; [K.], "Ueber die Patrimonial-Gerichtsbarkeit," vol. 114 (1841): 121–25; Eduard Pelz, "Die Verwaltung der Landgemeinde," vol. 122 (1845): 237ff. The Westphalian governor, Carl Freiherr von Vincke, wrote two books on the subject, advocating reform: *Ueber Communal- und Polizei-Verwaltung in den Landgemeinden Niederschlesiens* (Breslau, 1845), and *Die Patrimonial und Polizeigerichtsbarkeit auf dem Lande in den östlichen Provinzen des preussischen Staats* (Breslau, 1847). On the debate within the *Staatsrat*, see Alf Lüdtke, *'Gemeinwohl,' Polizei und 'Fes-*

descriptions of patrimonial jurisdiction as originating in the concern of a Hausvater for his subjects, one critic commented that in all his travels through the Prussian monarchy, and in numerous conversations with peasants in taverns and public houses, he had never heard anyone subject to patrimonial jurisdiction describe it as paternal. "In an uncountable number of cases, have I heard the complaint that the influence which the dominial lords exercised on their judges was so oppressive that they wished the king would completely set aside the last of this old, out-of-date dependency," he wrote.[103] Those who defended patrimonial courts now usually did so without recourse to paternalist images. Kleist-Retzow, for example, defended patrimonial courts in 1847 as essential to the ständisch system of political differentiation; without it, the "rule of money" would triumph, he predicted.[104]

In the late 1830s and in the 1840s, the patrimonial powers of noble estate owners became a focal point of social conflict, both reflecting and, in some cases, causing confrontations in the villages. The brutality of many village police was notorious. When a man named Meyer became the police official in a weaving village in Silesia, he observed that people would "quiver before his shadow." This he apparently managed to accomplish through the use of the most modern, "industrial" methods, a whipping machine, which, according to the sworn petition of 390 village residents to the Berlin Assembly in 1848, he kept in constant operation. Noble estate owners who abused peasants under the guise of their patrimonial police owners were rarely punished, although the state claimed to supervise their exercise of authority. One estate owner who beat a worker to death was sentenced to only a few months in jail for the offense, a sentence that was later commuted to a monetary fine.[105]

Peasants considered patrimonial judges as opponents. "The peasant has little or no confidence in justice," wrote one contemporary; "... he views the patrimonial judge as a man who stands on the side of the estate owner and represents his partisan interests."[106] Despite a ruling

---

tungspraxis': Staatliche Gewaltsamkeit und innere Verwaltung in Preussen, 1815–1850, Veröffentlichungen des Max-Planck-Instituts für Geschichte, 73 (Göttingen, 1982), 282ff.

[103] Eduard Pelz, *Die Patrimonialgerichtsbarkeit*, 8–9.

[104] Hermann von Petersdorff, *Kleist-Retzow: Ein Lebensvild* (Stuttgart and Berlin, 1907), 89–90.

[105] These incidents are cited in Bleiber, *Zwischen Reform und Revolution*, 106–7. On the violence often committed through patrimonial courts and police, see Alf Lüdtke, *'Gemeinwohl,' Polizei und 'Festungspraxis,'* 291ff.

[106] Cited in Bleiber, *Zwischen Reform und Revolution*, 104.

by the government in 1830 that cases in which an estate owner himself was a party could not be handled by the patrimonial judge, little changed. Almost all cases coming before the patrimonial court involved, if only indirectly, some interest of the estate owner, and no patrimonial judge who valued his livelihood could be ignorant of those interests or indifferent to them. Peasants viewed judges with the same suspicion and contempt with which they regarded the commissioners who came to settle the terms of their regulation.

Peasant resistance to the authority of their lords grew in the early 1840s. This was true especially in Silesia, which had a long tradition of peasant unrest and where the plight of the Silesian weavers in the early forties led to a contempt for authority throughout the province. The resistance was most frequently led by Dreschgärtner, Häusler, and Einlieger—the small-holding or landless peasants living on the lower margin of existence and aware that their position was deteriorating steadily. In 1845, the government sent troops into Upper Silesia because of the increasing number of cases of wood theft and poaching. Arson was not uncommon. One report, from March 1847, commented that scarcely a night passed without a case of arson. And an estate owner observed that "countless cases have demonstrated that a Knecht or a worker who feels himself unjustly punished, or out of mere wickedness, often seeks revenge against his lord through arson or some other act of mischief."[107]

A more common act of resistance, however, was the simple refusal to fulfill service obligations to the lords. In the ensuing confrontations, the lords called on the state for assistance, while the peasants demonstrated a remarkable degree of solidarity. In the summer of 1844, for example, 42 Häusler and Gärtner in the village of Neuwaltersdorff, in Upper Silesia, refused to perform their service obligations. The estate owner called for assistance from the Landrat, who, fearing violence, sent the police to the village; they arrested the ringleaders of the strike. However, as the leaders were being led off to jail, the other striking peasants invited the authorities to arrest them too, and the entire group marched to the county seat, Habelschwerdt, to demonstrate their support for those arrested. Four weeks later, when the police appeared in neighboring villages to put down a similar strike, they were greeted by peasants armed with pitchforks. Only later did they succeed in arresting the leaders there. Although the authorities grew nervous about these manifestations of resistance and the king ordered investigations to ascertain whether they were caused by "excesses," the

---

[107] Cited in ibid., 145.

CHAPTER 8

state always supported the demands of the noble estate owners. In 1846, Minister of Internal Affairs von Bodelschwingh worried about a peasant uprising's spreading from neighboring Austrian Galicia across the border into Silesia, but his only solution was to suggest stationing more troops in Silesia.[108]

These were years of scarcity and hunger throughout Germany. The harvest of 1842 had been poor, those of 1843 and 1844, somewhat better. But in 1845 and 1846, successive crop failures drove the price of grain up. What made the crisis especially severe for the rural population, however, was the fact that the potato blight struck at the same time. It appeared in western Europe in 1845; by 1846, it had spread to the eastern provinces of Prussia. Potatoes were the major source of nourishment for small-holding and landless peasants; indeed, much of the population growth during the first half of the nineteenth century had depended on the cultivation of potatoes, which could support up to one-third more persons than could grain cultivation on the same amount of land.[109]

Although in the short term the crisis of the mid-forties in Prussia was caused by harvest failures and the potato blight, in the long term it was brought about by the conjunction of three interrelated factors.[110] The first of these, we have examined in this chapter: the way in which the transformation of agriculture left a growing number of agricultural laborers with little or no land and dependent on wage earnings. A survey made by the agricultural department of the Prussian government in 1848 revealed the plight of these marginal rural workers.[111] The data were gathered by sending a questionnaire to 168 agricultural organizations throughout the monarchy; since these organizations were generally dominated by noble estate owners or large-holding peasants, their responses may have contained a bias that would make the conditions of workers employed by such landholders appear to be somewhat more favorable than they actually were. Still, the picture yielded by the survey was grim. Rural workers were grouped into three categories: (1) those with small plots of land who worked on the large estates under annual contracts for wages; (2) those who had perhaps a house and a small garden but no fixed labor contract with an estate owner; and (3) those with no land or cottage,

[108] Ibid., 156.

[109] Wilhelm Abel, *Massenarmut und Hungerkrisen im vorindustriellen Europa* (Hamburg and Berlin, 1974), 365; Jordan, *Die Entstehung*, 102–3.

[110] Schissler, *Preussische Agrargesellschaft im Wandel*, 182.

[111] Alexander Lengerke, *Die ländliche Arbeiterfrage* (Berlin, 1849), provides the published results of the government survey.

306

no contract, and work assured only in the peak seasons. The survey showed that the peasants in the first group, referred to as *Dienstleute* or *Feldgesinde*, would probably survive the crisis. The conditions of those in the second category, the *Häusler* or *Colonisten*, varied considerably among the provinces; in East Prussia, they would probably come through the bad times if they were "diligent" and "thrifty." In Brandenburg and Silesia, their condition was said to differ little from those in the third, and lowest, category. The *Heuerlinge* and *Einlieger*, who comprised the final category of the survey, were in a desperate condition. They worked only from late spring to early fall; other forms of income, such as weaving, were generally not available; and they were considered lazy and "inclined to drunkenness." Almost all reports stressed the enormous increase in numbers of persons in these three pitiful groups.

The second factor in the long-term development of the "hungry forties" was the enormous population growth referred to in the survey of 1848. Between 1816 and 1855, the Prussian population increased from 10.4 million to 17.2 million, a growth of 65.7 percent.[112] Some of this growth resulted from the elimination of the landlord's right to control the marriage of many classes of peasants on his estate and village; some was due to the increased productivity of the land, especially through the cultivation of the potato; and some was doubtless produced by an increased demand for labor resulting from the intensification and modernization of agriculture. But the rapid expansion of the population during Vormärz more than satisfied this demand, so that, from the end of the 1820s, the wages of agricultural labor steadily declined. The gradual movement away from payment *in natura* to monetary wages, especially as grain prices increased, depressed the level of the wages further.

Third, this inordinate increase in the population, particularly the landless rural poor, coincided with the demise of domestic industry.[113]

---

[112] Schissler, *Preussische Agrargesellschaft im Wandel*, 159; W. Köllmann, "Bevölkerung und Arbeitskräftepotential in Deutschland 1815–1865," in Köllman, *Bevölkerung in der industriellen Revolution* (Göttingen, 1974), 95. The contemporary observations gathered by Carl Jantke and Dietrich Hilger, *Die Eigentumlosen* (Munich, 1965), especially 149ff., offer graphic examples of the poverty of the propertyless. The rapid growth of the poorest element of the rural population is stressed in the reports published in Lengerke, *Arbeiterfrage*. On the subsequent decline of the wages and on the crisis in general, see Karl Obermann, "Wirtschafts- und sozialpolitische Aspekte der Wirtschaftskrise von 1845–1847 in Deutschland, insbesondere in Preussen," *Jahrbuch für Geschichte* 7 (1972): 141–74.

[113] Peter Kriedte, Jürgen Schlumbohm, and Hans Medick, *Die Industrialisierung vor der Industrialisierung: Gewerbliche Warenproduktion auf dem Land in der Formationsperiode des Ka-*

CHAPTER 8

Domestic industry was not widespread in the eastern provinces of Prussia; in most areas it was unknown, despite a number of proposals by officials to introduce it. Domestic linen weaving, of course, was well developed in Silesia and in parts of Prussian Saxony, but by the 1840s, the industry had collapsed and unemployment was widespread. Many smallholding peasants could not survive without the added income produced by weaving.

Conditions were awful for the rural poor everywhere in Prussia during the mid-forties, but they were especially deplorable in Silesia. One official report summarized the effects of three consecutive harvest failures: "In the first year of the scarcity, the livestock were sold in order to survive in the hope of a better year; in the second year, clothing and beds were sold or hocked; when, however, no potatoes grew in the third year, they fell helpless against starvation, and since they were weak physically and lacking in clothing, even if they could obtain work, they were incapable of performing it."[114] Disease followed famine. In 1847, an epidemic of dysentery was followed by typhus, which claimed an estimated 50,000 lives in Upper Silesia.

Neither the noble estate owners nor the government dealt with the catastrophe effectively. In County Rybnik, Upper Silesia, an estimated 20,000 people, one-third of the population of the county, were reported to be on the margin of starvation; when the county assembly met in 1847 to discuss the problem, only 12 out of 69 noble estate owners in the county bothered to attend.[115] Johann Hinrich Wichern, the conservative Protestant clergyman who founded Inner Mission to help the poor, reported that noble estate owners did perform some acts of charity during these years, but he suggested that it did not compare with the money they spent on horses, dogs, and the pleasures of the hunt.[116] The government also did little. Rudolf Virchow, at that time a liberal young physician, went to Upper Silesia to tend the sick; he complained bitterly in a letter to his father that Minister of Internal Affairs Bodelschwingh had, "through his disbelief and his obstinacy, sacrificed as many persons as a small war would cost."[117] Governor von Wedell reported in 1848 having ordered the establishment of orphanages for children who lost their parents in the epidemics; they would,

---

pitalismus (Göttingen, 1977), 310–12: English translation: *Industrialization Before Industrialization* (Cambridge, 1981). Schissler, *Preussische Agrargesellschaft im Wandel*, 182–83.

[114] Cited in Bleiber, *Zwischen Reform und Revolution*, 123–24.

[115] Ibid., 125–28.

[116] Ibid., 128.

[117] Maria Rabl, ed., *Rudolf Virchow: Briefe an seine Eltern, 1839–1864* (Leipzig, 1906), 129.

he added, "build from these children a class of useful rural servants." When, in another act of charity, Wedell signed a public circular letter appealing for private funds to assist the province, he was chastised by his superior, Bodelschwingh, who feared that the name of the provincial governor on such a letter might suggest that the government had done too little in the crisis.[118]

After returning to Berlin from Silesia in early March 1848, the young Virchow witnessed the outbreak of the revolution in Prussia. He wrote his observations on the conditions in Silesia under the influence of those events. He asked: "What is to be expected from a people that has struggled for centuries in bitter misery for its existence, that has never seen the time in which it benefited from its own labor, that has never known the joy of its own acquisition, the earnings of arduous labor, and that has always seen the fruit of its sweat fall into the purses of the landlord?"[119]

Another who criticized the government for failing to act in the crisis, the conservative estate owner and publicist Ernst von Bülow-Cummerow, was afraid he knew the answer to questions such as those posed by Virchow. In 1847, at the height of the crisis, and before the outbreak of the revolution, Bülow-Cummerow warned:

> The calamity that has been brought about by the harvest failures that so oppress the lower classes leads us directly to the concern that is widespread and well substantiated about the increase in the number of proletarians in the entire realm of the monarch.
>
> Ireland, indeed even England, shows where such an increasing number of proletarians leads, and how dangerous they can be when communist ideas, which are also spreading ever more widely here, take deep root; no one should deceive himself about this, especially since we do not have as a counterweight the strong constitution that England has.
>
> Only a few years ago, only a few proletarians were to be found here and there in the large cities, and communist ideas were completely unknown. . . .
>
> Although communist ideas in no way originate with the proletariat but with those who out of insanity or egotism work to overthrow the society, and they are especially to be found among young artisans, the chief danger lies in the existence of such a large mass of people who

---

[118] Cited in Bleiber, *Zwischen Reform und Revolution*, 126–29.

[119] Rudolf Virchow, *Mitteilungern über die in Oberschlesien herrschende Typhus-Epidemie* (Berlin, 1848), 19.

have nothing to lose and are always ready to fight against those who possess something.[120]

Bülow-Cummerow's chief concern here was neither to preserve the nobility from the intrusion of a market economy nor to renew the outworn bonds of paternalism between lords and peasants. Rather, his aim was to reassert the authority of the state so that it could provide the necessary protection for property. It required a new view of the state, one that recognized and utilized the power of public law in establishing authority in society.

[120] Ernst von Bülow-Cummerow, *Preussen im Januar 1847 und das Patent vom 3. Februar* (Berlin, 1847), 26–27. Friedrich William IV was so irritated by this book that he returned his gift copy to Bülow-Cummerow without opening it. K. A. Varnhagen von Ense, *Tagebücher*, 2d ed. (Leipzig, 1863), 4: 56.

9

POLITICS ON THE EVE OF REVOLUTION

CONSTITUTIONAL CONFLICT RENEWED, 1840–1847

The central problem confronting Prussia after 1840 was that the institutions of the state, established during the early years of the restoration, were incapable of accommodating the changes that had subsequently overtaken Prussian society. Within the state, a tension existed between the institutions of local authority and those of the central government. This tension intensified, in large part, because the promised constitutional development had never taken place. The landowning nobility continued to dominate the countryside through the Landräte, the county assemblies, and the provincial diets, but, except insofar as the Landräte carried out the orders of the central government, these local institutions remained isolated and largely ignored by the central administration. The provincial diets established in 1823 had little impact on the policies of the state; they met infrequently and only at the command of the king, their deliberations were not public, and their advisory powers were severely restricted.[1] They inspired little public confidence or interest, and they grew increasingly less representative with each passing year. Indeed, they were not even convened during the last three years of Frederick William III's reign. The pledge of a constitution, offered by Frederick William III in 1815, remained unfulfilled at the time of his death in 1840. In order to avoid convening a national diet, as the assumption of a new state debt would require according to the State Debt Law of 1820, the conservative ministry governed frugally.[2]

The bureaucracy that governed Prussia in Vormärz regarded these local ständisch institutions with suspicion and hostility, viewing them as obstacles to its rule rather than as bodies to be integrated into the governmental process. Even officials such as Gustav von Rochow, who began their careers by defending the ständisch institutions controlled by the landowning nobility, soon adopted the centralistic ethos of the

---

[1] See chapter 6.
[2] Reinhart Koselleck, *Preussen zwischen Reform und Revolution* (Stuttgart, 1967), 361.

CHAPTER 9

bureaucracy.³ The lines of command ran to the governmental districts, frequently bypassing the provincial governors, who were considered to be provincial officials. Claiming to embody the state as a whole, the bureaucracy (*Beamtenstand*) saw itself, and was commonly viewed by the public, as the guardian of the public interest, elevated above the conflicting interests of the other Stände. It was this claim that caused the Berlin philosopher Eduard Gans to say that the Prussian state was neither a patriarchal nor a constitutional state, but a guardian state.⁴

By 1840, this structure of the state was seriously out of touch with the society it governed. The population growth was most pronounced among those segments of the society utterly unrepresented by the local Stände—the landless rural peasantry and the urban poor. However, the requirement of landownership for membership in the provincial diets also excluded much of the new wealth and the educated bourgeoisie.⁵ The central administration, which had been a chief agent for economic modernization from the reforms of Stein and Hardenberg through the completion of the German Customs Union in 1834, became, during the late 1830s, timid and afraid to initiate change. A friendly observer referred to the "somewhat exhausted machinery of state" in 1840; the English ambassador to Berlin, Lord Russell, described the "state of decrepitude" of the Prussian government.⁶ But the paralysis of the central administration was more than exhaustion or disrepair; the government could not take the initiative in needed developments such as railway construction because it feared the consequences of convening a national diet to approve and fund a new state debt. Bülow-Cummerow, the Pomeranian estate owner who worked strenuously for the economic development of eastern agricul-

³ For Rochow's early political views, see Ernst Müsebeck, "Die märkische Ritterschaft und die preussische Verfassungsfrage von 1814 bis 1820," *Deutsche Rundschau* 174 (1918): 158–82, 354–76. The transformation of Rochow's views are interesting, for they run parallel to the changing emphasis of conservative thought in Vormärz. During the Hardenberg regime, he shared the views of his brother-in-law, Marwitz, in the defense of the landowning nobility and his belief in the traditional ständisch institutions. After entering the government, and especially after the July Revolution, he lost his confidence in the ständisch institutions for the state and saw the bureaucracy as the backbone of the state and its only defense against revolution. See especially Ludwig Dehio, "Wittgenstein und das letzte Jahrzehnt Friedrich Wilhelms III," *FBPG* 35 (1923): 229–31.

⁴ Cited in Koselleck, *Preussen zwischen Reform und Revolution*, 380; see also John R. Gillis, *The Prussian Bureaucracy in Crisis* (Stanford, 1971), 14ff.

⁵ Koselleck, *Preussen zwischen Reform und Revolution*, 340–42.

⁶ Cited in Friedrich Keinemann, *Preussen auf dem Wege zur Revolution* (Hamm, 1975), 8; see also Hans Branig, *Fürst Wittgenstein: Ein preussischer Staatsmann der Restaurationszeit* (Cologne and Vienna, 1981), 190.

ture, complained bitterly that the government would "prefer to sacrifice all of the advantages that a network of railroads would have for the country, for the security of the state, than to request of the Stände the funds necessary to undertake the construction."[7]

Precisely this fear of future change prompted Wittgenstein to draft a political testament for Frederick William III that would prevent his successors from changing the basic structure of the monarchy.[8] This testament reflected discussions that had taken place within the ministry throughout the 1830s. Enumerating the institutions created in Prussia during the restoration, it declared: "My subjects possess, in the well-ordered state administration, in the Council of State [Staatsrat], in the provincial diets, in the City Ordinance, and in the communal constitutions, the guarantee of undisturbed order and legality [*Gesetzlichkeit*]." These institutions, "the basic pillars of the monarchy," formed the "constitution of the state" and were not to be altered without the full consent of all the agnates of the royal house. The testament further provided that if it became necessary to convene a national diet to approve a new state loan, in accordance with the law of 1820, this national diet should be composed of sixty-four members—four each from the eight provincial diets and thirty-two members from the State Council.[9] Frederick William III died without finally signing the testament, but the knowledge that it reflected his desire caused Frederick William IV to give it great weight.[10]

Frederick William IV's ascension to the throne in June 1840 offered hope that the paralysis of the government would be overcome. One of the new king's close associates, Voss-Buch, predicted: "The stagnant water will plunge over the opened sluices and create a flood."[11] Many of the king's initial decisions pleased liberals and worried his conservative friends. He reinstated Ernst Moritz Arndt to the professorial

---

[7] See Herbert Obenaus, *Anfänge des Parlamentarismus im Preussen bis 1848* (Düsseldorf, 1984), 524.

[8] The background to the political testament, as well as the document itself, is offered by Dehio, "Wittgenstein und das letzte Jahrzehnt Friedrich Wilhelms III," 213–40. See also Branig, *Wittgenstein*, 190.

[9] Provincial diets comprising four estates were to have one member elected from each estate; provincial diets with only three estates were to elect two representatives from the first estate.

[10] For Wittgenstein's explanation for the failure of the king to sign the testament, see K. A. Varnhagen von Ense, *Tagebücher* (Leipzig, 1863), 3: 17, 31 January 1845. Frederick William IV's view is reported in Ernst R. Huber, *Deutsche Verfassungsgeschichte seit 1789* (Stuttgart, 1960), 2: 485.

[11] Cited in Herman von Petersdorff, *König Friedrich Wilhelm der Vierte* (Stuttgart, 1900), 31.

chair that had been taken from him after the Carlsbad Decrees. Three of the famous "Göttingen Seven"—Friedrich Dahlmann and the Grimm brothers—who had lost their positions in the constitutional conflict with the king of Hanover in 1837, received academic posts in Prussia. Frederick William IV halted the persecution of the "demagogues" and gave amnesty to many arrested for political actions. General Boyen, who had resigned from the ministry in 1819, was called back as a member of the State Council in July 1840 and named minister of war the following year.[12] Leopold von Gerlach found it "striking that the first step of the king was liberal," while his brother Ludwig ascribed the king's liberal gestures to his quest for "popularity."[13]

There was never any danger of the new king's becoming too liberal. But the one expectation for his reign that was shared by both the liberals and the circle of conservatives that had surrounded him as crown prince was his rejection of bureaucratic absolutism.[14] Varnhagen von Ense predicted the development of a party that would "work systematically against" the king, composed of "those who were previously in the state administration and, in addition, the largest part of the bureaucracy."[15] Wittgenstein, one of the adherents of bureaucractic absolutism, saw immediately that his own influence had ended with the death of Frederick William III and wrote the following to Metternich as early as in July 1840: "You are certainly more than correct that a transition of government is a difficult and dangerous epoch in the life of a state. . . . It is not clear to me whether the present king will move in the direction of his late father, however much this may be desired. The king certainly has the best intentions and the most benevolent attitudes. However, nature has endowed him with the most ingenious fantasies, and this is an enemy that is difficult to overcome, especially when one is not indifferent to popularity. I become more convinced each day that I am not useful to a government like the present one."[16] Rochow was powerful at the outset of Frederick William IV's reign and retained considerable influence until 1847, but he resigned his ministerial post in 1842.[17] In fact, the king did not wish to have powerful

---

[12] Keinemann, *Preussen auf dem Wege*, 8; Gillis, *Prussian Bureaucracy*, 15; Huber, *Verfassungsgeschichte* 2: 479.

[13] Leopold von Gerlach, *Denkwürdigkeiten* (Berlin, 1891), 1: 80; Ernst Ludwig von Gerlach, *Aufzeichnungen aus seinem Leben und Wirken, 1795–1877*, ed. Jakob von Gerlach (Schwerin, 1903), 1: 275. Varnhagen notes the conflicting reactions to the king's liberal gestures, *Tagebücher* 1: 232, 17 October 1840.

[14] Gillis, *Prussian Bureaucracy*, 15; Koselleck, *Preussen zwischen Reform und Revolution*, 363.

[15] Varnhagen, *Tagebücher* 1: 220, 28 September 1840.

[16] Cited in Branig, *Wittgenstein*, 193.

[17] Varnhagen predicted Rochow's influence on Frederick William IV even before the

ministers. He deeply believed in his divine right to rule and hoped to govern in a personal and direct fashion, like the prince idealized in Haller's doctrine. He once remarked to his friend and adviser Christian Karl Bunsen: "There are things that one only knows as king, that I did not understand as crown prince and only first experienced as king."[18] To Leopold von Gerlach, he confided, "In the four years of my reign, I have had the experience—and you can believe me that it is a sad experience—that I see things more clearly than my ministers and I can expect no advice from them."[19]

Throughout his long tenure as crown prince, Frederick William IV had always been closely associated with the restoration. His tutor, Ancillon, had stressed the importance of ständisch social distinctions. During the 1820s, he worked closely with Rochow, the Gerlach brothers, and Voss-Buch. He had been instrumental in Hengstenberg's appointment to the university faculty in Berlin, and he had encouraged the founding of *Das Berliner Politische Wochenblatt*. Above all, he was an admirer of the political doctrines of Haller; together with his inner circle of unofficial advisers led by the Gerlachs, Frederick William IV hoped to build a harmonious political order based on a monarch ruling by divine rights in consultation with the loyal Stände.[20] He dismissed "paper constitutions" as intruding on the patrimonial relationship between the king and his people.[21] He intended to "elevate" the Stände "through the force and authority of his person."[22] Critics commonly viewed his ideas as fantasies, and Alexander von Humboldt referred to Frederick William's wish "to build a small Middle Ages."[23]

---

death of Frederick William III: "People are increasingly inclined to think about the possibility of a change of sovereigns, and hopes and fears are expressed. The opinion is that under a new government, Minister von Rochow will be all powerful." *Tagebücher* 1: 175, 14 May 1840.

[18] Petersdorff, *König Friedrich Wilhelm IV.*, 2.

[19] L. von Gerlach, *Denkwürdigkeiten* 1: 104–5. Frederick William IV wrote Theodor von Schön that he believed his authority came from the "King of Kings" (28 December 1842). Hans Rothfels, *Theodor v. Schön, Friedrich Wilhelm IV. und die Revolution von 1848* (Halle, 1937), 243.

[20] The composition of this inner circle of advisers is related in Petersdorff, *König Friedrich Wilhelm IV.*, 17–18. See also Huber, *Verfassungsgeschichte* 2: 482–83.

[21] Frederick William first used the phrase "parchment constitution" in his cabinet order of October 4, 1840, directed to the East Prussian diet. Huber, *Verfassungsgeschichte* 2: 486. In a letter to Schön dated December 28, 1842, he again referred to written constitutions as "scraps of paper." Rothfels, *Schön, Friedrich Wilhelm IV.*, 243. He used the phrase repeatedly from 1840 to 1848.

[22] Caroline von Rochow, *Vom Leben am preussischen Hofe* (Berlin, 1908), 347.

[23] Humboldt's comment is related in Paul Heere, *Von Preussens Befreiungs- und Verfassungskampf: Aus den Papieren des Oberburggrafen Magnus von Brunneck* (Berlin, 1914), 346. Wittgenstein used the phrase "deplorable fantasies" in describing Frederick William's

CHAPTER 9

Frederick William's ideas simply did not correspond to the needs or the expectations of the society. Neither the institutions nor the ideology he had inherited was sufficient to cope with the society he had to govern. To "elevate" the Stände, he was willing to convene a national diet; indeed, immediately after his father's death, he proposed to announce a diet at the time of the ceremonial oath-taking with the provincial diets. Such a national diet would be organized according to the prescription of his father's political testament. His advisers and his brother, Prince William, vigorously opposed convening such a diet, so, for the moment, Frederick William dropped the idea.[24] Although he was willing to convene a national diet with extremely limited authority, he refused to do so in response to any requests made by the provincial diets.

The difficulty with Frederick William's vision of ständisch representation was that he did not want the authority of a national diet to go beyond that possessed by provincial diets since 1823.[25] This was even further than the bureaucracy was willing to go. As a result, his efforts to enhance the Stände met with opposition within the government and with demands by the diets for greater competence and broader representation. These demands he considered unthinkable and impertinent, and they further strengthened the resolve of the bureaucracy to oppose his desire for ständisch representation. Policies he considered generous seemed to produce opposition and ever-increasing demands, causing him to recoil from his own policies in irritation and frustration. It is in the nature of paternal government to expect gratitude from subjects; when it was not forthcoming, because the subjects believed they received only their due—or less—Frederick William reacted like a father angry and frustrated at his children's ingratitude. As a consequence, his government seemed to zigzag between liberality

---

ideas to Rochow. Rothfels, *Schön, Friedrich Wilhelm IV.*, 109; Varnhagen described the king's fantasies, *Tagebücher* 1: 220, 28 September 1840.

[24] Rochow wrote a long memorandum opposing the idea of calling a national diet, claiming that, except for a few persons in the East Prussian, Posen, and Westphalian diets, there was no sentiment in favor of a national diet. Even Frederick William IV doubted that convening only thirty-two representatives of the provincial diets would be recognized as sufficiently representative. See Obenaus, *Anfänge des Parlamentarismus*, 525–27. Varnhagen reported a conversation with K. W. Freiherr von Canitz und Dallwitz, the Prussian ambassador to Vienna from 1841 to 1845 and foreign minister from 1845 to 1848, *Tagebücher* 3: 95, 21 June 1845, in which Canitz complained bitterly of the poor advice Frederick William had received in 1840. By persuading him to postpone convening a national diet, Canitz charged, his advisers had destroyed his chances of a successful reign.

[25] Koselleck, *Preussen zwischen Reform und Revolution*, 363.

and reaction. After observing this indecision for two years, Varnhagen commented, "One asks where we are going and what it is that we want. No one knows and all officials fluctuate in uncertainty. . . . Middle Ages, liberalism, religiosity, strict surveillance and press freedom, noble advantage and civil equality [*Bürgerlichkeit*]—these all run side by side, with everything lacking limit and purpose."[26]

These conflicting currents of Prussian politics were evident from the first oath-taking ceremony for the new king in Königsberg in September 1840.[27] By long-standing custom, the king invited the Stände to declare their traditional privileges, which he then pledged to respect. The Prussian diet used this occasion to request, by a vote of 89 to 5, that the king honor his father's pledge of a constitution and establish a national diet. Frederick William was angered by the proposition, but Schön managed to reassure him of the diet's good will. Disappointed that his initial plans for a national diet had been rebuffed by his ministers, the king shared with Schön his hopes of convening, in due time, a meeting of all the provincial diets. After his audience with the king, Schön remarked to Alexander von Humboldt, "The king is more liberal than I am." In his official response to the diet, Frederick William expressed his intention to develop more fully the ständisch institutions of the monarchy. He did not accept the request of the diet, but he told the members that they had acted "completely within their rights."[28] The ever-prescient observer of Prussian political events, Varnhagen von Ense, commented on the meeting of the Königsberg diet, "The rejection of a ständisch constitution for the state has not made a good impression. I believe that the king will never be free of this issue during his entire reign; it will always recur."[29]

The ministry was angered by the actions of the Prussian diet. Prince

---

[26] Varnhagen, *Tagebücher* 2: 66, 1 May 1842. On May 17, 1842, Varnhagen wrote the following: "The king, who could not have escaped knowing how little he has succeeded in his intentions, how slow are the effects of his commands, blames the bureaucracy for these obstructions. He is pleased when the bureaucrats are criticized, but whoever criticizes them is also attacking royal authority. Thus, it is said that the king is the only revolutionary in the country because he makes the people dissatisfied and agitates them against the authorities. In fact, it is difficult to be a good subject, for there is no clear posture for such." Ibid., 72.

[27] For descriptions of the events in Königsberg, see Rothfels, *Schön, Friedrich Wilhelm IV.*, 108–10; Theodor von Schön, *Aus den Papieren Theodor von Schön* (Berlin, 1875), 3: 136–43; Obenaus, *Anfänge des Parlamentarismus*, 528–532; Heinrich von Treitschke, *Deutsche Geschichte im neunzehnten Jahrhundert* (Leipzig, 1882), 5: 42–49.

[28] Schön's comment to Humboldt is in Rothfels, *Schön, Friedrich Wilhelm IV.*, 110; the king's response to the diet is reprinted in Schön, *Aus den Papieren*, 3: 170–72.

[29] Varnhagen, *Tagebücher*, 1: 216, 16 September 1840.

CHAPTER 9

William wrote Schön that the request of the diet represented "the highest disloyalty to a new sovereign."[30] After returning to Berlin, Frederick William was increasingly influenced by Minister of Internal Affairs Gustav von Rochow. Rochow persuaded the king to issue a cabinet order on October 4 that virtually retracted the assurances that he had given the diet in Königsberg. Schön, in Berlin at the time, wrote dejectedly to his wife that "a completely different philosophy" prevailed in the capital city.[31] He initially considered resigning, but after returning to Königsberg, he decided to make an additional appeal to Frederick William. On December 14, he sent the king a copy of Stein's political testament (Schön was its actual author), accompanied by his commentary. Schön also wrote for private circulation the memorandum *Woher und Wohin?* (Whence and whither?) outlining his interpretation of the recent Prussian past and his proposals for the immediate future.[32]

Woher und Wohin? reflected Schön's continued allegiance to the principles of the Stein reforms. His brief review of Prussian history was critical of the politics of the restoration. By the end of the eighteenth century, he asserted, the Prussian bureaucracy governed the state very much like Catholic priests who served only for themselves, not for their congregations. The bureaucracy behaved "as though the people existed for it, rather than it for the people." With the spread of the Enlightenment, however, a new spirit developed within the state, bringing the reforms that ended both the heavy-handed rule of the bureaucracy and the "control of local authorities and noble estate lords who governed in a relatively patriarchal fashion." "The misfortunes of the years from 1807 to 1813 and the laws of that era demanded the independence of the people . . . and brought the people into an increasingly clear consciousness. The most beautiful fruit and most admirable manifestation of these times was the Prussian militia [*Landwehr*], created not by civil or military officials, but proceeding from the people and brought to maturity by the force of the people." Unfortunately, Schön maintained, the bureaucracy reacted to the reforms by seeking to sustain its own significance. "Step by step, the bureaucracy worked to retain its importance." Thus, Schön asserted, the city ordinance has been rendered "inconsequential," the communal ordinance insufficient, and the militia modified until it lost its original character. The provincial diets were originally greeted as a sign that

---

[30] Treitschke, *Deutsche Geschichte*, 5: 44–45.
[31] Rothfels, *Schön, Friedrich IV.*, vol. 3; Schön, *Aus den Papieren*, 3: 195.
[32] *Woher und Wohin?* is reprinted in Schön, *Aus den Papieren* 3: 230–39.

the king recognized the maturity of the people, but the bureaucracy had worked to limit and reduce popular influence; no general diet had emerged. The people's frustration had led to the request of the Prussian diet. It was the request, "not of the propertyless or the homeless, not of empty-headed youth," not of the "proletarians," but of "men of property, men of judgment and mature experience." The creation of a general diet, Schön argued in the spirit of Stein, would give the people a new independence; it would reduce the need for so large a bureaucracy, provide greater oversight of the expenditure of state funds, offer the insight of local affairs for the legislative process, and give the people a closer tie to the defense of the land. A general diet would revitalize "the public life of the land." In a sharp critique of the paternalist assumptions of authority, Schön concluded: "The age of the so-called paternalist or patrimonial government, in which the people is seen to comprise a mute mass preferring and allowing itself to be led, is not to be restored. If one does not seize the age as it is, and extract what is good from it, and shape its development, the opportunity will disappear."

Schön did not intend to publish his essay. He planned to have printed a few copies for friends and associates, among them the king.[33] However, Rochow, who had had secret agents reporting on liberal opinion in East Prussia throughout the period of his ministry, obtained a copy before it was circulated and shared it with the king. It strengthened Rochow's position and weakened Schön's. The king disliked the pamphlet, which he considered not only an attack on the government of his father, but an assault on his assumptions about the nature of his authority. "Truly," he wrote Schön, "I feel myself king 'by divine right' and will so feel, with your help, until the end of my days." He continued with a vigorous defense of paternalist rule:

I have not promised my Stände a resplendent government, but a paternal one, and I will keep my promise. Glitter and artifice I leave without envy to the so-called constitutional princes who, by means of a piece of paper, have become a fiction, an abstract concept, to the people. A paternal government, however, is a German prince's nature and duty, and because the dominion is my paternal inheritance, my *patrimonium*, I have a heart for my people, and I will therefore lead my children who are not yet of age [*unmündige*]. . . . You, my dear Schön, slander the noble name of paternal and patrimonial dominion

---

[33] Rothfels, *Schön, Friedrich Wilhelm IV.*, 112.

CHAPTER 9

by describing a form of government that you should have called the dominion of a steward or prefect.[34]

During the following months, Schön and Frederick William engaged in a remarkable exchange of views, with Schön continuing to assert that the Prussian people had attained the level of maturity that would permit an extension of the powers of the diets and the creation of a national diet, whereas the king articulated, once again, the rudiments of paternalist authority.[35] This correspondence was precipitated by the bitter feud that developed between Schön and Rochow. Determined to eliminate Schön's influence, Rochow employed secret agents to gather information that would implicate Schön with revolutionary sentiments. Schön was outraged when he learned that these agents had opened his private correspondence, and he wrote to Rochow accusing him of destroying popular confidence in the government by such tactics. Frederick William attempted to mediate the conflict between the two men, but his growing bitterness toward the East Prussian liberals caused him to side with Rochow in the fight. Schön ultimately resigned as provincial governor in 1842.[36]

A pamphlet entitled *Vier Fragen beantwortet von einem Ostpreussen*, published anonymously by Johann Jacoby in 1841 on the eve of the meeting of the Prussian diet, sharpened the differences between the East Prussian liberals and the king.[37] Jacoby, a Jewish doctor in Königsberg, sent copies of the pamphlet to the provincial diets throughout Prussia; it circulated widely and was discussed everywhere.[38] It became

[34] Published in ibid., 213–16.

[35] This correspondence is printed in Rothfels, *Schön, Friedrich Wilhelm IV.*, 216–45; see also Schön, *Aus den Papieren* 3: 267–87.

[36] For a description of the events leading to Schön's resignation, see Rothfels, *Schön, Friedrich IV.*, 116–23; Treitschke, *Deutsche Geschichte* 5: 158–64. For Varnhagen's interesting commentary on the dispute, see *Tagebücher* 1: 227, 351. He reported that Rochow "spoke of Schön with the most hateful expressions." Leopold von Gerlach, on the other hand, spoke of Schön's "mendacity and vanity, his hatred of Rochow and the entire world of the Berlin officials." *DZA II*, Rep. 92, C. v. Voss-Buch, no. 16, Bl. 13.

[37] [Johann Jacoby], *Vier Fragen beantwortet von einem Ostpreussen* (Mannheim, 1841). On Jacoby, see Edmund Silberner, *Johann Jacoby* (Bonn and Bad Godesberg, 1976); Peter Schuppan, "Johann Jacoby und die antifeudale Opposition in Preussen am Beginn der 40er Jahre des 19. Jahrhundert," *Jahrbuch für Geschichte* 7 (1972): 97–139; Edmund Silberner, "Johann Jacoby, 1843–1846: Beitrag zur Geschichte des Vormärz," *International Review of Social History* 14 (1969): 352–411.

[38] The pamphlet made an enormous impression. Varnhagen wrote, "The major question does not rest and will not rest; the aristocratic officials quake at the thought that the king might give in to the demands." *Tagebücher* 1: 275. The Russian ambassador sent it to Saint Petersburg with the observation that this "important pamphlet . . . is the manifesto of the liberal party." The chief of police in Königsberg reported to Rochow: "The

the most important expression of the liberal viewpoint during the constitutional conflict of the 1840s. Frequently compared to Sieye's *What Is the Third Estate?*, the pamphlet prompted numerous rejoinders and considerable support.[39] Jacoby attacked the strict censorship of the provincial diets, claiming that the censorship of reports on their deliberations made them into a "false representation" (*Scheinvertretung*). "An assembly that is watched in its affairs with such distrust, that conducts its business behind closed doors, and whose speeches can never be published must be seen as anything but an adequate organ for the people's needs." The king and the people—"until now separated by a standing army of soldiers and officials"—must be united through a true system of representation.[40] The government considered the pamphlet seditious and brought Jacoby to trial for high treason. Frederick William IV wrote to Schön about Jacoby: "I do not count baptized Jews among my East Prussians. That is a true consolation for me."[41]

Given this unpropitious beginning, it is not surprising that the government was concerned that the provincial diets of 1841 would provoke an extended confrontation over the constitutional question. These fears were ungrounded. Except for Posen, where the Polish national question surfaced, and Westphalia and the Rhineland, where religious questions came to the fore, the diets were relatively quiet.[42] Although Jacoby's *Vier Fragen* had caused a considerable stir in Prussia, at the king's request, Schön persuaded the diet not to submit another request for a constitution.[43] None of the other provinces did so either. After some initial excitement, the diets ceased to hold public interest. Varnhagen recorded in his diary: "The provincial diets begin

---

sensation that this writing makes here is completely extraordinary, and in general it is read and discussed with a very special interest." Schuppan, "Jacoby und die antifeudale Opposition," 120ff.

[39] Silberner, *Johann Jacoby*, 79–89. There were a large number of rejoinders to Jacoby's pamphlet, many sponsored by the government. Dr. L. von Henning, *Zur Verständigung über die preussischer Verfassungsfrage* (Berlin, 1845), and [Canitz], *Die Frage: Wohin? In Bezug auf die landständischen Verhaltnisse der preussischen Monarchie* (Berlin, 1843), are two such examples. On discussions of *Vier Fragen*, see Varnhagen, *Tagebücher* 1: 277, 2 March 1841. The comparison with Sieyes was made by Arnold Ruge. Schuppan, "Jacoby und die antifeudale Opposition," 116.

[40] Jacoby, *Vier Fragen*, 16.

[41] Rothfels, *Schön, Friedrich Wilhelm IV.*, 222. Jacoby was not a baptized Jew and remained active within the Jewish community. He was acquitted of the charge of treason. Silberner, *Johann Jacoby*, 44–59, 89–103.

[42] Keinemann, *Preussen auf dem Wege*, 22; Obenaus, *Anfänge des Parlamentarismus*, 542–43.

[43] Keinemann, *Preussen auf dem Wege*, 19; Rothfels, *Schön, Friedrich Wilhelm IV.*, 113ff.; Varnhagen, *Tagebücher* 1: 285, 30 March 1841.

to bore people. They are filled with pitiful phrase-mongering, purely servile obeisance, and, in the face of the protestations and panegyrics of the government, they possess not the slightest trace of free, manly speech."[44]

The provincial diets of the early 1840s demonstrated that the East Prussian nobility was exceptional for its liberalism. Brandenburg, Pomerania, and Saxony possessed the most conservative nobility, whereas the Rhineland had the most liberal diet.[45] The progressive posture of the landowning nobility in East Prussia had a number of causes. It undoubtedly had something to do with the fact that a number of East Prussian officials had studied with Kant and Kraus at Königsberg; it was also related to the fact that Königsberg was a major commercial city on the Baltic Sea, a center for the grain export to England, with a strong commercial class. But the liberal view of the landowning class in East Prussia undoubtedly was also related to the depth of the agricultural depression there in the 1820s and the fact that many estates changed hands during those years, with a more entrepreneurial group of landowners surviving. Their values corresponded more closely to those of the commercial interests, which, during the period of the British Corn Laws restricting the market for grain, were committed to free trade. Finally, the role of Schön himself cannot be ignored. He was revered by many noble estate owners for his role in saving what could be saved of their class in the depression. He carried enormous influence in the province. Schön's brother-in-law, Magnus von Brunneck, was one of the leaders of the liberal faction of nobles in the Prussian diet.[46]

Despite the quiet posture of the provincial diets in 1841, as Varnhagen had predicted, the constitutional question did not go away. The 1840s witnessed a tremendous growth of political consciousness in Prussia, well in advance of 1848.[47] Jacoby's two trials, in 1841 and 1845 (he was again arrested, tried, and again acquitted for two pamphlets that appeared in 1845), attracted widespread public attention.

---

[44] Varnhagen, *Tagebücher* 1: 285, 30 March 1841.

[45] Treitschke, *Deutsche Geschichte* 5: 145; Obenaus, *Anfänge des Parlamentarismus*, 543–44.

[46] See Peter Schuppen, "Ostpreussischen Junkerliberalismus und bürgerliche Opposition um 1840," in Helmut Bleiber, ed., *Bourgeoisie und bürgerliche Umwälzung in Deutschland, 1789–1871* (Berlin, 1977), 65–100; Koselleck, *Preussen zwischen Reform und Revolution*, 369–70.

[47] This theme is extremely well developed in Obenaus, *Die Anfänge des Parlamentarismus*, 594–648. For the increased attention that conservatives gave to the diets, see the correspondence of Leopold von Gerlach with Carl von Voss-Buch, DZA II, Rep. 92, C. v. Voss-Buch, no. 16, Bl. 8–9, 13, 15–16.

A flood of pamphlets on the constitutional issue appeared in these years, voluntary associations (*Vereine*) with local political concerns sprang up throughout the monarchy, and new newspapers provided a wider range of political perspectives than had been permitted in the past. This higher level of political consciousness was manifested in the number of petitions submitted to the provincial diets by the people. The Jacoby affair produced a significant petition campaign in East Prussia in 1841. But most of the petitions came in the two subsequent meetings of the provincial diets. In 1841, the Silesian diet received 100 petitions—less than the 128 received at its first meeting in 1825. But in 1843, the number of petitions submitted grew to 130, and in 1845, it reached 225. Forty of those submitted in 1845 called for legal or disciplinary action against officials.[48] The petitions represented a wide range of concerns, calling for broader representation, the elimination of the ten-year landownership requirement for election to the diet, and the publication of the deliberations of the diets. By 1845, a growing number of petitions addressed the problems faced by the poorer classes. The level of political action was notable; a striking report of the Silesian diet contrasted the political engagement of the 1843 diet with those that had preceded it.

In the six previous diets, a quarrel of the parties was, to a large extent, unthinkable. Scarcely did a burgher dare to raise his voice than he would be startled by the echo of his words and struck speechless in his best arguments. At times he would not be accorded the slightest honor of attention. The noble lords read the newspapers, conversed with one another in the assembly, or laughed with superior bonhomie in the reddened faces of the plebeians. Even in the sixth diet, it was not self-understood that the burghers joined in speaking; a report from peasants was not thinkable, even when one had the grace to inquire about peasant conditions.[49]

All this changed in 1843. Embryonic party factions began to appear in the diets of 1843 and 1845.

The government did not know how to handle this increased level of political activity; as a result, it pursued contradictory policies that at

---

[48] Ibid., 583ff. On the role of Vereine, see Thomas Nipperdey, "Verein als soziale Struktur in Deutschland im späten 18. und frühen 19. Jahrhundert: Eine Fallstudie zur Modernisierung," in his *Gesellschaft, Kultur, Theorie: Gesammelte Aufsätze zur neueren Geschichte*, Kritische Studien zur Geschichtswissenschaft, 18 (Göttingen, 1976), 174–205; Wolfgang Hardtwig, *Strukturmerkmale und Entwicklungstendenzen des Vereinswesens in Deutschland, 1789–1848*, Beiheft 9, *HZ* (1984): 11–50.

[49] Cited in Obenaus, *Anfänge des Parlamentarismus*, 569.

CHAPTER 9

times abetted the growth of interest in politics and at other times tried to restrain it. In 1841, Frederick William announced that the diets would be convened every two years. The government also relaxed the censorship of the deliberations of the diets, beginning in 1843. But when the diets of 1843 and 1845 produced numerous demands for broader representation, the ministry was tempted to reimpose censorship on the proceedings of the diets by requiring that they all be reported in a newspaper controlled by the government. Minister of Internal Affairs Count Arnim even suggested dropping the biennial regularity of the meetings.[50] When the Polish representatives in Posen requested greater representation for Poles in the diet, a national assembly for Prussia, and freedom of the press, the king was so angry that he publicly threatened to suspend permanently the Posen diet—a response that only served to reveal the arbitrary basis for the Stände.[51]

This growth of political activity that brought pressure on the provincial diets caused additional problems for the government. By localizing political action, it intensified the tension between the ständisch institutions and the central administration. This may be what prompted Varnhagen to comment that "within the near future, the king will either have to create a national diet or eliminate the provincial diets."[52] While decentralized provincialism had traditionally been a line of conservative defense by the landowning nobility, by the 1840s it was causing difficulty for the conservative government committed to the preservation of noble preeminence, for it was rendering the monarchy ungovernable. Ernst von Bodelschwingh, who served in the ministry from 1842 to 1848, foresaw serious difficulties as the need to consult the provincial diets increased. The government's task would be made much more "difficult," he declared, if in "the course of legislating it must consult eight diets and then, laboriously and often without happy success, rework the legislation into a unified whole."[53]

Although the creation of a national diet would simplify the task of consulting with separate provincial diets, it would also threaten to unleash forces that the government would find difficult to control. In

[50] Ibid., 589–90.
[51] Keinemann, *Preussen auf dem Wege*, 52; Varnhagen, in *Tagebücher* 2: 163, 14 March 1843, remarked on the king's threat to suspend the Posen diet: "The threat not to convene the Stände ever again shows undeniably that this body of the Stände rests on nothing and is based on any sudden fancy."
[52] Varnhagen, *Tagebücher* 1: 277, 2 March 1841.
[53] Cited in Obenaus, *Anfänge des Parlamentarismus*, 555.

some respects, the dilemma facing the government resembled that faced by Hardenberg in 1811. He found it hard to push through his financial reforms without the approval of a "representative" body, the Assembly of Notables. Convening such a body, however, had provided a forum for the conservative opponents of his reforms. Similarly, Frederick William IV and a number of his advisers recognized that a national diet, or even the anticipation of one, would be likely to provide the liberals with a platform for generating even more opposition to the government. Leopold von Gerlach thought it would be impossible to limit the responsibility of a national diet. "Any measure, such as the convocation of a general diet," he wrote, "would be most dangerous, if undertaken without necessity. The diet would not stop at consulting about a state loan but would act on anything it considered urgent."[54]

Faced with this dilemma, the government proceeded timidly by first convening the United Committee, composed of representatives from each of the provincial diets. Even the plans for this modest step sent shock waves of fear through some conservative circles.[55] Many viewed the formation of the United Committee as preliminary to a national diet. But the government severely limited the scope of the committee and established procedures to prevent it from acting in a parliamentary fashion or developing partisan factions. Only three issues were to be discussed: whether it was in the national interest for the state to extend the network of railroads, whether an increase in taxes would be warranted for this purpose, and how the government should proceed with legislation concerning private waterways. No recommenda-

[54] Gerlach, *Denkwürdigkeiten* 1: 99.

[55] The committee was composed of 12 representatives from each province in addition to the marshal. Obenaus, *Anfänge des Parlamentarismus*, 559. Treitschke, *Deutsche Geschichte* 5: 184, set the total at 98, with 46 from the nobility, 32 from the cities, and 20 from the peasantry. Trauttmannsdorff, the Austrian ambassador to Berlin, predicted ominously that the committee would satisfy no one. "If the United Committee now meets, it will be difficult to limit it to advice on legislation shared with it or to prevent it from submitting petitions and expressing all kinds of wishes. If the government does not comply, if the committee finds no concessions on the side of the government ... the committee will return dissatisfied or perhaps it will have to be sent home, spreading an unfavorable voice in the provinces and only contributing to an unfavorable meeting of the Stände at the next diet." Keinemann, *Preussen auf dem Wege*, 37. Leopold von Gerlach defended Frederick William IV against the criticism of the extreme conservatives. "They say that the king has excited the liberal party and helped it gain power, as was not the case in the previous government. It may be said in response: he could not continue as had his predecessor, and his ständisch measures, his relaxation of the limitations on the press, and more that could be included, I do not consider to have been mistakes." *Denkwürdigkeiten* 1: 86.

tions would be received by the king on issues not directly related to these topics. No petitions were to be directed to the committee. Members of the committee were seated in alphabetical order to prevent groupings according to political persuasions. Genuine debate was not permitted; committee members were called on by the marshal, in alphabetical order, and could speak only once on each issue. The minister who was present at the committee discussions could, through the marshal, close debate at any time.[56] The most important issue discussed was the manner of state support for railroad construction; to the government proposal of a state guarantee for the interest on railway investment, committee member Brust, from the Rhineland, insisted that there was no difference between a guarantee of interest and a state loan, which only a national diet, and not the committee, had the right to approve. Bodelschwingh responded that the committee was consultative only and that it did not have the authority to approve or reject anything. A few ultraconservatives objected to any railroad construction, but an overwhelming majority of the committee favored an extension of the network of railways and an increase in taxes.[57]

The committee adjourned after three weeks of inconsequential discussions. The government was generally satisfied with the outcome, but the meeting of the committee did nothing to quiet the calls for a national diet. By the end of 1844, the king had resolved to convene a meeting of all the provincial diets, but he had yet to convince his brother, William, and other members of his government.

Plans for a New Nobility

At the same time that the government groped for an acceptable constitutional structure that would better reconcile the state and the society in Prussia, it began to consider how, in the newly emerging society, it could preserve a landowning nobility.[58] These discussions are among the most interesting of any in the Vormärz, not merely because they show how aware the king and his ministers were of the link between preservation of the nobility and preservation of the monarchy (that relationship had been stressed by conservatives for some time) but also because they demonstrate how willing the government was to

[56] Keinemann, *Preussen auf dem Wege*, 47.
[57] Obenaus, *Anfänge des Parlamentarismus*, 556–63.
[58] The discussion that follows here is based on material found in DZA II, Rep. 2.2.1, no. 930. The only discussion of the official plans for a new nobility that I have seen are found in Treitschke, *Deutsche Geschichte* 5: 256–58. Paul Hassel, *Joseph Maria von Radowitz* (Berlin, 1905) 1: 439–41, gives Radowitz's views without dealing with the background.

consider consciously creating a new nobility, more compatible with the new wealth, but still buttressing the monarchy.

Between 1790 and 1848, the Hohenzollern policy of granting patents of nobility to commoners changed substantially.[59] First, by the 1840s, far fewer patents of nobility were awarded than had been the case at the end of the eighteenth century. Leaving aside the years 1798 and 1840, which were exceptional because Frederick William III and Frederick William IV elevated a large number of commoners to the nobility on the occasion of their coronation (Frederick William III granted 74 patents, his son, 43), each decade showed a decline in the number of commoners ennobled. From 1790 through 1806, 212 were ennobled; during the subsequent thirty-three years of Frederick William III's reign, 174 received noble titles. From 1841 through 1848, Frederick William IV granted only 24 titles, an average of only 3 per year, one-third the number granted, on the average, during the 1790s.

Second, and still more striking, is the fact that the ovewhelming majority of those given titles by Frederick William III were army officers and public officials. Fewer than 10 percent owned noble estates. Frederick William IV reversed this policy; well over 50 percent owned noble estates. Even allowing for the fact that the number of commoners owning noble estates increased markedly in the 1820s and 1830s, the figures show a clear preference for persons who owned noble estates. This tendency was obvious to keen observers from the outset. In commenting on the list of persons ennobled at Frederick William IV's coronation, Varnhagen noted: "It is noteworthy that the king also here, as in Königsberg, coupled all of the titles of nobility granted with ownership of land. It appears that he will put the nobility on the same basis as the English."[60] Estate ownership as a precondition for nobility was consistent with Frederick William IV's enthusiasm for Haller's doctrine of the patrimonial state in which land was the basis for authority; a landless nobility exercised no Herrschaft and therefore provided no inherent support for monarchy.

Frederick William's insistence on a landed nobility became the subject of discussions within the government from 1841 through 1847. At the time of his coronation, he created a number of new nobles whose titles were associated with the ownership of an estate; although they could retain the title for their lifetime, it could be inherited by their children only as long as the estate remained in the family. If it were

[59] The figures used here are drawn from Koselleck, *Preussen zwischen Reform und Revolution*, appendix 3, 676–79.

[60] Varnhagen, *Tagebücher* 1: 229, 15 October 1840.

sold, the noble title was to be revoked. This "principle of inheritance" became the basis for many of the discussions of the Commission for Noble Affairs, created by a cabinet order of July 21, 1841, which stated:

> The task of this commission shall first be the illumination of my intended principle of inheritance for new noble families and the conditions for their continued existence, which are linked directly to landownership as such; it is also the illumination of the historical character of the nobility in general, the needs of the present, and the requirements that must be met if the nobility is to preserve its political position and its true mission for the monarchy in these times.[61]

In 1843, Karl von Savigny, the minister of justice, reported to the other members of the ministry on the discussions on the commission. The commission, he declared, had proceeded with the assumption that the preservation of a landowning nobility was essential to the state. The question was how to do it. One method was to insist on entailed estates that could be inherited only by the oldest son, who alone would also acquire the noble title. This method, however, was completely contrary to the historic character of the German nobility, according to which all children of a noble father inherited the title whether or not they were excluded from the inheritance of the landed estate. Savigny reported that the commission believed the present situation called for the development of a "gentry," a union of the younger sons of nobles with those burghers who had recently acquired estates. As one of the founders of the historical school of law, which viewed law as a product of the history and custom of a people, Savigny expressed doubts about an effort to emulate the English gentry. "Even if one finds a perfect model in the English gentry," he commented, "it must be emphatically stated that it may be scarcely possible to transplant successfully into foreign soil a circumstance that is so unique and that has grown so slowly into maturity."[62] In the discussion following Savigny's presentation, the king reaffirmed his determination to link nobility to landownership and all agreed that the loss of land should deprive the family of its title.[63]

Reference to the English gentry formed the focal point for a long memorandum written in April 1844 for the commission by Christian Karl Bunsen, who at that time served as the Prussian ambassador to

---

[61] DZA II, Rep. 2.2.1., no. 930, Bl. 62.
[62] Ibid., Bl. 64.
[63] Those present were Boyen, Thile, Arnim, Voss-Buch, and the king. Ibid., Bl. 71–72.

England.[64] Bunsen analyzed the future of the nobility in Prussia by attempting to place it within the context of the major social changes that were under way in Europe and that had already transformed English society. "It is easy to perceive that if the present course of things continues," he wrote, "in the not too distant future, the great majority of noble estates in most provinces will be found in the hands of non-noble owners." These bourgeois estate owners will then form a constitutional majority in the provincial diets and will "exploit every opportunity to exhibit an anti-aristocratic spirit." "The commercial class will become better educated and more ambitious each year; indeed, in general, it can be said that it will steadily and persistently become richer and that it alone can build and maintain great fortunes. This fact dominates the entire future of Europe," he predicted. "In Prussia, this means that a commercial class, in control of the new wealth, will gradually monopolize the noble estates and thereby become, except for the high nobility [*Herrenstand*], the First Estate [*Ritterstand*]."

Bunsen compared this development to that which had taken place in England since the sixteenth century, the rise of the gentry. "The rich businessmen and manufacturers became 'country gentlemen.' Their rich and well-bred daughters married other landowners or perhaps even the son of a peer." These new landowners did not receive titles, but as they married other gentry or persons with titles, they were "assimilated into the families of peers and thereby into the provincial administration and the police," giving "the entire class of estate owners an aristocratic character."

A similar fusion of new wealth and old nobility was possible in Prussia, Bunsen believed. He based his confidence on three "realistic" factors: (1) "the properly acquired rights and the existing privileges" of the old and new nobility; (2) the constitutional structure of the provincial diets, which based membership in the noble Estate (Ritterstand) of provincial diets on the ownership of a noble estate for ten years or the direct inheritance of such an estate; and (3) the expansion of the definition of personal qualifications for service in the army and the state, which since the reform era had made it possible for commoners to achieve high rank. These factors had developed in such a way during the preceding two decades that they made it possible for a fusion of the old and the new elites to take place on the land. "The suitable moment is at hand to cast such a monarchical-aristocratic institution

[64] DZA II, Rep. 2.2.1., no. 930, Bl. 8–21.

into the democratic current of the times in such a way that it will be carried forward by that current," Bunsen declared.

Two separate efforts were necessary to create a noble "gentry" consistent with the traditions and the history of Prussia, Bunsen maintained. The first was to insist that in those provinces in which a high nobility (Herrenstand) comprised the First Estate, the younger brothers of those seated in this First Estate participate in the Second Estate (Ritterstand), alongside all the other lower nobility or commoners owning noble estates who were eligible for membership in this Second Estate. This would ensure that the "Second Estate of the monarchy will thereby maintain a significantly strong aristocratic character, which it will increasingly require." "What would have become of the English Parliament," he asked, "if the future peers and their brothers had not sat in the House of Commons?"

The second approach to the assimilation process required that those who purchased noble estates be given a title of nobility immediately, making them eligible to participate in the Ritterstand, as long as they were able to meet three conditions: (1) that the estate or complex of estates that they acquired be of sufficient size and income to correspond to the other estates of the province; (2) that they establish a limited entail (*Fideikommiss*), making the estate a possession of their entire family and assuring that it was not merely bought for short-term speculation; and (3) that the individual meet the "personal" qualifications for membership in the Ritterstand. Because the ownership of an estate was, according to Bunsen, "not without political significance," this third condition was of great importance. Persons elevated to the nobility should have the "education, culture, and noble life style that enable them to be nobles." They should have occupations in which they had been concerned with the "general" good, by which Bunsen meant they should have exercised some form of Herrschaft. Servile or artisan occupations, which had "only a personal interest," should be excluded from membership in the Ritterstand. Bunsen believed that the army reforms had given "the entire nation" the capacity for honor that would make commoners with the right experience eligible for this new nobility. He concluded:

In this way, no one is excluded, everyone is encouraged to noble undertakings and to live in a noble manner.... Thus, the nobleman can once again become a political reality and a power, not through possessions alone, but through the love and respect of the nation which surrounds him. The Ritterstand will become the flower and the spokesmen of the educated nation, instead of a noble caste that is neither loved nor desired and that, in the course of the century, is threatened with poverty and extinction. Finally, the crown holds the power to ennoble the feeling of independence of the upwardly striving, rich, and cultivated middle class [Bürgerstand], to harness and use it for the enhancement of the most conservative of all occupations—landownership. Such an institution appears to be a true realization of the royal idea accompanying that which was expressed at the coronation.

Bunsen's memorandum was a remarkable document. It showed the lengths to which some were willing to go in order to preserve a conservative landowning aristocracy—if the old nobility could not retain its estates, the commoners who purchased the estates should be ennobled and, through contact with the rest of the nobility and intermarriage, imbued with a "noble spirit." But the document was also remarkable in that it demonstrated that prior to the revolution of 1848 and well before German unification and industrialization, important members of the government already thought in terms of a necessary union of the old and the new elites that would work to preserve aristocratic domination and monarchical authority. The year 1848 would show that the middle class was not yet powerful enough to seize power, but some conservatives already in 1844 saw the import of its growing wealth.

Not everyone received the ideas for a new nobility with enthusiasm. Leopold von Gerlach worried that the heavy emphasis on landownership as a condition for receipt of a noble title would neglect the role of service and reward acquisitive values.[65] His brother, Ludwig, was concerned that the emphasis was placed exclusively on the preservation of the Ritterstand, the legal category of noble estate owners, rather than on the preservation of the nobility per se. He believed it was important to retain the "concept" of nobility, not merely its outward manifestations.[66]

During the two years following the submission of Bunsen's memorandum, the Commission on Noble Affairs worked to draft legislation encompassing the principles for future elevation to the nobility. The second and final draft of the law was completed in late 1846 or early 1847.[67] The draft followed the lines of the commission's previous discussion. "In the future," the proposed royal patent declared, "we will preferably award elevation to the nobility only to those persons who have owned a noble estate for ten years." They must have secured the future of this noble estate through entail. The provincial diets were to be consulted with regard to the "personal capacity" of the individuals

[65] DZA II, Rep. 92, C. v. Voss-Buch, no. 16, Bl. 5; no. 27, Bl. 50–52.
[66] DZA II, Rep. 92, C. v. Voss-Buch, no. 27, Bl. 69–75.
[67] DZA II, Rep. 2.2.1., no. 930, Bl. 31–36.

considered for noble titles. If, through partition, the estate ceased to qualify as a noble estate, its owner might retain his title for his lifetime, but the title could not be inherited by his children. Titles granted, for service to the crown, to persons who did not own a noble estate were lifetime titles and could not be inherited except if the son had also achieved a high service rank or had acquired a noble estate and met the other qualifications for nobility.

In referring to the local assemblies of noble estate owners (Ritterschaften) as the "nurseries" (*Pflanzschulen*) for the aristocratic development of commoners who owned noble estates, the "Motive" for the legislation explained its objectives: "The conclusion of the patent expresses the conviction that the realization of these principles will achieve the purpose of the law: namely, to increase the political significance of the nobility and thereby introduce a healthy accommodation, a moderation of the apparent separation between noble and non-noble estate owners."[68]

In May 1847, Cabinet Minister Thile sent the proposed law, together with the Bunsen memorandum, to Radowitz, friend and adviser of Frederick William IV. It is not clear why he sought Radowitz's advice, but it is possible that Thile wanted his support in persuading the king that the law was a bad idea. Thile's cover letter to Radowitz offered a summary of his misgivings and the reason for his opposition to the patent:

> If I am to offer my judgment of the entire matter quite honestly, I must acknowledge that I cannot agree with it and that I have opposed it as much as I am able. We will, in the future, have one nobility composed of those with unconditional rights of inheritance, one with conditional inheritance, one that is a purely personal or service nobility, and a half-nobility (gentry). To the nobility with unconditional inheritance rights will belong all the previous noble families, most of whom will be propertyless; those with conditional inheritance will be based on the ownership of property; and entry into the service nobility and the gentry will be attainable merely by speculating on land—that is the total picture that hovers before me and from which I cannot see anything healthy emerging.
>
> It is impossible to deprive the old nobility of its right to unconditional inheritance, even when it is propertyless; to link the new nobility to property ownership is most highly desirable and expedient; to try to create something for those who fall in between is, however, liable

---

[68] The "motive" is found in ibid., Bl. 37–43.

only to create confusion, division, and to obscure the original character of the nobility.[69]

Radowitz's analysis of the proposed law corresponded to that of Thile.[70] While the patent would achieve a certain fusion of the old nobility and a new aristocracy of the land, he believed, it did not make clear what should be the function of the old nobility in the alliance. The proposal did not ask the important question, "What must be done in order to secure the aristocratic principle in the new society? Consideration of this question would lead, on the one hand, to an investigation of the essence of nobility, to the conflict of noble and non-noble life styles, to the eternal conflict between honor and profit." He continued, "On the other hand, this question would lead to an examination of the obligations of the nobility and of the necessity to replace its older duties, which can no longer be fulfilled, with other duties that reach deeply into the organic life of the present age."

Radowitz used the opportunity provided by this consultation to write a personal note to the king advising against issuing the patent, which he feared would generate "mistrust and hatred."[71] He applauded the king's efforts to set aside "the previous system of government," which he characterized as "administrative absolutism," and to establish the basis for a true ständisch monarchy. But the issue of a new nobility, it was clear, did not stand high on Radowitz's agenda for the monarchy. Much else needed to be done, he declared: "The press must be emancipated," and the goverment must turn its attention to "the urgent social problems of the present—it must undertake generous measures against mass poverty through the organization of work and the regulation of emigration." It should lead in the organization of a German federation.

After the receipt of Radowitz's critical evaluation of the proposal, the ministry apparently set aside, at least for a time, the effort to create a new nobility. The following year the revolution of 1848 swept away the possibility of consciously building a gentry; the fusion of the two elites would take place, but in a different time and in a different way.

The United Diet

In December 1844, Frederick William IV announced to his advisers that he wanted to convene a national diet by 1847.[72] He believed the

[69] Ibid., Bl. 29–30.
[70] Ibid., Bl. 47–54.
[71] Ibid., Bl. 43–47.
[72] Obenaus, *Anfänge des Parlamentarismus*, 651ff.

provincial diets and the United Committee provided an "unstable footing" (*schiefen Fläche*) for public life in Prussia. Although Frederick William had intended to establish a national diet since 1840, he was pushed toward this decision throughout 1844 by his minister of internal affairs, Count Adolf von Arnim. Arnim had argued that it was necessary for the government to seize the initiative, to "show through its deeds that it has not for a moment abandoned the program of progress" announced in 1840.[73] Arnim insisted that a national diet would provide a necessary "element of unity" for the eight provinces and that it would produce the "needed reforms in a conservative, not a radical sense." He wanted to set aside the United Committee and establish a national diet with a first chamber comprising the 50 members of the high nobility with individual or collective votes in the provincial diets; a second chamber would be composed of 70 representatives from each of the three Estates of the provincial diets—10 each from the three larger provinces and 8 each from the five smaller provinces.[74] Arnim's proposal, finally submitted in May 1845, thus preserved representation by the Stände but granted equal representation to the noble estate owners, the towns, and the peasants. Arnim proposed to limit the diet to practical considerations, especially the state loan that would be required to construct the railroad to East Prussia. He hoped, as he put it, to "take the wind out of the sails" of the opposition.[75] Frederick William did not like Arnim's idea of creating a new institution and he did not wish to dissolve the United Committee; such actions, he feared, would be seen as creating a constitution rather than allowing one to develop naturally. Instead, he favored convening all of the provincial diets together. This would not create a new institution and would have the further advantage of retaining the numerical superiority of the landowning nobility. Discussions about the formation of a national diet continued throughout 1845 and 1846. A chief critic of the idea was Prince William, who reluctantly agreed to the plan on the condition that a diet include a separate chamber for the high nobility.[76]

The Patent of February 3, 1847, establishing the United Diet, re-

[73] Documents related to Arnim's constitutional plans are in STAP, Pr. Br. 37, Boitzenburg, 3946, 3947, 3960.

[74] STAP, Pr. Br. 37, Boitzenburg, 3947, Bl. 3–7. See also Obenaus, *Anfänge des Parlamentarismus*, 652.

[75] Cited in Helmut Asmus, "Die preussische Verfassungsfrage in Frühjahr 1847: Die ständische Gesetzgebung vom 3. Februar 1847 und die Vorbereitungen der grossbürgerlichen Opposition zum Vereinigten Landtag," *Jahrbuch für Geschichte* 7 (1972): 178.

[76] Obenaus, *Anfänge des Parlamentarismus*, 655; Treitschke, *Deutsche Geschichte* 5: 607–9.

flected the king's ideas.[77] It combined all of the provincial diets into a single body charged with advising the crown on a proposal to introduce new taxes and the approval of a state loan for railroad construction. Further, it declared that the United Committee would continue and be convened every four years. As with the provincial diets, the United Diet had the right to receive and consider petitions for the crown. Nowhere did the patent mention the promise of a constitution made in 1815. To assure that the patent could not be construed as a constitutional document, it avoided such phrases as "national diet" or "national assembly." No member of the government except the king signed the patent, because he wished to make it clear that it was a gift from him alone. He even wanted to prohibit the newspapers from using phrases that would make the diet appear to be a parliamentary body.[78]

The United Diet was a curious mixture of ständisch principles and popular representation. It was divided into two curia, the Curia of the High Nobility (*Herrenkurie*), composed of 72 princes, counts, mediatized German nobles, and members of the royal family, and the Curia of the Three Estates, composed of the 537 representatives from the other three estates of the provincial diets—noble estate owners, towns, and peasants. On the one hand, membership was determined by Stand, giving the diet a ständisch foundation; on the other hand, as in the case of the provincial diets, the United Diet operated as an undivided whole for most of its business. The plenum was an assembly of both curiae; it discussed the tax and state loan issues presented by the king. Other issues, such as petitions, were discussed separately and voted on separately by the two curiae. In the Curia of the Three Estates, voting was by head, not by estate; this made it resemble a parliamentary body. But the delegates were seated in the assembly according to province and Stand; a concession was also made to ständisch principles by permitting the curia to dissolve into its three constituent parts (*itio in partes*) if two-thirds of the membership of one particular Estate believed that it might be injured by a decision of the majority. This, too, followed the practice of the provincial diets. In addition, the United Diet conceded to the provinces a similar right to demand that the curia vote by provincial representatives if one province feared it would be injured by a vote of the majority. In cases in which such

---

[77] Eduard Bleich, *Der erste Vereinigte Landtag in Berlin 1847* (Berlin, 1847; facsimile ed., Vaduz-Liechtenstein, 1977), 1: 3–4. The patent itself merely established the diet in accord with the law on state debt, January 17, 1820. Other ordinances accompanied the patent, establishing the structure and procedure for the diet, ibid., 4–10.

[78] Treitschke, *Deutsche Geschichte* 5: 609.

CHAPTER 9

divisions took place, the recommendations of all of the constituent parts were forwarded to the king. This mixture of structures, then, allowed the United Diet to be considered as a ständisch assembly in which the Estates were separately represented, and, at the same time, to be viewed as a national assembly.[79]

It was precisely this ständisch profile and the limited power it gave to the United Diet that provoked widespread criticism of the February Patent. Liberals in the provincial diets considered boycotting the diet in protest. Magnus von Brunneck, a leader of the liberal nobility in East Prussia, wrote to Alfred von Auerswald that the members of the diet should, at the outset of the meeting, try to establish its legislative competence, and if they could not be satisfied, they should be prepared to leave. "I recommend that all representatives . . . see to it that they have the money for the return trip when they arrive so that they will not be embarrassed if we conclude after a few sittings to give up and go home." Theodor von Schön suggested that at the opening of the diet the representatives declare themselves incompetent to serve as a general diet and demand a new election for the provincial diets.[80]

As had been the case in 1840, this public discussion of a constitutional issue prompted a spate of pamphlets. The most famous of those attacking the February Patent was *Annehmen oder Ablehnen?* (Accept or reject?), written by a Silesian liberal, Heinrich Simon. Simon's polemic infuriated the king, who immediately initiated proceedings against him. " 'We asked you for bread and you give us a stone!' " began the provocative essay. "That was our painful outcry as we read through the Patent of February 3. . . . The ordinance of February 3 takes away from the people, without listening to them, the few ständisch rights that it has had and gives rights to the crown that it has never had."[81]

---

[79] The separate voting by Stand was not advantageous to the nobility because of the possibility that the two Stände of commoners, the towns and the rural communities, would vote against the landowning nobility. Therefore, voting by head, with the nobility controlling nearly half of the votes, was preferable. See Peter Eickenboom, *Der Preussische Erste Vereinigte Landtag von 1847* (phil. diss., Bonn, 1976), 128ff. Theodore Hamerow described the mixture of ständisch and representative categories in the United Diet as "neither fish, flesh, nor good red herring." *Restoration, Revolution, and Reaction* (Princeton, 1958), 91. The ultraconservatives were offended by the vote by head. Carl Wilhelm von Lancizolle complained that the voting by head count was a mistake "because it signifies an undifferentiated assembly" that resembled a national assembly. *Ueber Königtum und Landstände in Preussen* (Berlin, 1846), 536–37.

[80] Heere, *Aus dem Papieren Magnus von Brünneck*, 406ff.; Rothfels, *Schön, Friedrich Wilhelm IV.*, 191; Asmus, "Die preussische Verfassungsfrage," 191.

[81] Heinrich Simon, *Annehmen oder Ablehnen? Die Verordnungen vom 3. Februar 1847, beleuchtet vom Standpunkt des bestehenden Rechts* (Leipzig, 1847), 5ff. For the proceedings against Simon, see Asmus, "Die preussische Verfassungsfrage," 189.

Simon maintained that constitutional life was based on a social contract, so that the patent could be considered a proposal only until a popular assembly had approved it. Other liberal pamphleteers criticized the ständisch representation because, they argued, the Stände no longer existed but were based merely on forms of landownership. Conservative writers defended the patent. A historian of religion at Berlin, Peter F. Stuhr, defended ständisch representation as the only alternative to an assembly composed of "proletarians" and "inexperienced intellectuals." "Next to the general representation of the common consciousness, it is equally necessary to have representation of the individual circles of community life, which move in particular directions," he wrote.[82]

Not all of the landed nobility were pleased with the February Patent. Some resented the special position given the higher nobility through the creation of an upper chamber; from the older provinces came complaints that the newer provinces had been heavily favored in the selection of the high nobility for the upper chamber—a majority came from Silesia (25), Westphalia (12), and Saxony (7). Bülow-Cummerow worried that the requirement of a two-thirds majority of both chambers to pass petitions on to the king would give a small number of the high nobility the power to block the wishes of the Curia of the Three Estates and the will of the nation.[83]

Frederick William IV's opening address to the United Diet should be viewed against this background of criticism and opposition.[84] He appealed to the people for support against "all the indignities that I and my government have been subjected to during the last seven years" by the press. Determined to assert the divine right by which he ruled, he warned the delegates of an "insatiable mania for innovation" that would destroy the constitutional structure that had developed over time. Delegates to the diet were not to "represent opinions," but to represent the rights of the Stände. "There is no power on earth," the

---

[82] Stuhr wrote two pamphlets in 1847: *Die Preussische Verfassungsfrage vom weltgeschichtlichen Standpunkt aus betrachtet* (Berlin, 1847) and *Die Phantasien des Herrn Gervinius und seiner Freunde über die Geschichte und die Verfassung Preussens* (Berlin, 1847). An anonymous critique of the liberal views is also found in *Kritische Beleuchtung der Schift: Die Preussische Verfassung und das Patent von 3. Februar 1847 von G. G. Gervinius* (Leipzig, 1847). Liberal pamphlets included Ferdinand Fischer, *Preussens Herrenbank und Wahlgesetz* (Leipzig, 1847), and Friedrich Crüger, *Das Ständische Verfassungsgesetz für Preussen vom 3. Februar 1847* (Neuhausen, 1847).

[83] Eickenboom, *Erste Vereinigte Landtag*, 63; Treitschke, *Deutsche Geschichte* 5: 616; Ernst von Bülow-Cummerow, *Preussen im Januar 1847 und das Patent von 3. Februar* (Berlin, 1847), 266.

[84] The opening address (*Thronrede*) is in Bleich, *Der erste Vereinigte Landtag* 1: 20–26.

king declared, "that can succeed in making me transform the natural relationship between prince and people, whose inner truth gives it strength, into a conventional, constitutional relationship, and I will never allow a written piece of paper to come between the Lord God in Heaven and this land." Finally, with a phrase that captured the essence of his attitude but that angered the delegates who demanded that the United Diet become a legislative parliament, Frederick William declared that the diet's responsibility was to approve new taxes and the government loan, but that he would reconvene the diet in the future, "if I consider it good and useful, and I will happily do it often if this diet offers me proof that I can do it without injuring the rights of the crown."

The king's speech set the confrontational tone that characterized the remainder of the meeting of the diet. According to Varnhagen, several hundred delegates refused to applaud the king's address and nearly one-third considered leaving the diet immediately. Public criticism of the speech was common. "How stupid not to have left a backdoor open" and "we have received the closing address at the beginning" were expressions that circulated among the salons frequented by Varnhagen.[85] They reflected the uncompromising tenor of the royal address. The first agenda for the diet became, therefore, the discussion of how to respond to the king's opening address. It provided the liberals in the diet an opportunity to set forth their demands—regular and periodic meetings of the diet, unrestricted rights to petition the king, the right to approve all government loans and new taxes, consultative powers for all legislation affecting individual and property rights, and freedom for the diet from all the restrictions imposed on the provincial diets and the United Committee. Not all of these claims appeared in the liberal version of the address to the king, but the claim of the diet to be considered a national assembly was evident. A conservative address to the king was defeated and a compromise version overwhelmingly accepted. The king's response, upon receipt of the address, was less strident than his opening speech. He recognized that the competence of the diet could develop further in the future; although he refused to grant the right of the diet to convene regularly, he did promise to reconvene it within four years.[86]

[85] Varnhagen, *Tagebücher* 4: 60–63, 11–13 April 1847.

[86] The diet's address to the king and his response are found in Bleich, *Der erste Vereinigte Landtag* 1: 28ff. For details of the liberal proposal of Beckerath, the conservative proposal of Arnim, and the compromise of Auerswald, see Helmut Asmus, "Die Verfassungsaddresse der grossbürgerlich-liberalen Opposition im preussischen Vereinigten Landtag von 1847," *Zeitschrift für Geschichtswissenschaft* 22 (1974): 1326–40.

The issue of regular, periodic meetings became the central point of contention during the United Diet because it was critical to the claims of authority made by the diet. Members of the government joined by ultraconservatives considered periodic meetings to be an invasion of the royal prerogative. Liberals, on the other hand, insisted that regular, periodic meetings, whose convocations were not dependent on the will of the king, were fundamental to any constitutional order. Without regularly scheduled meetings, the diet could not claim to be a national diet representing the will of the people, but merely a body convened at the king's pleasure to advise on legislation or to approve new taxes or government loans. David Hansemann complained of effects of the uncertain status of representation in the Prussian diets:

What is one of the greatest weaknesses of the legislation on the rights of the Stände up to the present? It is the uncertainty, the lack of clarity, and the fact that they can be altered on grounds of expediency, even very quickly. And, therefore, we have, gentlemen, a very changeable constitution in Prussia because the views of it have changed often between 1815 and 1846. This impermanence of the constitution I consider to be a great misfortune, not only for the nation, but even more for the strength of the throne. . . . The force of the nationality will be awakened through a sense of justice.[87]

The "uncertainty" and "unclarity" of the rights of the Stände, about which Hansemann spoke, permeated the deliberations of the United Diet. Faced with the king's refusal to acknowledge the diet as a national assembly possessing the right of periodic meetings, those who wished to establish broader claims for the diet followed several other strategies. Georg Friedrich Freiherrn von Vincke, the leader of the Westphalian liberal faction, circulated the *Declaration of Rights* asserting the right of the diet to approve all future legislation in the state. Vincke's *Declaration* gained 138 signatures, but a number of liberals believed it went too far and refused to sign it.[88] A second approach was to withhold approval for the loans or guarantees of interest payments requested of the diet by the government. Opponents of the government reasoned that since the legislation of 1820 gave the authority to approve loans to a "national diet," and because the king had refused to acknowledge the United Diet as such an assembly, the United Diet lacked the competence to approve government loans. Accordingly, the

---

[87] Karl Biedermann, *Geschichte des ersten preussischen Reichstages* (Leipzig, 1847), 82.
[88] Ibid., 107; see also Obenaus, *Anfänge des Parlamentarismus*, 690; Treitschke, *Deutsche Geschichte* 5: 623–24.

CHAPTER 9

diet defeated the proposal for a loan guarantee for the construction of the eastern railroad by a vote of 360 to 179. Among those voting against the loan were a large number of noble estate owners from East Prussia, who stood to gain from the undertaking.[89]

A third effort of the diet to reaffirm its competence was to pass a resolution calling for a change in the February 3 Patent, so as to broaden the powers of the diet. Numerous proposals for changes were submitted; most called for a periodic and regular meeting of the diet, the elimination of the United Committee, an expansion of the rights of petition, and an enlarged competence of the diet to approve state debts. Both curiae of the diet ultimately agreed on a proposal, which received support even from the conservative members of the diet. The king's response came immediately; he did not foreclose the possibility of further modification of the February Patent but refused to eliminate the United Committee. Any further changes in the United Diet would be made after the meeting of the United Committee early in 1848.[90]

This struggle to establish the United Diet as a genuine parliamentary body appeared in many of the debates. It was evident, for example, in the interesting discussion of the government's proposal to exclude persons of "disrepute" (*bescholtenen Personen* or persons of *bescholtener Ruf*) from the ständisch assemblies. Persons of disrepute had been excluded from the county and provincial assemblies from the outset, but the basis for exclusion was never clear. The authority to declare someone unworthy of serving in a diet resided with the government, and there were strong suspicions that exclusions had been politically motivated. These suspicions focused in 1847 on the case of Count Reichenbach, whose election to the United Diet had been set

---

[89] Dietrich Eichholtz, *Junker und Bourgeoisie vor 1848 in der preussischen Eisenbahngeschichte* (Berlin, 1962), 119–24; Kurt Born, "Die Entwicklung der Königlichen Preussischen Ostbahn," *Archiv für Eisenbahnwesen* (1911), 879ff.; Obenaus, *Anfänge des Parlamentarismus*, 692. East Prussian liberal nobles were proud to claim that they placed principle above self-interest in the question of the eastern railway. Treitschke, *Deutsche Geschichte* 5: 625–26. As Bismarck pointed out, however, the eastern railway was also defeated because a number of conservative nobles questioned the "utility of the undertaking." Bleich, *Der erste Vereinigte Landtag* 3: 1468. Many noble estate owners agreed with Adolf von Rochow that the railroad brought few advantages to the society. "Stability of governments, faithful subjects, enduring peace"—these were not present in societies that had large railway systems, such as England. For the landowning nobility, the railroad provided a visible symbol of the penetration of industry; it cut through the rural landscape, slicing in half the integrated whole of their landed estates. See Eichholtz, *Junker und Bourgeoisie*, especially 41, 59.

[90] Biedermann, *Geschichte des ersten preussischen Reichstages*, 28off.; Obenaus, *Anfänge des Parlamentarismus*, 689–91.

340

aside by the governor of Silesia on the grounds that Reichenbach was under investigation for circulating forbidden political pamphlets; despite the confirmation of a good reputation by the other noble estate owners of his county, Reichenbach was excluded from the diet.[91] The new law proposed by the government was intended to clarify the grounds upon which persons could be excluded. Persons were to be considered of disrepute who (1) had lost the rights of honor as a result of a criminal conviction (the right to hold public office or to swear an oath, for example); (2) had been dismissed or expelled from the army as a result of the decision of a military honor court; (3) had been legally excluded from the exercise of civil or communal rights; and (4) had been judged to be in disrepute by the other members of their Stand. Further, the law held that persons who were under criminal investigation would not be allowed to exercise their ständisch rights until the investigation had cleared them of suspicion.[92]

Opponents of this broad definition of *disrepute* based their arguments on several grounds. Beckerath argued that the law failed in its two major requirements: to protect the rights of the individual and to preserve the institutions of the community. The rights of the individual could easily be transgressed by authorities who could launch a criminal investigation timed to prevent his participation in a ständisch assembly. "No one of public respect can be declared to have forfeited his rights if his unworthy behavior is not an established fact. It is contrary to any sense of justice for the punishment to precede the judgment," he declared. By the same note, the rights of a representative assembly would be violated if it allowed the government to determine who was worthy of participation. He insisted, "A ständisch assembly, arising from a legally executed election, forms a constitutionally constituted independent body. The most intrinsic nature of the vocation that it has to fulfill over and against the administration makes it necessary that its composition be not in the slightest way determined by the interference of the state authorities."[93] All representative bodies that have endured have retained the power to determine the credentials of their members, he maintained.

A second argument against the law, advanced by Auerswald, also stressed the integrity of a representative assembly. The honor of such an assembly was undivided, he argued; the dishonor of one member brought dishonor to the entire assembly. Therefore, the assembly as a

---

[91] On the Reichenbach case, see Biedermann, *Geschichte des ersten preussischen Reichstages*, 245–49.

[92] Ibid., 231–32.

[93] Bleich, *Der erste Vereinigte Landtag* 2: 208–9.

whole must pass judgment on the reputation of any of its individual members. "Although our ständisch legislature is differentiated, the king has also assembled us as a unity, in order to complete various functions in common. Thus, it would be proper, and do no injury to principle, for such an assembly of all four Estates to act in common in judging the honor of one of its members."[94]

These two arguments, taken together, essentially called for a liberal system of representation. Beckerath's insistence on an independent representative assembly, immune from executive interference, was tantamount to the demand for a separation of executive and legislative powers. Auerswald's call for a unified assembly acting on the credentials of its members essentially set aside the system of ständisch representation, for if peasants and townsmen were to pass judgment on the honor of nobles, ständisch differentiation no longer had its essential meaning.

The entire liberal attack on the law regarding disrepute in fact challenged the principle of ständisch differentiation. The obvious target for such criticism was that portion of the law that would exclude anyone as lacking good repute who had been convicted of a breach of honor by a military honor court. These courts, established to enforce a sense of noble honor in the army, could deprive an officer of his rank and honor for refusing to fight a duel that honor required. By defining such a loss of honor as disrepute, the law imposed a noble, that is ständisch, definition of honor on the whole society. Mevissen objected to the mixing of noble honor with the exercise of civil rights. "Consider how in the last century the honor of the noble Stand esteemed certain noble passions as worthy of honor, and how in this century, the concept of the honor of the nobility and the concept of a general civil honor are sharply differentiated. Even today there is a Stand for whom the duel is a matter of honor, while the greater part of society considers the duel to be a punishable crime. . . . I consider it impossible to resolve the conflict of noble honor and civil honor at this time in our state." Mevissen insisted that conviction for a criminal offense was the only basis for disrepute that would justify the loss of political rights.[95]

Conservatives argued that because membership in the diets was according to Stand, it was proper to apply ständisch definitions of honor and disrepute to their membership and that these were not concepts that could be evaluated by the assemblies in general. "The govern-

---

[94] Ibid., 210.
[95] Ibid., 201–2.

ment has established that someone may exercise his ständisch rights only as a member of a Stand, and I can see no reason that this Stand, out of which these rights arise, should not also be able to judge the most important question of whether one is in disrepute," declared Otto von Manteuffel. Another conservative noble defended the duel as a test of honor by quoting Guizot to the effect that the duel was the culmination of civilization; another described the duel as "so fused with the German character [*Wesen*] that we must preserve it from attack."[96]

The debate over honor and disrepute demonstrated the differences that existed between the concepts of honor held by the middle class and those of the nobility. It also gave evidence of the force of the middle-class criticism of traditional noble values. Opponents of the law distinguished the private from the public sense of honor. Mevissen put it most clearly: "Honor has two sides, the inner and the outer. The inner sense of honor rests on the sense of self [*Selbstgefühl*], on the sense of inner moral freedom, the inner worth, on the consciousness that the individual personality ought never be untrue to its convictions." This internal, private sense of honor, Mevissen believed, was paramount; it could exist whether it was acknowledged by others or not. It could not be shaken by any judgment of the world. There was also, he declared, a second meaning of the term *honor*, an outward meaning, the honor that one enjoys in the eyes of the world, in the respect one enjoys in society. "This respect rests on the opinion of society, that the individual person stands in a serene unison with the moral customs of this society in his sense of justice and his actions." It was this public meaning of honor, and it alone, that the law could judge, and for this reason, Mevissen believed that only a criminal conviction could deprive a person of his right to serve in a diet. For Mevissen and the other liberal opponents of the law, honor was specific to the individual. A person was honorable or dishonorable because of his actions; he earned the respect of society. The single code of honor that could apply in judging worthiness for service in the diets was obedience to the law, and this applied to everyone equally.[97] For the conservative supporters of the law, honor remained linked to Stand, to station and birth. Honor was based not merely on individual achievement or the respect one gained in society, but also on the Stand

[96] Ibid., 206–8, 218.

[97] Ibid., 201ff. For a general discussion of conflicting definitions of *honor* see "Ehre," in *Geschichtliche Grundbegriffe*, ed. Otto Brunner et al. (Stuttgart, 1975) 2: 1–63.

into which one was born. This differentiation of ständisch honor was contained in the Prussian General Law Code until 1850.[98]

Numerous amendments to the law dealing with disrepute were passed in the Curia of the Three Estates. The Curia of the High Nobility, however, approved the version as it had been presented by the government, modifying slightly the paragraph suspending rights of a person under investigation to require that the investigation be completed as quickly as possible.[99]

One of the most interesting discussions of the United Diet took place in the Curia of the High Nobility over a petition calling for a general reform of the system of patrimonial justice. The Ministry of Justice was itself preparing a measure to reform the patrimonial courts, so it supported the petition submitted by Prince Biron, from Kurland. The need for reform was widely acknowledged. Some court districts of the monarchy were responsible for supervising from 400 to 1,000 separate patrimonial courts, so careful supervision was virtually impossible.[100] Some patrimonial judges served a large number of patrimonial courts, so the intimacy on which the whole system was predicated was also in doubt. Moreover, the powers of the patrimonial courts varied widely, according to the traditions of the different provinces.

Discussion of the petition demonstrated both the continuing strength of paternalist images of authority and the need for reform if the system were to survive. The committee from the curia that examined the petition recommended that patrimonial justice be reformed but not eliminated. Patrimonial justice, the committee reported, was "a duly acquired individual right," "an essential moment . . . in the organism of our ständisch institutions."[101] Arguments in support of patrimonial justice repeated those that had been voiced during the previous four decades. Prince Lynar, from Silesia, stated, "I know myself, from personal experience and observation, patrimonial judges who understand and fulfill their important profession in all of its aspects and who fully deserve to be called patrimonial judges—paternal judges—because of their fatherly administration. They are the

[98] *ALR*, II/20/#538–690. For two case studies of commoners who purchased noble estates and who ran afoul of the prevailing notions of honor, see Robert M. Berdahl, "Junker and Burgher: Conflicts over the Purchase of Rittergüter in the Early Nineteenth Century," in *Mentalitäten und Lebensverhältnisse: Festschrift für Rudolf Vierhaus* (Göttingen, 1982), 160–72.

[99] Biedermann, *Geschichte des ersten preussischen Reichstages*, 241–44.

[100] Bleich, *Der erste Vereinigte Landtag* 2: 808.

[101] Ibid., 805.

friends, the protectors, the advisers of those under their jurisdiction; they seek to resolve all the conflicts submitted to them . . . and, insofar as it is possible, to know all of the personalities and relationships of those in their jurisdiction."[102] The king's brother, William, entered the discussion in defense of patrimonial justice more than once. He was convinced that the lower classes were better off in those regions where patrimonial courts still prevailed. Noble estate owners in the western provinces, he observed, "are all called only 'estate owners' [*Gutsbesitzer*], just as each peasant also calls himself an 'estate owner,' and they no longer have the slightest means at hand to influence the morality of those in their villages, and that, I believe, is a very large disadvantage. For if the estate owner lives with a fatherly caring relationship for his peasants, he can have only a beneficial effect."[103]

Only two members of the curia spoke in favor of eliminating patrimonial courts entirely, Count York and Count Dyhrn. Dyhrn argued that although patrimonial justice had numerous positive aspects, its foundation rested on the patrimonial state. "I believe this patrimonial state no longer exists," he declared. Therefore, patrimonial justice should also be eliminated. "It has been said here," he remarked, "that the last bonds that still exist between the noble estate owner and those who live on his estate will be torn asunder by the elimination of patrimonial justice. I must confess that I do not recognize any bonds any longer in the patrimonial courts."[104]

The upper chamber of the United Diet approved the petition calling for reform of the patrimonial courts, but it was never discussed in the Curia of the Three Estates. The elimination of patrimonial courts would take place only in the wake of the revolution of 1848.

As the debates on the definitions of *disrepute* and the reform of patrimonial justice demonstrated, liberals were frequently critical of the deep residual force that ständisch culture continued to exercise in Prussia. However, although the liberals continued to claim for the United Diet the rights of a national assembly, they never directly attacked the principle of ständisch representation in itself. There were no demands for popular representation. Despite the government's efforts to preserve both the ständisch and the provincial character of the assembly, and despite the fact that the diet was merely a meeting of all the provincial diets, it differed markedly from the provincial assemblies. In important respects, it assumed the characteristics of a parlia-

[102] Ibid., 812.
[103] Ibid., 817.
[104] Ibid., 813, 818.

mentary body. Stenographic reports of the debates were published, giving the public access to the diet's deliberations. Political factions—embryonic parties—developed, transcending provincial boundaries. Even before the diet convened, Hansemann rented a large apartment near the palace where he began to meet with delegations of liberals from other provinces. The pamphleteer Simon proposed to Hansemann that liberals rent rooms at the Hotel de Saxe so that they could more easily build a political club "in the French sense." Liberals also gathered at the hotel Russischer Hof. Conservatives congregated at the Englisches Haus, but they were less organized than their liberal colleagues. The conservative publicist F. Wülffing complained that the liberals planned strategy "until far into the night," but the conservatives lacked organization and leadership.[105]

It may be that the conservatives were disorganized. But it is also true that the landowning nobility, never a completely homogeneous group, was divided by the issues that faced the diet. Especially from East Prussia and Silesia came a group of noble estate owners who were eager to establish a national assembly that would assume many of the powers of a parliament. They were opposed by the landed nobility from Brandenburg and Pomerania, who continued to support Frederick William IV's views of the constitution.

The United Diet adjourned on June 26, 1847. It may be viewed as both the capstone and the ultimate failure of the government effort to construct a modern state based on ständisch institutions. The diet had opened with Frederick William IV's assurance that it completed "the noble edifice of ständisch freedom" that would prevent Prussia from dissolving into a constitutional system; as it closed, Count Schwerin observed that Prussia "would henceforth become a constitutional state."[106] The diet rejected the government's request for a state loan to build the eastern railway because the king refused to recognize the diet as a national assembly that would meet at regular, periodic intervals. It was an audacious act, referred to by the young conservative delegate Otto von Bismarck as extortion. Leopold von Gerlach lamented on May 7: "The diet has lasted nearly four weeks and one defeat follows another."[107] He later moderated his view slightly, but conservatives generally found little to cheer about in the decisions of the assembly.

The United Diet represented a new plateau of political conscious-

[105] Obenaus, *Anfänge des Parlamentarismus*, 704–5. Huber, *Verfassungsgeschichte* 2: 494.
[106] Bleich, *Der erste Vereinigte Landtag* 4: 2397.
[107] Leopold v. Gerlach, *Denkwürdigkeiten* 1: 118.

ness in Prussia, a fact that helps to explain the politics that emerged from the March days of the revolution of 1848. The diet directed political attention to the central administration and policies of the state in a way that had not been the case since the reform era. As a consequence, the provincial and county institutions, the locus of noble predominance, receded in importance. The emergence of political interests and factions that crossed provincial boundaries also contributed to the further dissolution of ständisch institutions in which the power of local noble estate owners was concentrated. If the authority of the crown was not directly weakened by the decisions of the diet, neither was it enhanced, as leading nobles in the monarchy echoed the observation made by Theodore von Schön in 1840, that the time of the patrimonial state had passed and that the monarchy had to be established on a new footing.

When the February Patent was first promulgated, Prince William declared: "A new Prussia will be formed. The old Prussia passes to its grave with the publication of this law. May the new be as majestic and great as the old was glorious and honorable."[108] An ideology predicated on localism, paternalism, and a structure of authority embedded in private law no longer sufficed for the "new Prussia" that emerged from the United Diet. Conservatism now required acceptance of the modern state and public law.

[108] Treitschke, *Deutsche Geschichte* 5: 609.

10

IDEOLOGY ON THE EVE OF REVOLUTION: FRIEDRICH JULIUS STAHL

Down to the 1840s, the conservative ideology of the Prussian nobility developed largely in response to the bureaucratic absolutism of the eighteenth century and the era of the Stein-Hardenberg reforms. First Adam Müller, then Carl Ludwig von Haller, elaborated a view of authority that corresponded to the daily experience of the landowning nobility: Herrschaft required the direct control of subjects by a paternal authority. The landowning nobility exercised patrimonial power over the peasants on their estates, and the king was the patrimonial ruler of the land. When exercised directly, by a king and his nobility, this Herrschaft was tangible and real for the subjects; when carried out by a bureaucracy, authority became abstract and impersonal. The abstract power of bureaucratic absolutism, these ideologists maintained, led inexorably to revolution. In its most extreme form, enunciated by Haller, this ideology of the patrimonial state denied altogether the public nature of the state; it transformed all authority into a hierarchy of private contracts between rulers and ruled, culminating in the private and personal rule of the prince.

Despite Frederick William IV's enthusiasm for Haller's patrimonial state, the events of the first years of his reign made it clear that such an ideology was no longer adequate. The state was a public institution, essential for providing the infrastructure on which both agrarian and commercial capitalism were built. As the agricultural entrepreneur from Pomerania Ernst von Bülow-Cummerow repeated in numerous pamphlets during the 1840s, the state alone could provide the legal structure, the credit guarantees, the roads and the railroads, and the instruments of social control necessary for the economic development of rural Prussia.[1]

The United Diet also demonstrated the inadequacy of the patrimo-

---

[1] See *Preussen, seine Verfassung, seine Verwaltung, sein Verhältniss zu Deutschland* (Berlin, 1842); *Ueber Preussens Landwirtschaftliche Kreditvereine, die Reformen, deren sie bedürfen und über ein tüchtiges System der Bodenbenutzung und Schätzung* (Berlin, 1843); *Das Bankwesen in Preussen* (Berlin, 1846); *Preussen im Januar 1847 und das Patent vom 3. Februar* (Berlin, 1847).

nial ideology. By insisting on regular and periodic meetings of the diet as a condition for approval of government measures, the diet essentially called for constitutional limitations on the power of the monarch. If the liberals in the diet did not raise the issue directly, their demand indirectly posed the question of where sovereignty resided. Moreover, the widespread public discussion of the constitutional question before and during the diet, as well as the emergence of political factions, indicated that the contested terrain had changed. The danger to the traditional landed elite came not from an unbridled bureaucracy, but from an ambitious entrepreneurial class.

By 1847, *restoration* no longer served as a meaningful word in the lexicon of Prussian conservatives. They needed an ideology that developed a theory of strong monarchical power without, at the same time, succumbing to bureaucratic absolutism. They needed an ideology that recognized the public character of the state, one that would allow them to accept and exploit a constitutional system.

The person chiefly responsible for developing a new ideology for Prussian conservatives in the 1840s was Friedrich Julius Stahl. More than anyone else, Stahl was responsible for reconciling Prussian conservatives to constitutionalism. Stahl's political ideology found the means of maintaining the personal character of authority within the context of public law. He offered a conservative theory of a modern state that could accommodate change and give a place for the new social forces, while it retained the personal element in authority embodied in monarchy and nobility.

Friedrich Julius Stahl

Stahl was an unlikely standard-bearer for the conservative nobility of Prussia, for he was, by birth, both Bavarian and Jewish. He was born Julius Jolson in 1802, the son of Valentin Jolson, a merchant in Würzburg; his mother was the daughter of Abraham Uhlfelder, a successful merchant and leader of the Jewish community in Munich. In 1805, Jolson received permission to move to Munich, so he and his young family moved into the Uhlfelder household. Julius's grandfather was a powerful patriarch, whose forceful presence made a deep impression on the young boy.[2]

---

[2] This brief biographical sketch is based on Gerhard Masur, *Friedrich Julius Stahl: Geschichte seines Lebens, Aufstieg und Entfaltung, 1802–1840* (Berlin, 1930). Masur never completed the second volume of this biography. See also Hans Peter Pyclik, *Friedrich Julius Stahl: A Study of the Development of German Conservative Thought, 1802–1861* (Ph.D. thesis, Minnesota, 1972).

CHAPTER 10

These were difficult years for Jews in Bavaria. Restrictions on Jews had been relaxed somewhat in Prussia in the eighteenth century, and Austria had granted them legal equality in 1781. In Bavaria, however, Jews were still denied citizenship and the corresponding rights of public worship and freedom of movement. They were excluded from public schools and subject to extraordinary taxes. Special allowances and privileges went to a few individuals who provided financial and commercial services to the state. Abraham Uhlfelder was such a person; he served as a business agent for several members of the royal court. In anticipation of Jewish emancipation, Uhlfelder urged his brethren to prepare themselves for citizenship by demonstrating their steadfast loyalty to the state. The edict of emancipation finally came in 1813; shortly thereafter, Julius's father volunteered for service in the militia and fought in the wars of liberation.

Emancipation made it possible for young Jolson to attend Wilhelms Gymnasium, a new preparatory school founded by the reform government. This school was intended to introduce the neohumanism of north German schools into conservative and Catholic Bavaria. The intellectual leader of this new school was Friedrich Thiersch, a Protestant called to Munich from Göttingen. Thiersch's teaching combined classical ideals with religious belief. Through him, the young Jolson became acquainted with the work of Friedrich Heinrich Jacobi, who had been a critic of Spinoza's rationalism and pantheism. Jacobi asked: is the supreme being merely the origin and prime mover of all things, or is it a personal intelligence? He concluded that God must be a free personality and that humankind, as the supreme creation, must also be free and independent. The idea of God as a free, creative personality became an axiom of Stahl's philosophy from the very beginning. Under Thiersch's tutelage, Jolson came to view the personal God of creation as the Christian God of revelation. Dissatisfied with Judaistic formalism, he decided to convert to Christianity. In 1819, against the wishes of his parents, he traveled to Erlangen, where he was baptized a Lutheran. He dropped the name Jolson and assumed the name Stahl; in honor of his godfather, Thiersch, he took Friedrich as his first name.[3]

---

[3] Stahl's motives for conversion were questioned by his contemporaries and by subsequent historians, especially during the Nazi period. The advantages of conversion were obvious. But, given the consistency of Stahl's religious commitment throughout the remainder of his life, there seems little reason to doubt the genuineness of his conversion. See Pyclik, *Stahl*, 14. The rest of Stahl's family eventually also converted to Christianity. Masur, *Stahl*, 37. For examples of literature stressing the Jewish traces in Stahl's writing, see Johannes Hedel, "Der Einbruch des jüdischen Geisten in das deutsche Staats- und

Also in the fall of 1819, Stahl began to study law at Würzburg. While a student at Würzburg, he joined a local chapter of the *Burschenschaften*, the student associations that had fallen under police surveillance because of radical political activities. At a secret meeting of the Burschenschaft in 1821, Stahl opposed efforts to politicize the association, arguing that its function should be solely educational. After a brief period in Heidelberg, he returned in 1822 to study in Erlangen, the Protestant university in Bavaria where, since 1820, Friedrich Wilhelm Schelling lectured in philosophy. In 1820, Schelling had become a sharp critic of Hegelian rationalism in terms that Stahl found attractive. Stahl's studies in Erlangen were cut short in 1824, however, by the government, which banned him from further study after it discovered that he had attended a clandestine meeting of the Burschenschaft. Stahl's appeal to the king and his insistence that he had opposed all political activity by the Burschenschaft gained him a reprieve: he could return to his formal study within two years, in 1826. Stahl spent the two years of his ban studying Hegel's philosophy as well as Savigny and the historical school of law.

After the ban on his formal education ended, Stahl completed his legal studies and took a position at the new *Hochschule* in Munich. At just this time, the winter semester of 1827–1828, Schelling returned to Munich and delivered his lectures on recent philosophy. The Schelling lectures attracted enormous attention; they gave Stahl the critical perspective he needed to construct his own philosophy of law. Schelling proclaimed the lectures as the transition from negative to positive philosophy. Negative philosophy was based on necessity, positive philosophy on freedom. The philosophy of necessity, Schelling maintained, was the product of rationalism as it had developed from Descartes through Spinoza, Leibniz, Kant, Fichte, and his own early philosophy; this system of rationalism reached its apogee in Hegel, who declared that the real was rational and the rational real. This identification of reality and rationality, Schelling argued, left no room for freedom, for if reality were rational, it was necessary, that is, it could not be other than it was. Turning away from rationalism, Schelling drew upon antirationalists such as Jakob Böhme, Johann Georg Hamann, and Friedrich Jacobi to assert that the endless variety of creation was evidence of God's freedom.[4]

Schelling's attack on rationalism provided Stahl with the tools he

---

Kirchenrecht durch Friedrich Julius Stahl," *HZ* 155 (1937): 506–41; Fritz Fischer, *Moritz August von Bethmann-Hollweg und der Protestantismus* (Berlin, 1937), 365.

[4] Masur, *Stahl*, 103–5.

needed to launch his own assault on Hegel's philosophy of law. He published in 1830 the first volume of his *Philosophie des Rechts*, the preface of which contained Stahl's acknowledgment of his debt to Schelling, whose lectures, Stahl wrote, "launched a completely new era of philosophy."[5] In 1830, Stahl also became the editor of a new government newspaper, *Thron und Volksfreund*, an organ intended to represent the king's position in the debate over the constitutional question in Bavaria. The newspaper lasted only nine months; Stahl then wrote for *Inland*, another government newspaper. In the course of his brief career as a publicist, Stahl developed the major arguments that would later form the basis for the monarchical principle. Stahl's academic career began in 1832 when he was appointed assistant professor in Erlangen; thereafter, he advanced rapidly. He was appointed professor of Roman law in Würzburg, and the following year he returned to Erlangen as professor for state and church law, a position that satisfied his highest expectations. During these years, he also wrote the second volume of his *Philosophie des Rechts*, the first part of which appeared in 1833 and the second part in 1837. Stahl was selected to represent the University of Erlangen in the meeting of the Bavarian diet in 1837, a position that cost him the confidence of King Ludwig I, for he joined other members of the diet in opposing some of the policies of the government. As a result of his opposition, the king withdrew Stahl's right to teach state law and permitted him to teach only civil law.

In 1840, Stahl accepted the chair at Berlin that had once been held by Hegel. His appointment coincided with the new government of Frederick William IV and, like the appointment of Schelling in Berlin the following year, was motivated by the king's desire to overcome the pervasive influence of Hegel that still lingered in Berlin nearly a decade after his death. Students who were disciples of Hegel, for example, jeered Stahl's inaugural lecture. But Stahl's appointment also displeased many of the Prussian conservatives who were still enamored with Haller. *Das Berliner Politische Wochenblatt* had been critical of Stahl's *Philosophie des Rechts*. Antagonized by Stahl's rejection of Haller's teaching as a primitive form of natural law theory and as a thoroughly false reconstruction of the Middle Ages, these Prussian conservatives believed Stahl was too attached to the historical school of law, which they considered relativistic and insufficiently Christian. Stahl reported to a friend the rumors that circulated in Berlin about him,

---

[5] The preface to each edition is reprinted in the third edition. See *Philosophie des Rechts* (Heidelberg, 1856), 1: xiv.

shortly after his arrival. Some claimed he would subordinate the state to the church, others that he was a pietist or an absolutist.[6]

Not until the publication of the booklet *Das monarchische Princip* in 1845 did the Prussian conservatives begin to recognize what Stahl could offer their political ideology. Thus, from the mid-1840s, Stahl became increasingly involved in Prussian politics. In 1847, as the United Diet debated a proposed revision of the law on Jewish emancipation, Stahl published the essay "Der christliche Staat und sein Verhältniss zu Deismus und Judentum," in which he argued against the extension of full rights of citizenship to non-Christians. When the revolution broke out in Berlin in March 1848, Stahl fled; he later returned and contributed booklets and essays to the conservative cause, as well as articles for the *Kreuzzeitung*, the newspaper founded by conservatives in the summer of 1848.[7] He was elected to the Prussian Chamber of Deputies and later awarded a seat in the House of Lords (*Herrenhaus*) of the Prussian Parliament. One of the most effective orators in Parliament, Stahl became a leader of the Prussian Conservative Party during the decade after 1848; with the beginning of the "new era" in 1858 under the regency, and later monarchy, of Prince William, the influence of Stahl's ultraconservative wing of the party waned. He died in 1861.

It would be too much to claim that Stahl spoke for all of the landed nobility or that his political theory satisfied all of his conservative compatriots. The Prussian nobility was never a unified and cohesive class, and less so in the 1840s than earlier. Some of Haller's enthusiasts were never completely converted by Stahl, no matter how closely they worked with him. Ludwig von Gerlach, for example, believed that Stahl's political thought was too abstract, too philosophical, and that it was not sufficiently grounded in the experience of Herrschaft. Gerlach complained that, in contrast to Haller, Stahl did not appreciate that Herrschaft came from above, not from below; Gerlach complained that God, for Stahl, was a moral force, a creative personality, but not the Father, Lord, and King. For Gerlach, monarchical power could be based only on the principle of fatherhood, just as God could

---

[6] Erich Kaufmann, in *Studien zur Staatslehre des monarchischen Prinzips*, in *Gesammelte Schriften* (Göttingen, 1960), 3: 2, wrote: "Out of the university of Hegel and the Hegelians, Berlin was to be the university of 'the philosophy of revelation' of Stahl and Schelling." On Stahl's reception in Berlin and the rumors circulated about him, see Ernst Salzer, "Stahl und Rotenhan: Briefe aus dem ersten an den zweiten," *Historiche Vierteljahrschrift* 14 (1911): 514–51. See also Pyclik, *Stahl*, 44ff.

[7] *Das monarchische Princip* (Heidelberg, 1845); *Rechtswissenschaft oder Volksbewusstsein?* (Berlin, 1848); *Die Revolution und die konstitutionelle Monarchie* (Berlin, 1848).

most clearly and tangibly be understood as a Father.[8] Gerlach never completely trusted Stahl's conservatism. Reflecting on Stahl in a letter to Heinrich Leo, the historian and conservative writer, Gerlach wrote the following in 1867:

> As you have correctly observed he [Stahl] for the most part fell into a vulgar constitutionalism and sought only to temper it in a conservative manner through Christian-moral feelings. In March 1848, he fled and was inclined to cast aside the entire study of law [*Staatsrechtswissenschaft*] as no longer useful. . . . It is painful to write this about a dear friend, who fought so bravely and in whose soul I took such delight and strength and edification in the midst of the fight. But you have forced me to do so. . . . His learning was weak and he had no firm ground beneath his feet; his opponents and his more insightful friends have both seen this also and have considered his conservative position to be relatively accidental; in 1850, he could just as easily have been a follower of Radowitz or of Bethmann.[9]

It was precisely this flexibility, lamented by Gerlach, that gave Stahl's political system its strength and that enabled him to redefine constitutional monarchy in a conservative manner. He was a more profound thinker than either Müller or Haller, although beneath the philosophical apparatus of his major work, *Die Philosophie des Rechts*, lay an ideological system that served both monarchy and nobility in Prussia. His political thought, formulated on the eve of the revolution of 1848, provided the framework for conservative thought well beyond 1848. What were the main elements of Stahl's political thought?

Stahl's Philosophy of Law

Stahl published a number of books, booklets, and collections of speeches in his lifetime, but the core of his thought, from which he derived everything else, was in his *Philosophie des Rechts*. This analysis of Stahl's thought, therefore, is drawn largely from the structure of

---

[8] *Von der Revolution zum Norddeutschen Bund aus dem Nachlass Ernst Ludwig von Gerlach*, ed. Hellmut Diwald (Göttingen, 1970), 1: 30–31.

[9] Ibid., 31. Radowitz had, prior to the revolution, advocated a reform of the German Confederation. After the revolution, he became the leading advocate of the Erfurt Union, a plan for the union of Germany under Prussian leadership, excluding Austria. Conservatives like Gerlach opposed the plan because it broke the longstanding conservative association with Austria and because it catered to the pressure of nationalism. Moritz August von Bethmann-Hollweg was the leader of the left wing of the conservative faction after 1848. He became a leader of the government during the "new era" after 1858.

this work.[10] Stahl divided *Die Philosophie des Rechts* into two major parts, with the whole comprising three large volumes. Given the scope of the entire work—the three volumes totaled nearly eighteen hundred pages in the third edition—it is natural that there was some overlap and repetition. On the whole, however, Stahl pursued a discrete objective in each volume. Part 1, subtitled "History of the Philosophy of Law," offered a history of political theory from antiquity to the nineteenth century. Part 2, subtitled "Legal and Political Philosophy on the Basis of a Christian Perspective," comprised two volumes. The first dealt with Stahl's views on the philosophical foundations of political theory, and the second offered Stahl's own theory of the state.

In his history of political thought, Stahl interpreted the work of previous thinkers through the prism of his own philosophy, selecting those aspects of their work that would clarify his own system. Thus, he paid little attention to the ancient Greeks and almost none to the Romans. He believed the Greeks were deprived of the capacity to develop a "historical ethos" because they lacked the concept of a personal God who transcended the temporal order. The Christian teleology of the medieval thinkers provided them with a view of history, but their "theocratic" philosophy led them to stress God's direct intervention in the temporal order.[11] While eliminating this "theocratic character" of medieval thought, the Reformation also based the temporal world on the will of God, but as it was expressed in his commandments, not as a result of direct intervention. In this way, the Reformation emancipated the individual; for the first time, "the otherworldly nimbus of external authorities and their unlimited power over faith and conduct disappeared, and man retained a sphere in which he stood directly under God and his conscience."[12]

Stahl believed, as did most conservative thinkers of his century, that

[10] Stahl made major revisions between the first and second editions, even changing the titles. First edition: *Die Philosophie des Rechts nach geschichtlicher Ansicht*, vol. 1, *Die Genesis der gegenwärtigen Rechtsphilosophie* (Heidelberg, 1830); vol 2, *Christliche Rechts- und Staatslehre* (Heidelberg, II/1: 1833; II/2: 1837). Second edition: *Die Philosophie des Rechts*, vol. 1, *Geschichte der Rechtsphilosophie* (Heidelberg, 1847); vol. 2, *Rechts- und Staatslehre auf der Grundlage christlichen Weltanschauung* (Heidelberg, II/1: 1845; II/2: 1846). The third edition has the same titles as the second and few changes, though obviously his emphasis changed here and there as a result of the revolution of 1848. Citations here, unless otherwise indicated, are from the third edition (Heidelberg, 1854–1856).

[11] He devoted only two pages to the Romans in his first volume. In the first edition, he paid little attention to the Middle Ages as well. He added to it in the second and third editions. For the discussion of ancient philosophy, see *Philosophie* 1: 8–49; for medieval philosophy, see 50–89.

[12] Stahl, *Philosophie* 1: 74–75.

rationalism led to revolution. This did not mean that he opposed the use of human reason, for he believed that reason was not incompatible with the Christian faith and that reason, too, was the result of God's revelatory creation.[13] However, he objected to any philosophy that viewed reason as the ordering principle of the universe, for it displaced the idea of a personal God and the authority he exercised.[14] Thus, a philosophical system that presumed to impose rational patterns of one's own making on the universe was bound to be revolutionary. Divorced from God, reflecting only the arrogance of human beings, such a philosophy would distort the basis for true human freedom. Therefore, Stahl devoted much of his history of political thought to a criticism of the "abstract philosophy of right," as he categorized rationalism.

Abstract philosophy, Stahl maintained, sought to reconstruct the world purely from the categories of reason. It assumed that the categories of human thought could be imposed on all phenomena and thereby explain reality. "It is as though one considered the eye as the source of light," he wrote, "and wanted to discover history, not through the observation of events, but by examining the inner construction of the eye and its various parts."[15] The genesis of all modern rationalist thought was Descartes's dictum *cogito ergo sum*. Whether Spinoza or Hegel spoke of a "universal Being," or Kant of "the unconsciousness," all rationalist philosophy came back to the same dualism, said Stahl, "the real being of the thinker (the I), and the pure determination of the thought." Stahl found this duality imcompatible. The individual determined essence through free, creative, living actions. Reason, as defined by the rationalist, on the other hand, was independent; as an objective reality, it was "complete from the beginning." What followed from reason was contained within it from the outset. The individual was a free and freely determining being; objective reason was objective necessity, and, therefore, unfree.[16] The two poles could not be joined.

Stahl translated this dichotomy between subjective thinker and objective reason into the distinction between objective rationalism and subjective rationalism. Objective rationalism, of which Spinoza was the first major representative and Hegel the most recent, denied the existence of a personal God and the creative independence of human beings in the temporal world. Because it viewed the entire world as

[13] Masur, *Stahl*, 147–49.
[14] Stahl, *Philosophie* 1: 102.
[15] Ibid. 1: 92.
[16] Ibid., 100–101.

the rational expression of God, so that "everything that happens cannot be other than according to this law, cannot be other than good and right," objective rationalism excluded the possibility of evil.[17] From such a point of departure, the development of an ethical system was impossible.

Subjective rationalism, the mainstream of abstract philosophy until Hegel, developed its ethical system on the basis of natural law. "One can say that logic is the heart of the new philosophy, causing its pulse to beat; natural law, however, is its face, in which its soul is reflected," Stahl wrote.[18] For Stahl, the belief in natural law was the most dangerous manifestation of rationalist philosophy, the vital link between rationalism and revolution.[19] Because natural law was ascertained by reason, with no explanation of where reason acquired its basic structure, morality and justice based on natural law were devoid of content. Kant resolved this problem by means of the categorical imperative, which assumed that the basic content of an ethical system was inherent in human nature. Stahl believed that Kant's error was his assumption that the true norms could be discovered by logic and that the necessity born of that human logic corresponded to transcendent values. Fichte went even further than Kant by suggesting that the individual's consciousness itself was reason; subject only to the logical necessity imposed by one's own consciousness, the individual's actions were free. For Fichte, the free "I" was the source of morality. Defining himself through his encounter with the other, the "non-I," the individual found the moral axioms in actual social existence. Kant and Fichte both demonstrated the central ethical rule of natural law theory, from which the basis of its entire social and political system was derived—"the maxim of coexistence": "each must limit his freedom so far as to allow that of the others to exist." "This is the highest, the only basic rule of natural law," Stahl wrote.[20]

The clearest example of the manner in which rationalist philosophy tried to reconstruct the world from reason, according to Stahl, was its concept of humanity in a state of nature. Natural-law theorists admitted that a state of nature, devoid of social existence, had never existed. It was a construct of reason, used to explain the origin of society and the state. According to this rationalist reconstruction, individuals were born into a state of nature with unlimited freedom; this was their natural right (*Urrecht*). The encounter with others who possessed the

[17] Ibid., 107.
[18] Ibid., 139.
[19] Herbert Marcuse, *Reason and Revolution* (New York, 1954), 360–74.
[20] Stahl, *Philosophie* 1: 248. Subsequent references in the text are from this edition.

same freedom and reason led to the "maxim of coexistence"—respect for the freedom and natural rights of others. The maxim of coexistence produced a social contract for the protection of these rights and from this contract developed the state. Stahl summarized the argument: "The state is ... the realization of the maxim of coexistence. Its purpose is the protection of the rights of the individual" (251). Whether states actually originated in this way was of little concern to abstract theorists, Stahl declared; all states were based on an implicit contract, which gave them the power to legislate. But for Stahl, the social contract also opened the door to revolution.

The principles of natural law also led to revolution, Stahl complained, because they demanded social equality. If people were born free and created the state in order to protect their freedom in a social setting, then it followed that each should have an equal measure of freedom in society. Inequality before the law would have to disappear, for legal inequality assumed that the state fulfilled purposes other than the preservation of freedom. For example, if it were important for one Stand "to exist for honor, as a representative of divine majesty, then it must have privilege from birth," Stahl declared. Setting such privileges aside in the name of individual freedom, he warned, would "lead to permitting women equal participation in the administration of the state" (139–40). Stahl considered natural-law theory as destructive in all spheres of life—the family, the social order, and the state.

It [natural law] is especially destructive for the state. It does not acknowledge the tasks that lie in the vocation of the state to provide a higher order over men, nor does it see the necessity of organic division of the ranks for the fulfillment of these tasks. It does not acknowledge the authority or the power originally inherent in the state for this vocation; rather, it considers the state as a random assembly of men merely for the protection of their freedom, with the necessity of equal rank and without any power except that which the members voluntarily grant it. (283)

Stahl's criticism of rationalism culminated in his attack on Hegel, whose idealism made reason, in the form of Absolute Mind, the pervasive, driving force of all being. Although Hegel was the most abstract of all of those Stahl put in the rationalist camp, he admitted that Hegel's political philosophy had avoided many of the errors common to natural law thinkers. "Hegel successfully fought the widespread errors of his day: the theory of Kant, which made the freedom of the individual and the mere respect for the existence of other men (the maxim of coexistence) into the exclusive principle of right and the state, and which considered marriage as merely a contract over sexual relations.... He successfully fought Rousseau's teaching of popular sovereignty" (471). Hegel had both overcome the mechanistic view of constitutional monarchy of the other rationalists and combatted the feudal, private-law theory of the state of Haller. However, Hegel's philosophy depersonalized the state; he made the state's authority into an abstraction, faceless and without personality.

Hegel's error, Stahl believed, was that he began with the same pantheistic assumption as Spinoza and Schelling, which considered God as the universal, the substance of the world, who had no existence apart from individual things. Likewise, for Hegel, individual things did not exist apart from God—the universal was the particular and the particular was the universal (425). Whereas neither Spinoza nor Schelling had offered a logical explanation for this union of the universal and the particular, Hegel believed he found the explanation by inventing the dialectic. In the dialectic, each thought suggested its opposite and was reconciled with its opposite in a higher synthesis. Hegel assumed that reason revealed itself in nature through the dialectical process. God, Absolute Mind, for Hegel, developed its consciousness through the dialectical process in history; thus, all of history was necessitated by the dynamic logic of the process. Stahl believed this denied the vitality of human creativity in time, rendering people unfree tools through which the Absolute Mind achieved consciousness. Stahl complained of Hegel's view: "Man does not come to know himself in the family, in the state, through philosophy, in God and the living God in him; rather, the system of thought—the thought of the family, of the state, and so on—comes to know itself in man, so that one could say, the mirror reflects itself in mankind" (459). Hegel's pantheism, his identification of Absolute Mind with everything, so that the is and the ought were identical, ultimately denied human freedom and depersonalized authority.

Stahl insisted that the Hegelian system could not be true if the theory of the dialectic were false. He argued that there was no basis for believing it to be true. It was not true that every proposition suggested its opposite. The idea of finitude suggested infinity, but it did not prove its existence. The notions of the dialectic were vague, the concepts of antithesis (*Gegensatz*) and unity were unclear. Some of the syntheses Hegel used as examples were, in fact, new formations, genuine fusions of the two opposing principles they reconciled; other syntheses simply eliminated one of the opposing principles and reconfirmed the other (442–44). For Stahl, the dialectical method failed, and with the failure, Hegel's system collapsed.

CHAPTER 10

Hegel's state was the product of the dialectic, the higher synthesis that resulted from the opposition of the free individual (the one) and the collection of individuals in society (the many) (437). The state stood as the universal providing the overarching unity to the conflicting particular interests manifested in civil society. But, Stahl charged, the unity took place at the level of abstraction. "The dissonance, which cuts through the real world, appears here merely as abstract, and it finds its reconciliation in an abstraction," he wrote (462). For Stahl, the dissonance grew from the fact that human beings were free but incomplete personalities struggling for their fulfillment. The dissonance, for him, was that humankind was alienated from God and could be reconciled to God only by God's personal intervention.

In summarizing his criticism of Hegel and the entire history of the philosophy of abstract speculation, Stahl repeated his objection to its failure to grasp the true meaning of human alienation. In doing so, he laid the groundwork for his own Christian philosophy.

> Finally, speculative philosophy has made that which is deepest and truest of the natural and moral cohesion of the world, and that which is completely closed to vulgar rationalism, into its center: the need for and the reality of a reconciliation of mankind with the power that is above man. But it also possessed only a shadow of this highest truth. Instead of the reconciliation and union of living personalities, the divine and the human, through the living deed, it was satisfied with the reconciliation of the logical moments and their conceptually unified presentation. (482)

As a Christian, Stahl considered the human condition to be the result of the Fall, which had alienated humankind from God and rendered human beings incomplete. The source of reconciliation, the "personality of God," became the unifying principle of Stahl's philosophy. By *personality*, he meant a living entity, not an abstract concept as it was for Hegel, or "merely abstract self-consciousness," as it was for Fichte. "Personality alone is true being, simultaneously concrete and spiritual," Stahl wrote at the outset of his second volume of *Philosophie*. Personality was the unifying essence of both God and human beings; it was the "absolute unity" that brought all parts into a meaningful whole.[21]

---

[21] The term Stahl used, *Persönlichkeit*, is difficult to translate into English because the term *personality* is laden with psychological baggage. Stahl spoke of the "personality of God," in the image of which, "the personality of man" was created. He used the term in its theological meaning to signify that God was a person, whose Fatherhood was indicated by the fact that one addressed him in prayer with the familiar "*Du*." For this theological

Because personality was free, creative individuality, its manifestation, was the freely creative act. The world was the freely willed creative act of God. He was everywhere present and active in his creation, but he was not identical with creation itself, as the pantheists maintained. Conceiving of God as a free personality separate from the world did not limit his power or render him finite, as the pantheists alleged, for, according to Christian faith, God was in the world, but not of it. Creation was an act of free personal will by God, not the result of abstract reason; thereby all creation remained free and not bound by logical necessity.[22] This, Stahl believed, was the basis of freedom. God was a dynamic creator, unfettered by necessity.

Created in the image of God, the human being was also a personality, a free individuality. As a free personality, the individual had the capacity to reshape and restructure the substance of the world, God's creation, and thereby to become a cocreator.[23] As a free personality, the human being was endowed with a free will; if one were in complete union with God, living in the kingdom of God, one would freely will God's will. However, because of the Fall, humankind was not in complete union with God, so one also chose evil. Only willing God's will enabled humans to approach his fulfillment. "It is the task of man to be a true and complete person," Stahl declared.[24] While this was never achievable on earth, one had the obligation to establish on earth a "moral world" in which the will of God would be clear. The civil order (the state and the law) was responsible for creating the moral world, while the church fostered the faith; both throne and altar thus contributed to the realization of the human purpose on earth.[25]

The development of a moral order, as a part of creation, was closely linked, for Stahl, with God as personality. "Morality is the fulfillment of man in himself (naturally as a result of his will), or the revelation of the divine essence in man."[26] Morality sprang from two sources: obedience and, growing from obedience, love. "Love, although it rests on the foundation of obedience, is the higher means of fulfillment than mere obedience. The fullness of religion is not contained in the mere

---

explanation of the term, see Kurt Galling, ed., *Die Religion in Geschichte und Gegenwart: Handwörterbuch für Theologie und Religionswissenschaft*, 3d ed. (Tübingen, 1965), 5: 227–28. For Stahl's formulation of the concept, see especially *Philosophie*, II/1:14ff.; for his rejection of Hegel's use of the term, see 1: 461.

[22] Ibid., II/1:22ff.

[23] On this theme, see Dieter Grosser, *Grundlagen und Struktur der Staatslehre Friedrich Julius Stahls* (Cologne and Opladen, 1963), 48–50.

[24] Stahl, *Philosophie*, II/1:23.

[25] Ibid., II/1:82.

[26] Ibid., II/1:71.

obedience to God, but also the love of God; the fullness of morality does not consist of mere duty, but also of love of others. . . . Man is creative in obedience and faithfulness to duty, he is divine in his love." But, Stahl insisted, the object of love was never an abstraction, but ultimately always a person.[27] True morality required a personal God; moral action, motivated by the love of God, brought one closer to one's essence, the image of God. Only the love of God, therefore, made one free.

History was the cocreation of humankind and God in the temporal order. It was the creation of God insofar as God had a plan for history—the moral development of human beings, their gradual realization of their divine image through moral action. It was through history that humankind would be prepared for the kingdom of God, and as cocreator, humankind had the responsibility to build the framework in the temporal order that would lead to moral fulfillment.[28] Here Stahl both drew and differentiated himself from the historical school of law. Natural-law theorists had erred in thinking that ethical norms could be derived from reason; with the historical school, Stahl insisted that ethical norms were always mediated through history. But he believed that the historical school of law had ignored the ethical content in the law and had succumbed to relativism because it considered all law merely the product of history and custom. For Stahl, law had ethical content insofar as it reflected the will of God for the establishment of a moral kingdom on earth. Law created the context for the moral world. Civil society, which for Stahl combined law and the state, was not merely the product of sin; "in its essence, it is much more a moral objective."[29] Only in its empirical form was law a response to sin; a perfect moral community would still be a community of law, but its coercive aspects would be unnecessary.

In his discussion of law, Stahl was concerned to distinguish, as Haller had not, between private law and public law. Both forms had the common objective of creating a moral order. Private law was enveloped by the public law of the state; it existed because the state provided the secure framework for private relationships to develop. Private law dealt with the relationships of private individuals—the integrity and freedom of the person, the law of property, and the fam-

---

[27] Ibid., II/1:106–8.
[28] Grosser, *Grundlagen und Struktur der Staatslehre Friedrich Julius Stahls*, 65; Stahl, *Philosophie*, II/1:48ff.
[29] Ibid., II/1:147.

ily.³⁰ In his definition of the rights of the individual, Stahl demonstrated his essential conservatism. Everyone possesses innate rights, Stahl declared, which originated in "man as an image of God." These rights included the integrity of the person—protection from bodily harm and from the "destruction of the person" through slavery. Stahl drew a distinction between slavery and hereditary serfdom, since serfs remained legal persons.³¹ He declared everyone to be equal before the law but allowed for inequalities of rights as a result of the need for social differentiation. "The plan for a moral world requires the inequality of rights. As men have different positions and responsibilities, so they must have different rights."³² Stahl also argued for the preservation of different acquired rights, in large part to justify the claims that were legitimated by time.

Public law, the domain of the state, was the subject of the final volume of Stahl's *Philosophie des Rechts*. Throughout this volume, Stahl elaborated his idea of the personal nature of authority, what he called "the personality of Herrschaft." For Stahl, the state formed an "ethical kingdom" (*sittliches Reich*), established to fulfill the commandments of God and to prepare people for their life to come in "the kingdom of God." Because God revealed himself in his commandments, the state was the manifestation of the authoritative aspects of God's personality; Stahl also therefore referred to the state as a "kingdom of personality."³³ Neither an organism composed of interdependent persons nor a community (*Gemeinde*) composed of independent and equal persons, the state was a union of independent persons under a single personality. At the center of the state stood "a real, natural personality," the king (9–10). The state articulated its authority through public law, which reflected the "personality of Herrschaft" as God's commandments reflected the personality of God. "The formative principle of public law is the personality of Herrschaft. It runs through all the institutions of Herrschaft," Stahl maintained (18). In this complex formulation, Stahl managed to assert the divine origin of earthly authority without returning to the older tradition of divine-right monarchy.

By conceiving of the state as an institution of public law that was the creation of both human beings and God, Stahl avoided many of the errors he identified in earlier political thinkers (176).³⁴ As a human

---

³⁰ On the differences between public and private law, see ibid., II/1:300–309; on the general principles of private law, see ibid., II/1:310ff.

³¹ Ibid., II/1:318–20.

³² Ibid., II/1:331.

³³ Stahl, *Philosophie*, II/2, 1. Subsequent references in the text are from this edition.

³⁴ See also Grosser, *Grundlagen und Struktur der Staatslehre Friedrich Julius Stahls*, 76–78.

creation, the state was governed by a personal ruler and was closely tied to the institutions of civil society; as a creation of God, the state was provisory but endowed with a moral purpose of preparing humans for the kingdom of God. Stahl thus differed from the natural-law theorists of popular sovereignty on the one side and Haller on the other. The state was a public institution that was neither the creation of the will of its members nor the private domain of the prince. In his first volume he had already made this point: "Publicness [*Öffentlich*] [of law] is, in truth, not that which exists for the people and is completed by the people and according to its will, but that which exists for the purpose of a higher order . . . above the people no less than above the prince."[35] By defining the state as a moral institution, Stahl, like Hegel, elevated the state above civil society. Unlike Hegel, however, Stahl believed the state was inextricably involved in the special interests of civil society; "society and the state, the social and the political realms are distinguishable, but inseparable," he wrote.[36]

In his discussion of civil society, Stahl displayed the same conservative prejudices that had been common among the Prussian nobility since the turn of the century or before. In many respects, his conservatism on these issues seemed to contradict the positions that he developed elsewhere in his *Philosophie*. He complained, for example, that codification of law dissolved the bonds of convention that had existed in the past, especially in rural society; the spread of centralized, written law had caused the rural population to ask why, if the law was so alterable, it could not be changed more to the advantage of the peasantry (33). He lamented the fact that both peasant and noble lands had become "rolling wares," bought and sold by speculators. He believed it was "morally and politically best" to preserve the landowning peasantry by prohibiting the partition of lands, rather than to create a larger class of landless day laborers dependent only on the large landholders (65). "The organic connection of the landowners and the workers, that is, that which is based on connection of an enduring inner relationship between them, is certainly better than the mere mercantile connection between them, according to which they remain strangers." It was important that the old families, peasant as well as noble, retain the possession of the lands of their ancestors. At one point Stahl criticized the agrarian legislation in terms reminiscent of Adam Müller: "The so-called emancipation of landownership, this slogan of the liberal doctrine, is a meaningless thought, a pure phantom.

[35] Stahl, *Philosophie* 1: 566.
[36] Stahl, *Philosophie*, II/2:52. Subsequent references in the text are from this edition.

If the freedom of landownership is to have any sense, it can be only in the fact that each rural worker should farm his own land without foreign capital and thereby gain the profit of his labors for himself" (67–68). Also, like many other conservatives, Stahl complained about the decline of the handicraft system and railed against the development of factories. Even if industry were an unavoidable, providential development, he claimed, "it would be an error to assume that it ... has been an absolute gain for society. Thus far, industry and machine production are a calamity for the human race" (72–73).

Stahl skillfully defended both the creation of a new landowning aristocracy or gentry and the preservation of the old feudal nobility of birth. He recognized that the nobility's monopoly of military service, wealth, land, education, and culture—"the origin and effect of Herrschaft"—had been successfully challenged by the other classes in the society. The nobility no longer could claim to be the dominant Stand; like other Stände, its role in civil society depended on its special profession (*Beruf*). But the preservation of the unique identity of the nobility was important for society precisely because aspects of its traditional "profession" remained necessary. Stahl believed that the nobility provided historical continuity that was essential for the social cohesion of society; without the special place of the nobility, society "dissolves into a mass of the people." A chief element of this continuity was represented in the ownership of land over the generations of a family. "A landowning aristocracy in the continuous possession of land represents especially that element of continuity, the historical side of national life" (105–7). But, Stahl acknowledged, the nobility no longer held a monopoly of landownership; therefore it had to be an open aristocracy, as the Ritterschaft was defined in the provincial diets of Prussia. Stahl's defense of an open aristocracy corresponded to the plans for a gentry discussed in the government of Frederick William IV. He believed new titles of nobility should be tied to the ownership of an estate (116–17).

Stahl went even further and presented a case on behalf of what he referred to as the "romantic nobility," the old feudal nobility of birth, some of whom no longer owned land. This nobility, "the residue of the Middle Ages," as he put it, was often ridiculed by public opinion. To Sieyes's question, posed in 1789, of whether the nation would be poorer without this nobility, Stahl answered with a resounding yes (111). This nobility provided civil society with a moral dimension that was important in its contributing to the "ethical kingdom" that was the state. "Exactly this nobility has a significance for the nation that cannot remain disregarded. It possesses in its particular, characteristic spirit, the personal sacrifice of the princes, and a specific concept of honor and noble ethics that we designate with the term 'knightly.' . . . There is a moral individuality and, indeed, a highly noble individuality in this Stand and therefore it should not be eliminated." He readily admitted that "what is often most visible" about the nobility was the "wretched Junkerdom" instead of "true knighthood." But the outward ethics of the bourgeoisie were no better. The bourgeoisie also had a "dark side," often filled with "baseless pride of wealth, profanity of judgment, . . . the spirit of the railroad: 'where I have paid, I am equal to everyone. . . .'" The moral spirit of both Stände was required for balance in the society, Stahl maintained (111–13).

Both forms of nobility, the landowning aristocracy and the nobility of birth, played important roles in the moral life of the state. Both should be maintained. But this could not be done, Stahl believed, by the continued insistence on archaic forms of privilege that were unacceptable to "the spirit of the age." The nobility could not preserve itself by laws providing differential punishment for injuries suffered by or committed by its members; it could no longer justify many of its tax exemptions, the claims of special status as "nobly born" members of the Ritterschaft, or preferential rights to public offices (117–18).

Although Stahl objected to Haller's conception of the state as a series of private contracts based on landownership, he defended the patrimonial police and judicial powers of the noble estate owners long after the latter had been eliminated in the wake of 1848. Stahl thought it proper that whoever owned a large estate exercised legal jurisdiction over its inhabitants, limited only by state sanction and supervision. To replace the estate owner's power with bureacratic officials would transform an "organic relationship into a mechanistic one." However, Stahl admitted, because of the emancipation of the peasantry, "the authority of the landowners cannot be continued in the old manner" (119–20). The dependency and service obligation of the small peasants, declared Stahl, were largely a "memory of an earlier bond of obedience and piety." Moreover, as citizens of the state, peasants were immediate subjects of the king. The problem was to reconstitute the essentials of the estate owners' former "organic" authority in a manner consistent with the new circumstances. Stahl rejected the establishment of self-governing communities in which the large landowners were outnumbered by small holders. It would be far better to transform the patrimonial relationship into an official one along the lines of the English justice of the peace. But Stahl still allowed a wide latitude for patrimonial power and paternal relationships.

Where the property relationship is such that the large landowner manages his estate with day laborers who also live on his estate, the old and necessary authoritative rights must belong to him by virtue of his possession and with a strong additional claim of property right. For it is really a close union . . . similar to that of a housefather [Hausvater] over his family and servants or a master over his journeymen and apprentices. There is nothing more unnatural than to place such a relationship under the concept of a community [Gemeinde] and then permit the inhabitants—the day-wage laborers together with their employer—to elect the village council. (127)

Although the state was not identical with civil society, it existed to order and advance these elements of social life—the relationships between the Stände—that comprised civil society. The separation from civil society accomplished two objectives for Stahl: it elevated the state as an "ethical kingdom" and it demarcated the limitations on the state's capacity to intrude into the private sphere of its citizens. For Haller, where no distinction existed between the public and the private sphere, the prince was theoretically empowered to order all aspects of his "private" state; Müller's definition of the state as "the totality of human affairs" also fused the public and the private. Stahl's separation of state and society corresponded more closely to liberal theory. It also enabled him to define the state as a *Rechtstaat*, a state under the rule of law (132ff.). The limitation of the state power by law protected the sphere of free individual conscience. Although the king, too, was limited by law, the Rechtstaat was not, for Stahl, a state of laws instead of people. The king, though limited by law, was also the author of law; he stood at the core of the state as the "personality of Herrschaft." "The Rechtstaat stands above all in opposition to the patriarchal, to the patrimonial, to the mere police state," whose characteristics, Stahl believed, involved the arbitrary exercise of power. It was also different from the "popular state" (*Volksstaat*) of Rousseau and Robespierre. Stahl, along with the early liberal thinkers Karl Theodor Welcker and Robert von Mohl became an originator of the idea of the Rechtstaat, which became a central feature of liberal ideology in Germany throughout the remainder of the century. But Stahl's Rechtstaat suffered from the same lack of content that troubled the liberal theory of the state; placing both king and citizenry beneath the law did not define the law itself. Stahl only insisted that the law conform to God's commandments.

The two primary aspects of the state, as Rechtstaat, were authority and law. Authority was exercised by the king, who did not rule on the basis of his own private will or purpose, but according to the laws and ethical purpose of the state. As the king was "the personification of the state," the "personality of Herrschaft," he alone was sovereign, for sovereignty was as indivisible as the human personality (239, 189). Citizens were obliged to obey his commands because he was sovereign. But because the state was an ethical kingdom based on the divine commandments, citizens were also obliged to obey because God subjected them to earthly authority.[37] Since, for Stahl, freedom consisted of obedience to God's will, the state authority provided the context for the achievement of human freedom. Stahl's Rechtstaat, no less than that of the liberals, combined freedom with authority. Stahl permitted no active resistance to authority.

In 1845, Stahl published a separate booklet, *Das monarchische Princip*, which he later included as a chapter in the second edition of his *Philosophie*.[38] This booklet was Stahl's contribution to the constitutional debate in Prussia in the 1840s, and it won the attention of a number of conservative nobles. It articulated a constitutional position accepted by many nobles during the United Diet of 1847 as a reasonable compromise and represented a central ideological position of conservative nobles after the revolution of 1848. Thus, the publication of *Das monarchische Princip* not only represented the central thesis of Stahl's political thought, but also facilitated his entry into Prussian politics in 1847 and after.

Stahl wrote *Das monarchische Princip* in part to reassure Prussian conservatives that not all constitutional development needed to follow the same lines as had the English parliamentary system, which had grown from specific historical circumstances in England. "It cannot be denied that the English constitution is a preview [*Vorbild*] of the European future," he admitted, "but only from the viewpoint of its constitutional character [*staatlichen Charakters*], not from the viewpoint of the supremacy of parliament."[39] The future would give the state a more pronounced public character, but it need not bring the triumph of popular sovereignty. Prussia was also moved by these currents of the age, he believed, carrying it away from the old ständisch constitution, away from the patrimonial state. But, Stahl believed, it was still possible to retain the authority of a personal monarchy.[40]

In order to differentiate the Prussian pattern from the English experience, Stahl developed his monarchical principle in contrast to the

[37] Stahl cited the Scripture Romans 13:1–5.
[38] *Philosophie*, 2d ed., II/2:321–73; 3d ed., 372–423.
[39] Stahl, *Das monarchische Princip*, 34.
[40] Ibid., iv–viii.

English parliamentary system. The English Parliament had developed rights that made it independent of the crown. Among these were the right to initiate legislation, to reject tax bills, to approve the military budget annually, and the requirement that ministers be responsible to Parliament. These rights gave the English Parliament the upper hand; in England, it was sovereign.[41]

Stahl recognized that the budgetary power of a parliamentary body was crucial to determining the locus of sovereignty. He insisted that the monarch, not the representative assembly, must retain unchallenged budgetary power. The representatives had the right to approve taxes but not determine how taxes would be allocated, for that was in the administrative power of the king. But the representatives did not have the power to deny all taxes and thereby cripple the government; if a disagreement developed between the crown and the assembly over tax policy, all previous taxes should remain in effect. The crown had the power to continue to collect and allocate taxes. Only the king initiated legislation in Stahl's system; the representatives had the right to petition him to initiate legislation, but they could not introduce it themselves. Stahl distinguished between basic laws, laws that affected the fundamental structure of the society, on the one hand, and laws that were largely administrative, on the other. The king was obligated to consult the representation in the former, but not in the latter. The assembly could lodge complaints with the king about his ministers but did not have the power to remove them. They remained responsible to the king. For Stahl, the essence of the monarchical principle was contained in the phrase "authority, not majority"; it was the phrase with which Prussian conservatives later saluted his contribution to their cause.[42]

Rejecting the old ständisch system of representation, Stahl argued that a representative assembly should combine a new ständisch system, based on occupation or profession, with the idea of a unified popular representation. He wrote as follows:

Every healthy representation of our age must represent the national unity and the ständisch differentiation; it must represent the practical state of affairs and occupational dispositions, "the land," and it must represent the embodiment of man, "the people." It must, therefore, form an essential contrast to the system of the French chambers, but

[41] Ibid., 2–12.

[42] In 1852, the conservatives gave a banquet in honor of Stahl's fiftieth birthday. They presented him with a silver cup inscribed with the motto "Authority, Not Majority." Stahl expressed his pride at being a spokesman for the Prussian nobility. See Pyclik, *Stahl*, 7.

CHAPTER 10

no less of a contrast to the old German diets. The representative principle only errs when it is separated from the ständisch principle, as there [France], and it errs no less when it is separated from the principle of popular unity, as here [Prussia].[43]

Although the representative assembly possessed only advisory power, it did represent public opinion. Stahl was the first conservative thinker to give weight to public opinion. He did so because he considered the state to be an ethical kingdom, which had an obligation to shape and elevate the moral fiber of its people. The role of public opinion was twofold: it was necessary for the government to test public opinion to see if its policies conformed to the "moral-intellectual" imperatives, and it was necessary for the government to lead the opinion of the people through its ethical example. His idea of representation of public opinion was two-way, from the people to the government and from the government to the people. In this respect, his view resembled that advanced by Hardenberg more than three decades earlier.[44]

These were the main themes of Stahl's political philosophy. The monarchical principle was intended to provide the king with undiminished sovereign authority, while it allowed for the introduction of public law and a constitutional system that limited both the king and his people. The essence of the monarchical principle was the "personality of Herrschaft."

Stahl's Role in Developing Conservative Ideology

Stahl's theory of the state revolved around several key concepts that recurred regularly in his writing. Depending on his purposes, he defined the state as "the personality of Herrschaft," "the ethical kingdom," or "authority and law." The interrelationship of each of these concepts is important for our understanding of Stahl's contribution to the development of conservative thought.

Like other conservatives, Stahl viewed "abstract rationalism" as the ultimate enemy, the source of revolution. His political system contained a criticism of all forms of government that emanated from rationalist thought because they reproduced arbitrary rule that failed to educate people to the full meaning of the law and therefore had revolutionary consequences. Whether it devised laws from the dictates of

[43] Stahl, *Das monarchische Princip*, viii.
[44] Stahl, *Philosophie*, II/2:487ff. Edmund Burke had recognized the importance of public opinion but worked within the framework of the English parliamentary system.

370

abstract reason or from pragmatic experience, bureaucratic absolutism attempted to rationalize the laws of the state, to eliminate local institutions and practices that produced a differentiated system of justice. It produced legal codes that, even when based on custom and convention, suggested that law was essentially the act of an arbitrary sovereign will. The governance of the state by bureaucracy exposed the arbitrary nature of absolutist law and prepared the soil for revolution. A second form of "rationalism," natural-law theory, which viewed the state as a social contract, was the primary source of revolution. Whether in conjunction with bureaucratic absolutism, epitomized by Frederick II's statement, "I am the first servant of the state," or in Rousseau's idea of the general will, natural-law theory maintained that positive law grew from the social contract and that people could therefore change positive laws as they perceived their needs to change. In this system, too, Stahl believed, law became arbitrary because it was subject to radical revision. The third version of rationalist natural-law theory, perhaps its crudest form, came from the pen of Haller, whose law of nature was simply the domination of the stronger. Thus, Haller conceived of the state as the private acquisition of the prince; law was arbitrary, subject to his will.

Stahl built his political system in opposition to these forms of rationalism. By defining the state as the personality of Herrschaft, he tried to salvage the personal connotations of Herrschaft that had long been central to the conservative ideology. The notion of personality offered two major advantages. One, personality was individualized, creative, personal, and human. It suggested that all Herrschaft had a human face, that it was exercised by a person, not an agent or an abstraction. It could be understood by its subjects in concrete, personal terms. This was the side of Herrschaft that Marwitz had stressed when he considered the paternalistic role of the nobility essential—the state was an entity that the peasants grasped only as they came to know it from their immediate landlords. The second advantage was that it implied that Herrschaft was indivisible; to divide a personality was to destroy it. Sovereignty existed in the will of a single individual, shared by neither feudal lords nor popular parliaments.

But the personality of Herrschaft that Stahl described was not the personal, face-to-face Herrschaft that the noble lords exercised on their estates, although Stahl made substantial concessions to estate owners on this issue. It was not private, but the Herrschaft of public law. The king's personality, his undivided sovereignty, was expressed through public law. This law was created by the actions of men and of God. It was created in the temporal order, that is, history. Thus public law was not arbitrary or subject to radical and frequent change. It was a reflection of the commandment of God, revealed through history and articulated by the personality of the king.

An example of how Stahl conceived of this personal Herrschaft was offered in his discussion of the constitutional oath. In the past, Stahl observed, kings swore an oath to uphold the "constitution" of the land—the rights and privileges developed by the subjects over time. In response, the subjects swore an oath of loyalty and obedience to the king. The oath was a transaction between persons, as it was to remain in the oath sworn by soldiers to the king throughout the history of the monarchy. The king swore an oath, before God, to uphold the law, the subjects swore an oath, before God, to obey the king. Stahl argued against the swearing of oaths to the new constitutional documents because they were subject to change, "mere experiments and no one knows if they will succeed."[45]

Because the state was an "ethical kingdom," the function of the law was to educate, to enable the citizens to develop as moral human beings. For this purpose, the law had to be public, generalized to apply to everyone, including the king, because true moral education involved not merely obeying the law, but "loving" the law and the lawgiver, that is, internalizing its commandments. Law that was arbitrary, subject to change, could not be internalized. An arbitrary father could not be obeyed because his will was unknown and unpredictable. This is why Stahl believed that the nobility was important in the moral education and preservation of the state, for its "profession" was to demonstrate the historical, the unchanging dimension of community life. If true to its profession, Stahl believed, the nobility possessed honor and inspired respect for the sovereign; it had internalized the essence of the law.

The state's responsibility for the moral education of the people also accounted for Stahl's view of representation as flowing in both directions, from the people to the king and vice versa. The king had always to be aware of the opinion of the public because his actions were measured against a standard of morality that was understood by that portion of the public that had, presumably, internalized the law—those who were seated in a diet. At the same time, through these representatives, the personality of Herrschaft was to be transmitted to the people to educate them in the ethical kingdom.

Although Stahl rejected the rationalist political thinkers who had preceded him, he joined them in the same discourse. His definition of

[45] Ibid., II/2:300.

the state as an "ethical kingdom" bore a superficial resemblance to Kant's view and that of German liberalism in general. For Kant, true human freedom was achieved through obedience to the ethical commandment of the categorical imperative. For Stahl, moral law was more concrete and originated outside the individual; it was the commandment of God as revealed in history and the personality of the king. But Stahl also believed that "the full and positive realization of the moral idea is the essence of freedom."[46] The state, as an ethical kingdom, a Rechtstaat, was responsible for providing the temporal context for moral development. Stahl's emphasis on individuality and the creative force of the human personality owed much to the liberal neohumanism of the early nineteenth century.

Although he drew close to many of the doctrines of liberal middle class, Stahl demonstrated an astonishing indifference to and ignorance of the issues related to economic change. His discussion of property was superficial and his attack on industry lacked the insight that Müller had acquired much earlier. His exclusion of the proletariat and the capitalist class from national representation may have pleased his noble supporters, but it revealed a remarkable naiveté about the balance of forces within civil society.

Stahl's political thought was the last serious effort to develop a formal ideology in defense of traditional monarchy and nobility before the revolution of 1848. Although it addressed problems that grew out of the political dialogue of Vormärz, its real service to the conservative cause came after the revolution, when the conservative nobility had to adjust to constitutional government, political parties, and parliamentary elections. The assurances Stahl had offered in *Das monarchische Princip* in 1845 proved to be correct. It was possible to construct a constitutional monarchy that would not inevitably evolve into a parliamentary democracy.

[46] Ibid., II/2:136.

EPILOGUE

In the years that separated the Stein-Hardenberg agrarian reforms from the revolution of 1848, the Prussian nobility established and consolidated the modern basis for the political power it would exercise at least until the end of the Second Empire in 1918. It is to this period that we must look if we are to understand the basis for continuity in German history between the nineteenth and twentieth centuries and if we are to grasp the full import of what Hans-Ulrich Wehler has called the "long catalog of heavy historical burdens" of the German past. These "historical burdens" were above all present "in the influence of pre-industrial leadership groups, norms and ideals; in the tenacity of the German ideology of the state; in the myth of the bureaucracy, and in the superimposition of ständische inclinations and class contrasts."[1]

By 1848, all of the major factors that enabled the Prussian nobility to retain its enduring political influence were in place. The privations associated with the Napoleonic wars and the severe agrarian depression of the 1820s had purged from the ranks of the noble estate owners most of those who were overwhelmed with debt or who were incapable of adapting their estate organization to the requirements of modern, capitalistic agriculture. The emancipation of the peasantry was far from complete by 1848, but that process of "regulating" the peasantry, of separating the peasant holdings from those of the noble estate owners, and the gradual transformation of the rural population into a wage-earning class, demonstrated that the noble landowners had little to fear from an emancipation process that they controlled. The noble landowners were the real winners of the agrarian reforms. The transformation of the lord-peasant relationship had brought with it the need to alter as well the political and juridical structures in the countryside and had undermined the traditional paternalistic justification for the nobility's authority. But that informal, traditional paternalistic rationale had been replaced by a formal ideology of conserva-

[1] Hans-Ulrich Wehler, *Das Deutsche Kaiserreich*, 2d ed. (Göttingen, 1975), 238–39.

tism that had incorporated the same fundamental notions of authority into an ideology of the state. This migration of personalized, paternalistic authority from the private estate and village to the realms of public law and to the state itself, as in the political thought of Stahl, was accompanied by recovery of political power within the state by the landowning nobility. From the 1820s through the 1840s, the influence of the landowning nobility in the court and central government grew. The institutions of the restoration were embossed with ständische characteristics, to the extent that even the liberal *Staats-Lexikon* published by Rotteck and Welcker recognized that "the Stände form the skeletal structure of society." In short, as Hanna Schissler has written, "There could hardly have been a worse time to try to take away the Junkers' power than the revolution of 1848."[2]

The outbreak of the revolution in March 1848 threw many conservatives into confusion. Stahl, for example, fled from Berlin at the first sign of strife, earning the contempt of some of his fellow conservatives, which he never was able to overcome completely.[3] On the land, noble estate owners dealt with the peasantry in a variety of ways. Some, faced with insurrection and rebellion, fled; others granted extensive concessions to their peasants; still others found the peasantry calm and loyal. Otto von Bismarck, for example, armed his loyal peasants on his estate of Schönhausen before hurrying to Potsdam to urge the king to organize a counter-revolutionary army supported by the peasantry.[4]

Very quickly, however, the initial trauma and confusion subsided and conservative nobles began to regroup in order to wrest control from the liberal ministry that had gained power in March. Those like Stahl who had fled returned and took up the banner of counter-revolution. Nobles were in the forefront of all the counter-revolutionary activities; their success demonstrated how firmly the Prussian nobility had established its control in the decades prior to 1848. Several actions in the spring and summer of 1848 epitomized the politics of the Prussian nobility as it had developed in the preceding decades; each of the

---

[2] Hanna Schissler, "Die Junker: Zur Sozialgeschichte und historischen Bedeutung der agrarischen Elite in Preussen," in H.-J. Puhle and H.-U. Wehler, eds., *Preussen im Rückblick*, Sonderheft 6, *Geschichte und Gesellschaft* (Göttingen, 1980), 106.

[3] Hellmut Diwald, ed., *Von der Revolution zum Norddeutschen Bund* (Göttingen, 1970): 1: 31; William O. Shanahan, *German Protestants Face the Social Question* (Notre Dame, Ind., 1954), 195.

[4] Otto Pflanze, *Bismarck and the Development of Germany: The Period of Unification, 1815–1871* (Princeton, 1963), 62.

actions also demonstrated that the political arena after 1848 was to be fundamentally different from before.

The most important catalyst to the counter-revolution was the creation of the Kamarilla, the close circle of unofficial conservative advisers who gathered around Fredrick William IV at Potsdam. The Kamarilla formed on March 30, 1848, immediately after the king had acquiesced to the demands of liberals by appointing a ministry headed by the Rhenish merchant Ludolf Camphausen.[5] Its membership was drawn from the conservative nobles who had gained positions of influence through their associations with Frederick William IV during the 1830s and 1840s, above all Leopold von Gerlach, Baron Senfft von Pilsach, and Hans von Kleist-Retzow; it also included a relative newcomer to the political scene, Otto von Bismarck. Immediately after its inception, the Kamarilla began to insulate the king from his liberal official ministry; in response to the Kamarilla's first advice, the king informed his ministry that he would remain in Potsdam and not return to Berlin until complete order had been restored. Throughout the spring, summer, and early fall of 1848, the Kamarilla insinuated itself into the process of decision making, bolstering the resolution of the king and working to undermine the actions of the more liberal ministries. It continued to work its influence until finally, on November 2, the king appointed Count Brandenburg as head of the ministry, and the stage was set for the successful counter-revolution.

The significance of the Kamarilla lay not in the fact that a few people who were close friends and confidants of the king gathered around him to counteract the actions of the official government. That strategy was not new and Frederick William had been especially susceptible to it since his days as crown prince. Although Frederick William had always vacillated in his conduct of policy, and he was especially bewildered during the turbulent March days, he never wavered in his view of the divine basis of royal authority; this gave the Kamarilla the opportunity to exercise its influence. The true significance of the Kamarilla lay in the fact that its members recognized that although the basis of royal authority may still have been intact, the framework for politics in Prussia had changed. This realization provided the foundation of a conservative political movement and ultimately the formulation of a conservative political party in Prussia.

The revolution pushed politics into the public arena in a way that had never before been the case in Prussia. The demand for a popu-

---

[5] Erich Jordan, *Die Entstehung der konservativen Partei und die preussischen Agrarverhältnisse von 1848* (Munich and Leipzig, 1914), 150–55.

larly elected constituent assembly and the calls for a German National Assembly led Ludwig von Gerlach to conclude that Prussian conservatism needed a newspaper that could represent the views and interests of the conservative nobility and the throne. Within a week of the Berlin barricades, Gerlach was at work on plans for the newspaper; before the end of March, Gerlach had outlined his ideas, begun to organize the financial support necessary to launch the project, and conducted conversations with Hermann Wagener, who would be the first editor of the newspaper. Gerlach wanted to call the newspaper the Iron Cross, but it was decided to call it the *Neue Preussische Zeitung* instead; with an iron cross as the centerpiece of its masthead, however, the newspaper came to be called the *Kreuzzeitung*. After several exemplar issues, it began regular publication on July 1, 1848. Among its regular contributors were Ludwig von Gerlach, Stahl, and Bismarck.[6]

From its inception, the *Kreuzzeitung* differed from the conservative newspapers that preceded it. Although it retained a Christian orientation and many of its contributors, including its editor, Wagener, had come from Prussia's pietistic circles, it was not primarily a church publication in the way that Hengstenberg's *Evangelische Kirchen Zeitung* had been. It was clearly intended to be a political newspaper. The *Kreuzzeitung* was aimed at a wider audience than that of the *Berliner Politische Wochenblatt* that Radowitz had published in the 1830s; its articles were less intellectual and more intended to shape the political opinions of a more active and broadly based conservative populace than had been the case with the *Wochenblatt*. The *Kreuzzeitung*'s razor-sharp and often personal attacks on liberal politicians and their policies were clear indications of how the rules of the game of politics had changed since the revolution.

Local organizations throughout the eastern provinces also contributed to the development of a conservative movement in Prussia. Most of these organizations were devoted to the preservation of the rights and privileges of noble estate owners. In the summer of 1848, the activities of these local unions (*Vereine*) made possible a large assembly of landholders in Berlin, which came to be called the Junker Parliament. The Junker Parliament met to combat the agrarian legislation proposed by the liberal ministry. By mid-July, the Prussian constituent assembly, gathered in Berlin, had received more than 500 proposals and more than 6,500 petitions, more than two-thirds of which called for the final elimination of the remaining feudal obligations of the

---

[6] Ibid., 161ff. See Bernhard Studt, *Bismarck als Mitarbeiter der Kreuzzeitung in den Jahren 1848 und 1849* (Bonn, 1903).

peasantry.⁷ Most of the petitions called for the elimination, without compensation to the noble estate owners, of all of the rents and work obligations to which the peasants who had not been "regulated" were still subject. In July, the ministry of Auerswald and Hansemann appealed to the landowners to make "sacrifices" in order to preserve the "position of landownership in the state" and "to fashion a peaceful and friendly" relationship with the peasantry. The government submitted to the constituent assembly several measures dealing with lord-peasant relations. First, it proposed that all limitations "on the free disposition of persons or property" which were "a consequence of hereditary bondage" or as a consequence of "improper expansions" of the obligations of the peasantry be eliminated without any compensation to the landowners. Second, continuing obligatory service and rent payments, "the chief feudal obligations," would also be eliminated, but with compensation to the landlords at the rate of eighteen times the annual value of the rent. The government would establish banks to enable the peasants to amortize this compensatory payment over a number of years. Finally, as of January 1, 1849, the government proposed to end all exemptions on land taxes enjoyed by the noble estate owners.⁸

This proposed legislation, and above all the loss of tax exemptions, activated the resistance of the landowning nobility all over Prussia. From Saxony came petitions and pamphlets denouncing the proposals as an attack on property rights and thus bearing "the character of communism." In Pomerania, Hans von Kleist-Retzow, Heinrich von Putkamer, Otto von Bismarck, and Ernst von Bülow-Cummerow led the campaigns against the proposed reforms. Bülow-Cummerow convened three hundred landowners from Pomerania, Prussia, Posen, and Saxony on July 24 in Stettin, calling themselves the Union for the Preservation of the Rights of Estate Owners. This union sent an appeal to Frederick William IV and its representatives went to Berlin to meet with the king. Subsequently, Bülow-Cummerow called for a meeting of landowners in Berlin, which convened on August 18 and 19; giving itself the clumsy title General Assembly for the Preservation of the Interests of the Landowners and the Maintenance of the Prosperity of All Classes of the People, it was clear that the gathering was primarily concerned with the interests of the noble estate owners, so it

---

⁷ Gerhard Becker, "Die Beschlüsse des preussischen Junkerparlaments von 1948," *Zeitschrift für Geschichtswissenschaft* 24 (1976): 891.

⁸ Ibid., 891–92.

was more commonly and appropriately dubbed simply the Junker Parliament.[9]

The Junker Parliament submitted three separate addresses to the king opposing the elimination of peasant service obligations and rents and noble exemptions to land taxes. The appeals hit the mark, demonstrating clearly the continuing influence of the landowning nobility. On August 28, Frederick William IV forwarded the appeals to Minister Auerswald asking that the agrarian legislation be set aside. "I find the present moment inappropriate to carry out the proposed plans," the king wrote. He considered it "unpolitical" for the existing National Assembly, in which the large landowners were barely represented, to consider legislation that would not aid "the truly neediest classes of the rural population but would only provide an advantage to the more prosperous peasants at the expense of the large landowners."[10] The proposals were dropped. Peasant emancipation was not completed until March 2, 1850, when a conservative government won the credit for it. The tax exemptions of the east Elbian nobility remained until 1861 and were eliminated then only in exchange for compensation.

The Junker Parliament was significant for more than its success in preventing the adoption of the agrarian reforms offered by a liberal ministry. The debates within it revealed the dialectical tension that had been present within the conservative politics of the Prussian nobility since early in the century and that would characterize conservatism throughout the rest of the century. In his address opening the Junker Parliament, Bülow-Cummerow charged that the government had fallen into the hands of radicals and communists who had no regard for the rights of traditional property. In contrast to the higher purposes served by Hardenberg's tax plans of 1811, made at a time when the state faced a crisis threatening its very survival, the proposals submitted by the liberal government served no higher interest of state; rather, they were gratuitous attacks on the property rights of noble estate owners. The impending legislation demanded that estate owners sacrifice "their entire wealth," Bülow charged. For Bülow, the preservation of nobility depended on the preservation of its unique rights of landownership. He concluded unabashedly: "The material interests have a significance that transcends all others; to the extent that we carry through with them, we sustain constantly a firm foundation beneath us."[11]

[9] Jordan, *Die Entstehung der konservativen Partei*, 260ff.
[10] Becker, "Die Beschlüsse des preussischen Junkerparlaments," 918.
[11] Jordan, *Die Entstehung der konservativen Partei*, 265.

EPILOGUE

Ludwig von Gerlach objected to this abject defense of the material privileges of the landowning nobility. Drawing on the teachings of Haller and to a lesser extent Stahl, he appealed to his fellow nobles with the view that "property is a political concept, an office founded by God in order to preserve his law, and the kingdom of his laws. It is always to be thought of in the closest connection with duties which are to be fulfilled by it; only in this connection, only as an office, is it holy. . . . Pleasure without duty, property as merely the means of pleasure is not holy, but dirty. Were property nothing more than this, communism is correct." The opposition to the proposed reforms, he warned, should not stem from the mere defense of property as an inherent right of the individual, but as an obligation, a duty, for only this conception of property would preserve the nobility and its power to ennoble the nation. Gerlach concluded, "*Mere* conservation—this negative posture—the front facing the manure pile, the back turned to the demands of the state, is a position that can perhaps be excused in the peasant. . . . To sacrifice, to seize the field, to conquer is the strongest form of defense—the back to the manure pile, the front toward the enemy—that is noble."[12]

Gerlach's critique of the emphasis on the material interest of the nobility in 1848 was reminiscent of Marwitz's critique of his fellow nobles in 1812. The same tension between unadorned advocacy of economic privilege and the ideological representation of the nobility's special role in society would also run through the history of the Prussian conservative party throughout the 1850s; it would be central in the reorganization of the party in 1876, and in the politics of the *Bund der Landwirte* in the 1890s, thus providing an essential element in the continuity of German history. This continuing tension was a reflection of the complex dialectic between the nobility's material foundation and the ideology of its authority that had emerged in the politics of the Prussian nobility during the first half of the nineteenth century.

[12] Diwald, *Von der Revolution zum Norddeutschen Bund*, 1: 54.

INDEX

Adams, John Quincy, 34
agrarian crisis: causes of, 265–66, 306–10; effect of, on landownership, 273–78
agriculture: capitalist, 5, 6, 71, 155–56, 177–79, 293–96; grain production, 77–78, 267–68; reformation of, 77, 84–90, 144–57, 282–86
Allgemeines Landrecht. *See* general law code of 1794
Ancillon, Johann Friedrich, 193, 197, 198, 200–201, 204–7, 220, 230, 258, 315
army, 92–94
Assembly of Notables, 112, 127–32, 144, 148, 156, 199, 254, 325
Aufklärung, 162; opposition to, 163

Bauer. *See* peasantry
Beneckendorff, Karl Friedrich, 42, 47, 52–53, 59
Bismarck, Otto von, 14 n.1, 244, 346, 375, 376–78
Bourdieu, Pierre, 5, 6
Brunner, Otto, 11, 13, 45, 52
Bülow-Cummerow, Ernst von, 147, 278, 309–10, 312–13, 348, 378, 379
Burke, Edmund, 163, 164, 170, 172

capitalism: critique of, 260–62
Colerus, Johann, 46, 50
conservativism: and constitution of the land, 130–34; ideology of, 6, 158–81; and ideology of Haller, 231–46; and ideology of Müller, 169–81; and ideology of Stahl, 349–73; influence of Ancillon on, 204–7; influence of Gerlach on, 253–58; and pietism, 250; during the restoration, 216–17
constitution, 182–83; controversy surrounding, 321–23; of the land, 130–34

courts, patrimonial, 57–62, 121–22, 123, 240, 304–5, 344–45

diet, national: controversy surrounding, 311–13; creation of, 316–17, 324–26, 333–35; opposition to, 190–92; representation of peasantry in, 191–93
Diet, United, 334–47, 348, 353, 368
diets, provincial, 90, 91, 186, 189; authority of, 209–10; and commission for ständisch affairs, 208–10; and constitution, 317; and county government, 213–20; creation of, 198, 199–204; and Frederick William IV, 317–26; and the general law code of 1794, 104–6; and political concerns of nobility, 210–12; reactions to, 202–3
Dohna, Count Alexander von, 115, 194–95, 202, 269, 270, 274, 281
domination: ideology of, 4; symbolic, 159, 220–23; system of, 46. *See also* Herrschaft; paternalism

Edict of Regulation, 142, 149–52, 155
Emancipation Edict, 110, 115–23, 131, 133, 144–45, 156, 194, 203, 281, 301; February Ordinance, 118–21, 145–48. *See also* peasantry: regulation of
Enlightenment. *See* Aufklärung
Ense, Varnhagen von, 314, 317, 321, 322, 324, 327, 338
Epstein, Klaus, 7, 63

Finance Edict, 124–28, 134
Frederick II, 18, 21, 36, 60; and agricultural reform, 78, 84–85; and general law code of 1794, 98–99; and preservation of peasantry, 93–97
Frederick William II, 105–6

381

Frederick William III, 107; and constitutional monarchy, 182–83, 193, 197, 311; and Emancipation Edict, 115; and military defeat of Prussia, 107–9; and regulation of peasantry, 151

Frederick William IV: governmental policies of, 313–22, 324–26; and liberalism, 314, 316, 317, 320–23; and paternalism, 319–20, 327; and the United Diet, 333–35

Garve, Christian, 47–53, 56, 63–64
Gemeinde. *See* village community
Gendarmerie Edict, 132, 141–43, 159, 213
General Commissions, 287–91
general law code of 1794, 11, 28, 30, 41, 60, 74–75, 97–106, 131, 203, 234, 345
Gentz, Friedrich von, 162, 163–67
Gerlach, Leopold von, 208, 246, 253, 314, 315, 325, 331, 346, 376
Gerlach, Ludwig von, 208, 243, 246, 251, 252–58, 314, 331, 353–54, 377, 380; influence of Haller on, 254–57
Gramsci, Antonio, 66; and crisis of hegemony, 159–62
Gutsherrschaft, 19, 20

Habermas, Jurgen, 66–67
Haller, Carl Ludwig von, 232–46, 250, 254–63, 315, 327, 348, 352, 353, 359, 362, 366, 371; conservative ideology of, 244–46; influence of, on Frederick William IV, 315, 327; versus Müller, 243, 244, 246; and paternalism, 236–38; and patrimonial state, 238–42; and social contract theory, 234–36
Hardenberg, Karl August, Fürst von, 112; and constitutional conflict, 183–98; reforms, 123–43, 149–52, 156; State Council, 189–90. *See also* Stein, Karl; Stein-Hardenberg reforms
Harnisch, Hartmut, 35
Hausväterliteratur, 45–48, 50, 54
Hegel, G.W.F., 165, 356–60
Herrschaft: and constitutional monarchy, 363, 368–70, 371–73; definition of, 10–11, 45, 54–65, 150, 156; symbolic, 65–76
Huber, Ernst R., 7

Humboldt, Wilhelm von, 185, 188, 196, 202, 228

Jacoby, Johann, 209, 320–21, 322, 323
Jews: restrictions on, 211–12, 350
Junker. *See* nobility

Kamarilla, 253, 376
Klein, Ernst Ferdinand, 99, 103, 105
Klewitz, Wilhelm von, 190–91
Koselleck, Reinhart, 190, 202, 279

Landschaft, 78–80, 97, 187, 266, 274–77, 293; during reform, 108–9
Landtage. *See* diets, provincial
Lette, Wilhelm Adolf, 301–3
liberalism, 314, 316, 317, 320–23; and the United Diet, 338–47

Maikäferei, 246–47, 248, 251, 252
Mannheim, Karl, 6, 161
Martiny, Fritz, 22
Marwitz, Friedrich August Ludwig von der, 50–51, 69–70, 75, 126, 128, 129, 132, 133, 134–43, 159–60, 164, 189, 202, 213, 225, 230, 231, 255, 371, 380
Mayer, Edward, 275
Mecklenburg, Prince Carl von, 225–27
Montesquieu, 99–100, 205, 239
Müller, Adam, 132, 158–81, 189, 205, 231, 243, 244, 246, 255, 348, 354, 364, 367; conservative ideology of, 169–81; his critique of capitalism, 169, 173–79; his defense of paternalism, 174–75; intellectual development of, 163–67; his response to reforms, 167–68

National Assembly, 132–33, 142, 143, 156
Neumann, Sigmund, 7
nobility, 14–28; authority of, 55–56; and bureaucratic absolutism, 90–97; its concept of honor, 75, 226–29, 340–44; conservativism of, 130–34, 140–41, 379–80; and constitution of the land, 130–34; and county government, 212–20; emergence of, 16–20; and the general law code of 1794, 104–6; hunting privileges of, 72–73; impact of reforms on, 154–57; Junker Parliament, 377–80; and landownership, 14, 21–25, 79–

84, 152–54, 327–33, 364–67; and liberalism, 322; marriage patterns of, 25–28; its opposition to constitution, 193–95; its opposition to Emancipation Edict, 117–23; its opposition to reforms, 130–43, 149–54, 188–89; and pietism, 248–52; political concerns of, 210–12; versus reform bureaucrats, 108–15; representation of, in provincial diets, 329–31; rights of, 299–300; symbols of, 223–26, 279
noble estates, 18–24; allodialization of, 23–25; economic development of, 18–20; effect of agricultural reforms on, 85–90; effect of depression on, 264, 266–67; effect of peasant regulation on, 287–89; and land speculation, 79–84; ownership of, 82–83, 273–78, 279; size of, 15–16; as village communities, 44–47. *See also* village community

paternalism, 44–54; and capitalism, 262–63; and constitution of the land, 130–34; in county government, 217–20; critique of, 318–19, 344–47; defense of, 174–75, 178; during the depression, 281–82; effect of land speculation on, 80–84; ideology of, 5, 158–60, 348–49; limitations of, 51–54; and patrimonial state, 238–42; and peasant regulation, 291–92; and pietism, 258–59; and village community, 303–5
peasantry, 29–43; and agricultural reform, 293–96; effect of agrarian crisis on, 307–10; effect of agricultural reforms on, 85–90, 93–96; effect of depression on, 265, 280–82; and Emancipation Edict, 115–23; and the general law code of 1794, 102–4; its groups identified, 28–34, 41–43; hereditary rights of, 287, 289–93; how perceived, 47–51; protection of, 93–97, 152; regulation of, 145–54, 286–300; its representation in county government, 214–16; its representation in national diet, 191–93; its representation in provincial diets, 199–201; resistance of, 40, 51–53, 118, 121–22, 142, 304–6; rights and obligations of, 18–20, 28–43, 377–80
pietist movement, 247–53

Pocock, J.G.A., 161
provinces, Prussian, 9–10; effect of depression on, 267–71; organizational structure of government of, 185–89

Raumer, Friedrich von, 147–49, 164
Recess of 1653, 21, 90, 91, 194
Rechstaat, 367–68, 373
Reformation, 17
Regulation Edict, 149–52, 155
Rehberg, August Wilhelm, 163–64
revolution of 1848, 37, 333, 374–76
Rochow, Gustav von, 192, 194, 199, 200, 203, 208, 224–26, 301, 311, 314, 315, 318–20
Romanticism, 179
Rosenberg, Hans, 19, 73, 96

Scharnweber, Christian Friedrich, 120, 142, 146, 147–51, 155
Schön, Theodor von, 115–17, 144, 146, 151, 156, 167, 187, 188, 202, 203, 210, 264–65, 271–75, 281, 317, 336, 347; his role in government of Frederick William IV, 318–22
Schroetter, Frederick von, 115–16
Sider, Gerald, 159–60
Smith, Adam, 165, 168, 173, 175
Stahl, Friedrich Julius, 244, 348–73; Christian philosophy of, 360–62; conservative ideology of, 370–73; his criticism of rationalism, 356–60; critics of, 353–54; political ideology of, 354–70
Stand: commission for ständisch affairs, 207–10; concept of, 220–30; and distinctions between groups, 73–75; and the general law code of 1794, 102–6, 203; and the patrimonial state, 243–45; and the reform movement, 108–10; and representation in government, 112–15, 136–40, 180–81, 200–201, 203, 259–60, 315–19, 334–39, 369–70; and representation in the United Diet, 334–47; and symbolic domination, 75–76, 220–21
Stein, Karl, Freiherr vom und zum, 110–14, 133, 142, 146; and the reform movement, 110–15; Emancipation Edict, 115–23; Nassau Memorandum,

Stein, Karl (*cont.*)
110–12. *See also* Hardenberg, Karl August; Stein-Hardenberg reforms
Stein-Hardenberg reforms, 97, 106, 139, 220–21, 231
Svarez, Carl Gottlieb, 60, 99–103

Teutonic Order, Knights of the, 17, 18, 20
Thadden, Adolf von, 247, 249–51, 255
Thaer, Albrecht, 88–90, 120, 149, 177, 283
Thompson, E. P., 4, 52, 67

towns: decline of, 17–20

United Committee, 325–26

village community, 41, 44–45, 51, 55–57, 62–65; governmental structure of, 301–5

Weber, Max, 12
Wittgenstein, Ludwig Josef Johan, 197–98, 208, 313, 314
Wolff, Christian, 99–101